OXFORD EARLY CHRISTIAN STUDIES

General Editors

Henry Chadwick   Andrew Louth

THE OXFORD EARLY CHRISTIAN STUDIES series includes scholarly volumes on the thought and history of the early Christian centuries. Covering a wide range of Greek, Latin, and Oriental sources, the books are of interest to theologians, ancient historians, and specialists in the classical and Jewish worlds.

Titles in the series include:

Origen and the Life of the Stars
A History of an Idea
A. Scott (1991)

Regnum Caelorum
Patterns of Future Hope in Early Christianity
Charles E. Hill (1992)

Pelagius' Commentary on St Paul's Epistle to the Romans
Translated with introduction and commentary by
T. S. de Bruyn (1993)

Arator on the Acts of the Apostles
A Baptismal Commentary
Richard Hillier (1993)

Ascetics and Ambassadors of Christ
John Binns (1994)

Athanasius and the Politics of Asceticism
David Brakke (1995)

Eunomius and the Later Arians
R. P. Vaggione (*forthcoming*)

The Christology of Theodoret of Cyrus
P. B. Clayton (*forthcoming*)

Arnobius of Sicca
Religious Conflict and
Competition in the Age of Diocletian
Michael Bland Simmons (*forthcoming*)

Ambrose of Milan and the End of the Nicene–Arian Conflicts

DANIEL H. WILLIAMS

CLARENDON PRESS · OXFORD

Oxford University Press, Great Clarendon Street, Oxford OX2 6DP

Oxford New York
Athens Auckland Bangkok Bogota Bombay
Buenos Aires Calcutta Cape Town Dar es Salaam
Delhi Florence Hong Kong Istanbul Karachi
Kuala Lumpur Madras Madrid Melbourne
Mexico City Nairobi Paris Singapore
Taipei Tokyo Toronto
and associated companies in
Berlin Ibadan

Oxford is a trade mark of Oxford University Press

Published in the United States by
Oxford University Press Inc., New York

British Library Cataloguing in Publication Data
Data available

Library of Congress Cataloging in Publication Data
Ambrose of Milan and the end of the Arian-Nicene conflicts /
Daniel H. Williams.
(Oxford early Christian studies)
Includes bibliographical references and index.
1. Ambrose, Saint, Bishop of Milan, d. 397—Views on Arianism.
2. Arianism—Italy—Milan Region—History. 3. Milan Region (Italy)—
Church history. I. Title. II. Series.
BR1720.A5W45   1995   273'.4—dc20   94-29847
ISBN 0-19-826464-X

3 5 7 9 10 8 6 4 2

Printed in Great Britain on acid-free paper by
Ipswich Book Co. Ltd., Suffolk

To my parents

Gayle and Morris,
partners in making a dream become reality

PREFACE

THIS book is the revised product of a Ph.D. dissertation written at the University of Toronto The conflicts between Christian confessional groups in the fourth century present quite a number of historical, theological, and prosopographical challenges which the current renewal in fourth-century studies has only begun to address. In particular, rekindled interest in the doctrine of the Trinity and in the traditional credal formulations of God's identity mandate historically sensitive research if we are successfully to recover the mind of the early Church on these subjects. It is hoped that this volume will make a useful contribution in bringing further clarity to the forbidding complexities of the fourth-century Trinitarian debates.

I am much indebted to the Rt. Revd Dr Rowan Williams, who first suggested the idea of publishing my dissertation. Without his encouragement I doubt if this project would ever have taken its present form. I must also express my gratitude to Professors Timothy Barnes and Joanne McWilliam, who, from the start of this undertaking, offered helpful guidance through its many revisions. Dr Barnes freely shared the proofs of his *Athanasius and Constantius* (Cambridge, Mass., 1993), which helped me avoid some serious errors in my own analysis of events in the 360s. Professor Henry Chadwick graciously read the typescript and offered valuable criticisms for which I am very grateful. Whatever other lapses in judgement may be detected by the reader are entirely my own doing.

I also want to express my thankfulness to the pastors and people of Lorne Park Baptist Church in Mississauga, Ontario. During our six-year sojourn as foreigners in a foreign land, they provided us with countless gifts of emotional support and enrichment. Concerning matters of computer technology, special thanks must go to Mr Jeffrey Miles for his many hours spent converting my documents into a usable form.

No book is written in a vacuum. The members of my family contributed much to its production by their encouragement and by allowing me the space to devote the many hours necessary in meeting writing deadlines and goals. Thank you, Ryan and Chad, for being so patient and understanding while I finished my 'big project'. Most of all, I am grateful to my wife Cindy, who willingly journeyed with me every step over the miles and years, and whose partnership in this project, as in many others, made it possible.

D. H. W.

CONTENTS

ABBREVIATIONS

CAP	A. Feder (ed.), *Collectanea Antiariana Parisina* (*fragmenta historica*) of Hilary of Poitiers (Vienna, 1916)
CCSL	*Corpus Christianorum, series latina* (Turnhout, 1954–)
CSEL	*Corpus scriptorum ecclesiasticorum Latinorum* (Vienna, 1866–)
C. Th.	T. Mommsen and P. M. Meyer (eds.), *Theodosiani libri XVI cum Constitutionibus Simondianis* (Berlin, 1905)
DHGE	A. Baudrillart (ed.), *Dictionnaire d'histoire et de géographie ecclésiastique* (Paris, 1912–)
DTC	A. Vacant, E. Mangenot, and E. Amann (eds.), *Dictionnaire de théologie catholique* (Paris, 1903–50)
EOMIA	C. H. Turner (ed.), *Ecclesiae Occidentalis monumenta iuris antiquissima* (Oxford, 1899–1939)
FC	*Fathers of the Church* (New York, 1947–)
GCS	*Die griechischen christlichen Schriftsteller der ersten drei Jahrhunderte* (Leipzig and Berlin, 1897–)
Hahn	A. Hahn and G. Hahn (eds.), *Bibliothek der Symbole und Glaubensregeln der alten Kirche* (Breslau, 1897)
HE	*Historia ecclesiastica*
ILCV	E. Diehl (ed.), *Inscriptiones Latinae Christianae veteres* (Berlin, 1925–31)
JEH	*Journal of Ecclesiastical History*
JRS	*Journal of Roman Studies*
JTS	*Journal of Theological Studies*
LRE	A. H. M. Jones, *The Later Roman Empire*, vols. i–ii (repr. Baltimore, 1986)
Mansi	J. D. Mansi (ed.), *Sacrorum conciliorum nova et amplissima collectio* (Florence, 1759–98)
MGHAA	*Monumenta Germaniae historica, auctores antiquissimi* (Hanover and Berlin, 1877–1919)
NPNF	P. Schaff and H. Wace (eds.), *Nicene and Post-Nicene Fathers of the Christian Church*, 2nd series (repr. Grand Rapids, 1983–7)
Patrology, iv	A. di Berardino (ed.), *Patrology*, iv: *The Golden Age of Latin Patristic Literature from the Council of Nicea to the Council of Chalcedon* (Westminster, Md., 1988)
PG	*Patrologiae cursus completus, series Graeca* (Paris, 1857–86)
PL	*Patrologiae cursus completus, series Latina* (Paris, 1844–64; 2nd edn. 1878–90)

PLRE	*The Prosopography of the Later Roman Empire*, vol. i, A. H. M. Jones, J. R. Martindale, and J. Morris; vol. ii, J. R. Martindale (Cambridge, 1971, 1980)
PLS	*Patrologiae cursus completus, series Latina, Supplementum* (Paris, 1958–)
PWK	*Pauly-Wissowa-Kroll: Realencyklopädie der klassischen Altertumswissenschaft* (Stuttgart, 1893–1978)
RB	*Revue Bénédictine*
RE aug.	*Revue des études augustiniennes*
Regesten	O. Seeck, *Regesten der Kaiser und Päpste für die Jahre 311 bis 476 n. Chr.* (Stuttgart, 1919)
RHE	*Revue d'histoire ecclésiastique*
RIC	H. Mattingly *et al.* (gen. eds.), *The Roman Imperial Coinage* (London, 1923–81)
RSR	*Recherches de science religieuse*
SC	Sources chrétiennes
VA	*Vita Ambrosii*
VC	*Vigiliae Christianae*
ZKG	*Zeitschrift für Kirchengeschichte*

INTRODUCTION

THE last two decades have witnessed the rise of a renewed interest and literature on the subject of fourth-century Arianism. Scholarly output has been so prodigious that a recent survey of works published between 1979 and 1988 has aptly characterized this period as 'Arius redivivus'.[1] While the focus of many major studies has had more to do with re-evaluating Arius' thought and the early stages of Arianism,[2] significant contributions are by no means lacking on the origin and development in the later fourth century of groups who were also called by their opponents 'Arians'.[3] These new inquiries, despite the tenaciousness of the stylized portrait of Arianism as a monolithic system of belief, have shown that what writers in the patristic era collectively called 'Arianism' represents several distinctly different theological viewpoints. The result is that we are completely justified in designating the term Arianism a misnomer; one which was rhetorically conceived in a polemical context and whose continued use has served only to cloud historical description of those groups who were at most indirectly related to the theology espoused by the presbyter Arius.[4]

The metamorphosis of anti-Nicene ideology and ecclesiology produced

---

[1] A. M. Ritter, 'Arius redivivus? Ein Jahrzwölft Arianismusforschung', *Theologische Rundschau*, 55 (1990), 153–87. Ritter presents the most comprehensive analysis of the specialized literature to date.

[2] The major studies are R. C. Gregg and D. E. Groh, *Early Arianism: A View of Salvation* (Philadelphia, 1981); R. Lorenz, *Arius judaizans? Untersuchungen zur dogmengeschichtlichen Einordung des Arius*, FKDG 317 (Göttingen, 1979); R. C. Gregg (ed.), *Arianism: Historical and Theological Reassessments: Papers from the Ninth International Conference on Patristic Studies* (Philadelphia, 1985); R. Williams, *Arius: A Heresy and Tradition* (London, 1987).

[3] e.g. T. A. Kopecek, *A History of Neo-Arianism*, 2 vols. (Philadelphia, 1979); W. A. Löhr. *Die Entstehung der homöischen und homöusianischen Kirchenparteien: Studien zur Synodalgeschichte des 4. Jahrhunderts* (Bonn, 1986); M. R. Barnes and D. H. Williams (eds.), *Arianism after Arius: Essays on the Trinitarian Controversies of the Fourth Century* (Edinburgh, 1993).

[4] Although this term still functions as a generally recognized and shorthand label in the absence of anything better, its historical inaccuracy and theological inadequacy (cf. Barnes and Williams, *Arianism after Arius*, 'Introduction') should be understood by the reader.

a distinct movement in the second half of the fourth century, commonly called Homoianism by modern scholars, whose western adherents identified themselves with the theology derived from the Ariminum creed (359). M. Meslin's *Les Ariens d'Occident 335–430* (1967) still remains the authoritative study on this type of Latin Arianism. Meslin's major achievement was to show how western Arianism, like Nicene Christianity, developed in a Latin milieu, and produced within its own communities a whole range of devotional, exegetical, and polemical literature. These documents stand as strong witnesses to the internal vigour of their faith. In addition, the very valuable Arian fragments from which Meslin and others have been able to form their reconstructions—especially the Arian *scholia* from the Paris Latin MS 8907 and the polemical treatises in the Verona MS LI—have been the object of a series of new studies by R. Gryson,[5] who has also edited a new critical version of the extant fragments.[6]

As further strides are made in the analysis of Latin Arian literature and organization, it is no longer feasible to assume that Homoianism flourished solely on account of the influx of Arian refugees into western cities due to the Gothic invasions, or because of the political patronage of sympathetic emperors.[7] Certainly western Arian bishops took full advantage of imperial support or protection from their enemies when it was available. No one can deny the episcopal opportunism which characterized the political activities of Valens of Mursa and Ursacius of Singidunum (though no more than Athanasius). But it is equally true that the association of bishops which subscribed to the Ariminum creed as the most orthodox expression of the Church's *regula fidei* possessed a doctrinal agenda which informed their political and ecclesiastical endeavours. The faith which they defended was, in their eyes, not Arian but the traditional faith of the apostolic Church. Hence, Auxentius of Milan is quick to point out in his

---

[5] The fragments themselves are not a new discovery. F. Kauffmann, *Aus der Schule des Wulfila: 'Auxentii Dorostorensis epistula de fide, vita et obitu Wulfilae' im Zusammenhang der 'Dissertatio Maximini contra Ambrosium'* (Strasbourg, 1899); C. H. Turner, 'On MS Verona LI', *JTS* 24 (1922–3), 71 f.; B. Capelle, 'Un homélaire de l'évêque arien Maximin', *RB* 34 (1922), 81–108. R. Gryson, *Le Recueil de Vérone (MS LI de la Bibliothèque Capitulaire et feuillets inédits de la collection Giustiniani Recanati): Étude codicologique et paléographique* (The Hague, 1982); *Littérature arienne latine*, 3 vols. (Louvain, 1980).

[6] *Scripta Ariana Latina* (= *CCSL* lxxxvii) (Turnhout, 1982). For another critical edition of the *scholia* by Gryson, see *Scolies ariennes sur le concile d'Aquilée*, SC 267 (Paris, 1980).

[7] On the contrary, Y.-M. Duval has argued that Latin Arian literature became more abundant from the moment imperial assistance no longer actively supported the Homoian communities. 'Sur l'Arianisme des Ariens d'Occident', *Mélanges de science religieuse*, 26 (1969), 146.

defence to the Emperor Valentinian I in 364 that 'we faithfully preserve that which is catholic and of the Gospels, which the Apostles have
delivered'.[8] Nearly twenty years later the Gothic Bishop Ulfila, who
signed the Homoian creed at Constantinople (360), is just as conscientious about emphasizing the traditionality of his beliefs: 'semper sic
credendi et in hac fide sola et vera.'[9]

The picture of Latin Arianism emerging in current scholarship carries
important implications for how we are to reinterpret the controversy
between Homoians and Nicenes in the later fourth century. The problem, however, is that historical opinion regarding the development of the
Nicene faith in the west has only begun to question the conceptions put
forth in the nineteenth century. In brief, the prevailing view has been that
the western Church was generally committed to the Nicene faith,
or 'orthodoxy', at an early date, and that Arianism posed little, if any,
serious threat to its final domination as the Christian faith of the Roman
Empire. One finds these conceptions formulated in the works of H. M.
Gwatkin, *Studies of Arianism* (1882), and the *History of Dogma* by Adolf
von Harnack, both of whose conclusions have been perhaps the most
influential on the course of researches in reconstructing the Nicene–
Arian conflict.

Speaking of the aftermath of the Nicene council, Gwatkin writes:

From one point of view the victory was complete. Arianism was defeated all along
the line . . . To the Athanasian cause, on the other hand, the gain was enormous.
It was an invaluable advantage to have begun the contest by obtaining a definite
condemnation of Arianism from the highest authority. In the West, this was
enough to array conservative feeling in steady defence of the great council. Even
in the East, the authority of Nicaea was decisive as against Arians and conserva-
tives alike. Its creed was a watchword for the next half century.[10]

Central to Gwatkin's thesis is his view about Arianism's religious beliefs.
Arianism is described as an illogical compromise of Christianity and
Paganism: the worship of Christ as a demigod was nothing short of 'a
clear step back to heathenism'.[11] One should not be surprised therefore to

---

[8] Hilary of Poitiers, *Contra Auxentium*, 15 (*PL* x. 618c).

[9] *Scholia*, 308ʳ, 63 (Gryson, *Scolies*, 250). Ulfila's disciple Auxentius of Durostorum
twice mentions 'tradition' as the criterion of his orthodoxy (*Scolies*, 179).

[10] *Studies of Arianism, Chiefly Referring to the Character and Chronology of the Reaction
which Followed the Council of Nicaea* (Cambridge, 1882), 53.

[11] This theological connection between Arianism and Paganism is reflected in G. L.
Prestige, *Fathers and Heretics* (London, 1958), 68, 91. The same relation is predicated of
'Sabellianism'.

find Arians looking to their Pagan contemporaries for support against the positions of their opponents. More than one modern scholar has seen in Palladius' (of Ratiaria) attempt to use Pagan judges for resolving a conflict between Nicenes and Homoians in 386 clear evidence that Arians were partial to Pagan religious ideas.[12] But not only was Arianism motivated theologically by an alien religious system, according to Gwatkin, it also lacked an internal piety, producing a theology which was more philosophical and rational than Christian.[13] This accusation, which became a standard criticism in the assessment of Arian thought until just recently,[14] produced the conclusion for Gwatkin that Arianism could not have endured on its own religious merits as a viable faith. As such, whatever moments of predominance the Arians enjoyed over their Nicene opponents are said to be the result of court intrigue and military outrage: 'all authorities are agreed that Arian successes began and ended with Arian command of the palace.' Such a system could never have succeeded in the western Church. Not only was the west predisposed to the Nicene faith, but 'Christians were fewer and more rigid, more practical and more inclined to stand aloof from heathenism, so that the genuine Christian conception had more room to unfold itself'. The results are entirely predictable. 'In the West indeed Arianism scarcely had any legitimate footing at all.'[15]

Harnack comes to the same conclusions about Arianism even if for different reasons. Not unexpectedly he interprets Arian theology as a new form of Hellenism which employed biblical terminology solely as religious veneer in order to support its theoretical structure. In a way that is reminiscent of Newman's *The Arians of the Fourth Century* (1833), Harnack sees a relation between Arius' views and the 'Aristotelian rationalism' predicated of the school of Lucian and Antiochene theology.[16] Current philosophical presuppositions and Judaizing exegesis congealed in Arius to create a unique blend of teaching which was both contradictory and totally foreign to catholic Christology. So Harnack writes, '[I]t is only as a cosmologist that he is a strict monotheist, while as a theologian he is a polytheist.'[17] Conversely, the Alexandrian tradition, as exemplified by Athanasius' theology, is the very epitome of revealed and acceptable

---

[12] See Ch. 7 n. 14.   [13] *Studies of Arianism*, 271.
[14] G. C. Stead, 'The Platonism of Arius', *JTS* 15 (1964), 16–31; M. Wiles, 'The Philosophy in Christianity: Arius and Athanasius', in G. Vesey (ed.), *The Philosophy in Christianity* (Cambridge, 1989), 41–52.
[15] *Studies of Arianism*, 3.   [16] Williams, *Arius*, 6 ff.
[17] *History of Dogma*, trans. from the 3rd edn. by N. Buchanan, vol. iv (New York, 1961), 40.

religion, and Athanasius is said to have 'exposed the inner difficulties and contradictions [of Arianism], and in almost every case we may allow that he has right on his side'. It is evident that Harnack sees the dynamics of the Arian–Nicene struggle as two combatants uniformly arrayed against each other. Homoian doctrine, for example, bears all the trademark sins of Arius: the Homoian formula propounded at Ariminum had no theological conviction behind it but only 'resolved faith in Jesus Christ into a dialectical discussion'.[18] The Church in the west, in stark contrast to the ecclesiastical affairs of the east, when once it rejected the teachings of Photinus of Sirmium, 'remained firm' in its orthodoxy.[19] Like Gwatkin, Harnack assumed that Latin Homoianism rapidly disappeared once it lost its imperial support under Constantius II since it was devoid of any 'understanding of the inner essence of religion'. That Arianism survived at all in the west was due only to the patronage of the Empress Justina and the pro-Homoian court of Valentinian II.[20]

In what follows below, I will demonstrate how these twin conceptions of a uniform, essentially pro-Nicene west and a religiously lifeless, politically manipulative Arianism have continued to colour many modern analyses of the Trinitarian conflicts in the later fourth century. Scholarly work has only begun to integrate recent gains in the understanding of Latin Homoian life and literature with our views of western anti-Arian rhetoric, politics, and the writings of its leading proponents. Indeed, few major studies can be found that directly address the subject. M. Simonetti's *La crisi ariana nel IV secolo* (1975) is perhaps the most comprehensive historical survey since Gwatkin's *Studies in Arianism*. The former presentation is obviously sensitive to the stages of accretion and alteration as the development of the 'Arian crisis' in the decades which followed the council of Nicaea is discussed. Simonetti avoids completely the traditional arguments for Nicene triumphalism, even though he does operate on the assumption that the Nicene creed largely prevailed in the west before 360.[21] It has been correctly noted, however, that Simonetti tends to see the issues from the vantage point of the eastern bishops and pays most of his attention to the ecclesiastical and theological developments of the controversy, sometimes at the expense of important political aspects.[22]

An equally massive literary survey of the (so-called) Arian controversy in English by the late R. P. C. Hanson appeared in 1988.[23] Insightful

[18] Ibid. 80.   [19] Ibid. 70–1.   [20] Ibid. 103.

[21] *La crisi ariana nel IV secolo*, Studia ephemeridis 'Augustinianum' 2 (Rome, 1975), 380.

[22] J. Lienhard, 'Recent Studies in Arianism', *Religious Studies Review*, 8 (1982), 333.

[23] The Search for the Christian Doctrine of God: The Arian Controversy 318–381 (Edinburgh, 1988).

commentary is provided by Hanson on the various Nicene and anti-Nicene writers of the period and their respective theologies. Moreover, an entire chapter is devoted to the identification of Homoian Arianism, making important distinctions between it and Eunomianism—one of the many notable attributes of this book.[24] Following a similar format of presentation to *La crisi ariana*, Hanson begins with the controversy surrounding Arius and concludes with the council of Constantinople (381) under the chapter heading of 'The Controversy Resolved'. It is plain that Hanson's main effort is doctrinal analysis and not historical reconstruction as such. He deals very little with the way anti-Arian polemics were affected by the political context or how we ought to calculate the successive stages of conflict which ultimately led to the final demise of Homoianism. But in the same year that Hanson's book was released, a more narrowed examination of the Homoians and their political vicissitudes was published by H. C. Brennecke: *Studien zur Geschichte der Homöer: der Osten bis zum Ende der homöischen Reichskirche* (Tübingen, 1988), which does take into account the unfolding of religious tensions beyond the level of theological conflict.

Brennecke's approach to the source materials represents the state of scholarship that has superseded the older presuppositions of Nicene–Arian dynamics. His studies have revealed just how much the characterizations of the fifth-century pro-Nicene historiographers have prejudiced all subsequent investigations of this period. Brennecke has also added greater clarity and emphasis to the distinctions which existed between Homoians and the followers of Aetius and Eunomians. The fact that both groups are treated equivocally as Arians by ancient historians is another instance of hostile polemic[25] and has sorely confused the efforts of modern commentators to unravel the attending problems. Brennecke creates some confusion, however, when he argues that, because of their theological opposition to Eunomianism, Homoians were *de facto* anti-Arians; a state of affairs which was exacerbated and hardened by the Emperor Julian's persecution of Homoians (though not of the 'Anomoians').[26]

The author has little to tell us about western Homoians and their opponents for, as the title asserts, he has chosen to limit his focus upon the fortunes of Homoianism in the east, concluding at the end of the Emperor Valens' *imperium*, which was abruptly terminated by his death

---

[24] pp. 555–97. Hanson's assessment of Homoianism and its sources are evaluated in Ch. 3.

[25] *Studien zur Geschichte der Homöer*, 88 ff.

[26] Ibid. 2. See Ritter's criticisms, 'Arius redivivus?', 173–6.

at the battle of Hadrianople on 28 August 378. When Brennecke does speak about Latin Homoianism he overstates its dissolution as inevitable, declaring that it 'could never have taken a truly general hold in the west', and attributing the rise and fall of this anti-Nicene movement solely to the advocacy of Constantius' administration.

That Nicene Christianity had gained complete ascendancy in the west by the time the Emperor Theodosius entered Milan in the autumn of 388 needs little discussion. Exactly how and when this ascendancy was established is another matter. The intent of this book is to address these issues and offer a new interpretation of the evidence by undertaking a close examination of the years 360–87 with the goal of showing that the 'triumph' of Nicene Christianity in the west cannot be interpreted as an inevitable process which began at the Nicene council (325) and culminated with the councils of Aquileia and Constantinople (381). Using such a paradigm for understanding this period makes the mistake of assuming a level of continuity which did not exist. On the contrary, it seems western bishops had little loyalty to or practical use for the Nicene creed until the late 350s and that it did not become a generally 'western' creed until after the council of Ariminum (359). Read from this perspective, Jerome's famous statement regarding the outcome of the Ariminum council, 'The entire world groaned and was amazed to find itself Arian,'[27] is completely anachronistic. Furthermore, it will be seen that the council of Aquileia in 381, commonly understood as a western counterpart to the decisive council of Constantinople which met that same year, is not the terminus that ended the conflict between Homoians and Nicenes; if anything, it escalated the tensions and bitterness which already existed.

Among the many important personalities during this period, Ambrose of Milan is certainly the most central and the most apotheosized. There is no question that the bishop was influential, politically and ecclesiastically, in effecting a decisive hegemony in the west for pro-Nicene theology. But the glorification of his later career has all but obscured the process by which he reached this position of eminence. Detailed study of Ambrose's election to the Milanese episcopacy (374) and the years following reveals a figure who was often hard-pressed by his Homoian adversaries—an image scarcely recognizable if one depends on hagiographical sources for historical reconstruction. The striking fact that modern analyses of Ambrose's anti-Arian publications, with the exception

---

[27] *Dialogus contra Luciferianos*, 19 (*PL* xxii. 172C).

of large-scale biographical studies, are surprisingly rare in Ambrosian scholarship may indicate just how effectively the 'later' Ambrose and his struggle with heretical opponents was impressed on the memory of patristic sources—and upon subsequent interpretations of the bishop's early life. Even after the council of Aquileia, the city of Milan becomes a stage where the most intense struggle for ecclesiastical survival is played out. The evidence suggests that a revival of Homoianism occurred during the years 385–6, and that Ambrose was being sorely pressured by the pro-Homoian court of Valentinian II to surrender one of the city's basilicas to Homoian hands. Of all the figures of the later fourth century, Bishop Ambrose stands in the greatest need of historical demythologization and reconsideration of his earlier polemical writings.

But one cannot grasp the bishop and his age without first walking through that labyrinth of councils, creeds, and imperial edicts which dominate the study of the fourth century, and which make it so daunting. Major studies by T. D. Barnes and Peter Brown have provided us with abundant demonstration of the interpenetration of ecclesiastical and imperial politics.[28] The fourth century after Constantine was a time which saw an unprecedented transposition of social and political forms of power into the hands of the Christian Church.[29] Bishops increasingly took their place as the new élite of the Roman Empire: possessing authority as arbiters in legal disputes,[30] presiding over the manumission of slaves in church, acting as advisers to the emperor, and as foreign diplomats or emissaries of the court. To grasp the Ambrosian epoch therefore is to delve into a complex web of theological and ideological change that the student must be prepared to unravel. This is the context of the rise and decline of Homoian theology in the Roman world, and it forms an essential backdrop for understanding the eventual permanence of the Nicene creed and the glorification of those who defended it. For this reason it will be necessary to develop the historical situation in some depth before an appreciation of Ambrose and the scope of his contributions can be achieved.

---

[28] Respectively, *Athanasius and Constantius: Theology and Politics in the Constantinian Empire* (Cambridge, Mass., 1993); *Power and Persuasion in Late Antiquity: Towards a Christian Empire* (Madison, Wis., 1992).

[29] G. W. Bowersock, 'From Emperor to Bishop: The Self-Conscious Transformation of Political Power in the Fourth Century A.D.', *Classical Philology*, 81 (1986), 298–307.

[30] *C. Th.* I. 27. 1 (23 June 318?); I. 27. 2 (13 Dec. 408). On the performance of the 'episcopalis audientia' as a central and problematic aspect of pastoral activity, see the detailed analysis by K. Raikas, 'St. Augustine on Juridical Duties: Some Aspects of the Episcopal Office in Late Antiquity', in J. C. Schnaubelt and F. Van Fleteren (eds.), *Collectanea Augustiniana* (New York, 1990), 467–83.

Years before the advent of Ambrose, the area of northern Italy functioned as a predominant geographical source for the origination of anti-Arian literature, along with Illyricum. Rich in diversity and intensity, these writings demonstrate the varying degrees in which tensions between Nicenes and Homoians played a fundamental part in forming confessional and ecclesial consciousness after 360. One can only wonder at the assessment of such a scholar as Hanson, who declared, 'Arianism cannot have been much in evidence in N. Italy'[31] at this time. Even Hilary of Poitiers found it necessary to route his pro-Nicene campaign through north Italy because of the strong opposition. The versatile body of anti-Arian literature written by such north Italian bishops as Eusebius of Vercelli, Filastrius of Brescia, Zeno of Verona, and others must claim our attention in an examination of religious conflict in the late fourth century. The contributions of these writers, Eusebius in particular, whose career sheds very important light on the ecclesiastical situation of the west after Ariminum, have yet to be thoroughly integrated into a reconstruction of the period. The early chapters of this book will provide a partial remedy for this deficiency.

Is there a point at which we can say the conflict between Nicenes and Homoians was brought to a culmination so that there was a cessation of hostilities? Any answer to this question has first to distinguish the levels or layers of the controversy. Because we are not discussing only the doctrinal issues which were at stake, our *terminus ante quem* cannot be determined by a confessional-conciliar model. The limitations and inadequacies of a strictly doctrinal-historical approach will became obvious given the scope and variety of evidence available to the modern interpreter. It is hazardous to speak of an end to the Nicene–Arian controversies in an ecclesiastical sense since Arian Christianity continued to thrive as a minority movement in various quarters of the Roman Empire, well attested by the existence of fifth-century Arian and anti-Arian treatises.[32] Using a different means of calculation, it is possible to identify a major turning-point (or turning-points) amidst the controversy when the agitations between pro-Nicenes and anti-Nicenes ceased to occupy the political energies of imperial administrations as they had done from the days of Constantine. I will propose that two events, both in the west, were central

---

[31] *The Search*, 530.
[32] e.g. Maximinus' edited collection of Arian works, Augustine, *Contra sermonem Arianorum* (dated by B. Daley to 419, 'The Giant's Twin Substances: Ambrose and the Christology of Augustine's *Contra sermonem Arianorum*', in R. Teske and J. Lienhard (eds.), *Collectanea Augustiniana* (Villanova, forthcoming); id., *Contra Maximinum Arianum*, II (*c*.427).

for breaking the continuing threat which Homoianism posed to Nicene supremacy: the discovery of the relics of Protasius and Gervasius in Milan (386), which effectively undermined whatever local support was enjoyed by the pro-Homoian administration of Valentinian II; and, more importantly and generally, the invasion of Italy in 387 by Magnus Maximus. The first event galvanized enthusiastic popular support for Ambrose and his cause in Milan, while the second event effectively ended Homoianism as a political force and a religious alternative in the west. It was at this point, I suggest, that the ostensible 'triumph' of Nicene Christianity was complete; tyrannical catholicism had now come to stay, first in the person of Maximus, then in that of the eastern Emperor Theodosius, who entered Milan a year later and enacted the kind of strict anti-heretical legislation which had been decreed six years earlier in Constantinople.

The above interpretation is grounded on the presupposition that the dynamics of conflict between western Nicenes and Homoians cannot be adequately grasped by a knowledge of doctrinal or conciliar development alone. As the intricacies of this (or any) period are discovered, it becomes more apparent that theological exchanges tell only part of the story. Polemical literature in particular was often composed in light of the current political, military, and social situation, and its message and purpose are best evaluated by rediscovering that situation. This approach to the historical task will be the one taken in this book and is aptly summarized by Rowan Williams: 'Orthodoxy is constructed in the processes of both theological and political conflict; which means that understanding it fully should involve understanding these conflicts.'[33] Such a view does greater justice to acknowledging the complexities of religious struggle and conciliation in the later fourth century. It informs us also that the constitution of orthodoxy is indebted to an interrelation of factors, some of which are only indirectly related to the issue of right belief. Our evaluation of the theological syntheses produced must take these factors into account no less as an integral part of the development of doctrine.

---

[33] *The Making of Orthodoxy: Essays in Honour of Henry Chadwick* (Cambridge, 1989), p. ix.

I

The Council of Ariminum and Homoian Supremacy

WHEN Ambrose of Milan wrote against his Arian opponents in the 370s and 380s, he was engaging a theological position which he believed could be clearly distinguished from his own pro–Nicene faith. These 'Arians', as they are described, adhered to the Ariminum creed wherein Christ was said to be a creature: 'God sent his son made (*factum*) of a woman, made under the law; therefore, they read "factum" in the same sense as "created" (*creatum*).'[1]

In reality, the creed nowhere asserts the creaturehood of the Son; instead, it declares that the Son is like (*homoios*) the Father who begat him as the Scriptures teach.[2] But even if Ambrose slurred the beliefs of his opponents in order to demonstrate the implications of their heresy, he was quite correct in identifying the Ariminum creed as a confessional rallying point for the majority of western anti-Nicenes. As an alternative to the theology of consubstantiality and its interpreters, the Ariminum creed was accepted as an authoritative doctrinal standard by such leading bishops as Auxentius of Milan, Palladius of Ratiaria, and the renowned missionary to the Goths, Ulfila. Its fundamental place in Latin-speaking Arianism was perhaps best revealed when that same creed was named in a law issued by the government of Valentinian II in 386 as a counter-standard of faith to the Nicene creed.[3] It is evident then that Ambrose, like other pro-Nicenes of his day, was opposing a recognizable platform of theology that was central to the identity of the Homoian Church.

This situation differs quite noticeably from that which characterized Nicene and anti-Nicene opposition during the 330s, 340s, and most of the 350s. In these earlier decades, the issues of contention were much more canonical-ecclesiastical than theological, involving a conflict of

---

[1] *Contra Auxentium*, 25 (= *Ep*. LXXVa) (*CSEL* lxxxii. 3. 98. 297–8).

[2] As preserved in Theodoret, *HE* II. 21. 3–7 (*GCS* xliv. 145–6). This is the Niké creed which was brought back to the council of Ariminum and adopted by the assembly. Cf. the letter sent to Constantius by the pro-Homoians at Ariminum. *CAP* A VI (*CSEL* lxv. 87–8).

[3] *C. Th.* XVI. I. 4. See Ch. 7 for details.

personalities more than fixed opposing doctrinal systems. The arguments for this last point have been sufficiently emphasized[4] not to require extensive elaboration here apart from a few demonstrations. It can be shown that the events which led up to the council of Ariminum, and its counterpart council in the east, Seleucia, were responsible for the rise of a distinctive Homoian theology and coalition, as well as for a correspondingly new emphasis on the Nicene creed by those who had politically supported the cause of Athanasius or who favoured a single hypostatic tradition. These resulting new movements, Homoian and Neo-Nicene,[5] constitute a new epoch in the Trinitarian controversies of the fourth century, and eventually affected a consolidation and simplification of polemics utilized by defenders on both sides. For the present chapter, however, our goal is to provide a brief background of the ecclesiastical situation before Ariminum, and then turn our attention to the councils of Ariminum (359) and Constantinople (360) which produced the doctrinal-ecclesiastical identities relied upon by polemicists in subsequent years.

I. ECCLESIASTICAL AND DOCTRINAL DEVELOPMENT BEFORE ARIMINUM

(a) *The status of the Nicene creed 325–360*

Not only did the promulgation of the Nicene creed in 325 fail to solve the Christological disputes which were dividing the eastern bishops, the creed, with its controversial use of *homoousios* as a means of expressing the commonality of the Son's essence with the Father, had gained little currency in the Church as a generally recognized authoritative statement of orthodox sentiment. Even the most vocal advocates of the doctrine of *homoousios* were not united on its meaning as applied to divine being. Marcellus of Ancyra, in his zealous opposition to the eastern view that the Word was a distinct and secondary hypostasis, is said to have explained that the Word and the Spirit went forth from God as they were needed, and that, in the end, they would return to God.[6] This view, as it is distilled from

---

[4] J. N. D. Kelly, *Early Christian Creeds* (3rd edn., London, 1972), 236 ff.; Hanson, *The Search*, 239 ff.

[5] This latter term will be used to designate the flowering of the Nicene faith after the councils of Ariminum (359) and Constantinople (360).

[6] J. Lienhard, 'Basil of Caesarea, Marcellus of Ancyra and "Sabellius" ', *Church History*, 58 (1989), 157–9; J. Pelikan, *The Emergence of the Catholic Tradition (100–600)*, vol. i (Chicago, 1971), 209.

the fragments of Marcellus' *Contra Asterium* and from the two anti-Marcellan treatises which Eusebius of Caesarea wrote in reply,[7] appears to conceive of the substantial unity of the Father and the Son (and the Spirit) in terms of a numerical identity which temporarily expands into a Triad but without any division. The degree to which Marcellus still retained this position by the time he submitted a doctrinal brief to Julius of Rome in 340 continues to be debated, since he seems to have lost the sharper edges of his modalist theology in this document.[8] It is not unlikely that Marcellus purposely modified his position to avoid further controversy, as Epiphanius himself suggests, although J. Lienhard has recently argued that Marcellus did not have a coherent system in the *Contra Asterium*, and the view of an expanding and contracting Godhead was never at the heart of his theology.[9] Nevertheless, this understanding of Marcellus' more offensive ideas is that which prevailed in the eastern mind-set of the fourth century. A summary of his views produced by Basil of Caesarea in the 370s very closely corresponds to the earliest teaching attributed to Marcellus[10] as the popular form of doctrine to which the eastern bishops most objected and which they condemned at the council of Constantinople in 336 and at consecutive councils thereafter.[11] Another strong proponent of the Nicene formula and member of that council, Eustathius of Antioch, had already been deposed for what also appear to be charges of Sabellianism.[12]

When a Roman synod under Julius' direction in 340 found Marcellus (and Athanasius) not guilty of the charges against them and readmitted them to communion, the eastern bishops were infuriated and used the occasion of the dedication of Constantine's Golden Basilica in Antioch a

---

[7] The fragments are found in vol. iv of *Eusebius Werke*, ed. K. Klostermann (*GCS* xiv), 'Die Fragmente Marcells', 185–215. In the same volume are Eusebius' two polemical works against Marcellus, *Contra Marcellum* (1–58) and *De ecclesiastica theologia* (60–182). Cf. J. Lienhard, 'Marcellus of Ancyra in Modern Research', *Theological Studies*, 43 (1982), 486–503.

[8] In Epiphanius, *Panarion haereses*, 72. 2. 1–3. 5 (*GCS* xxxvii. 256–9).

[9] Lienhard, 'Basil of Caesarea', 159.

[10] Basil claims Marcellus denied the real existence of the Son, that he misinterpreted the title Logos as 'mere word', that the Word went forth as needed and temporarily, and would return again to its source, and that the Word neither existed before its going nor will it exist after its return. *Epp.* LXIX. 2; CXXV. 1; CCLXIII. 5.

[11] Hilary, *CAP* A IV. 1. 3 (*CSEL* lxv. 50); Socrates, *HE* I. 36 (*PG* lxvii. 172B–73B).

[12] The date for Eustathius' deposition is contested. H. Chadwick ('The Fall of Eustathius of Antioch', *JTS* 49 (1948), 27–35) has argued for a date of 326, and T. D. Barnes for 327 ('Emperors and Bishops, A. D. 324–344: Some Problems', *American Journal of Ancient History*, 3 (1978), 53–75, esp. 59). Hanson supports a more traditional dating of 330/331 ('The Fate of Eustathius of Antioch', *ZKG* 95 (1984), 171–9; *The Search*, 209–11).

year later to respond to the Roman decision. In particular, the so-called 'Third Creed' of the Dedication Council of Antioch condemns Marcellus by name, as does the more official 'Second Creed' by implication.[13] The fact that Marcellus was never formally condemned by a western council reinforced the suspicion in the mind of the eastern bishops that defenders of single hypostasis theology were necessarily tainted with Sabellian tendencies.[14] This suspicion was repeatedly expressed in subsequent doctrinal statements issued by eastern councils at Serdica (Philippopolis),[15] and especially at the council of Sirmium in 351, when a disciple of Marcellus, Photinus—another strong advocate of the unity of the Godhead—was formally deposed for teaching, *inter alia*, that the Son of God originated at the time he was born of Mary and from that time forth was called Son and Christ.[16] Such were the problematic results of *homoousios* doctrine. With good reason did Hilary of Poitiers warn his fellow bishops years later in *De synodis* that *homoousios* was not an automatic symbol of orthodoxy, given the ease with which it was used for Sabellian or other heretical interpretations.[17]

Athanasius certainly did not share Marcellus' early interpretation of the unity of divine essence. His defence in the third *Oratio contra Arianos* that the Father and Son share an identity of nature is studiously qualified by anti-Sabellian language.[18] Politically speaking, Athanasius showed no disposition to vindicate Marcellus after the latter's condemnation in 336. His cause only became linked with Marcellus when the two met in 340 in Rome, and their conjunction does not appear to have been for theological

---

[13] Hahn, nos. 155 and 154.

[14] In AD 371 Basil complains to Athanasius that the heresy of Marcellus still has not been formally anathematized in the west, especially at Rome. And even though they (i.e. Romans) have never ceased to condemn Arius, they have brought no charge against Marcellus, 'who displayed an impiety diametrically opposed to that of Arius' (*Ep*. LXIX. 2 (trans. R. Deferrari, *Saint Basil: The Letters* (Cambridge, Mass., 1950), ii. 44)). The mixed reviews and confusion over Marcellus' reputation are especially evident in Epiphanius' prologue, *Pan. haer.* 72. 1. 1–2.

[15] Hilary, *CAP* A IV. 2–3 (*CSEL* lxv. 49–51).

[16] Athanasius, *De synodis*, 27 (27) (*PG* xxvi. 740C). Photinus had been condemned before 351 at least twice in the west: at Milan in 345 and Rome in 347 (*CSEL* lxv. 142).

[17] Hilary, *De synodis*, 67–71 (*PL* x. 525A–527B).

[18] *Oratio contra Arianos*, III. 23. 4 (*PG* xxvi. 372A). Moreover, C. Sansbury has noted that Athanasius stood closer to Eusebius of Caesarea in his view that the Son as 'firstborn of all creation' (Col. 1: 15) was a reference not simply to his humanity but to the condescension of the pre-existent Word. 'Athanasius, Marcellus, and Eusebius of Caesarea: Some Thoughts on their Resemblances and Disagreements', in Gregg (ed.), *Arianism: Historical and Theological Reassessments*, 281–2. I remain unconvinced by the arguments of C. Kannengiesser that the third book of *Contra Arianos* is spurious.

reasons. Indeed, Athanasius' notoriousness seems to have had virtually nothing to do, at least directly, with an offensive doctrine. The letter of Julius in response to the Dedication Council (341) indicates that Athanasius was being charged with crimes, whereas Marcellus had been charged with *impietas*.[19] Likewise, in the long conciliar letter which was published by the eastern bishops at Philippopolis (343), Athanasius is not condemned on the same grounds as Marcellus or on account of Homoousian theology, but for 'villainy' (*facinora*) and various deeds which are described as 'scandalous conduct and shameful acts' (*flagitia criminaque*).[20]

It is of particular significance that Athanasius exhibits almost no inclination to use the Nicene watchword, *homoousios*, for over two decades after the council. Nor is his adherence to Nicene theology the principal cause for his enemies' attacks, despite Gwatkin's insistence that the Nicene faith figured heavily in Athanasius' struggles.[21] We cannot assume (as does Gwatkin) that Athanasius, Marcellus, and their supporters represented a Nicene 'party' or common cause against an equally united group of opponents called 'Arians'.[22] Not until the publication of the *De decretis* (*c*.352/3) did Athanasius begin to champion publicly the terminology of the Nicene creed as a language uniquely necessary for the preservation of orthodoxy. Whereas he had regularly used the less offensive term *homoios* to express the essential unity of the Father and Son (below), Athanasius now explained that the unscriptural but less ambiguous term *homoousios* was necessary to specify the shared nature which exists between the Father and the Only-begotten.[23] Such language was most effective in exposing the heretical intent of those who wished to speak of the Son as 'created' or 'originated' as an expression of the Son's creaturehood. Commensurate with a new emphasis on Nicene terminology was the elevation of the council of Nicaea to the status of an 'ecumenical council', having

---

[19] *Apologia contra Arianos*, 30; 32 (*PG* xxv. 297C; 300A; 301A).

[20] For the nature of these charges see the detailed discussion in Barnes, *Athanasius and Constantius*, 36 ff.

[21] *Studies of Arianism*, 53 ff.

[22] This latter group, usually dubbed the Eusebians in current literature (taken from the sobriquet applied by Athanasius to Eusebius of Nicomedia and his followers, cf. 'The Eusebians and the Court', *NPNF* iv, p. xxxiv), can best be described as 'a loose and uneasy coalition' (R. Williams's phrase) whose strongest theological influence came from Eusebius of Caesarea and whose strongest political bond was their attitude toward Athanasius (R. P. C. Hanson, 'Arius', *JEH* 39 (1988), 235).

[23] *De decretis*, 20 (*PG* xxv. 449D; 452D). On the occasion and dating of this treatise, Barnes, *Athanasius and Constantius*, 110–12; app. IV.

declared in its confession the 'faith of the catholic Church' which has
been handed down from the beginning.[24]

Despite this conciliar declaration, the reassertion of the Nicene faith
did not serve to lessen the differences which existed between proponents
of a single hypostatic theology. We know, for instance, that Athanasius
separated himself from Marcellus about the time of Photinus' condemnations. A section of narration in Hilary's dossier of texts which pertains
to this period, unfortunately in fragmented condition, provides sufficient
evidence to show that Athanasius' decision was probably linked with new
suspicions being cast on Marcellus as a result of the investigations of his
disciple Photinus.[25] Perhaps the only thing Athanasius and Marcellus
ever had in common was their hatred of the Eusebians and the goal of
being restored to their sees.

In the Latin west, acknowledgement of the Nicene formula did not
begin to manifest itself until the mid-350s. While the creed was recognized as an orthodox standard, its priority neither forbade the manufacture
of new confessions nor did it serve to determine the language of subsequent
western creeds. At the western council of Serdica (343), Bishop Ossius of
Cordoba, famous for his pre-eminent position at the council of Nicaea,
felt no compunction in framing a new formula whose composition was
completely void of any reference to the Nicene council or its creed.[26]
After the council, Ossius and Protogenes wrote to Julius of Rome reas-
suring the latter that their purpose in issuing the Serdican formula was
not to replace or introduce any innovations to the Nicene creed.[27] An
entirely new formula, even if it was not proposed as an official creed, was
necessary because the brevity of the earlier creed made it more suscep-
tible to the subtle dialectics of those 'disciples of Arius' wishing to overthrow the doctrine of one hypostasis. The term *hypostasis* was employed
in the Serdican creed as that which the Father, Son, and Holy Spirit
share, but interestingly *ousia* suffered scorn as a name used by the heretics
(Theodoret, *HE* II. 8. 39). Outside Rome, the Nicene creed appears to

---

[24] *De decretis*, 27 (*PG* xxv. 465D; 468A). Cf. *Epistula ad episcopos Aegypti et Libyae*, 5; 7;
De synodis 14; 21. H. Chadwick has pointed out that, although the term 'ecumenical' had
already appeared in the letter of the Egyptian synod of 338, and in the *Vita Constantini* (III.
6), it did not yet carry the later ecclesiastical implications which designated an ecumenical
council as a special category of synod. 'The Origin of the Term "Oecumenical Council" ',
JTS 23 (1972), 132–5.
[25] *CAP* B II. 9. 1 (*CSEL* lxv. 146). See n. 16.   [26] Kelly, *Early Christian Creeds*, 257.
[27] Their communication to Julius is summarized in Sozomen, *HE* III. 12. 6 (*GCS* I. 116).
Despite Hartranft's footnote, *NPNF* ii. 290 n. 5, which states that this letter is not extant,
it is preserved in *PL* lvi. 839B–840A and *EOMIA* i. 644. An English translation of the letter
and the creed is in S. G. Hall, 'The Creed of Sardica', *Studia Patristica*, 19 (1989), 173–84.

have been known but not relevant to the confessional needs of western bishops. The fact that Hilary of Poitiers says he had never heard the Nicene creed recited before his exile in 356 ('fidem Nicaenam numquam nisi exsulaturus audivi')[28] should not perhaps be taken prima facie, and is probably an indication that Hilary's first exposure to a recitation of the creed was at the ecclesiastical proceedings at the western synods of Arles (353) and Milan (355). Hilary's situation was not unique. What happened at these synods exemplifies the convictions of western bishops concerning the Nicene faith.

Both synods were concerned with the Emperor Constantius' efforts to establish ecclesiastical harmony by encouraging the inculcation of eastern conciliar decisions in the west. The issues in contention were not so much theological as ecclesiastical-political; in particular, the condemnation of Athanasius, Marcellus, and Photinus.[29] After the subscription of all the bishops present at Arles to these condemnations, with the exception of Paulinus, letters from Liberius (now the bishop of Rome) to Constantius[30] and to Eusebius of Vercelli[31] demonstrate the existence of an offensive movement on the part of some western bishops to reverse the decisions of Arles in order to instate the Nicene creed as the basis of orthodoxy. The movement had little effect, however. When Eusebius of Vercelli presented the Nicene creed for signatures at the synod of Milan,[32] he was working on the assumption that those western bishops would recognize the creed

---

[28] *De synodis*, 91 (*PL* x. 545A).

[29] Several pieces of evidence have been linked together in order to show that the events at Arles and Milan followed a similar pattern. In *Chronicle*, II. 39, Sulpicius Severus observes, 'an edict was published by the emperor so that whoever did not subscribe to the condemnation of Athanasius, he would be thrust into exile' (39. 1 (*CSEL* i. 92. 9–10)). Councils were said to have met in the Gallic towns of Arles and Biterrae (more commonly spelled Baeterrae), where the participants were forced to subscribe against Athanasius (92. 12–13), and the same method was followed at Milan, 'nihil invicem relaxabat' (92. 18–19). A letter from the Milanese synod (355) to Eusebius of Vercelli communicates the same information except that it reveals the condemnations of Marcellus and Photinus had accompanied that of Athanasius, 'Epistola synodica', 2 (*CCSL* ix. 119. 10–15). K. M. Girardet has convincingly shown that the 'edictum' of Sulpicius can be identified with the requirement laid on Eusebius in the 'Epistola synodica', and probably represents the enforcement of the decrees passed at the council of Sirmium 351 ('Constance II, Athanase et l'Édit d'Arles (353)', in Charles Kannengiesser (ed.), *Politique et théologie chez Athanase d'Alexandrie* (Paris, 1974), 71–81).

[30] In Hilary, *CAP* A VII. 6 (*CSEL* lxv. 93. 1–4).

[31] 'Appendix II B', 3 (*CCSL* ix. 122–3).

[32] 'Liber I ad Constantium', 8 (*CSEL* lxv. 186–7). H. C. Brennecke's attempts to prove the apocryphal nature of this story are not at all convincing. *Hilarius von Poitiers und die Bischofsopposition gegen Konstantius II: Untersuchungen zur dritten Phase des arianischen Streites (337–361)* (Berlin, 1984), 178–82.

as an acceptable symbol of orthodoxy and rally to its necessity. Instead, an emotional outburst from Valens of Mursa, a long-time opponent of Athanasius, easily scuttled the plot to introduce the creed, and the synod concluded with a majority of western bishops endorsing the decisions made at Arles.[33] It would appear that very few bishops in the west held deep-rooted convictions about not disowning Athanasius, especially if the possession of their sees was at stake. And, despite a sudden resurgence of the Nicene creed in the face of opposition, the actions at the synods of Arles and Milan and later, with general acceptance of a Homoian creed at Ariminum, betray how peripheral the Nicene creed had been in the task of theological definition over the last three decades.

(b) *The rise of a 'Homoian' creed*

The fragmentary nature of ecclesiastical affilations before Ariminum is attested by the plethora of credal and theological statements issued during this period. Even after the outward show of conformity by western bishops at Arles and Milan to the doctrinal perspective as probably expressed in the creed of Sirmium 351, a small group of influential bishops in Sirmium, composed of Valens of Mursa, Ursacius of Singidunum, and Germinius of Sirmium, published a theological declaration in 357 whose effect raised the mounting intensity of western abhorrence to the repeated incursions of eastern confessional theology even higher.

The most startling feature of this confession[34] is its explicit prohibition of the terms *homoousios*, *homoiousios*, or even *ousia*. The chief reason given for the ban is that such language is not found in Scripture; a complaint commonly echoed in earlier formulas such as 'second Antioch' or the so-called 'Long-lined Creed' (*ekthesis Makrostichos*) of 344, which sought to emphasize the words of Scripture as the only basis for credal affirmations. For these reasons, Athanasius had been compelled to defend the language used in the Nicene creed in his *De decretis*.

A second rationale for the ban announced at Sirmium is as noteworthy as the ban itself. Concerning the generation of the Son, a kind of agnosticism was expounded, since 'it is beyond human understanding, nor is

---

[33] There is not exact agreement among ancient sources as to which bishops were deposed at Milan, but the list certainly includes Dionysius of Milan, Eusebius of Vercelli, Lucifer of Cagliari, along with two of his clergy. See Sulpicius, *Chron.* 39. 6–7 *(CSEL* i. 92–3); Rufinus, *HE* i. 20 *(PL* xxi. 493A); Socrates, *HE* ii. 36 *(PG* lxvii. 301A); Sozomen, *HE* iv. 9. 3 *(GCS* l. 148).

[34] Preserved in Hilary, *De syn.* 11 *(PL* x. 487–9). Greek versions are found in Athanasius, *De syn.* 28 *(PG* xxvi. 740C–743A) and Socrates, *HE* ii. 30 *(PG* lxvii. 285B–289A).

anyone able to explain (*enarrare*) the nativity of the Son, of whom it is written: "Who will explain his generation?" (Esai LIII. 8). For it is clear that the Father alone knows how he begot his son, and the son how he was begotten by the Father.'[35] This enforced silence, which so offended western sensibilities and which prompted Hilary of Poitiers to apply the sobriquet 'Declaration of Ignorance' (*ignorantiae decretum*), introduced a deliberate ambiguity about the generation of the Son. Given the accented subordinationism in the new Sirmium declaration, as well as the absence of the standard anti-Arian anathemas which had characterized most creeds since the Dedication Council, it is no surprise that the imposed silence on the generation of the Son was received with great suspicion.

The declaration is said to have been imposed upon all the churches with imperial sanction: 'now heresy bursts forth with the acclamation of civil authority . . . and seeks to impose a form of faith (*credendi formam*) on the churches.'[36] Even so, the body which issued the statement does not appear to have been a formal council,[37] and we should not understand the confession it produced as a creed in the usual sense. Despite the fact that it was widely promulgated in the west, it is never cited by later creeds, and its unique form, such that 'it does not conform to any of the usual creed patterns',[38] lends support to the view that the declaration was not meant to be a formal creed of the Church as it stood. More likely, the confession served as a position paper and rallying point which marked the beginning of a new affiliation of pro-Homoians that eventually established a separate ecclesiastical identity. By espousing a more radically articulated subordinationism and maintaining a silence on the standard anathemas of Arianism, the proponents of this theology placed themselves outside the sentiments of earlier Eusebian tradition. But it is hardly appropriate to think of these bishops as a coherent group, or 'Homoians', who issued an official formula. Indeed, nowhere does the declaration from Sirmium teach that the Son was *homoios* to the Father, as Hanson erroneously reports.[39]

Reaction to the Sirmium Manifesto was swift and strong in the west. The prohibition of substance language and placing of certain epistemological restrictions on the Son's generation, thus seeming to limit his

---

[35] *De syn.* 11 (*PL* x. 488B–489A).

[36] *De syn.* 78 (*PL* x. 530C–531A). Eudoxius, hurriedly elected to the see of Antioch in 357, responded favourably to the manifesto, writing a letter to congratulate Valens, Ursacius, and Germinius (Sozomen, *HE* IV. 12. 5–7).

[37] *Contra* Brennecke, *Hilarius von Poitiers*, 312, and M. Simonetti, *Patrology*, iv. 34.

[38] Kelly, *Early Christian Creeds*, 285.

[39] 'A Note on "Like according to the Scriptures"', *ZKG* 98 (1987), 230.

divinitas, did much to elevate the consciousness of many western bishops to the necessity of establishing a centrally recognized standard for orthodoxy. Publication of the Sirmium confession resulted in an outpouring of Latin treatises arrayed against it by Hilary of Poitiers,[40] Phoebadius of Agen,[41] and, perhaps, Marius Victorinus.[42]

Imperial approbation was then given to another confession whose language was more conciliatory and typified that of earlier creeds. In the spring of 359 another working group of bishops proposed a confession of faith which maintained the ban of *ousia* but stated that the Son was 'God from God, like the Father who begat him' and 'like the Father in all things'.[43] This application of *homoios* to describe the relation of the Son and Father was a borrowing of traditional language that was well known and used among various groups of combatants. Athanasius, for example, freely employed the phrase 'like the Father' or 'like the Father in all things' in *Oratio contra Arianos* and elsewhere to express the unity of the Father and Son.[44] In most instances where the phrase is used, John 14: 9 is quoted ('he that has seen me has seen the Father'), and it is clear that *homoion to patri* is meant to denote an essential unity. The expression 'like in all things to the Father' also appears in the Macrostich Creed, itself a document of *rapprochement* on the part of the easterners in 344.[45] Even though the creed asserted the subordination of the Son, it also insisted on the inseparability of the Father and Son and on 'one dignity of the Godhead'.[46] Historically, the *homoios* phrase had a strongly conservative

---

[40] Hilary wrote *De synodis* partly in response to the declaration or 'blasphemia' (*De syn.* 10–11), and most probably against 'liber I' of the dossier texts later called by Jerome 'Adversus Valentem et Ursacium, historiam Ariminensis et Seleuciensis synodi continens' (in *CSEL* lxv). For the argument that 'liber I' was written against the 'blasphemia', see D. H. Williams, 'A Reassessment of the Early Career and Exile of Hilary of Poitiers', *JEH* 42 (1991), 212–17.

[41] *Liber contra Arianos* (*PL* xx. 13–30).

[42] While it has been generally concluded that the first letter from Candidus to Victorinus and the latter's response (*CSEL* lxxxiii. 1. 1–48) are motivated by the Sirmium Manifesto, there is virtually no internal evidence to substantiate such a date. The entire correspondence may have been just as easily a product of the circumstances surrounding Liberius' exile following the council of Milan (355). The chronology of Victorinus' works as presented by Hadot is in need of a revision.

[43] This is the 'Dated Creed', sarcastically labelled by Athanasius on account of its mention of the date ('in the consulate of the most illustrious Flavii, Eusebius and Hypatius, in Sirmium on the 11th of the Calends of June') in the preamble. Athanasius, *De syn.* 8 (*PG* xxvi. 692B–693B); Socrates, *HE* II. 30 (*PG* lxvii. 280A–285A).

[44] *Expositio fidei*, 1 (*PG* xxv. 201A); *Orat. c. Arianos*, I. 2. 40 (*PG* xxvi. 96A); II. 15. 17 (181C); II. 16. 22 (192C); II. 18. 34 (220B); III. 25. 20 (365A).

[45] For background, see Kopecek, *A History of Neo-Arianism*, i. 87–95.

[46] Athanasius, *De syn.* 26. 6–7 (*PG* xxvi. 732B–733B).

application, as in the Macrostich, but it could also designate essential likeness, which is how it was understood by Athanasius and later, by Hilary of Poitiers. In the *De synodis* (358), Hilary sanctions the use of 'like in all things to the Father' as an acceptable means of expressing the equality of Father and Son. 'By declaring, most beloved brethren, that the Son is like (*similem*) the Father in all things, we are proclaiming nothing other than equality [between the two]. Likeness (*similitude*) means perfect equality.'[47]

This assurance may have had an important impact on those western bishops present at Ariminum a year later. The purpose of writing *De synodis*, as Hilary tells us in the introduction (chs. 1–10), was to warn his unsuspecting Gallic colleagues about the subtle heresy which was behind the Sirmium 'blasphemia' (357) and how it should be strenuously resisted in collusion with orthodox eastern bishops at the upcoming dual councils. But little did Hilary know that a new creed had been proposed to the emperor, namely the 'Dated Creed', which used the phrase 'like in all things' to express something very different from what he had taught his fellow bishops.

The group which met in Sirmium and issued the first Homoian creed in 359 was a strange *mélange* of bishops. Basil of Ancyra had come there hoping to seal the emperor's agreement with a confession of faith proposed at Ancyra which claimed the Son was 'like-in-essence' (*homoiousios*) to the Father.[48] Instead, he encountered the 'Illyrian trio'—Valens, Ursacius, and Germinius—Pannonian bishops who were very often in attendance at the imperial court in Sirmium and who had already convinced Constantius of the necessity of a new creed as the best means for establishing ecclesiastical harmony at the forthcoming eastern and western councils.[49] Also present were Marcus of Arethusa, George of Alexandria

---

[47] *De syn.* 73 (*PL* x. 528A).

[48] This Homoiousian creed (preserved in Epiphanius, *Pan. haer.* 73. 2. 1–12 (*GCS* xxxvii. 268–84) was the result of a synod convened by Basil at Ancyra which had met in order to condemn Eudoxius' activities in support of Aetius' doctrinal position (Sozomen, *HE* IV. 13. 2–6 (*GCS* l. 156); cf. Philostorgius, *HE* IV. 8 (*GCS* xxi. 61–2)). A delegation was sent from Ancyra to Sirmium and was able to secure Constantius' agreement against Aetius and with their confession. Sozomen preserves Constantius' letter in response to the Homoiousian delegation (*HE* IV. 14. 1–7 (*GCS* l. 156–7)). To formalize the creed drawn up at Ancyra, Basil repaired to Sirmium to arrange for a council. On the rise and fortunes of the Homoiousians, see Löhr, *Die Entstehung der homöischen und homöusianischen Kirchenparteien*, 63–75.

[49] According to Sozomen's sole account, the idea of convening a 'second Nicaea' originated with Constantius for the purpose of uniting the eastern and western churches. The motivation for this decision appears to have been the affair over Aetius at Antioch and the threat of being confronted with even more doctrinal variations (*HE* IV. 16. 1 (*GSC* l.

(Athanasius' replacement), and a certain Pancratius of Pelusium. According to Germinius in a communiqué which he wrote years later, a discussion was held in the presence of the emperor in May concerning the many dissensions over the faith. It resulted in the drafting of a new document which was accepted by all present; 'in that profession it was written thus: "the Son is like the Father in all things just as the Holy Scriptures say and teach." '[50] This formula was, of course, the 'Dated Creed', which also acknowledged the incomprehensibility of the Son's generation and reiterated the ban on the use of *ousia* in reference to deity. Just as in 357, the grounds for this prohibition were that the Scriptures nowhere contain it—a justification which is repeated four times throughout the creed.

2. THE COUNCIL OF ARIMINUM AND ITS LEGACY

The two synods of 359 did not begin at the same time. Indecision over the eastern location made it impossible for enough bishops to converge at Seleucia until September.[51] Ariminum (Rimini), on the other hand, had long been announced as the site for the western synod, so that proceedings commenced there in late spring, probably in the third or fourth week of May.[52] It is not necessary to rehearse all the details of the western synod since standard accounts by modern historians are readily accessible, and more or less tell the same story.[53] More pertinent to our purposes here is a careful consideration of how and why the synod of Ariminum

158–9)). Constantius' close participation in conciliar developments throughout 359 is somewhat unique. This is not to say, as E. D. Hunt reminds us, that the influence of the Homoian bishops rendered Constantius incapable of exercising independent judgement ('Did Constantius II Have "Court Bishops"?', *Studia Patristica*, 21 (1989), 87). Prior to Theodosius I, emperors never presided nor even sat as a member of a church council, 'except in the extraordinary circumstances of 359, when Constantius took an abnormally prominent role in theological debate, a role which had no precedent' (Barnes, *Athanasius and Constantius*, 169).

[50] 'Epistula Germini ad Rufianum, Palladium et ceteros', in *CAP* B VI. 3 (*CSEL* lxv. 163).

[51] 27 Sept. 359. Hilary, *In Constantium*, 12. 9–10 (*Hilaire de Poitiers: Contre Constance*, ed. A. Rocher (Paris, 1987), 192); Socrates, *HE* II. 39 (*PG* lxvii. 332B–333A).

[52] It is difficult to place the exact beginning of the council. In the *fragmenta* of Hilary there is preserved a letter of Constantius to the council at Ariminum giving final instructions on matters of procedure (A VIII (*CSEL* lxv. 93–4)). The letter is dated 28 May ('datum V. Kal. Iunias Eusebio et Ypatio conss.') and is the second communication of the emperor to this council.

[53] See Brennecke, *Homöer*, 23–39; G. Fritz, 'Rimini (concile de)', in *DTC* xiii. 2708–11; J. Zeiller, *Les Origines chrétiennes dans les provinces danubiénnes de l'Empire Romain*, Studia Historica 48 (2nd edn., Rome, 1967), 284–7, for interpretations of the evidence.

came to endorse fully an edited version of the Dated Creed. As we will see later in this chapter, it was the creed which was endorsed at Ariminum, along with several qualifying statements, that sparked such controversy in the west for the rest of the century, so that its final and formal ratification at Constantinople in 360 was virtually ignored by westerners.

There is no doubt that the course of events at Ariminum turned on the result of unforeseen circumstances which occurred when an embassy sent by that council met with its opponents in the town of Niké. We can see, in retrospect, that Niké acted as a kind of divide separating the synod into two sessions which were strikingly different from one another. This difference is aptly illustrated in a remark by Sulpicius Severus: 'in this way the council was concluded; having a good beginning but ending with a disgraceful outcome.'[54]

Considering the outcome of the first session at Ariminum, it appears that the warnings of Hilary and Phoebadius had had some impact on their western colleagues. The unveiling of the Dated Creed in the midst of the council by Valens and his fellows[55] was rejected out of hand by the majority of bishops, though not because it was thought to contain heretical doctrine. Rather, it was felt by the majority that no other creed or addition need be considered except 'that which has been received from the beginning', namely the Nicene creed. A profession of faith made by this majority group of bishops, only preserved in the historical fragments of Hilary, states their position unambiguously.

For we believe it is pleasing to all catholics that we ought not to withdraw from an accepted confession (*symbolo*) which we, in collaboration with everyone, recognize; nor are we about to retreat from that confession which we have received from God the Father, through the prophets and through our Lord Jesus Christ, being taught by the Holy Spirit and the Gospels, and by the apostles, and through the tradition of the fathers according to the succession of the apostles unto the proceedings held against heresy at Nicaea, which was cast aside at that time, but now is established permanently.[56]

The rest of the confession forbids anything new to be added, or the term *substantia* to be deleted. Hilary supplies the further detail that all 'catholics' subscribed to the document, but those 'who came against it' were condemned.[57] In the subsequent synodical letter,[58] and in a another letter to

[54] *Chron.* II. 44. 8 (*CSEL* i. 98).
[55] Socrates, *HE* II. 37 (*PG* lxvii. 308A–B); Sozomen, *HE* IV. 17. 6–7 (*GCS* l. 163–4).
[56] *CAP* A IX. 1 (*CSEL* lxv. 95).   [57] *CAP* A IX. 2 (*CSEL* lxv. 96).
[58] *CAP* A IX. 3 (*CSEL* lxv. 96–7). Cf. Athanasius, *De syn.* 11. This letter is dated 20 July.

Constantius,[59] the council explains how it excommunicated and deposed
the principal chiefs of the minority party: Valens, Ursacius, Germinius,
and Gaius (of Sabaria).[60] Contrary to the interests of unity and peace
which the emperor had pointedly requested of the council, these men
were said to have fostered discord and strife among the churches by
introducing their innovation (i.e. the Dated Creed), and by despising the
decree drawn up by so many saints, confessors, and martyrs. But, even
more damnable, we are told that Valens, Ursacius, and those with them
refused to assent to certain propositions put forth by the council ana-
thematizing Arianism and other heresies.[61] This last statement lends cre-
dence to a proposal by Y.-M. Duval, that the majority adopted a series of
anathemas in this first session of the council roundly condemning Arius,
the temporal generation of the Son, ditheism, and adoptionism. Duval
has shown that two manuscripts discovered in the Bibliothèque Nationale
of Paris (Lat. 2341, fos. 148ᵛ-149; Lat. 2076, fos. 50ᵛ-51ᵛ) which contain
these anathemas, or the 'Damnatio Arii', also include a copy of the Nicene
symbolum in the preamble.[62] This has significance in that most modern historians tend to attribute the anathemas to the second session of Ariminum,
as described in the *Dialogus contra Luciferianos* by Jerome, where the
fatigued and wearied bishops are said to have adopted a series of anti-
Arian statements. As far as we know, the condemnations were strictly an
oral exercise. No document was presented in the second session for

---

[59] *CAP* A v (*CSEL* lxv. 78–85). The letter is also preserved in Athanasius, *De syn.* 10 (*PG*
xxvi. 696B–700B); Socrates, *HE* II. 37 (*PG* lxvii. 312C); Sozomen, *HE* IV. 18. 1–15 (*GCS* l.
164–7); Theodoret, *HE* II. 19. 1–13 *GCS* xix. 139–43).

[60] *CAP* A v. 2; A IX. 3 (*CSEL* lxv. 83; 97). In Athanasius' translation of both documents,
the name Auxentius (of Milan) appears among the condemned (*De syn.* 9; 11 (*PG* xxvi. 696A;
697C). Cf. Socrates, *HE* II. 37 (*PG* lxvii. 316A). We would expect Auxentius to have been
present at Ariminum, but it is strange that Hilary never makes mention of this fact in his
Contra Auxentium, which he wrote in 364. He certainly would have utilized such a polemically
valuable piece of information if it were available. But even when Auxentius attempts to
discredit Hilary's episcopal credentials at Milan on the basis that he was once condemned
by Saturninus, Hilary employs no such similar rebuttal of Auxentius at Ariminum (ch. 7).
Nor does Auxentius' name appear in the new delegation which was formed after the second
session of Ariminum. The identity of the Homoian bishop Gaius is uncertain. M. Meslin
contends this is the same Gaius who was bishop of Sabaria. *Les Ariens d'Occident 335–430*
(Paris, 1967), 64–6.

[61] Athanasius, *De syn.* 9 (*PG* xxvi. 693C–D; 696A). Cf. Sozomen, *HE* IV. 17. 7 (*GCS* l.
164. 3–5).

[62] 'Traduction latine inédite du symbole de Nicée', *RB* (1972), 9–17. Duval gives the
texts on pp. 10–12. The text of the *symbolum* most closely resembles the text given by
Hilary in *De syn.* 84. More importantly, the wording of an addition to this text ('prophetica
et evangelica . . . doctrina') appears in the confession of the first session of Ariminum
(*CSEL* lxv. 95); see n. 61).

signatures beside the Homoian formula. Nor was there a presentation of the Nicene creed. It is not certain about the degree to which the western bishops were 'stubbornly faithful to the doctrine and to the vocabulary of Nicaea', as Duval asserts, but it is reasonable to conclude that the two documents (the 'Damnatio Arii' and the *symbolum*) pertain to the events of the first session rather than the second.[63]

When ten delegates from the majority at Ariminum were chosen to go to the emperor with the synodical letter, they were strictly charged by their colleagues to make no compromise with 'the Arians'.[64] Ten delegates from the minority group also went as self-appointed representatives of the council. When the delegates arrived in the town of Niké in Thrace they were not received by the emperor, who had, they were told, been called away suddenly on account of a barbarian uprising on the frontier. In the mean time, pressure was laid on those delegates[65] representing the majority of bishops at Ariminum to reach an agreement with the minority party; the result was a dramatic reversal on their part. By 10 October 359 the hard-line position of the majority had been overturned by their own delegates. Restutus (or Restitutus) of Carthage, the leader of the majority delegation, tells how the two groups met together ('in comminus positi') at Niké, and explains that the excommunication of Valens, Ursacius, Germinius, and Gaius was a grave error that should be annulled. Furthermore, Restutus claimed they had also experienced mutual agreement over 'the catholic faith in these matters according to their profession',[66] which was none other than the formula recently drawn up at Sirmium. It declared that *ousia* should be abolished on the grounds that it was ambiguous and non-scriptural and confessed that 'the Son was like the Father'. A small but significant alteration had taken place. The traditional phrase 'in all things' had been removed; perhaps at the behest of Valens, who is said to have tried unsuccessfully to excise the phrase several months before at Sirmium.[67] A copy of the new formula which was approved at Niké is preserved in Theodoret,[68] and is virtually the

---

[63] So Duval, 'Traduction latine', 8 f. Duval has also suggested (p. 23) that a textual 'rupture' between Constantius' Letter to the Council of Ariminum (*CAP* A VIII) and the decision of the council (A IX) exists and it is possible that the *symbolum* and 'Damnatio Arii' originally had their place there.

[64] Sulpicius, *Chron.* II. 41. 8 (*CSEL* i. 95).

[65] Pseudo-Athanasius reports that the bishops were insulted, threatened with not being allowed to return to their dioceses, and treated with violence. *Ad Afros*, 3 (*PG* xxvi. 1033C).

[66] *CAP* A V. 3. ii (*CSEL* lxv. 86. 14).

[67] Epiphanius, *Pan. haer.* 73. 22. 6 (*GCS* xxxvii. 295).

[68] *HE* II. 21. 3–7 (*GCS* xliv. 145–6).

same creed which was ultimately approved by the assembly that gathered in Constantinople in 360.[69]

If the creed which the majority delegates accepted at Niké was less orthodox than the one proposed at Ariminum in July, it was not troubling to the delegates themselves. In his historical chronicle, Prosper of Aquitaine seems to be referring to the events at Niké when he records: 'The synod at Ariminum . . . at which the ancient faith of the fathers was condemned by the betrayal of the initial ten delegates, and thereafter, by everyone.'[70] But the exclusion of 'in all things' was not the point of betrayal; the emphasis placed on the significance of its omission by modern historians is much exaggerated. When both sets of the delegates returned to Ariminum, the majority was horrified, not so much that a new form of the 'Dated Creed' had been introduced, but that the Nicene faith had been omitted and replaced with another creed.[71]

The second session of the Council of Ariminum does not suffer from a lack of documentation. In fact, it is the second half of the council which receives most of the attention in accounts by Jerome, Rufinus, and Sulpicius Severus by reason of the drastic capitulation which took place. Apart from the inclusion or exclusion of minor details, the accounts from these three sources are congruent enough with one another to draw a reliably composite picture of the events.[72]

What is perhaps one of the most striking features of the second session is how quickly the pro-Nicene majority became a minority. There was some initial resistance to the delegates who returned from Niké in that they were denied communion with the others,[73] but this seems not to

---

[69] Athanasius, *De syn.* 30 (*PG* xxvi. 745C; 748A–C).

[70] *Chron.* 1104 (*MGHAA* i. 456). (= Jerome, *Chron.* AD 363 (*PL* xxvii. 689–90).)

[71] This may substantiate Meslin's point (*Les Ariens*, 286) that none of the condemnations of the first session is aimed at the doctrine which was being presented to the council at that very moment. Not a word is spoken with regard to the *homoios* theology, nor about the omission of *homoousios*. Rather, there is just a strong reassertion of orthodoxy, suppressing the difficulties born from recent doctrinal speculation.

[72] Y.-M. Duval, 'La "Manœuvre frauduleuse" de Rimini à la recherche du *Liber adversus Vrsacium et Valentem*', in *Hilaire et son temps: actes du colloque de Poitiers, 29 septembre–3 octobre* (Paris, 1969), 62–3. It also seems to me that the difference between Sulpicius Severus and Jerome with regards to the conclusion of the council which is stressed by Fritz ('Rimini', 2710) is a matter of emphasis and not a contradiction. Jerome (*Dial. c. Lucif.* 19) has everyone returning to their sees in complete harmony and gladness, whereas Sulpicius (*Chron.* II. 44. 8) claims only that neither party could say that it had conquered. This might leave the impression that the council ended in disharmony. Cf. Theodoret *HE* II. 21. However, the fact that only one delegation went to Constantinople (unlike Seleucia) indicates that the council was at least ostensibly unified at the end.

[73] Sulpicius Severus, *Chron.* II. 43. 4 (*CSEL* i. 96. 26–7).

have persevered for any appreciable amount of time. Already by the end of November or early December, opposition to the Niké creed was whittled down to a mere twenty bishops.[74] According to Jerome's discussion of the circumstances, the reason lay in the apparent orthodoxy of the creed.

For at that time, nothing seemed so characteristic of piety, nothing so befitting a servant of God, as to follow after unity, and to shun separation from communion with the rest of the world. And all the more because the current profession of faith no longer exhibited on the face of it anything profane . . . [main points of Niké creed are then recounted] . . . There was a ring of piety in the words, and no one thought that poison was mingled with the honey of such a proclamation.[75]

Sulpicius too notes how speedily the pro–Nicene bishops, after the return of the delegation, 'rushed in flocks over to the other side'. But he stresses that the reason was 'partly because of the weakness of their character, and partly because of weariness of being threatened with expulsion into foreign lands' ('imbecillitate ingenii, partim taedio peregrinationis evicti').[76] No doubt both factors were true. The ignorance of most western bishops as to the real issues underfoot at the council is a point stressed on countless occasions in subsequent years. It is equally true that the praetorian prefect Taurus, who was present at all the proceedings, had received authority to banish any recalcitrant bishops, provided the number did not exceed fifteen. Constantius had already shown at Arles and Milan that he was prepared to endorse the deposition of disagreeable bishops with exile.[77]

Not only was the creed brought back from Niké perceived as faithful to the teaching of the catholic Church, but even the omission of *ousia* seems originally not to have been a major bone of contention among the bishops who had initially appealed to the Nicene creed. A second letter to Constantius, which is sent under the name of the whole council,[78] tells how those who had endorsed the use of *ousia* and *homoousios* changed their minds, and agreed that such names were 'unworthy to God, since they are never found in Scripture'.[79] In the same letter, such denials give way to hyperbole: the use of these terms is potently described as a

---

[74] *Chron.* II. 43. 4 (*CSEL* i. 96. 32–97. 2). Ch. 44. 1 states that the proceedings at this time were in their seventh month.

[75] *Dial. c. Lucif.* 17 (trans. in *NPNF* vi. 328).

[76] *Chron.* II. 43. 4 (*CSEL* i. 96. 30–1).

[77] Cf. Athanasius, *Historia Arianorum*, 76 (*PG* xxv. 785A).

[78] But to which Hilary appends: '[id est Migdonius, Megasius, Valens, Epictetus et ceteri, qui haeresi consenserunt]' (*CAP* A VI (*CSEL* lxv. 87. 5–6)).

[79] *CAP* A VI. 1. ii (*CSEL* lxv. 87).

sacrilegium and they are said no longer to have a place in sound doctrine. The council also indicated that its position was now unified with the eastern council (Seleucia); a claim which the pro-Homoian bishops may have used manipulatively.

The council of Ariminum seems to have ended on a note of outward unity and harmony. Even certain resistant bishops[80] finally subscribed to the Niké formula, once Valens assented in dramatic fashion to a series of anti-Arian anathemas. At this point, writes Jerome, 'all the bishops and the whole church together received the words of Valens with clapping of hands and stamping of feet'.[81] We have no reason not to trust Jerome's report on the ending of the council, particularly since he declares that he is basing his account on the *gesta* of the council which were open to public scrutiny.[82]

Among the anathemas affirmed in the midst of the assembly, Valens is said to have claimed that the Son of God was not a creature like other creatures. Despite the fact that the sincerity of his testimony was accepted prima facie by all, it is this statement in particular which Sulpicius singles out as containing a secret guile:

Then Valens . . . added the statement, in which there was hidden cunning (*occultus dolus*), that the Son of God was not a creature as were other creatures; and the deceit (*fraus*) of this profession bypassed the notice of those hearing. Even though he denied in these words that the Son was like other creatures, the Son was, nevertheless, pronounced to be a creature, only superior to other creatures.[83]

Jerome too claims that, underneath Valens' acclamation of orthodox-sounding anathemas, there was deceit. Specifically, it was regarding his denial that the Son of God was not a creature as other creatures.

After these proceedings, the council was dissolved. Everyone returned with gladness to their own provinces . . . But evil does not lie hidden for very long, and the sore, poorly bandaged and festering with pus, erupts again. Later Valens and Ursacius and their other allies in wickedness, distinguished priests of Christ of

---

[80] Phoebadius of Agen and Servatio of Tungri are mentioned as the leaders of those who had not yielded. *Chron.* II. 44. 1 (*CSEL* i. 97).

[81] *Dial. c. Lucif.* 18 (*PL* xxiii. 171C–172A).

[82] Ibid., 'Quod si quis a nobis fictum putat, scrinia publica scrutetur. Plenae sunt certe Ecclesiarum arcae, et recens adhuc rei memoria est' (*PL* xxiii. 172A). It is possible that Jerome is grossly exaggerating the means by which the deeds of Ariminum were preserved; his penchant for the fantastic is well known. But his statement here is not implausible. We should expect that a great many bishops who had been present at Ariminum were still alive when Jerome wrote the *Dialogus* (*c*.380). Moreover, Jerome was not the only one who was familiar with the synod's *acta*, as shown later in this chapter.

[83] *Chron.* II. 44. 7 (*CSEL* i. 97–8).

course, began to wave their palms saying they never denied that Christ was a creature, but that He was 'like' other creatures.[84]

Had the bishops at Ariminum been deceived into accepting the Niké creed through a fraudulent display of anti-Arianism on the part of Valens? Was there a *fraus* committed as Sulpicius and Jerome claim? Or was Valens only accused of deceit by later orthodox writers once the west had decidedly regrouped around the *homoousios* doctrine and so opposed the council of Ariminum? The Athanasian tendency to depict Valens and Ursacius as villains and crypto-Arians has been largely influential on the way in which historians recount the council of Ariminum. For H. M. Gwatkin, Valens' action at the western council was simply another example of the Homoian intrigue. And the resistance of those orthodox bishops in the second session 'had to be overcome by a piece of villainy almost without parallel in history'.[85] J. Zeiller's description differs only in tone: 'Valens très habilement leur soumit une addition qui semblait appuyer la pensée orthodoxe: "Le Fils n'est pas une créature", en y ajoutant ou se réservant d'y ajouter ensuite: "comme les autres", ce qui était l'expression même du système arien.'[86] In Zeiller's view, there is no question that the bishops at Ariminum were cunningly deceived by Valens.

An opposite interpretation of the documents is provided by M. Meslin, who is critical of the idea that Valens willingly or knowingly committed fraud. In *Les Ariens d'Occident 335–430* Meslin has tried to present Valens and Ursacius not as unscrupulous schemers, but as sincere theologians— a view that has been criticized in at least one review of the book.[87] We should not be surprised, therefore, to find Meslin attempting to exonerate Valens from conventional charges of deceit or suspicious behaviour at Ariminum. Instead, he believes it is probable that Valens never affirmed that the Son is a creature, since neither Valens nor Ursacius is ever credited with making such a statement. Nor is it likely, in Meslin's view, that Valens would have risked ruining the compromise situation which was established in the second half of the council by attempting suddenly to introduce a clause that could be interpreted as Arian.[88]

In defence of Meslin's interpretation, it should be observed that Valens did unambiguously declare in the second session of Ariminum that he was not an Arian and utterly abhorred their blasphemies.[89] Such a disavowal

---

[84] *Dial. c. Lucif.* 19 (*PL* xxiii. 172B) (trans. from *NPNF* vi. 329 (altered)).
[85] *Studies of Arianism*, 178.   [86] *Les Origines chrétiennes*, 287.
[87] See Duval, 'Sur l'Arianisme des Ariens d'Occident', 148.
[88] *Les Ariens*, 287.   [89] *Dial. c. Lucif.* 18 (*PL* xxiii. 180B–C).

should be taken literally. For the Niké creed was not a traditional Arian formula in the sense of sharing the views which are condemned in the Macrostich Creed or in the anathemas of Sirmium 351. And it is hardly surprising that anyone in the middle of the fourth century should deny a connection to Arius or to the name Arian. Another Homoian bishop, Palladius of Ratiaria, makes the same denial at the council of Aquileia in 381. Neither Valens nor Palladius saw themselves as points on a line that stretched back to Arius. The Homoian formula was understood by its authors as completely informed by the tradition of the Church; its chief desire being to remain true to biblical language, albeit in a very wooden fashion. We should expect that Valens, while eschewing Arianism at Ariminum, would strive to leave the Homoian proposition untainted by anathemas which might dilute its character. If Valens and his associates were 'sincere theologians', they were sincere in this respect. Does this mean, therefore, that we ought to reinterpret Jerome's and Sulpicius' cry of fraud as simply the result of hostile polemic?

An examination of later documents hostile to Ariminum is instructive on this point. They show that the existence of deceitful practices employed at Ariminum (actual or not) was well attested in the west. Chief among these is the letter from the synod of Paris which met probably in the summer of 360.[90] The letter, addressed to the (anti-Homoian) eastern bishops who were at Seleucia and Constantinople, was sent in response to a communiqué sent by these bishops to the west by means of Hilary of Poitiers. The latter seems to have unobtrusively left Constantinople in the beginning of spring of that year.[91] His plea to Constantius for an opportunity to reconsider the grounds for his banishment[92] reveals that the bishop from Poitiers was present in Constantinople at the time of the council. Based upon the report of the eastern bishops and the testimony of Hilary, the synod of Paris, in the strongest of terms, condemned the 'deceit of the devil (*fraudem diaboli*) and the conspiracy of the heretics against the Lord's church'.[93] It also declared that those western bishops who subscribed to the acts of the council did so out of ignorance. The combination of these two themes is underlined in Liberius' letter to the Italian bishops (AD 362/3), when he describes the majority of bishops at

---

[90] Y.-M. Duval, 'Vrais et faux problèmes concernant le retour d'exil d'Hilaire de Poitiers et son action en Italie en 360–363', *Athenaeum*, NS 48 (1970), 264; Zeiller, *Les Origines chrétiennes*, 302.

[91] Duval, 'Vrais et faux problèmes', 262–3.

[92] *Liber II ad Constantium*, esp. 1–2 (*PL* x. 563D–565B).

[93] 'Incipit fides catholica exposita apud Pariseam civitatem ab episcopis Gallicanis ad orientales episcopos', *CAP* A I. 1 (*CSEL* lxv. 43. 19–20).

Ariminum as 'ignorantes', and tells how they were deceived by 'those who nullified (*offenderunt*) the plain meaning with an oblique and malign subtlety of obscure reasoning, through which they masked the veil of truth, making it appear that darkness was light and light was darkness'.[94]

It is unlikely that the western bishops at Ariminum realized they were subscribing against the Nicene faith. Nevertheless, Hilary sardonically refers to the difference between the two sessions: 'They condemned the sound faith which they defended earlier, and received the treachery which they condemned earlier.'[95] A decade later the great disparity between the two sessions of the council is still being rehearsed by Ambrose in his attack on Homoianism,[96] and in a letter to Valentinian II he bypasses the argument for the numerical superiority of Ariminum by explaining how sound decisions of the majority bishops in support of the Nicene creed were altered only by the illegitimate tactics (*circumscriptionibus*) of a few.[97] There was no question that the deception of the majority bishops at Ariminum is what accounted for the radical transformation of the synod's opinion in the second session.

Having established the existence of a strong tradition among western writers that the majority bishops at Ariminum signed the Homoian formula on the basis of a *fraus*, we are still left with the question of the precise nature of this deception. Admittedly, the moment of the reputed *fraus* is difficult to pinpoint, and indeed may not be any one event. But at least two accusations appear with some regularity. The first has to do with a questionable tactic which Sulpicius reports was used on those bishops at the second session of the council who had not yet yielded to the Niké formula.

When they began to make some movement toward solving their differences, and little by little Phoebadius was weakening, he was at last overcome by a proposal offered. For Valens and Ursacius affirmed that the present confession was composed in accordance with catholic understanding, which was put forward by the easterners under the authority of the emperor, and could not be repudiated without sacrilege. And who can bring an end to the discord if those matters acceptable to the easterners are not acceptable to the westerners?[98]

---

[94] *CAP* B IV. 1 (*CSEL* lxv. 157. 7–9). A letter by a synod of Italian bishops sent to their colleagues in Illyricum that same year stresses the same points as Liberius (B IV. 2 (*CSEL* lxv. 158. 8)).

[95] *CAP* A V. 2 (*CSEL* lxv. 85).

[96] *De fide*, I. 18. 122: 'This also was the first confession of faith at the council of Ariminum and the second correction after that council. The letter sent to the emperor Constantius testifies to this confession, and the councils which followed declared the correction' (*CSEL* lxxviii. 51–2).

[97] *Ep.* 75. 15 (*CSEL* lxxxii. 3. 80).   [98] *Chron.* II. 44. 4 (*CSEL* i. 97).

Only when Phoebadius and the other bishops with him heard that the Niké formula had been approved by the Seleucian council and the emperor did they finally consent to the formula with certain qualifications. This is the very point which the council of Paris makes to its like-minded colleagues in the east when it mentions how the western bishops were deceived: 'For a great number who were present either at Ariminum or Niké, were forced into a silence over "ousia" by the authority of your name.'[99] The western bishops were obviously under the impression that the entire bloc of eastern bishops had subscribed to the Homoian formula. Not until Hilary returned to the west and reported on the actual events at Seleucia did the western bishops realize that the position of their eastern colleagues had been falsely represented. Interestingly, the homoiousian delegates at Seleucia were finally convinced to accept the Acacian 'homoian' formulary when they were told that the western bishops had approved it.[100]

A second, and perhaps more significant, accusation against Valens' actions at Ariminum was his denial that the Son of God was a creature as other creatures. As pointed out above, both Sulpicius and Jerome claimed that there lurked in Valens' words to the assembly a secret guile. In a lengthy article,[101] Y.-M. Duval has argued that this accusation is the key to the *fraus* committed at Ariminum since it is this accusation which becomes central in later descriptions of the deception. Duval's documentation is extensive and it is impossible to reproduce the steps of his argument in full, although his treatment of three principal texts, fundamental to his case, is worth reciting. In a passage from Jerome's *Dialogus contra Luciferianos* which was cited earlier,[102] Duval observes that the discovery of deceitfulness did not come until after the council was dissolved. Only then did Valens and his associates begin 'to wave their palms saying they never denied that Christ was a creature, but that He was "like" other creatures'. It is to this moment that Jerome directed his famous epitaph, 'Ingemuit totus orbis, et Arianum se esse miratus est' ('The entire world groaned and was amazed to find itself Arian'). Sulpicius verifies the fact that it was only later that the bishops at Ariminum realized their mistake.[103] At what point then were the supposed true

---

[99] *CAP* A I. I (*CSEL* lxv. 43. 22–44. 2). Barnes underestimates the significance of this argument in his treatment of the capitulation of the majority at Ariminum. *Athanasius and Constantius*, 169 f.

[100] Sozomen, *HE* IV. 23. 5–6 (*GCS* I. 177).

[101] 'La "Manœuvre frauduleuse" ', 51–103.

[102] n. 84.   [103] *Chron.* II. 44. 8 (*CSEL* i. 98).

intentions of Valens unveiled? According to Duval, the *fraus* was not revealed until the council of Constantinople (360). An important passage from Hilary of Poitiers, which was written after this council, tells how the western delegates, conducted by Valens, joined themselves to the heretical 'delegation from the eastern synod' (the Acacians) without a moment's hesitation. To reveal their hypocrisy, Hilary gives an example from the discussions which the three delegations[104] held at Constantinople: 'When you were demonstrating why you said the Son of God is not a creature, you answered that the saints at Ariminum did not say that Christ is not a creature, but that he is not a creature like the others.'[105] However exceptional in nature, the Son was implied to be a creature and 'so the Son was foreign (*alienus*) to the Father and Christ to God'.

Hilary's testimony has much support for it. Very probably he is not putting words in Valens' mouth since his account so closely mirrors the reports we have from Sulpicius and Jerome about the events at Ariminum. Moreover, a rescript from Germinius of Sirmium addressed to Rufianus, Palladius, and others shows that Valens' intentions were far more radical than his words seemed to indicate. Germinius' own theological evolution is itself a question that requires further study,[106] but it seems that by 366, which is the date of the rescript, the bishop of Sirmium no longer identified himself theologically with Valens and his colleagues. After defending his own position that the Son is like to the Father 'per omnia' (in all things), he reproaches Valens for claiming the Scriptures teach that Christ is a creature ('"facturam" et "creaturam"').[107] Not without some irony, Germinius stresses further that Valens either forgot or intentionally concealed the fact that 'similis per omnia' figured in the formula which he signed on 22 May 359.[108]

The third piece of evidence which we will choose from Duval's discussion comes from Ambrose of Milan and the third book of his *De fide*. To quote Duval, 'Il a accusé ses adversaires de chercher à tromper les esprits simples. L'exemple qu'il donne n'est autre que l'anathématisme sur la

---

[104] A single delegation, ostensibly unified, came from Ariminum. From Seleucia there arrived representatives from the Acacians, supporting the Homoian confession, the Homoiousians, and those who professed the dissimularity of the Son's substance to the Father, led by Aetius and his disciple Eunomius.

[105] *CAP* B VIII. 2 (2) (*CSEL* lxv. 176).

[106] For a preliminary investigation, see D. H. Williams, 'Another Exception to Fourth Century Typologies: The Case of Germinius of Sirmium', *Journal of Early Christian Studies* (forthcoming).

[107] *CAP* B VI. 2 (*CSEL* lxv. 162. 28–9). [108] *CSEL* lxv. 163. 10–11.

créature.'[109] Indeed, Ambrose appears to be citing the *gesta* of the council of Ariminum when he directly quotes, ' "Qui dicit", inquiunt, "Christum creaturam secundum ceteras creaturas, anathema sit." ' (' "Whoever says", they declared, "Christ is a creature just as other creatures, let him be accursed." ')[110] Simple people (*simplices*) heard these words, Ambrose notes, and trusted them as worthy of belief. But in doing so, they became snared by the hook of ungodly deceit. It would have been sufficient to condemn anyone who says that Christ is a created being. By adding ' ". . . in the manner of other creatures", you do not deny that Christ is a creature, but that he is a creature like [all others]'. The implication, according to Ambrose, is that 'you say indeed he is a creature, even if you assert he is superior to other creatures'.[111]

To conclude, we need not maintain the Athanasian conception of Valens and Urscacius in order to support the likelihood that some manner of duplicity occurred at Ariminum. We certainly might expect that the majority of bishops who attended the council would cry foul once they found out that a different interpretation was given to the documents they had signed. At the same time, we have seen how Valens and his immediate circle favoured a strong subordinationist theology which would naturally lend such an interpretation to the acts of Ariminum. Valens' investigation of his own ally and friend Germinius of Sirmium, who some years later continued his anti-Nicene stance but disagreed over the exclusion of the qualifying phrase for the Son's likeness to the Father, 'in all things', demonstrates just how devoted Valens was to the maintenance of this perspective. There is no doubt then that the pressure for uniformity exerted by the prefect Taurus and the misrepresentation of eastern attitudes by Valens were the most compelling reasons for the bishops at Ariminum to have signed the Homoian creed brought back from Niké.

Following the dissolution of the council at Ariminum, a new delegation was formed and was sent to Constantinople for a joint council which

---

[109] ' "La Manœuvre frauduleuse" ', 92.

[110] *De fide*, III. 16. 130 (*CSEL* lxxviii. 153–4). Compare Jerome, *Dial. c. Lucif.* 18: 'Si quis dixerit creaturam Filium Dei, ut sunt caeterae creaturae, anathema sit' (*PL* xxiii. 171C). We have already seen that Ambrose must have had access to the minutes of the council (cf. *De fide*, I. 18. 122).

[111] *De fide*, III. 16. 132 (*CSEL* lxxviii. 154). Particularly striking is how Ambrose links this terminology to Arius himself: 'He says the Son of God is a perfect creature, but not as other creatures.' ('Dei filium creaturam dixit esse perfectam, sed non sicut ceteras creaturas.') Meslin (*Les Ariens*, 318 n. 113) is surely correct to see here a reference to Arius' letter to Alexander: 'creaturam dei perfectam sed non sicuti unam creaturam', according to the translation of Hilary (*De trin.* IV. 12) (cf. Athanasius, *De syn.* 16 (*PG* xxvi. 709A)).

convened in January 360[112] with the two delegations from Seleucia.[113] The 'epistle of the western bishops' which declared 'That the Son is like to the Father according to the Scriptures' was presented to the assembly and all parties in attendence were compelled to sign.[114] Thus, the formula from Niké attained official status as the creed of the Roman Empire with the added provision that all other formulas, past and present, were declared null and void. It is this formula which Ulfila, the so-called 'bishop of the Goths' (Sozomen, *HE* iv. 24. 1), took back to upper Moesia (secunda) as the faith of the Christian emperor and Romans everywhere.

The decisions of Constantinople were now widely promulgated, issued under the authority of an imperial edict.[115] For the west, however, the council whose decisions were invoked by supporters and detractors alike was not Constantinople, but Ariminum. It was Ariminum where the Homoian creed was first revealed, but, more importantly for the pro-Nicenes, it was Ariminum where the betrayal of the faith occurred.[116] This mixed legacy of the western council becomes one of the great water-sheds in Latin literature over the next half-century for determining orthodoxy or heresy—depending on which session of the council is being invoked. Thus, an unnamed group of Italian bishops will declare (*c*.363) that they have renounced the decrees of Ariminum, and, in order for their episcopal colleagues in Illyricum to establish communion with them, they must not only subscribe to the Nicene faith, but must also send 'an annulment of the council of Ariminum without ambiguity'.[117] About the same time we find at the church of Sirmium legal action being taken against three laymen for confessing the consubstantiality of the Son to the Father. It is demanded that they sign the *symbolum* of Ariminum as a demonstration of their pure faith or face the consequences of prison.[118]

---

[112] Kopecek's contention (*A History of Neo-Arianism*, i. 229 f.) that there were two councils at Constantinople, one in Dec. 359 and one in Jan. 360, cannot be sustained. Cf. Brennecke, *Homöer*, 40–56, for treatment of events at Seleucia and Constantinople.

[113] Both the Homoiousian majority and a group led by Acacius that supported a Homoian-type of confession sent delegations to Constantinople. J. Lienhard, 'Acacius of Caesarea: *Contra Marcellum*: Historical and Theological Considerations', *Cristianesimo nella storia*, 10 (1989), 4–7.

[114] Philostorgius, *HE* iv. 12 (*GCS* xxi. 65. 22–8). Cf. Sozomen, *HE* iv. 23. 7 (*GCS* l. 177–8).

[115] Lucifer, *De non parcendo*, 26 (*CCSL* viii. 245. 13–15); Socrates, *HE* ii. 37 (*PG* lxvii. 320C).

[116] Witness Rufinus' epitaph in reaction to the standardization of the Homoian formula with absolutely no mention of Constantinople (*HE* i. 21 (*PL* xxi. 495A)).

[117] *CAP* B iv. 2 (*CSEL* lxv. 158. 22).

[118] *Altercatio Heracliani laici cum Germinio episcopo Sirmiensi*, ed. C. Caspari, Kirchenhistorische Anecdota 1 (Christiania, 1883), 131–47 (= *PLS* i. 345–50).

The fact that the *gesta* of the council of Ariminum were widely known must have contributed to the resiliency of its tradition. Jerome's remark, that accounts of the synod could be found in the archives of many churches, is easily vindicated: citations from or personal knowledge of the *gesta* are abundant in western literature, including the Italian synodical letter to Illyricum,[119] Marius Victorinus,[120] Auxentius of Milan, who appended a copy of the *acta* to his confession of faith which he sent to Valentinian I,[121] Ambrose (his use of the *gesta* cited above), and that which forms the substance of the debate between Augustine and Maximinus in 417.[122]

Regardless of the fact that the council of Ariminum and its proceedings were condemned by a number of synods in Gaul,[123] such as Paris, and Italy, its conclusions continued to be perceived as binding by the Homoian community. Typical is the assertion made in AD 366 by Valens, Ursacius, Gaius, and Paulus in a letter to Germinius which describes the catholic faith as that 'which was set forth and confirmed by the holy council of Ariminum'.[124] In the west there is evidence that the authority of the council of Ariminum came to stand in juxtaposition to the council of Nicaea. Damasus of Rome, and later Augustine, will have to rebuke existing claims that Ariminum eclipsed Nicaea since the decisions of the former were ratified by a greater number of bishops.[125] The competitive relationship between the two councils is particularly apparent in Ambrose, who experienced strong opposition from the Homoian faction early in his episcopate in Milan. It seems his Homoian accuser, Auxentius of Durostorum, claimed the authority of Ariminum in support of his confession that Christ was not a creature as other creatures, to which Ambrose retorts, in his defence to Valentinian II, 'Thus it is written by the synod of Ariminum; and with justification I loathe that assembly, following rather the profession of the Nicene council from which neither death nor the sword will be able to separate me.'[126]

---

[119] In *CSEL* lxv. 158. 16–18.

[120] *De homoousio recipiendo*, 4 (*CSEL* lxxxiii. 1. 282–3) (Duval, 'La "Manœuvre frauduleuse"', 82 n. 154).

[121] Hilary, *Contra Aux.* 15: 'In order that Your Piety may truly understand those things done at the council of Ariminum, I have sent them along, and I ask that you command these to be freely read . . .' (*PL* x. 618c).

[122] *Collatio cum Maximino*, I. 2 (*PL* xlii. 710).

[123] Sulpicius Severus, *Chron.* II. 45. 5: 'frequentibus intra Gallias conciliis' (*CSEL* i. 98. 29).

[124] *CAP* B IV. 5 (*CSEL* lxv. 159. 18–19).

[125] Respectively, *Ep.* 1 'Confidimus' (*PL* xiii. 348c); *Collatio cum Max.* I. 2 (*PL* xlii. 710).

[126] *Ep.* XXI. 75. 14: 'Hoc scriptum est in Ariminensi synodo; meritoque concilium illud exhorreo sequens tractatum concilii Nicaeni, a quo me nec mors nec gladius poterit separare'

We have chronicled the events and their implications which led to the establishment of a Homoian identity that was crystallized through the successes of the council of Ariminum. During this process, we found that the churches in the west were not unified theologically in an indebtedness to the Nicene creed as a general confessional standard. By the winter of AD 360 one can speak of what Gwatkin called the 'Homoian supremacy'[127] in the west, though for only a very short time. Even before the death of Constantius (3 November 361), one is confronted with the fragmentary evidence of a mounting opposition to the recent successes of the Homoian bishops, a process that resulted in a hardening of theological affiliations. And by the beginning of the reign of Valentinian I, only three years later, the credal affirmations of the late 350s have formed into definable parties— Homoian and Neo-Nicene, *inter alia*—with distinct churches, liturgies, and literature. As the parties took shape, so did the controversy which produced them. Not surprisingly, there is no lack of polemical literature appearing in the aftermath of Ariminum, allowing us to chart with some precision the contours of the conflict over the next two decades. We will attempt to throw new light on this period and on the leading ecclesiastical luminaries who arose in its midst.

(*CSEL* lxxxii. 3. 79). The dramatic confession which was intended by this statement is apparent when compared to Rom. 8: 35–9 (Vulgate): 'quis nos separabit a caritate Christi; tribulatio an angustia . . . an gladius. Certus sum enim quia neque mors neque vita . . . poterit nos separare a caritate Dei.'

[127] *Studies of Arianism*, 180.

2

Early Pro-Nicene Campaigns: Hilary of Poitiers and Eusebius of Vercelli

THE Homoian confession of faith had triumphed in the Roman Empire, but only at great cost to itself. Valens and Ursacius and the other leaders of the new Homoian coalition had created many enemies for themselves on account of the severity of the methods employed at the councils of Ariminum and Constantinople. Moreover, the prohibition of all 'substance' language at these councils directly contributed to an unparalleled counter-reaction in the west which asserted the primacy of the Nicene creed as the only orthodox standard of faith. A number of other factors also provided impetus for the sweeping success of the pro-Nicene movement. Surely the political chain of events after 360 must play a large role in our understanding since the rise of a Neo-Nicene reaction in the west can be charted in direct relation to the loss of control over Britain and the Gauls which Constantius experienced as Julian, still Caesar, advanced in political power. Julian was content to allow, even encourage, anti-Homoian sentiment in hopes of unsettling Constantius' position in particular and weakening the catholic Church in general.[1] To comprehend the rapid changes in the ecclesiastical situation, one can point to leading personalities who were largely responsible for bringing about the west's opposition to Homoian theology: we will look at two in particular, Hilary of Poitiers and Eusebius of Vercelli.

Chief among the early leaders of the anti-Homoians was the exiled bishop Hilary of Poitiers, whose relatively obscure career was suddenly illuminated by his daring political and literary activities after 358/9. Following his return from exile in Asia Minor, Hilary's significance as one of the pre-eminent apologists of the Neo-Nicene movement in the west, especially in Gaul, is indisputable. The bestowal of the title 'doctor ecclesiae'[2] on Hilary underscores the value which later generations placed

---

[1] Julian's hatred both of his uncle's political power and of Christian supremacy over Pagan religion informed his political policies during 360-3. G. W. Bowersock, *Julian the Apostate* (Cambridge, 1978), 18.

[2] See J. Daniélou, 'Saint Hilaire évêque et docteur', and B. de Gaiffier, 'Hilaire docteur de l'Église', both in *Hilaire de Poitiers: évêque et docteur (368-1968)* (Paris, 1968), 17; 27-37.

on his theological contributions. While our literary inheritance from Hilary is rich and, for the most part, well preserved,[3] the course of his activities after the council of Constantinople (360) cannot be traced with any certainty. Most of the modern literature that deals with his career addresses the issues that precede his exile or the works which were produced in exile.[4] Only a few studies are available which focus on the difficult task of critically reconstructing Hilary's movements following his departure from Constantinople. A large part of the problem has to do with the fragmented state of our sources, which provide little more than a glimpse into the flurry of anti-Arian councils and polemics taking place in the west during the early 360s. It is during this time that Hilary's acclaim reached its height. Given the importance of these years (359–363/4), we are obliged to undertake whatever recovery of information is possible about Hilary's political and literary activities, especially because his writings represent our main source for charting the rise of Nicene dominance in the west. What follows is a brief survey of the evidence pertaining to the role which the bishop of Poitiers played in the Neo-Nicene reconstruction following the council of Constantinople and just prior to his meeting with Eusebius of Vercelli in Italy.[5]

I. HILARY OF POITIERS AND HIS LITERARY AND POLITICAL ACTIVITIES AGAINST HOMOIANISM

The surprising degree of mobility which Hilary enjoyed in exile is well established by his own admission.[6] He was in attendence at the council of Seleucia (359),[7] and immediately after is found in Constantinople,

---

[3] C. Kannengiesser, 'L'Héritage d'Hilaire de Poitiers', *RSR* 56 (1968), 450 ff.

[4] The major studies are J. Doignon, *Hilaire de Poitiers avant l'exil* (Paris, 1971); C. F. Borchardt, *Hilary of Poitiers' Role in the Arian Struggle* (The Hague, 1966); Brennecke, *Hilarius von Poitiers*. The latter two works provide a limited discussion of the issues concerning Hilary's return from exile and his consequent literary labours. The recent publication of a new critical edition of the *In Constantium* by André Rocher, *Hilaire de Poitiers: Contre Constance*, SC 334 (Paris, 1987) is a much needed and welcome study on a seminal work of Hilary which was written after the latter returned to Gaul. It is unfortunate that Rocher's historical analysis tends to perpetuate a dependence on traditional views about Hilary's career at several critical points.

[5] A more summarized version can be found in D. H. Williams, 'The Anti-Arian Campaigns of Hilary of Poitiers and the "Liber contra Auxentium" ', *Church History*, 61 (1992), 7–22.

[6] *De synodis*, 63 (*PL* x. 552C).

[7] Sulpicius, *Chron.* II. 42. 1–4 (*CSEL* i. 95); *In Const.* 12 (Rocher, 192. 1–11). His alleged influence with the Homoiousian party during the debates of the council is overestimated by older research, which has been influenced by Sulpicius' inflation of Hilary's importance in exile.

probably having accompanied the Homoiousian delegates who were commissioned by the council at Seleucia to represent its decisions.[8] Once he was in the capital city, however, it appears that Hilary received no invitation to join the proceedings nor had any opportunity to sign formally against the Homoian formula which had become the new basis of ecclesiastical unity. To his dismay, the emperor had agreed to reject all other confessional formulas, including the more moderate homoiousian theology of his eastern colleagues, and all delegates from the western and eastern councils were required to sign the anti-ousian formula from Niké.[9] Constantius could now celebrate his tenth consulate as one who was on the verge of an ecclesiastical triumph that would exceed even that of Nicaea. In the early weeks of January 360, as other bishops were arriving in Constantinople for a council to ratify the new doctrinal unanimity of east and west, Hilary made a drastic move: he composed a letter, addressed to Constantius, for the purpose of securing a personal audience.[10]

In the first part of this document, Hilary attempts to convince the emperor that he had been exiled (at the synod of Biterrae (Baeterrae) in 356) on the basis of false charges. If he were given the opportunity directly to confront his accuser (presumably Saturninus, bishop of Arles, who also happened to be present in the city), he could prove his innocence.[11] But more pressing on the bishop's mind was the present controversy which racked the 'whole world' due to the recent councils (Ariminum and Seleucia). In the letter, Hilary expresses his belief in the obligation of a Christian emperor to defend the orthodox faith, that is, Nicene theology. The problem, in his view, originated from those bishops who did not counsel the emperor with sound doctrine but, 'either from audacity, or opportunity, or error, the immutable constitution of apostolic doctrine was confessed fraudulently, or boldly bypassed so that the truth, with its usual significance of confessing the Father, and the Son and the Holy Spirit, was eluded.'[12] Hilary is acutely aware that a council has convened in the city and is just beginning to debate the faith. He

---

[8] *Chron.* II. 45. 3 (*CSEL* i. 98).

[9] Philostorgius, *HE* IV. 12 (*GCS* xxi. 65. 22–8); Sozomen, *HE* IV. 23. 7 (*GCS* l. 177–8).

[10] This letter is the so-called 'Liber II ad Constantium' (*CSEL* lxv. 197–205). Since it has now been shown that the so-called 'Liber I' is really part of the western synodical letter from Serdica, the title 'Liber II' cannot be accurate (see Rocher, 24 ff.). Henceforth the letter will be identified simply as *Ad Constantium*.

[11] *Ad Const.* II. 2. 1–2: 'I am in exile not for a crime but on account of schism and false reports submitted to you, pious emperor' (*CSEL* lxv. 198). The actual content of these charges continues to vex scholars. See T. D. Barnes for a summary of the modern approaches and some of the problems involved: 'Hilary of Poitiers on his Exile', *VC* 46 (1992), 129–30.

[12] *Ad Const.* II. 4 (*CSEL* lxv. 199. 10–14).

urges Constantius, therefore, to give him an opportunity to address the assembly so that the truth may be clearly preached for the sake of unity, eternity, and the peace between the east and west.

Hilary's pleas went unheard. The Homoian formula from Ariminum was endorsed by the synod and on 15 February 360 Constantius, along with those bishops present, consecrated the Great Church at Constantinople, named the 'Sophia', which his father had begun a generation earlier.[13] No panegyrics delivered on that occasion have come down to the present day, but we can be sure that parallels were drawn between the two emperors on their respective abilities to unify the empire politically and religiously.

We do not know how long Hilary remained in Constantinople: at some undisclosed point the bishop of Poitiers left the city for his homeland. Unfortunately the circumstances of his return to Gaul are complicated by conflicting information.[14] Of the two explanations offered by Sulpicius Severus, scholars have generally preferred the account in his *Chronicle* to that in the *Vita Martini*.[15] The former explains that Hilary 'was ordered to return to Gaul as a seed-bed of discord and an agitator of the east while the sentence of exile against him remained uncancelled'.[16] But this passage is equally problematic. If Hilary had been 'an agitator of the east', it is very difficult to understand how he would have been allowed to return to Gaul and freely incite turmoil in a region which was already in a state of agitation against Constantius' policies. Just as suspicious is the exaggerated importance which Hilary is purported to have in the east by such an interpretation. Undoubtedly this latter difficulty is due to the common historiographical problems one encounters when viewing the later 'Arian controversy' through the anachronistic accounts of most of our sources. Regarding Hilary's departure from Constantinople, we may wonder how Sulpicius could be so ill-informed, unless, with Meslin, we attribute his explanation more to 'la vision hagiographique' at this juncture than to a concern for historical detail.[17]

---

[13] *Regesten*, 207.

[14] Y.-M. Duval treats this question and weighs the various evidence in detail in 'Vrais et faux problèmes', 253–66.

[15] 'when the holy Hilary learned through the penitence of the king that authority was granted him to return . . . (VI. 7 (*CSEL* i. 117)). There is no evidence that Constantius ever 'repented' of his actions toward religious dissenters in addition to the sheer unlikelihood of such an event.

[16] *Chron.* 45. 4 (trans. in *NPNF* xi. 118). For its acceptance, see, *inter alia*, P. Galtier, *Saint Hilaire de Poitiers: le premier docteur de l'Église* (Paris, 1960), 71; Borchardt, *Hilary of Poitiers' Role*, 173; E. Griffe, *La Gaule chrétienne à l'époque romaine* (2nd edn., Paris, 1964), 260; and most recently Rocher, 'Introduction', *Contre Constance*, 26.

[17] 'Hilaire et la crise arienne', in *Hilaire et son temps*, 37.

In all likelihood, Hilary set out for Gaul without having received any expressed approval in the early spring of 360. It must be admitted that there is no one text which supports this alternative; however, we can point to two important changes after the council of Constantinople which make a plausible case. The first is a sudden change in the political climate of Gaul, and the second is a radical difference in the way Hilary perceived the emperor and his goal to unify the empire doctrinally. We will consider these in order.

While Julian was wintering at Paris, he was proclaimed Augustus early in 360 by his troops.[18] Constantius' attempt to deflate Julian's recent military successes by ordering the Gallic auxiliaries to the Persian front had backfired. The army refused to leave its *patria* and hailed Julian as the Augustus of the west. It was clearly a rebellious act, dramatically signalled by the immediate departure of the praetorian prefect, Florentius, who fled so quickly that he left his family behind.[19] Despite Julian's assurance of complete co-operation, Constantius refused to accept the new situation, appointing Nebridius in Florentius' place as a means of retaining his authority in the Gauls.[20] But the move had little effect. Julian's sway in that part of the west as an Augustus was uncontested, and by the end of July his position was secure enough for him to leave on a short campaign to the Rhine.[21]

It is not improbable that Hilary would have heard the news of the usurpation, perhaps in Constantinople. Exactly how he would have responded to such reports we cannot be sure. In a passage which continues to perplex scholars, he seems to hint at the idea that Julian reserved a certain sympathy for the circumstances of his exile,[22] so much so that it has been suggested that the *Ad Constantium* was written by Hilary as an indirect attempt to court the western ruler's favour. This view cannot be pushed too far since the letter was almost certainly written before news of

---

[18] Ammianus Marcellinus, *Res gesta* xx. 4.4 ff. (ed. W. Seyfarth, *Ammiani Marcellini Rerum gestarum libri qui supersunt*, vols. i-ii (Leipzig, 1978), 188 ff.) (hereafter 'Ammianus'); Socrates, *HE* iii. 1 (*PG* lxvii. 373B). At least Julian wished to claim that the initiative began with the army.

[19] Ammianus, xx. 8. 20–1 (Seyfarth, 203).

[20] Ammianus, xx. 9. 5, 8 (Seyfarth, 204, 205) (in March).

[21] Ammianus, xx. 10. 1 (Seyfarth, 205). Further evidence of Julian's sovereignty can be seen from the coins minted at Arles and Lyons in honour of his quinquennalia (6 Nov. 360), which depict the portraits of the two Augusti (Bowersock, *Julian the Apostate*, 53).

[22] *Ad Const.* ii. 2. 1: 'nor do I have an insignificant witness to my complaints; namely my religious lord, Julian, your Caesar, who endured more grievous injuries than I in my exile from evil persons' (*CSEL* lxv. 198). As Meslin points out, Hilary would have scarcely been able to say anything false in such a context ('Hilaire et la crise arienne', 24).

Julian's proclamation reached Constantinople. Nevertheless, it is true that Julian was still overtly showing favour to the Christians at this time;[23] in particular, he was interested in winning the support of those who had suffered under Constantius by granting political immunity and recalling exiled bishops in his jurisdiction.[24] Julian was well aware, as Socrates informs us, that Constantius had rendered himself odious to the proponents of Homoousian theology.[25] There is no doubt that Julian was acting on this knowledge to increase his political base long before Constantius' death.

At the very least we can presume that Hilary would not have risked returning to the west independently, unless he were convinced by some means that Julian's policies were sufficiently distanced from those of Constantius. What we know of Hilary's actions in the east, therefore, can plausibly be linked to the changing political-religious situation in the west. There is also literary evidence from Hilary's own pen that recent circumstances in Constantinople warranted drastic action on his part. At Constantinople, Constantius' overt communion with the leading Homoian bishops of the west and the Acacians from Seleucia appears to have instigated radical changes in Hilary's thinking about the past and present religious politics of the emperor. The *In Constantium*[26] represents a manifesto of revolt against Constantius' policies and reveals an individual ready to be martyred for his faith.

Thanks to the recent edition of this work by A. Rocher, issues concerning content and background have been sufficiently treated. Its occasion and date are much more controversial and will require some further comment. According to Rocher, the *In Constantium* had a double objective. The first was to dispose of the honoured idea of the emperor as one who defends the catholic faith. Second, Hilary sought to dissipate the illusion that the Homoian formula imposed at Ariminum was inoffensive and indifferent to the faith.[27] One is immediately struck by the sharp difference in attitude

---

[23] Julian celebrated the Epiphany, 6 Jan. 361, in the church of Vienne (Ammianus, XXI. 2. 5; Seyfarth, 219).

[24] Socrates (*HE* III. 1 (*PG* lxvii. 376C–377A)) and Philostorgius (*HE* VI. 7 (*GCS* xxi. 75)) place the edict after Constantius' death (3 Nov. 361). But a passage from the *Historia acephala* (3. 2–3 (A. Martin, *Histoire 'acephale' et index syriaque des lettres festales d'Athanase d'Alexandrie*, SC 317 (Paris, 1985), 150)) may imply that this edict, not published in Alexandria until Feb. 363, stems from an earlier pronouncement that had already been in effect in the west.

[25] *HE* III. 1 (*PG* lxvii. 376C–377A).

[26] The manuscript evidence (see Rocher, 142–4) establishes that the preferred title of the work is *In Constantium*, as Jerome referred to it (*De viris illustribus*, 100), over the traditionally accepted *Contra Constantium*.

[27] Rocher, 'Introduction', 76.

between the *In Constantium* and the letter which Hilary had addressed earlier to Constantius in Constantinople. The *Ad Constantium* contains the usual flatteries of protocol in the prologue. Throughout the letter Hilary excuses the emperor's actions on account of his heretical counsellors and because, despite Constantius' sincere desire for truth, he was being 'deceived' by false reports.

In the *In Constantium* such excuses are replaced with severe accusations. The ratification of the Homoian faith at Constantinople is proof that Constantius listens and does what his pseudoprophets say: 'You receive with a kiss priests who have betrayed Christ.'[28] For this reason Hilary announces at the beginning of his manifesto: 'But we fight against a deceiving persecutor, against a flattering enemy, against Constantius, the antichrist.'[29] Given what he has seen and heard, he can no longer endure to remain silent as before. Repeatedly Hilary expresses his desire to stand boldly as a 'confessor' before Constantius just as he would before Nero or Decius, for this is what Constantius had become. It is absolutely clear that Hilary is ready to become a martyr for the Nicene faith—which is precisely why, *contra* Rocher,[30] the *In Constantium* is more likely to have been published in the period immediately following Hilary's return to Gaul than after Constantius' death.[31] Constantius is presented no longer as a legitimate emperor, now that he is an 'antichrist' and an 'enemy to divine religion'. Nor is there any reason why Hilary must be constrained by the laws of such a ruler, including the terms of his banishment. The overall impact of the treatise when taken seriously seems to offer a justification for Christian civil disobedience; the defence of the true faith has taken precedence over adherence to an unjust system.[32] The rhetorical effect of Hilary's diatribe locates the emperor at the centre of religious policy-making—a dubious assertion even about Constantius. One can sense the intensity of the writer's resentment when he taunts Constantius

---

[28] *In Const.* 10. 13–14 (Rocher, 186).   [29] *In Const.* 5. 1–3 (Rocher, 176).

[30] Rocher offers a complicated schema for successive stages of redaction (29 ff.), suggesting that it was not published as a whole until after Constantius' death (per Jerome). He contends that Julian's position politically was not strong enough for Hilary to have written such things with immunity. In effect, the *In Constantium* is a result of Julian's edict (Feb. 362), and was probably written 'en hommage de reconnaissance' to Julian as benefactor and liberator of Gaul (p. 52).

[31] If the document was not published until the winter of 361/2, the complete absence of any reference to the many anti-heretical councils which had already met in Gaul becomes too problematic to explain.

[32] The much debated phrase in *In Constantium*, 11, 'fugere sub Nerone mihi licuit' ('it was permitted for me to flee under Nero'), can be applied to the present context only with great strain.

with the words, 'Who are you to order bishops and forbid the form of apostolic preaching?'[33] This does not necessarily mean that Hilary agreed to or actually supported Julian in his usurpation as Brennecke concludes.[34] But the sudden shift of political circumstances in Gaul opened an unexpected door for Hilary, once he had renounced all fealty to the emperor and his antichristian policies, to return to his homeland—probably by late spring of that same year.

From the *Vita Martini*, we may postulate that Hilary arrived at Rome and proceeded to Gaul from there.[35] It is very possible that he met with Liberius while in the city, perhaps to inform the latter of the events at Seleucia and Constantinople.[36] He may have shown Liberius the letter which he was bringing from the Homoiousians to illuminate the westerners, as he did at the synod of Paris, about the 'deceit of the devil and the conspiracy against the Lord's church' perpetrated by the Homoians at Ariminum. The course of the discussion between Hilary and Liberius may have also centred on the circumstances of Liberius' exile and return to Rome. The compulsion laid upon the Roman bishop to submit to the bishops favoured by the imperial court would have corresponded perfectly to the case Hilary was building against his enemies. Liberius then supplied his visitor with documented proof of his unfortunate situation: by the time Hilary compiled the second section of the *Liber adversus Ursacium et Valentem*[37] eight letters of Liberius appear in the collection which are related to Liberius' opposition to the heretics and his capitulation to their views in exile.[38]

Leaving Rome, Hilary returned to his see in Poitiers.[39] Beyond this point we are not able to trace the Gallic bishop's whereabouts with any precision. Hilary's call for action, as manifested in the *In Constantium*, did not go unheeded by his colleagues. Sulpicius reports that, after Hilary's

---

[33] *In Const.* 16. 4–6 (Rocher, 200).   [34] *Hilarius von Poitiers*, 362.

[35] Martin arrived too late to join him (*Vita Mart.* 6. 7 (*CSEL* i. 117)). Despite its hagiographical character, the material pertaining to Hilary here is probably accurate enough to use in historical reconstruction.

[36] So supported by Duval, 'Vrais et faux problèmes', 263; Meslin, 'Hilaire et la crise arienne', 39; T. Holmes, *The Origin and Development of the Christian Church in Gaul* (London, 1911), 181.

[37] Brennecke, *Hilarius von Poitiers*, 363–4, is probably correct in thinking Hilary compiled the second book of the *Adversus Ursacium et Valentem* after he returned to Gaul, and probably after the synod of Paris (summer 360). His contention is unproven, however, that Hilary already had access to Liberius' letters while in exile and in time for the publication of book 1 of the *Adversus*.

[38] Accepting Feder's proposed list of letters in *CSEL* lxv. 191–2.

[39] *Vita Mart.* 7. 1 (*CSEL* i. 117).

return from exile, the creed which had been received at Ariminum was condemned by a spate of anti-Homoian synods held throughout Gaul.[40] From the collection of documents of this period in Hilary's dossier, we know that one of these synods convened in Paris.[41] It was not the first synod to meet since Saturninus, Hilary's arch-nemesis, had already been excommunicated by some previous assemblies.[42] The Parisian synod cannot be dated with certainty, and scholarly estimations range between the spring of 360 and the middle of 361. Much of the question hinges on whether the meeting of the synod is related to Julian's presence in the city, but we need not consider the intricacies of this problem here.[43]

Hilary's influence on the synod, as seen from its decisions, is clearly perceptible. Sensitivity to eastern concerns with western vocabulary and thought is apparent here. The synod's affirmation of *homoousios* is associated with a studied rejection of neo-Sabellianism; thus confirming its distance from Marcellan theology. Besides condemning the temporal generation of the Son, the similitude between Father and Son is accepted but in the sense of true God from true God, 'so that not a singularity of divinity (*unio divinitatis*) but a unity (*unitas*) of divinity is understood'. After its affirmation of Nicene theology, the Gallic synod undertook the excommunication of the known leaders of the Homoian movement, although most of the condemned bishops were from other provinces, with the result that their sentences were hardly enforceable. The immunity which Auxentius of Milan continued to enjoy in north Italy from anti-Arian prosecution is a good case in point. It was a different situation *in Gallias* however, and the synod proceeded to take action against all those bishops considered apostate and who had been installed in the sees of exiled bishops under the reign of Constantius. These were to be shut off from communion and removed from their ill-gotten episcopates.[44] If Julian was supporting such decrees with governmental enforcement, as it is likely he was, the measures taken against bishops sympathetic to the Niké creed were undoubtedly very successful. Small wonder that Sulpicius could triumphantly report that in just a short time 'our regions of Gaul were set free from the stain of heresy'.[45]

---

[40] *Chron.* II. 45.5 (*CSEL* i. 98. 29–31).

[41] In the *Adversus Ursacium et Valentem* there is a synodical letter to the eastern bishops (presumably the Homoiousians of Seleucia and Hilary's colleagues while he was in exile), *CAP* A I (*CSEL* lxv. 43–6).

[42] *CAP* A I. 4 (4) (*CSEL* lxv. 46). Paternus of Périgueux had also been deposed by a Gallic synod (*Chron.* II. 45. 7), perhaps before the meeting at Paris.

[43] See Duval, 'Vrais et faux problèmes', 264–5 for details.

[44] A I. 4 (3) (*CSEL* lxv. 45. 20–5).   [45] *Chron.* II. 45. 7 (*CSEL* i. 99. 5–7).

Concomitant with his ecclesiastical–political campaign against the Arians, Hilary's continued literary activity was no less aggressive. He is said to have 'also published books excellently written concerning the faith, by which he diligently exposed the cunning of the heretics'.[46] What were these books 'de fide'? Almost assuredly, the reference is to the twelve books written by Hilary which we know as *De trinitate*.[47] No other work by Hilary better suits the description nor was as popular among subsequent generations of defenders of Nicaea. The exact dating of the work is notoriously difficult: slim internal evidence indicates that it was written, or at least much of it, in exile, but scholars are not agreed whether to place its completion before or after he returned to Gaul.[48] From the theological programme which Hilary follows it is clear that the document itself is a fruit of his exile. This is evident in the pattern of logic which he pursues. In book v. 1 he rejects the polar extremes in Trinitarian doctrine, namely Arianism and Sabellianism, while preserving the soundness of the 'core' truth they both pervert. This is a feature of argumentation which he acquired in the east, operating similarly to the macrostructure in *De synodis*.[49] But it was never published in the east. Apart from the obvious fact that Latin readers were the intended audience for *De trinitate*, our ancient sources indicate that the treatise was issued in the context of Hilary's reclamation activities in the west.[50] This is compatible with what we know of his earlier stated efforts to reform and re-educate his western

---

[46] Rufinus, *HE* I. 31 (*PL* xxi. 501).

[47] A chief difficulty lies in the fact that we do not know what title Hilary gave to the work, or if he gave any. Jerome knows the work only as 'duodecim adversus Arianos confecit libros' (*De viris illust.* 100 (*PL* xxiii. 738B). It is not a title, as the translation in the *NPNF* iii. 380 indicates). Interestingly, John Cassian, a compatriot of Hilary, knows the work as *De fide* (*De Incarnatione Domini contra Nestorium*, VII. 24). The present title, *De trinitate*, is not found until MSS of the 6th century. P. Smulders, 'Remarks on the Manuscript Tradition of the *De trinitate* of Saint Hilary of Poitiers', *Studia Patristica*, 3 (= Text und Untersuchungen 78) (1961), 131.

[48] On the evidence see Borchardt, *Hilary of Poitiers' Role*, 42; Smulders, 'Remarks on the Manuscript Tradition', 131–2, although, in his preface to the *CCSL* edition of *De trinitate* (1979), Smulders is less sure when and where Hilary finished it ('Praefatio', *CCSL* lxii. 3). On the question whether all twelve books of *De trinitate* were an intended whole, see the convincing arguments of E. P. Meijering, *Hilary of Poitiers: On the Trinity, De trinitate 1. 1–9, 2, 3* (Leiden, 1982), 2 ff.

[49] For the theology of the *De trinitate*, see J. Moingt, 'La Théologie trinitaire de S. Hilaire', in *Hilaire et son temps*, 159–73; Smulders, *La Doctrine trinitaire de S. Hilaire de Poitiers* (Rome, 1944). Smulders thinks (281 n. 11) *De trinitate*, VII, was written about the same time as *De synodis*.

[50] Rufinus (*HE* I. 30–1) positions his discussion about Hilary's 'libros de fide' in the context of Hilary's restoration activities throughout the west. Socrates (*HE* III. 10) simply states that Hilary wrote his books 'shortly after the recall of those who had been banished' (trans. in *NPNF* ii. 84), namely after Feb. 362.

brethren upon his return from exile. It is also commensurate with the words of Hilary's manifesto against Constantius that the time for keeping silent is past. Unlike the irenic spirit which pervades *De synodis*, the *De trinitate* is a polemical treatise designed to refute the scriptural exegesis and theological arguments of the Arians. We may conclude therefore that Hilary returned to the west with the nearly finished manuscript of *De trinitate*, and published it sometime in 361 or perhaps 362 after the recall of the banished bishops by Julian.

Hilary's journeys for the propagation of Nicene orthodoxy, now backed by the decisions of the Gallic synods, took him beyond the borders of Gaul. It seems that the bishop of Poitiers carried into Italy his campaign of restoring bishops and churches which had succumbed to the anti-ousian decrees at Ariminum. Rufinus provides the sketchy information that 'once he returned [from exile] and situated himself in Italy, Hilary strove for the restoration of the churches, endeavouring to recover the faith of the fathers'.[51] But when exactly did Hilary arrive in Italy and begin his efforts of reclamation? Modern scholarship, implicitly following Rufinus, has generally assumed that he did so very soon after the synod of Paris. The problem is that Hilary's entry into the Italian prefecture cannot have been as straightforward as our sources suggest. A closer look at the political tensions between Julian and Constantius assists us in making a more precise determination of when Hilary could have carried his crusade outside Gaul.

Throughout the year 360, Constantius still controlled all of Italy in the person of his praetorian prefect Taurus. Taurus had served in this same office since 355 and was wholly devoted to the emperor's policies.[52] Without the benefit of Julian's jurisdiction it was impossible for Hilary to wield any ecclesiastical authority. In 361 the political situation changed very rapidly, as Julian openly challenged Constantius' control of the west. Early in the year Nebridius, who had been appointed by Constantius, abandoned his post in Gaul and the prefecture was filled by one who was loyal to Julian.[53] Julian wasted no time in moving his armies eastward and may have reached Sirmium as early as May or June.[54] Before the advance

---

[51] *HE* I. 30 (*PL* xxi. 501A).

[52] Flavius Taurus was *praefectus praetorio Italiae et Africae* from 355 to 361, when he was forced out by Julian's advance. For his continued faithfulness to Constantius he shared the consulate with Florentius in 361. *PLRE* i. 879–80.

[53] Ammianus, XXI. 5. 12, 8. 1 (Seyfarth, 224, 227). This is probably Decimius Germanianus (*PLRE* i. 392, 1050), who was immediately followed by Fl. Sallustius. Bowersock, *Julian the Apostate*, 58, needs to be modified on this particular.

[54] J. Szidat, 'Zur Ankunft Iulianus in Sirmium 361 n. Chr. auf seinem Zug gegen Constantius II', *Historia*, 24 (1975), 375–8. The more conventional interpretation of

of Julian's forces, both Taurus and Florentius (praetorian prefect of Illyricum) fled to Constantius.[55] These significant political changes should not be construed to mean that most of Italy was firmly in Julian's hands by the middle of 361. When two of Constantius' legions captured at Sirmium were being sent to Gaul for safe keeping, they rebelled at Aquileia and threatened to cut off Julian in the rear.[56] Fighting did ensue and continued until the publication of Constantius' death (3 November 361). Moreover, Rome remained loyal to Constantius until his death: Tertullus, the *praefectus urbis*, was not replaced by Julian until the autumn of 361.[57] We can surmise, therefore, that Hilary could have done little outside the Gauls before Constantius' death.

In light of the above scenario, Hilary is not likely to have extended his pro-Nicene efforts into northern Italy until late 361 or early 362. And it was in northern Italy, sometime at the end of 362, that he came into contact with the 'Confessor' of Vercelli, one whom he had not known previously. As a result of their joint campaigning throughout the west, we are told that 'the darkness of heresy was chased away'.

2. EUSEBIUS OF VERCELLI

Without any doubt, Hilary of Poitiers became one of the west's most celebrated theologians and anti-Arian figures of the fourth century. This was largely due to his substantial literary activity, most of which was widely circulated soon after his death.[58] We should not be surprised at the historical eminence ascribed to him by a compatriot such as Sulpicius Severus, who, in chronicling the aftermath of the council of Constantinople, mentions only Hilary as one who set the west free from the guilt of heresy.[59] But from historians less prejudiced in this way, we know that Hilary was joined in his reclamationary activities by another western bishop, who returned to his homeland with the personal status of a

---

Ammianus has Julian not leaving for Sirmium until July (so J. Bidez, *La Vie de l'empereur Julien* (Paris, 1965), 192–3).

[55] Ammianus, XXI. 9. 4 (Seyfarth, 228–9).

[56] Ammianus, XXI. 11. 1–3, 12. 1–20 (Seyfarth, 232, 233–5).

[57] Ammianus, XXI. 12. 24 (Seyfarth, 238).

[58] See Kannengiesser, 'L'Héritage d'Hilaire de Poitiers', 435–50, for a survey of 4th–5th-century cognizance of Hilary's writings. In particular, Jerome was thoroughly acquainted with Hilary's works and includes him in a list of prestigious Latin ecclesiastical writers (*Ep.* LXX. 5). Ambrose is heavily indebted to Hilary's *De trinitate*, taking extracts from each of the twelve books *sine nomine*, for the construction of his own *De fide*.

[59] *Chron.* II. 45. 7 (*CSEL* i. 99).

confessor and defender of Nicene orthodoxy. Rufinus, for example, explains how Hilary of Poitiers and Eusebius of Vercelli were both responsible for freeing the west from the darkness of its heretical shroud. 'Thus, those two men, like bright lights of the world, spread their radiance in Illyricum, Italy, and the Gauls with the result that everything hidden in corners and places concealing the darkness of the heretics was chased away.'[60]

It is curious that the bishop from Vercelli has received so little attention for his role during this period; a point which modern historians have been slow to recognize. Nearly ninety years ago C. H. Turner made the observation, '[A]t least this much may be said confidently, that Eusebius must have been a more important personage than we are accustomed to think'[61]— a remark that has gone relatively unnoticed. Overshadowed by the bulk and significance of Hilary's contributions, Eusebius of Vercelli has received only minimal study as an important figure in the western opposition against the Homoians after Constantinople (360). In some surveys of this era, he appears not at all.[62] Part of the problem is undoubtedly due to the tiny literary heritage which is connected to Eusebius. Jerome attributes only one publication to him, a translation into Latin of Eusebius of Caesarea's commentaries on the Psalms, now lost.[63] Despite this assessment, three letters are also known to have come from the pen of Eusebius, two of which have been transmitted in a ninth-century *vita*[64] and are generally considered authentic. The third letter is found in Hilary's collected *fragmenta historica* (*CSEL* lxv. 46–7). Its authenticity was contested in the earlier part of this century as a Luciferian forgery,[65] although the

---

[60] *HE* I. 31 (*PL* xxi. 501). The last two books of Rufinus' *Ecclesiastical History* must be utilized with caution. On their tendentious reporting and limits of reliability, see F. Thelamon, 'Une œuvre destinée à la communauté chrétienne d'Aquilée: l'Historique ecclésiastique de Rufin', in *Aquileia nel IV secolo*, Antichità Altoadriatiche 22 (Udine, 1982), 255–71.

[61] 'On Eusebius of Vercelli', *JTS* 1 (1900), 126.

[62] i.e., G. Haendler, 'Auswirkungen des arianischen Streites', in *Von Tertullian bis zu Ambrosius* (Berlin, 1978).

[63] *De viris illust.* 96 (*PL* xxxiii. 735B; *Ep.* LXI. 2 (*PL* xxii. 603).

[64] The first is a response to Constantius' invitation to attend the council of Milan (critical edition in Bulhart, *CCSL* ix. 103), and the second is a long letter written from his Scythopolitan exile and secretly sent to the faithful at Vercelli and nearby parishes (*CCSL* ix. 104–9).

[65] J. Saltet, 'La Formation de la légende des papes Libère et Félix', *Bulletin de littérature ecclésiastique*, 3/7 (1905), 222–36; 'Fraudes littéraires schismatiques lucifériens au 4ᵉ et 5ᵉ siècles', *Bulletin de littérature ecclésiastique*, 3/8 (1906), 300–26. J. Chapman, 'The Contested Letters of Pope Liberius', *RB* 27 (1910), 325 f. Simonetti ('Eusebius of Vercelli', *Patrology*, iv. 63) and Hanson (*The Search*, 508 n. 2) have recently affirmed this view but neither offers any new arguments.

arguments in favour of this view do not stand up under close examination and can be rightfully discounted.[66]

Until the early part of this century, these three letters were deemed to be the total literary inheritance from Eusebius. Now this inheritance has been substantially enlarged by the attribution to him of the first seven books of *De trinitate*; a work previously identified with the name of Athanasius or Vigilius of Thapsus.[67] There is at present no agreement over the question of authorship, though the position taken here is that no conclusive argument can be marshalled against the view which names Eusebius as the writer of the (shorter recension) first seven books of *De trinitate*.[68] If this work is correctly attributed to him, the tendency to underrate his role in this period can be more effectively challenged. None the less, Eusebius' historical significance is derived from his politico-ecclesiastical activities, particularly his seminal role in the Neo-Nicene campaign to regain those bishops lost at Ariminum. The problem is that most of his efforts are undocumented and the sparsity of our source data allows us only a limited picture. Even so, the small amount of data available suggests a picture of Eusebius who was more than a 'great helper to Hilary', as Gregory of Tours epitomized him.[69] It is no small matter that Eusebius had been commissioned by the synod of Alexandria to carry its conciliar decisions back to the west, where he is said to have restored many sees to Nicene sentiments, and that he may have been instrumental in loosening the long-standing Homoian grip on the see of Sirmium. It would seem that a more comprehensive reconstruction of Eusebius' career is in order,

---

[66] The Luciferian forgery argument is based on the harsh estimation which Eusebius had of Ossius and those bishops who lapsed at Ariminum. In particular, Chapman (and Simonetti) argues that a passage from the letter addressed to Gregory of Elvira, reveals a discreet reference to the Luciferian sect in Spain. The phrase 'Cunctos lateri tuo fideliter adhaerentes' is supposedly a description of Gregory's sect, whereas the second group, 'Dignare nobis scribere quid malos corrigendo profeceris, vel quantos fratres aut stantes cognoveris, aut ipse monendo correxeris' (*CSEL* lxv. 47. 8–12), are those who fell. Two separate groups are indicated in the second phrase: the 'malos', who are the Arians, and the 'quantos fratres', who share the same faith but stand in need of correction. There is no question that Eusebius felt strongly about the capitulation which occurred at Ariminum, but the passage here indicates a distinction between repentant and unrepentant bishops—a distinction which the Luciferians did not make. Duchesne, Wilmart, Feder, and Bardy have all defended the genuineness of the letter.

[67] *CCSL* ix, pp. vi ff. P. Schepens tries, unsuccessfully, to argue for an eighth book attributable to Eusebius. 'L'Ambrosiastre et saint Eusèbe de Verceil', *RSR* 37 (1950), 295–9.

[68] App. III.

[69] *De gloria beatorum confessorum*, 3: 'Eusebius vero Vercellensis episcopus magnum huic Hilario adjutorium contra haereses fuit' (*PL* lxxi. 831C–832A).

since, apart from the introductory work of V. C. de Clercq,[70] no contextual analysis of his contributions, taking both political and literary factors into account, exists to date. Such an undertaking would exceed the purposes and limitations of this present work, but some preliminary investigations are in order.

(a) *Eusebius at the council of Milan (355)*

Like many church figures of the fourth century who became renowned for their defence of orthodoxy, the biographical details of the life of Eusebius are filled with later hagiographic ornamentation which has little or no relation to historical fact. We know almost nothing reliable about his early life. It is wholly unlikely that Eusebius was a catechumen during the reign of Diocletian when he came to Rome with his parents: a detail from his *Vita*.[71] And the insistence that he had always remained chaste even while he was a catechumen is a predictable by-product of the strong ascetic traditions which permeate the fifth- and sixth-century sermons celebrating *de depositione vel natale* of Eusebius.[72]

The Roman connection may not be completely fictitious. Eusebius is reputed to have first served as a lector at Rome,[73] presumably under the bishopric of Julius, though we possess no further data to determine the date of his accession to the see at Vercelli. Not until the events surrounding the council of Milan (355) do we learn anything substantial about Eusebius himself. Like other western bishops at this time, he might have always remained cloaked in the silent folds of undocumented history if the circumstances of open rebellion against the emperor and an ensuing exile had not propelled him into prominence.

Even if he was already a bishop, it is more than likely that Eusebius did not attend the synod at Arles (353).[74] We may also assume that he did not

---

[70] His studies on Eusebius include two encyclopedia articles ('Eusebius of Vercelli, St.', *New Catholic Encyclopedia*, v. 637, and 'Eusèbe de Verceil (saint)', *DHGE* xv. 1477–83), and a brief examination of the Eusebian correspondence in *Ossius of Cordova: A Contribution to the History of the Constantinian Period* (Washington, DC, 1954), 430–3.

[71] *Bibliotheca hagiographica Latina*, ed. Socii Bollandiani, vol. i (Brussels, 1898–9), 412–13. Dekkers (*Clavis Patrum Latinorum* (2nd edn., The Hague, 1961), 25) places the composition of the *Vita* in the 8th or 9th century.

[72] For the list and brief description of these *sermones*, see J. Lienhard, 'Patristic Sermons on Eusebius of Vercelli and their Relation to his Monasticism', *RB* 87 (1977), 164–72.

[73] *De viris illust.* 96 (*PL* xxiii. 735B).

[74] Cf. Liberius' greeting in his first letter to Eusebius, which offers proof of Eusebius' untarnished record: 'Dearest brother, your unconquerable faith has provided me with a comfort in this present life; having followed the precepts of the Gospels you have in no way dissented from fellowship with the apostolic see' (*CCSL* xi. 121. 2–4).

subscribe to the conciliar letter which, as Liberius informs us, was circulating throughout Italy after Arles.[75] This made him a good candidate to join an episcopal reactionary movement that another Italian, Lucifer of Cagliari, was spearheading to overturn the decisions of Arles. The entire episode grants us a valuable look at the theological and ecclesiastical disarray which characterized the west before Ariminum.

Part of the Liberian correspondence clearly datable to this period informs us of the events that led up to the council of Milan (355). From this material, there are three letters not found in Hilary's *fragmenta* addressed to Eusebius of Vercelli.[76] Liberius was thoroughly convinced of the need for a new council after the débâcle at Arles. Athanasius, along with Marcellus and Photinus, had been condemned *in absentia* for a second time and all the bishops present had capitulated to this decision except Paulinus of Trier, who was banished on the spot. The decisions of the council brought personal loss to the Roman bishop as well. In a brief letter to Ossius he sorely laments the ruin of one of his trusted legates, Vincentius of Capua, who 'not only accomplished nothing [at Arles], but was himself misled by their pretence (*simulationem*)'.[77] Bishop Ossius would have been equally grieved since Vincentius, with another Roman presbyter Victor, had signed the Nicene creed,[78] and later the Serdican creed,[79] at Ossius' side. For propaganda purposes, Vincentius' change of heart may have been used to subvert the resistance of the remaining pro-Athanasian bishops in the west. Very soon after Arles Liberius felt the need to write to Caecilianus, bishop of Spoletium, lest the example of Vincentius hinder Caecilianus' perseverance in the truth.[80]

But other Italian bishops were not so easily intimidated. Foremost among them was the radical defender of Athanasius, Lucifer of Cagliari, who, after arriving at Rome, persuaded Liberius to support his plan of personally proceeding to the court of the emperor to request the convening of a new council.[81] It is under these circumstances that Liberius writes to Eusebius, hoping to elicit his participation in the execution of this new enterprise. The letter to Eusebius can be dated to the middle of 354.[82]

---

[75] *Ep. ad Const. per Luciferium*, 4 (*CSEL* lxv. 92. 5–7).

[76] See App. I, 'A Chronology of Letters Attributed to Liberius of Rome'.

[77] *CAP* B VII. 6 (*CSEL* lxv. 167. 12–13).   [78] Socrates, *HE* I. 13 (*PG* lxvii. 109A).

[79] Vincentius' name appears as no. 14 on the list of subscriptions (*CSEL* lxv. 134).

[80] *CAP* B VII. 3–4 (*CSEL* lxv. 166).

[81] 'Liberius episc. dilectissimo fratri Eusebio', 1. 3 ('App. II B. 1'; *CCSL* ix. 121).

[82] Girardet ('Constance II, Athanase et l'Édit d'Arles', 66) places it in 353/4, though 354 is far more probable. It is very likely that the synod met in Arles at a time commensurate with Constantius' celebration of his tricennalia, 10 Oct. (*Regesten*, 200). The emperor wintered in Arles until the the end of March and is not found at Milan until early autumn.

Briefly Liberius explains the lapse of Vincentius and how the rest of the bishops throughout Italy are being forced to follow the policies established by the easterners (i.e., the anti-Athanasians). Lucifer is then introduced as 'our brother and fellow-bishop . . . from Sardinia',[83] a reference which would have had special meaning to Eusebius, since he too was said to have originated 'de Sardinia'.

The immediate reaction of Eusebius to Liberius' request is positive. And the 'second' letter which is addressed to Eusebius in the Liberian corpus is the result of the Roman bishop's response to this news as reported to him by his carrier Callepius. It is intended primarily to commend Lucifer, his presbyter Pancratius, and his deacon Hilary to Eusebius' fellowship. Liberius again assures Eusebius that they are of like mind on matters of faith, and are in agreement that the public laws should not condemn someone absent—doubtless a reference to action taken at Arles. The repeated emphasis on the commonalities that exist between the two parties reveals Liberius' continued attempt to draw Eusebius into participation. In this he is successful. Sometime after the arrival of Lucifer and his fellows, Eusebius informed Liberius of his approbation for their mission now that he had spoken with Lucifer face to face. Liberius sent a third letter to Eusebius in a reply to his communication, though the latter is no longer extant.[84] 'My mind is greatly eased upon the reading of your letter; indeed, that cause which God favours can progress even further because you did not abandon our brothers, and now I am confident' (lines 8–11). Liberius also expresses his anticipation that as a result of their efforts a council will be held (*celebrari*), so that all who had been deceived in the earlier convention may be reformed. What Liberius really means by *reformari* is spelled out more precisely at the end of another letter which he addressed to the emperor under the care of Lucifer, Pancratius, and Hilary. In it he beseeches Constantius to bring together the bishops in an assembly 'so that all matters confirmed by the judgement of godly bishops may be established in an exposition of the faith, which was confirmed among a great many bishops at Nicaea where your father of holy memory was present.'[85] Liberius is appealing for nothing less than a complete capitulation on the part of the anti-Nicenes, which, given the credal formulation of the previous twenty-five years, shows how naïve he really was about the issues. Such *naïveté* was not unique in the west in the 340s and 350s.

---

[83] 'Liberius . . . fratri Eusebio', 1. 2 (*CCSL* ix. 121. 10).

[84] App. II B. 3. 1 (*CCSL* ix. 122–3. 6–9).

[85] *CAP* A VII. 6: 'Ad Constantium Imp. per Luciferium episcopum' (*CSEL* lxv. 93. 1–4).

Sometime at the end of 354 or early 355, the Emperor Constantius issued an invitation to all western bishops for the purpose of convening a council at his winter quarters in Milan. Obviously Liberius' request via Lucifer had been granted. With a personal letter of appeal from Liberius and the promised support of several leading Italian bishops—perhaps Eusebius and Fortunatianus of Aquileia were among these—Constantius was sufficiently convinced by the delegation that another assembly was warranted. Unfortunately, the documentation at our disposal for the proceedings which took place at the council of Milan is partial and fragmented.[86] The work of reconstructing the course of events relies heavily on the extant correspondence between Eusebius and members of that council.[87] It will become more obvious that the conclusions proposed below are very different from those of de Clercq, who has published the most complete synthesis of Eusebius' activities at the council.

The first letter which is attributed to the pen of Eusebius is in the form of a brief reply to Constantius' invitation to the council. In his response, Eusebius tells the emperor openly that he has also received letters from his brothers and fellow bishops explaining the reason (*ratio*) for the council and requesting that he embrace their purposes.[88] For the sake of the peace of the Church, he promises to come to Milan with all haste.

But when did Eusebius actually arrive at the council and find himself at odds with Valens and other anti-Athanasian bishops? The question is worth investigating since de Clercq, in his analysis of the three letters from the council of Milan to Eusebius, has concluded that Eusebius could not have been present at the opening of the council and may not have come until he was so requested by Lucifer and even by the anti-Athanasian bishops themselves. Of the three letters in question, the first is from Lucifer and his delegation, the second from the council itself, and the third from Constantius urging compliance to the decisions of the council.[89]

According to de Clercq's scenario, the pro-Arian bishops Valens, Ursacius, Germinius, and Eudoxius (bishop of Germanicia) took immediate charge of the proceedings. Even though there is no indication in the sources, as admitted by de Clercq, Eusebius somehow foresaw this chain of events, and, perhaps fearing the council was going to be another

---

[86] The only two narratives of the council which exist are: (1) an unfinished commentary by Hilary of Poitiers on the epistle from the council of Serdica (western) to Constantius (*CSEL* lxv. 184–7). We have already noted in Ch. 1 that the criticisms about the authenticity of this passage are unfounded; (2) Sulpicius Severus, *Chron.* II. 39, though his interest, like other historical notices of the council, is concerned with its final results.

[87] For a complete listing of Eusebius' letters, see App. II.

[88] *CCSL* ix. 103. 5–7.   [89] In Bulhart's edition under app. II A 1–3.

repetition of Arles, he stayed away. At length the Luciferian party sent him a pressing invitation, although this was not sufficient. 'Strangely enough, the opposing party also wanted his presence and even sent a delegation with an imperial order to bring him to Milan.'[90] De Clercq cites the narrative of the council from Hilary's commentary, 'Eusebius of Vercelli . . . was ordered to come to Milan', in order to establish the fact that Eusebius was ordered by the emperor to Milan. 'Eusebius was forced to obey', says de Clercq; but when he does arrive, he is refused admittance to the sessions for ten days. De Clercq believes this was so that Valens and 'his nobodies' could work on the recalcitrant bishops. Once he was admitted, Eusebius took the side of the Roman delegates, as Hilary notes.[91]

We have already seen from Eusebius' first letter (to Constantius) that he freely responded to Constantius' summons, which leaves the inference that Hilary's account is overstated at least on this point. We now turn to the three letters written to Eusebius. Let it be granted, for the moment, that Lucifer's letter is chronologically first, not the letter from the council of Milan as ordered by Bulhart's critical edition. In this short communication from Lucifer, Pancratius, and Hilary, Eusebius is reminded how no opportunity ought to be given to 'the head of the devil' by allowing the Arian dogma to spread. He is asked 'as soon as possible' to come and be present, for even now the poison is spreading.[92] Reading this first section of the letter certainly gives the impression that Eusebius has not yet come to the council. Of course, these words could conceivably have been written before the council began, and the letter could be simply another encouragement for Eusebius to join them in their mission. Yet in the second section of the same letter we find that not only had the council begun, but that it seems Eusebius had already been there.

For the Lord and his Christ knew that just as the name of God in the ruins of Simon was glorified at the coming of the most blessed apostles, so, after Valens was repulsed at your coming, the scheme (*machina*) of the Arian blasphemy was thwarted and destroyed from within.'[93]

To anticipate the conclusion, it will be proposed that the best interpretation of this passage in the light of other forthcoming evidence is that Eusebius did come to Milan at the beginning of the council, but once he

---

[90] *Ossius of Cordova*, 432; 'Eusèbe de Verceil (saint)', 1479. The idea that Eusebius did not come to Milan until later is followed by W. Rusch, *The Later Latin Fathers* (London, 1977), 20.

[91] 'Textus Narratiuus S. Hilarii' (Feder's title), *CSEL* lxv. 187. 6–7.

[92] App. II A 2. 1 (*CCSL* ix. 120. 1–4).   [93] App. II A 2. 2 (*CCSL* ix. 120. 4–8).

experienced the conflict with Valens and his allies which resulted in their retirement to the imperial palace ('after Valens was repulsed at your coming'), he left the city and returned to Vercelli. To place it in context, the above passage is surely an allusion to the episode documented in Hilary's account of how Eusebius at Milan initially thwarted the plans of the anti-Athanasians by suddenly presenting the Nicene creed for signatures before any other business could be transacted.[94] Both Hilary and Sulpicius note that the effect of this opposition was to force Valens and his party to retreat to the palace and re-group. Even public opinion in Milan was then turned against 'heretics', it is reported, which required them to remain under imperial protection.[95] The result, nevertheless, was that anti-Athanasian policies—repetitious of Arles—were promulgated by this group in the name of the whole council. Once they had taken refuge in the imperial palace, any further dialogue was cut off. Eusebius of Vercelli recognized this impasse and the futility of going on with the proceedings.

Careful reading of the next two letters which Eusebius received demonstrates that the council had (1) made certain decisions, but was still in progress, and (2) had to inform Eusebius of these decisions, preferring his compliance with them. In ostensibly affectionate terms, a conciliar letter informed Eusebius that they who have been taught 'the divine precepts of the Lord' are sending to him fellow bishops Eustomius (or Eudoxius) and Germinius, who were apparently at the council. The purpose of this delegation was to persuade Eusebius to embrace the decisions of the council for the sake of 'concordia', 'which is pleasing to God and of unity'. Among the decisions made by the council is the condemnation of the heretics Marcellus, Photinus, and also Athanasius, whose 'sacrilege is named nearly all over the world'.[96] Now once again this condemnation has been reaffirmed under the aegis of the emperor. Eusebius is admonished to be in agreement with the council over these matters, lest he seem not to be complying with the truth and sharing in the error of the condemned. Further elaboration and explanation is to be provided by episcopal delegates from the council when they arrive.

Once this conciliar letter is put in its proper context, there is no longer any need, with de Clercq, to wonder why Eusebius should have received a communication from the opposing party. Nor is there any evidence that the purpose of the delegation was to bring Eusebius to Milan. A third letter to Eusebius from Constantius confirms the fact that Eusebius was

---

[94] *CSEL* lxv. 187. 9–11.   [95] Sulpicius, *Chron.* ii. 39. 4 (*CSEL* i. 92. 22–3).
[96] App. ii a 1. 2 (*CCSL* ix. 119. 13–15).

not in Milan at the conclusion of the council; he is asked to accept the decisions of the council which were brought to him by the episcopal delegates. Frequent use of the past tense seems to indicate that some time has elapsed between the arrival of the delegation and the sending of this letter. For now the council is described as having met in Milan and an account is given of how it reached a decision in unanimity.

it was especially evident at the synod of Milan [that] in each matter the most wise bishops were decided (*decreverunt*) in the unanimity of harmony. Even those few delegates from separate provinces contributed (*protulerunt*) to the unanimity with a common willingness and in like manner confirmed the due respect of the law.[97]

Eusebius is warned with an icy cordiality not to reject the agreement of his brothers about which he has been informed, and to adhere to it in firm unity.

In sum, Eusebius did come to Milan as he pledged for the start of the council, but left once his tactic to establish harmony by requiring allegiance to the Nicene creed failed, resulting in such division that dialogue between opposite parties was no longer possible. All three letters to Eusebius, as discussed above, originate from the period following his departure from the council. From Eusebius himself there is only silence.

(b) *Eusebius in exile*

Ancient historians are in agreement that Eusebius of Vercelli was exiled at the council of Milan.[98] He was not alone in this fate. The host bishop, Dionysius, and Lucifer of Cagliari along with his presbyter and deacon were also banished because, says Athanasius, 'they refused to subscribe to my condemnation'.[99] The remaining bishops conformed to the decisions of the council, though Athanasius mentions only Vincentius of Capua, Fortunatianus of Aquileia, and Heremius of Thessalonica, who were induced to agree, it is said, by force. About Heremius we know nearly nothing, but the mention of Fortunatianus comes as a surprise. His

[97] App. II A 3. 3 (*CCSL* ix. 121. 16–20). The 'law' here refers to the decisions of previous councils such as Sirmium (351) and Arles (353).

[98] Sulpicius, *Chron.* II. 39. 4 (*CSEL* i. 92); Rufinus, *HE* I. 20 (*PL* xxi. 493A); Socrates, *HE* II. 36 (*PG* lxvii. 301A); Sozomen, *HE* IV. 9. 3 (*GCS* l. 148. 17).

[99] *Apologia ad Constantium imperatorem*, 27 (*PG* xxv. 629A). Cf *Apologia pro fuga sua*, 5; *Hist. Ar.* 43–5. Athanasius includes the banishment of Liberius, who was in fact exiled soon after the council had promulgated its decisions when he refused to sign the same document which was presented to Eusebius; that is, the conciliar letter issued from the council of Sirmium (351), not the Sirmium 'blasphemia' of 357 as contended by Löhr, *Die Entsehung der homöischen und homöusianischen Kirchenparteien*, 53–4.

resignation to the anti-Athanasians must have provided a big boost for that movement in Italy. In fact it is he who finally convinced Liberius to change position sometime after the council and to favour the more reasonable policies accepted by the emperor.[100] Like Liberius' delegate Vincentius, Fortunatianus is found on the register of subscriptions at the council of Serdica.[101] For reasons unknown the bishop of Aquileia forsook his allegiance to what may have appeared as a lost cause and signed against Athanasius and the others at Milan. We can speculate with some confidence that the fear of exile and replacement with an Arian bishop was a strong inducement to sign. He had probably observed how the stubbornness of Dionysius, bishop of Milan, resulted in his immediate deposition, banishment, and replacement with Auxentius, another avid anti-Athanasian from Cappadocia.[102] As far as we know, Fortunatianus never reverted to his former position. He undoubtedly signed the Homoian formula at Ariminum and seems to have maintained ties with the new Homoian movement until his death.[103]

Despite the inducements of the episcopal embassy sent to Eusebius from the council of Milan and Constantius' letter urging conformity to the council's decrees, he refused. He was condemned and ordered into exile along with Dionysius and Lucifer and his clergy. Their punishment, deemed as a sacrifice for the true faith, must have nevertheless shocked the western churches, and provided the stimulus which began to spur them out of complacency. As a result of these depositions a new kind of martyr was formed: 'a noble and unparalleled confession reveals to God those worthy of approval, and already has he chosen his martyrs for future glory', so Liberius later declares in a letter to the 'confessors' from Milan.[104] A formidable *inimicus* has attacked the Church and, with it, an old warfare is renewed.

Inasmuch as you have finally obtained glory, you are able to know even better thereafter that if any are crowned in persecution, they were given to know the bloody swords of the persecutor. Against you, who are devoted soldiers of God in all things, has the enemy—false brothers—struggled [but] you have snatched victory from their treachery.

---

[100] Jerome, *De viris illust.* 97 (*PL* xxiii. 735C; 738A).

[101] His signature is listed as no. 37 (B II. 4; *CSEL* lxv. 137).

[102] *Hist. Ar.* 75 (*PG* xxv. 784B).

[103] In one of his letters to the priest Chromatius and his friends in Aquileia, Jerome congratulates them on cleansing the city of 'the poison of the Arian heresy' (*Ep.* VII. 6), which, as Kelly notes, gained brief re-entry presumably by the compromises of Valerian's episcopal predecessor Fortunatianus (*Jerome: His Life, Writings and Controversies* (London, 1975), 31).

[104] *CSEL* lxv. 164–5; *CCSL* ix. 123.

Just as in former days soldiers of God have been raised up to do battle with the forces of tyranny that oppose the Church. Whether the exiles themselves ever received the letter is unimportant. The fact that the true faith now has its own confessors or martyrs (they are not distinguished here) provides it own self-authenticating proof. Designating those bishops exiled at Milan (and Arles) as martyrs would doubtless have helped to galvanize the spirit of the churches against heretical persecutors. Whether or not Liberius was consciously trying to excite social reaction by the use of such language, one thing is plain: he believed that these 'confessors' now possessed special merits which could help him in his own troubled situation as pressure to sign was brought to bear upon him. He asks for their prayers, 'because you, being completed, are closer to God'.

Exiled to Scythopolis on the outskirts of Palestine and completely cut off from the outside world, Eusebius probably never received Liberius' letter. In a long epistle which we have from his pen, Eusebius reports to the congregations under his jurisdiction[105] that after he arrived, being placed under the custodianship of the bishop, Patrophilus, he was prohibited from sending messages of any kind or receiving visitors. In fact, Eusebius claims he had to smuggle this letter out secretly with Syrus the deacon, who came 'to see the holy places and was not found with the other brothers'.[106] Bishop Epiphanius (of Salamis), who happened to be visiting a certain Joseph in Scythopolis, a former *comes* of Constantine and now a Jewish convert to Christianity, confirms the state of isolation in which Eusebius had been placed.[107] The cruel treatment which Eusebius reports that he received, reveals how ugly were the lengths to which Christian enmity in the fourth century was prepared to go. And we have no reason to doubt the historical reliability of his report.[108] Such circumstances were not uncommon; one may recall Athanasius' description of the sufferings of Ossius at the hands of his persuaders.[109] Even if it is the

---

[105] This included Vercelli and several other nearby towns: 'Dilectissimis fratribus et satis desideratissimis presbyteris, sed et sanctis in fide consistentibus plebibus Vercellensibus, Novariensibus, [E]pore[d]iensibus nec non etiam Dertonensibus' (*Ep.* ii; *CCSL* ix. 104).

[106] II. 9. 1–2 (*CCSL* ix. 109).   [107] *Pan. haer.* xxx. 5. 1–8 (*GCS* xxv. 339–40).

[108] In the letter to his congregation, Eusebius reflects on the period when he first arrived in exile and how the devil inflamed the *Ariomanitas* against him. Despite their opposition, he says, 'they were not able to persuade us', so that they tried by violence and, later, by intimidation. Finally the devil so mobilized all of them that they 'seized and imprisoned us out of duty to their infidelity, claiming that all this power was delivered to them by the emperor' (II. 3. 2 (*CCSL* ix. 105. 66–8)). Eusebius briefly describes for his readers some of his sufferings, which included solitary confinement (II. 3. 3–4 (105–6)). Only after a four-day hunger strike was Eusebius allowed to have the company of his clergy again.

[109] *Hist. Ar.* 45 (*PG* xxv. 749A).

case that such accounts are the products of hostile critics, like Epiphanius' vile characterization of Patrophilus (*haer.* 5, 6), we know that they were not wholly exaggerated.

We must now turn our attention to the third letter traditionally attributed to the pen of Eusebius which he wrote in exile to Gregory of Elvira.[110] From internal evidence, the letter must have been written after the council of Ariminum since it speaks of the 'many [bishops] who fell at Ariminum', but it pre-dates the death of Constantius (November 361).[111] In brief, the letter is a response to some previous correspondence sent to Eusebius by Gregory. There is no record of Gregory's communication, although the contents of Eusebius' letter indicate that Gregory informed him how he had opposed Ossius, upon the latter's return to Spain, presumably for his compliance in appending his name to the Sirmium declaration of 357.[112] At the same time, Gregory is congratulated for having withstood those lapsed bishops who entered into communion at Ariminum with Valens, Ursacius, and their fellows. Eusebius expresses his gratefulness that Gregory has remembered him in exile by writing of his resolution to resist heretics and that he has remained strong in the faith.

Wilmart's suggestion that Eusebius is responding to Gregory's treatise *De fide* cannot be correct.[113] Eusebius plainly says, 'I received the letter of your Sincerity', besides the fact that Eusebius is responding to a short report about the ideological position Gregory has recently taken. It is likewise tempting to suppose that Gregory's communication to Eusebius correlates with Jerome's remark that, after the council of Ariminum, some sent 'letters to those confessors who, for the sake of Athanasius, were in exile'.[114] The date and content of Eusebius' letter certainly lend themselves to this possibility. But it should not be overlooked that Jerome was speaking about bishops who were returning from the council of Ariminum. If Gregory is among these returning bishops, then he must have signed the formula at Ariminum. Eusebius' letter seems to indicate that Gregory did not attend the council, since he is congratulated for his

---

[110] 'Domino sanctissimo fratri Gregorio episcopo Eusebius in domino salutem' (*CSEL* lxv. 46–7; *CCSL* ix. 110).

[111] This is the allusion in the text to Constantius: 'omnis spes Arriomanitarum non in suo haud unito consensu, sed in protectione pendet regni saecularis' (*CCSL* ix. 110. 16–17). That Eusebius is still in exile ('Nos vero tui consacerdotes tertio laborantes exilio hoc dicimus') is the most obvious proof that Constantius has not yet died.

[112] Ironically Ossius is called a 'transgressor' by Eusebius (*CCSL* ix. 110. 2). See Barnes, *Athanasius and Constantius*, 130, on the means of extortion used against Ossius and Liberius.

[113] 'La Tradition des opuscules dogmatiques de Foebadius, Gregorius Illiberitanus, Faustinus', *Sitzungsberichte*, 1 (1908), 2 ff.

[114] *Dial. c. Lucif.* 19 (*PL* xxiii. 172C).

opposition to 'the many bishops who fell at Ariminum'. Any correlation between Gregory's action and Jerome's notice is therefore very doubtful.

The experiences which Eusebius, Lucifer, and other western bishops endured in exile must have moulded them into serious, perhaps embittered, opponents of the Homoian faith which meanwhile had become the official dogma of the Roman Empire. In Eusebius' letter to Gregory, he says that he is writing from his third place of exile, though he does not say exactly where he is. Piecing together several bits of information, it is generally thought that, after leaving Scythopolis, Eusebius was taken to Cappadocia (based on a *testimonium* preserved in Jerome), and from there to the upper Thebaid in Egypt.[115] Continuing to follow the trail of the exiled bishop, the next reliable notice we possess locates him in Alexandria involved with a synod of bishops.

(c) *The synod of Alexandria and Eusebius' return to the west*

The news of Constantius' death reached Alexandria on 30 November 361.[116] Only three days earlier, George, who had been appointed to assume the see after Athanasius' sudden flight in 356,[117] re-entered the city. A wave of popular discontent, mainly religious in origin, had caused him to flee Alexandria some three years before. Now his imperial patron was dead and his life was in danger again. According to the *Historia acephala*, the announcement of Constantius' death provoked an outbreak of mob violence against George so that he had to be placed under protective custody. The indignant crowd consisted mostly of elements from the Pagan community, whose hostility had been aroused by George's enforced prohibition of Pagan sacrifices and the taxation of long-standing civic cults.[118] On 24 December the prison house where he was being held was stormed and both he and an accompanying imperial *comes* were lynched.[119]

---

[115] *De viris illust.* 96. See de Clercq, 'Eusèbe de Verceil (saint)', 1480; Rusch, *Later Latin Fathers*, 20; Simonetti, 'Eusebius of Vercelli', *Patrology*, iv. 62.

[116] *Historia acephala Athanasii*, 2. 8 (Martin, 148. 40–2).

[117] *Hist. Ar.* 75 (*PG* xxv. 784C); *Apol. de fuga*, 24–5 (*Athanase d'Alexandrie: Apologie pour sa fuite*, ed. J. Szymusiak, SC 56 (Paris, 1958), 114–15). He did not actually assume the see until Feb. of the following year.

[118] C. Haas, 'The Alexandrian Riots of 356 and George of Cappadocia', *Greek-Roman and Byzantine Studies*, 32 (1991), 290 f.

[119] *Hist. acephala*, 2. 10 (Martin, 148). I am following A. Martin, who notes that the *comes* Diodorus (Ammianus, XXII. 11. 9) was the one killed with George, since he was probably charged by the emperor to accompany George to Alexandria (*Histoire 'acephale' et index syriaque*, 189 n. 65). The redactor of the *Historia* confuses the *comes* Diodorus and Dracontius,

Julian was now emperor of the entire empire and following Constantius' death he wasted little time in undoing the religious policies of his precedessor. His ostensibly neutral attitude toward such matters had cloaked his zeal for Pagan religion—at least for the first few months of his reign. Two general edicts published early in the new year effected religious toleration for both Pagans and Christians. By 4 February an imperial proclamation was announced in Alexandria which allowed the reopening of temples and resuming of sacrifices.[120] A second edict, not published by the prefect Gerontius until five days later, declared a general amnesty for all Christian bishops who were in hiding or in exile for religious offences.[121] Now the 'confessors' of Arles and Milan, as well as bishops condemned at other councils under Constantius, were permitted to return to their towns and have their property restored. But the edict did not automatically entail that these bishops were to be restored to their former sees. Marcellus returned to Ancyra and Meletius to Antioch only to find that the episcopal chair was occupied. In both cases, as perhaps elsewhere, conflict over these sees ensued—something that Julian was counting on.[122] Not all bishops returned, however, for there were some who had died in exile.[123] Athanasius was allowed to return to Alexandria and assume the bishopric in response, so it seems, to a special edict issued by Gerontius.[124] Within a matter of weeks, Athanasius entered the city, where he was greeted with an exuberant homecoming celebration.[125]

When Julian's edicts reached Egypt, Eusebius of Vercelli and Lucifer of Cagliari were at that time dwelling in the Thebaid. Eusebius directly proceeded to Alexandria, where the so-called (erroneously) 'council of Confessors' had been convoked. Lucifer elected not to attend but sent

who was the *monetae praepositus* according to Ammianus (XXII. 11. 9). Cf. Julian, *Ep.* 21; Sozomen, *HE* IV. 30. 2. The violence on this occasion seems to have been first sparked by George's desecration of the Serapeum in Alexandria.

[120] *Hist. acephala*, 3. 1 (Martin, 148; 150); Ammianus, XXII. 5. 2; Julian, *Ep.* 15. This countermands a law specifically prohibiting such activities issued by Constantius at Milan on 20 Feb. 356 (*C. Th.* XVI. 10. 6).

[121] *Hist. acephala*, 3. 2 (Martin, 150).

[122] Socrates, *HE* III. 1 (*PG* lxvii. 377A); Sozomen, *HE* V. 5. 1 (*GCS* l. 198).

[123] Such as Paulinus of Trier and Rhodanius of Toulouse (Sulpicius, *Chron.* II. 45. 9 (*CSEL* i. 99)) and Dionysius of Milan (Ambrose, *Contra Aux.*, 18 (*CSEL* lxxxii. 3. 93. 210–12)).

[124] *Hist. acephala*, 3. 3: 'Postmodum (the publication of the imperial letter) autem et prefecti Gerontii edictum propositum est, per quod vocabatur episcopus Athanasius ad suam reverti ecclesiam' (Martin, 150. 11–14).

[125] Gregory of Nazianzus, *Orationes* XXI. 27 (*Grégoire de Nazianze: Discours 20–23*, ed. J. Mossay, SC 270 (Paris, 1980), 166). Sozomen erroneously places the death of George after the return of Athanasius.

two deacons as representatives carrying his pledge to assent to whatever the synod might decree.[126] This important detail reminds us that Lucifer's initial attitude toward the upcoming synod was positive; perhaps presuming the synod would share his own intransigence toward a hasty compromise. It also confirms the like-mindedness toward their opponents which Lucifer and Athanasius had shared until that point. Several years earlier, Lucifer had sent Athanasius a copy of his two books *pro Athanasio*, at the latter's request. And in response to these strongly worded pamphlets, Athanasius wrote that he could see in them 'an apostolic likeness, prophetic trustworthiness, a magisterium of truth, doctrine of the true faith . . . a triumph over the Arian heresy'.[127] We may deduce that Lucifer had every confidence that a synod under Athanasius' leadership would arrive at decisions acceptable to him, whereupon he immediately took himself to Antioch.

Our knowledge about the Alexandrian synod, which met in the middle of 362, is founded solely upon two documents: a text transmitted under the title of 'Epistola Catholica', which had been consigned to the dubious writings of the Athanasian corpus since the fifteenth century and was recently identified by M. Tetz as a genuine fragment from the opening of the synodical letter produced by that assembly,[128] and another letter from the synod known as the 'Tomus ad Antiochenos' (hereafter *Tomus*). The latter document shows that we must distinguish within the course of the synod (1) a primarily Egyptian and larger session which dealt with the broader questions of faith and discipline facing local churches, and (2) a smaller assembly which met after the departure of most of the bishops and was solely concerned with the Antiochene question.[129] It is this smaller assembly which issued the *Tomus*.

In no uncertain terms the 'Epistola Catholica' set forth that the Trinity is *homoousios* as established by the great council of Nicaea. Whoever does not subscribe to this is condemned just like the Arians, whose actions reveal the devil standing behind them. The primary ecclesiastical-political

---

[126] Socrates, *HE* III. 6 (*PG* lxvii. 389A); Sozomen, *HE* V. 12. 2 (*GCS* l. 211). The *Tomus* cites two deacons, Herennius and Agapetus, sent by Lucifer (IX. 3).

[127] 'Epistulae duae ad Luciferum' (*PG* xxvi. 1181D–1186B). Quotation from the second epistle (1184B). The authenticity of the letters has been questioned by Saltet in *Bulletin de littérature ecclésiastique*, 3/8 (1906), 303–6, on the grounds that only a Latin version of the letters is known. There has been no general support for his scepticism.

[128] 'Ein enzyklisches Schreiben der Synode von Alexandrien (362)', *Zeitschrift für neutestamentliche Wissenschaft*, 79 (1988), 262–81. Tetz provides a critical edition and German translation of the text, pp. 271–4 (paragraph breaks are his).

[129] M. Tetz, 'Über Nikäische Orthodoxie', *Zeitschrift für neutestamentliche Wissenschaft*, 66 (1975), 196.

concern at the main session of the synod was how to deal with those bishops who were seeking to dissociate themselves from the compromise they had made at Ariminum and Seleucia. Now that Constantius was dead, the problem became paramount. Should those bishops who lapsed at the double councils be considered Arian heretics and stripped of their sees? Opinions varied among the assembly at Alexandria. A more rigoristic party present is said to have declared that no one in a priestly office who defiled himself in any way with the contagion of heretical communion ought to be received.[130] Judging from the tone and expression of Eusebius' letter to Gregory of Elvira (above), we may imagine that Eusebius too first came to the synod 'with unquestionably hostile feelings towards the weaker brethren who had come to terms with Arianism'.[131] At the same time, it is necessary to distinguish between the unyielding rigorist attitudes which characterized the post-Antiochene party, later known as 'Luciferians', from those attitudes of men like Eusebius and others at the synod. Once the gravity of the situation was fully set forth to the bishops present, we know that Eusebius and Lucifer's two delegates were in complete agreement with the rest of the synod to extend a conditional pardon to the fallen bishops.

In his letter to Rufinianus, written soon after the close of the synod, Athanasius describes this pivotal decision in concise terms: acquitting those 'not deliberate in impiety, but drawn away by necessity and violence, that they should not only receive pardon, but should occupy the position of clergy'.[132] Just as important as the decision itself was the reason which follows in the same paragraph: 'For they assured us that they had not gone over to impiety; but lest certain most impious persons should be elected and ruin the churches they elected rather to acquiesce in the violence and to bear the burden, than to lose the people.' It is a very probable reason, witnessing to a dynamic we have seen at work in previous councils, such as at Milan (355). The Alexandrian synod had to face the reality that abandoning the majority of those who sought pardon risked losing them entirely to the Homoian camp.

The same synod also concerned itself with at least three other matters that were more theological in nature: the consubstantiality of the Holy Spirit, the east–west division over the definition and orthodoxy of 'hypostasis', and the Christological problem over the true humanity of the

---

[130] Rufinus, *HE* I. 28 (*PL* xxi. 498C).

[131] C. B. Armstrong, 'The Synod of Alexandria and the Schism at Antioch in AD 362', *JTS* 22 (1921), 212.

[132] *Epistola ad Ruf.* (*PG* xxvi. 1180B–C) (trans. from *NPNF* iv. 566).

incarnate Son. At the close of the synod, two bishops from the assembly, Asterius (of Petra) and Eusebius (of Vercelli), were designated as special emissaries to declare and disseminate the decrees of the synod: Asterius in the east and Eusebius in the west, each presumably bearing a version of the 'Epistola Catholica'. But the two did not leave Alexandria until the conclusion of a second and smaller meeting of bishops who concerned themselves with the continued tensions that existed in Antioch between the partisans of the Eustathians, now headed by Paulinus, and the Meletians, who were seeking communion with the pro-Nicenes in Antioch.[133] The issue which confronted the synod was a very sensitive one. Despite the Meletian compromises with anti-Athanasians in the past, here was an opportunity for the synod to receive those who repented of their previous affiliations—applying the same principle which had been exercised for 'lapsed' bishops at Ariminum and Seleucia. When Eusebius and Asterius arrived in Antioch, carrying with them the *Tomus* which outlined the synod's conditional acceptance of the Meletian party, Lucifer's ordination of Paulinus was discovered, and the irreconcilable situation this had created with the Meletians. The Meletians had already begun to hold their own assemblies completely segregated from the Eustathians and from Lucifer, who obviously favoured the latter. Eusebius saw the utter futility of hoping to effect a reconciliation, and, seeing no reason to remain—he departed.

The bishop of Vercelli commenced to fulfil that commission which he had received at the first session of the synod at Alexandria. It is certain that he returned to the west by a land route, publishing the decisions of the synod all along the way. 'Now as Eusebius travelled about the East and Italy, he performed the office of a priest like that of a doctor. Each one of the churches, once it abjured its infidelity, Eusebius restored (*revocabat*) to the health of a right faith.'[134]

Beyond this brief description, we do not have any certain information about the places Eusebius might have visited. Only one tantalizing possibility presents itself. There is evidence that Eusebius passed through Illyricum on the way to Italy:[135] from a document that purports to be the minutes of a debate (in AD 366) between the bishop Germinius and three pro-Nicene laymen at Sirmium, Eusebius is said to have visited that city.[136] The 'orthodox' position in the *Altercatio* over the Holy Spirit's

---

[133] For the problems between and history of these parties in Antioch, see the standard and still useful work by F. Cavallera, *Le Schisme d'Antioche* (*IV* e–*V* e) (Paris, 1905).

[134] Rufinus, *HE* I. 30 (*PL* xxi. 501A).   [135] Socrates, *HE* III. 9 (*PG* lxvii. 405A).

[136] *Altercatio Heracliani laici cum Germinio episcopo Sirmiensi*, ed. Caspari, 136.

divinity as a partaker of the same nature as the Father and the Son is consistent with one of the decisions made at Alexandria, though it need not directly stem from it. If Eusebius did visit Sirmium on the way home, it was not for the last time. We know that, once Eusebius returned to Italy, he and Hilary of Poitiers combined their efforts in a joint campaign which took them as far east as Illyricum. At one point in the *Altercatio*, the layman Heraclianus' knowledge of the Homoousian teaching is, according to a cynical statement of Germinius, attributable to the influence of both Eusebius and Hilary: 'That Eusebius, an exile, taught you this; and Hilary also, who has now come from exile.'[137]

What is particularly fascinating about the *Altercatio* is the lack of hostility which Germinius, long-time ally of Valens and Ursacius and signatory of every Homoian formula since 357, exhibits over the mention of Eusebius' name.[138] This attitude may be due, in part, to Germinius' more moderated Homoian theology. More directly it seems to emphasize that Eusebius' mission, along with Hilary, in the western provinces was not so much polemical as pastoral. Eusebius had been charged to renew and restore relations not with bishops who were Homoians through confessional allegiance, but with those who had succumbed to the pressure of signing the disputed creed. Even if a kind of polemical evangelism had been part of Eusebius' mission, it would have proved to be virtually impossible. For the rest of Julian's short reign, imperial politics took a studiously neutral position with regard to this controversy, and the religious policies of Jovian and Valentinian I were, practically speaking, no different. This suggests, interestingly, that an attack on Auxentius of Milan by Hilary in 364[139] was more of an exception in this period of Nicene revitalization than the rule, and its failure to achieve Auxentius' deposition was proof that new political attitudes toward Christian strife over these issues were reigning.

The last we learn of Eusebius' movements is his return to Italy and meeting with Hilary. It is also very likely, despite the silence of our sources, that Eusebius met with Liberius at Rome. Favouring this proposition is the recognition that Eusebius, having a formal assignment from Alexandria to the west, would first seek out an audience with the Roman pontiff. He may have possessed a letter from the synod for Liberius. In

---

[137] Ibid., (Caspari, 134).

[138] This is an especially intriguing characteristic of the work since the catholic redactor of the *Altercatio* deliberately set about magnifying Germinius' Arianism. M. Simonetti, 'Osservazione sull' Altercatio Heracliani Cum Germinio', VC 21 (1967), 39–58.

[139] See Ch. 3, pp. 78–80.

a communication to the Italian bishops written in 362/3,[140] Liberius is aware of the Alexandrian decision regarding penitent bishops and his knowledge may be due to Eusebius' visit. Exhorting his fellow bishops to receive everyone who 'comes to his senses', Liberius writes, 'for this reason severity must be repudiated. It is proper for me to consider everything with moderation, especially since all those of Egypt and Achaia received many by using such a standard.' Now Rome had lent its weight to the Alexandrian proclamation.

Once Eusebius and Hilary met, the combined weight of the decrees from Alexandria and the Gallic synods convinced them of the value of journeying together. It is perhaps due to their efforts, directly or indirectly, that we hear of the assemblage of councils throughout the west in the mid-360s coming to a general agreement over the reconciliation of compromised but 'orthodox' bishops, and condemnation of leading Arian personalities.[141]

Not all advocates of Nicene Christianity were convinced that the policy of receiving penitent bishops into communion literally 'snatched the world from the jaws of Satan' (Jerome's phrase), as later protestations by Luciferians and other rigorist groups attest.[142] But on the whole, the conciliatory strategy provided an important period of reorganization and revitalization of anti-Homoian bishops and churches after the death of Constantius. Should we conclude, therefore, that from this chain of events 'the Arian cause was lost'?[143] Or, as Hefele summarizes, 'En Occident se firent surtout sentir les salutaires effets de cette série de conciles; l'arianisme disparut presque complètement de ces contrées'?[144] In what follows we shall see how the views represented by such remarks have served remarkably well to prohibit historians from coming to grips with the intensity of the controversy that occupied the west for the next two decades.

---

[140] *CAP* B IV (*CSEL* lxv. 156–7). Feder's dating.

[141] *CSEL* lxv. 157. 3–5. The 'Achaeans' are known to have enthusiastically followed the decisions of the Alexandrian synod. Basil of Caesarea (*Ep.* 204) speaks of a letter he received from Athanasius after the synod regarding the reception of penitent bishops which cites 'all the bishops both of Macedonia and Achaea as his supporters in this view' (Deferrari, iii. 171).

[142] The entreaty of Marcellinus and Faustinus, two stalwart defenders of Lucifer's policies, complains of Hilary as having 'shown favour to the transgressors' (*Ep.* 2. 24 (*CSEL* xxxv. 12)). Basil of Caesarea also reports of needing to defend himself against charges of Arianism due to his receiving into communion those bishops who had compromised themselves with 'the heresy of the Arians' (*Ep.* 204).

[143] J. L. Gonzalez, *A History of Christian Thought*, vol. i (Nashville, 1970), 285.

[144] *Histoire des conciles* (Paris, 1907), i. 2. 968.

3

Homoians and Anti-Homoians in North Italy

W HEN Athanasius responded to the Emperor Jovian's letter in 363 with the words, 'indeed, the whole world holds the apostolic faith',[1] the Alexandrian bishop was describing the successes of Nicene theology to an already sympathetic ear. And it was an exaggeration at the very least. Just five years previously, Hilary of Poitiers had glumly observed while in exile that 'the greater part of the ten provinces of Asia where I am staying do not really know God'.[2] Sulpicius Severus, looking back at this same period, remarked how widespread the 'Arian' heresy had become in the world, especially in Illyricum.[3] There can be no doubt that after the death of Constantius the pro-Nicenes had quickly galvanized themselves against the Homoian movement, breaking the sway which the council of Ariminum had over the west. Did that mean western Arianism was practically moribund by the time of Jovian's reign, as G. L. Prestige once claimed?[4] Part of the answer to this question is closely linked to one's interpretation of the status of western Homoianism and the intensity of (or lack of) polemical response which it evoked from pro-Nicenes of the 360s and 370s. Since the publication of M. Meslin's *Les Ariens d'Occident 335–430*, it is no longer as easy to overlook the durability of western Arian communities and their literary influence as it once was. As we shall see below, more recent scholarship in Latin Arian literature has rightly called many of Meslin's theses into question, but his fundamental contribution—that the energy and challenge of western Arianism to the pro-Nicenes was not solely dependent on the Gothic penetration of the Roman Empire, but was equally developed in its Latin milieu—must still be reckoned with in a study such as the present one. It may be that Homoian communities were fewer in number than Nicene after the passing of Constantius, but they were no less cohesive and vibrant communities, spawning theological, exegetical, homiletical, and polemical literature of which sizeable fragments have come down to us today. In fact, it now appears, as Y.-M.

---

[1] *Ad Jovianum*, 2 (*PG* lvi. 817A).
[2] *De synodis*, 63 (*PL* x. 522C–523A) (trans. from *NPNF* ix. 21).
[3] *Vita Mart*. 6. 4 (*CSEL* i. 116). [4] *Fathers and Heretics*, 75.

Duval has observed, that this literature became more abundant from the moment when the Homoians were abandoned by imperial authority.[5] Western Homoianism was hardly a lame duck even after the death of Constantius and the temporary loss of imperial patronage. So widespread was pro-Homoian literature in the west that Hilary of Poitiers, in his tract *Contra Auxentium* written in the reign of Valentinian I in 364, complains that the Arian opposition to the Nicene faith is considerably augmented: 'all of the churches contain full records (*chartae*) of their most impious blasphemies, and even complete books.'[6]

Any reconstruction of anti-Arian activities and literature will have to take this 'new' picture of western Arianism seriously. But we want to know if this inner vitality and literary productivity of the Homoians translated into a measurable external influence on their pro-Nicene opponents. When one takes a fresh look at the evidence for Homoian activity, literary and political, and the cumulative reaction which such activity produced in the Neo-Nicenes, it is possible to see a connection. What follows is a presentation of evidence often overlooked which will help prepare the reader to view the dynamics of anti-Arian polemics in a new light. This task will involve a careful examination of the political and ecclesiastical context of Homoian–Nicene tensions as found in available literature from this period.

I. HOMOIAN CHRISTIANITY IN ILLYRICUM AND ITALY AFTER CONSTANTIUS II

The political climate between the reigns of Julian and Gratian has been rightly emphasized by most historians of this period to play a fundamental part in the shaping of the controversy. After Julian's death (26 June 363), Jovian, a Christian, was reputed to be favourable to Nicene Christianity. This is confirmed by his gracious recall of Athanasius from banishment[7] as well as by a conciliar letter from a joint council of Meletians and Acacians which obviously sought to curry favour with the emperor by espousing the Nicene creed.[8] In practice, however, the emperor's partiality

---

[5] 'Sur l'Arianisme des Ariens d'Occident', 146.   [6] *Contra Aux.* 7 (*PL* x. 613B).

[7] *PG* lvi. 813. Regarding the correspondence between Jovian and Athanasius cf. Rufinus, *HE* ii. 1 (*PL* xxi. 508C).

[8] Socrates, *HE* iii. 25 (*PG* lxvii. 452B–453A); Sozomen, *HE* vi. 4. 6–10 (*GCS* 1. 241–2). L. W. Barnard identifies three Arian embassies sent to Jovian with the intent of opposing Athanasius' reoccupation of the Alexandrian see, all of which were rebuffed. 'Athanasius and the Emperor Jovian', *Studia Patristica*, 21 (1989), 384–9.

meant little: Jovian is said to have shunned religious controversy, declaring that he would not elevate one sect at the expense of another. Following his untimely demise (17 February 364), the new Emperor Valentinian pursued a similar course. Despite the fact that he too embraced the Nicene form of faith, it is well attested that he rigorously upheld a public policy of religious neutrality in the western half of the empire.[9] This is an important point whose force ought not to be glossed over too quickly. Not only did such a political stance allow for the maintenance of positions acquired by Nicenes and Homoians prior to 364, as Simonetti observes,[10] but it also effectively stifled any significant progress of the controversy until after the emperor's death (375) and the partisan politics of Gratian's later administration. Even so, Valentinian is depicted in a wholly benevolent light by later historiographical tradition as a defender of the Nicene faith in stark contrast to his brother Valens, who ruled the eastern half of the empire and openly favoured the 'Arians' by giving Homoian bishops important sees and suppressing Nicene opposition.[11]

On one hand, the period of the 360s allowed the pro-Nicene movement to consolidate the revitalization programme it had begun under Julian. Athanasius may be given to exaggeration, but his boast to Jovian, that 'churches in every quarter' have now assented to the Nicene faith, cannot be far from the truth. On the other hand, the Neo-Nicenes under Valentinian could do little about those Homoian bishops who tenaciously held their sees. We know of no successful deposition of an Arian bishop until the council of Aquileia condemned Palladius of Ratiaria and Secundianus of Singidunum in 381. The only way for a see to be opened for the election of a candidate favourable to Nicaea was through the death of the Homoian incumbent. A brief look at the careers of the leading western Homoians illustrates these observations more vividly.

The infamous and now aging Illyrian bishops Valens of Mursa and Ursacius of Singidunum had been repeatedly condemned by pro-Nicene assemblies at Paris (360) and other synods in Gaul and Italy,[12] and then

---

[9] Socrates, *HE* IV. I. 29; Sozomen, *HE* VI. 6; Theodoret, *HE* III. 16; Zosimus, *Historia nova* IV. 4 (henceforth Zosimus). It is the foremost attribute which Ammianus remembers about Valentinian's reign (XXX. 9. 5). Sozomen (*HE* VI. 21. 7) adds that Valentinian left questions of dogma or ecclesiastical policies entirely to the bishops.

[10] *La crisi ariana*, 380.

[11] Cf. Socrates, *HE* IV. 2, 6, 12, 15, 17; Sozomen, *HE* VI. 9. 1; 13, 15. I. Letters 256 and 257 of Basil describe Valens' persecution of pro-Nicene monastics. See Brennecke's illuminating assessment of Valens' other alleged brutalities against anti-Homoians, *Homöer*, 181 ff.

[12] *Ad Epictetum*, I (*PG* lvi. 1052A). Along with Gaius, possible bishop of Sabaria (Zeiller, *Origines chrétiennes*, 141, 175), and Auxentius of Milan.

on at least one other occasion by a Roman synod under Damasus in 371.[13] Nevertheless, Valens continued to preside over the see of Mursa as late as the reign of the Emperor Valens (364–78). Nor had the bishop's influence been abated by the series of condemnations. In 367 we find Valens, assisted by another Homoian bishop, Domninus of Marcianopolis (metropolitan of Moesia Secunda), successfully interceding on behalf of Eunomius with the eastern emperor.[14] It is the last act of Valens known to us from the sources; presumably he died soon afterwards—still in control of his see. Ursacius also maintained a grip on his see until his death *c.*366, and was succeeded by another anti-Nicene, Secundianus, who joined the side of Palladius of Ratiaria at the council of Aquileia. Germinius of Sirmium, metropolitan of Pannonia Secunda and close colleague of Valens and Ursacius (cf. Hilary, *De syn.* 81), was still bishop in 366,[15] after having held since 351 the see to which he was appointed following the deposition of Photinus. Not until Germinius' death (early 370s?) did a bishop favourable to Nicene theology become elected to that see.

We should not interpret the apparent stability of these and other Homoian sees as if a pro-Nicene presence were completely lacking in Illyricum. A synodical letter from an assembly held in north Italy addressed to an unidentified body of Illyrian bishops attests to the existence of churches hostile to Homoianism in that region. The letter (dated by Feder to 363/4), which was probably written in response to the Illyrians' report of certain churches leaning toward the Nicene position,[16] mandates that communion can be established only by subscription to the Nicene creed and complete separation from Ariminum. Six or seven years later, another Italian synod, this time at Rome, sent to Nicene bishops in Illyricum the results of its decision to condemn publicly Auxentius and all supporters of Ariminum.[17] No pro-Nicene councils are known to have

---

[13] *Ad Afros*, 3 (*PG* lvi. 1033B); Mansi, iii. 447. The recent verdict that *Ad Afros* may not be Athanasian does not affect the value of its witness to and dependency on this Roman synod. For its inauthenticity, see C. Kannengiesser, '(Ps.-)Athanasius ad Afros Examined', in H. C. Brennecke, E. L. Grasmück, and C. Markschies (eds.), *Logos: Festschrift L. Abramowski*, Beihefte zur Zeitschrift für neutestamentliche Wissenschaft 67 (Berlin, 1993), 264–80.

[14] Philostorgius, *HE* IX . 8 (*GCS* xxi. 119). Kopecek, *A History of Neo-Arianism*, ii. 429–30 provides the background for Eunomius' exile to Mauretania.

[15] Confirmed by the *Altercatio*, which is dated to 13 Jan. 366, and by his correspondence with other Illyrian Homoians later in the same year.

[16] 'Item Exemplum Epistulae Episcoporum Italiae', *CAP* B IV. 2 (*CSEL* lxv. 158. 9–11).

[17] Sozomen, *HE* VI. 23. 7–15 (*GCS* l. 266–8); Theodoret, *HE* II. 22 (*GCS* xliv. 147–50).

met in Illyricum until Anemius became bishop of Sirmium (immediately following Germinius' death), but the above correspondence allows us to suppose that there were many active pro-Nicene churches in that region, probably at least as many as Homoian.

Despite the fact that we have these traces of a vigorous anti-Ariminum presence in Illyricum, it is puzzling that we possess almost no known anti-Arian treatises from this part of the western empire.[18] The only exception is the *Altercatio Heracliani cum Germinio*, which is the reported minutes of a trial of three catholic laymen at Sirmium and which has been substantially reworked by a catholic editor.[19] Is the silence of anti-Arian works from this region purely circumstantial or is it a monument to the strength of Homoianism: 'les jours de la domination arienne',[20] until the reign of Theodosius? We cannot say for sure. Generally speaking, we have very few extant writings from Illyricum, so any silence on the Arian conflict should not be over-interpreted. We have seen that, even if the Homoians were not as numerous as the Catholics, they did hold influential sees, and thereby were able to maintain themselves as a substantial ecclesiastical power. Certainly this is an important consideration for the continued influence of Homoianism in the Illyrian provinces, and it is equally pertinent to the situation in north Italy, the other major centre of Homoian activity in the later 360s and 370s.

Unlike the Illyrian bishoprics, the establishment of Arianism in Italy owed much of its influence to the religious politics of the Emperor Constantius. In fact, as Meslin points out, '[l]es bouleversements apportés en Italie par la politique religieuse de Constance furent les plus importants de tout l'Occident'.[21] A few examples from our fragmentary evidence reveal a relatively strong anti-Nicene presence in Italy, both during and after Constantius' rule over the west.

At the relegation of Maximus, bishop of Naples (otherwise unknown), to exile, a certain Zosimus was consecrated to the see, probably at the hands of Valens and his associates. According to the Luciferian writer of the *Libellus precum*, Zosimus had formerly been an adherent of the 'catholic faith' but, for reasons unknown, received his see through the support of heretics. In reality, the actual commitment of Zosimus to Arian doctrines is unclear, since it appears that some time after Constantius' death he

[18] Cf. Dekkers, 'Scriptores Illyriae', in *Clavis Patrum Latinorum*, 133–56.
[19] See Simonetti, 'Osservazioni sull' Altercatio Heracliani cum Germinio', 44.
[20] Zeiller, *Origines chrétiennes*, 307.   [21] *Les Ariens*, 36.

began to favour a pro-Nicene position.[22] The case of Zosimus should not be considered unique. There were many like him who, in order to preserve their episcopates, went along with the prevailing political winds.

Far more persistent in their devotion to an anti-Nicene persuasion are two other Italian bishops briefly mentioned in an extant rescript of the Emperor Gratian in 378.[23] Florentius of Puteoli (Pozzuoli) is said to have been condemned and presumably deposed from his see; an episode which Pietri places at the end of Liberius' episcopate.[24] While the reasons for the action taken against Florentius are not revealed, the rescript does state that he returned to the church some fifteen years later, when 'he tried to contaminate it again' (*rursus contaminare conatur*). The inference is surely doctrinal, and almost certainly related to anti-Nicene doctrines which Florentius may have been preaching earlier at Puteoli. His return sparked deep division in the church as he reclaimed a large number of adherents: 'with his persuasion he led astray (*depravat*) a multitude of lost souls.'[25]

In north Italy, the church of Parma is said to have been so disrupted by its bishop that the latter was deposed by an unidentified Roman council. But the bishop was not so easily removed. A later Roman council in 378 laments to the emperor that 'the bishop of Parma, who was ejected from the church according to our judgement, nevertheless retains his see shamefully'.[26] The same rescript from the Emperor Gratian to the *vicarius* Aquilinus echoes this complaint of the Roman council and emphasizes the need for more severe measures.

The bishop of Parma . . . by the judgement of the holy synod (*sanctorum praesulum*) was ejected from the church which he disturbed, anticipating the empty glory of a more severe sentence; if there was anything your predecessor of devoted vigour should have done, he ought to have expelled him well beyond the boundaries [of the city].

Even though the texts do not specify the identity of the bishop nor the nature of his offence, it is most probably Urbanus of Parma, an

---

[22] *Ep. Marcellini et Faustini (Liber Precum)* II. 62 (*CSEL* xxxv. 23). According to this much embellished account, Zosimus converted to the Nicene faith after Lucifer returned from exile and came to Naples, 'ad quem Zosimus venire temptavit illa forte fiducia, qua scilicet iam de impietate correxisse videbatur'.

[23] In the *Collectio Avellana*, 13. 6–7, 'Gratianus et Valentinianus Augg. Aquilino vicario' (*CSEL* xxxv. 55–6).

[24] *Roma Christiana: recherches sur l'Église de Rome, son organisation, sa politique, son idéologie de Miltiade à Sixte III (311–440)* (Rome, 1976), i. 730 n. 4.

[25] *CSEL* xxxv. 56. 7–8.

[26] Quoted from F. Lanzoni, *Le origini delle diocesi antiche d'Italia: studio critico* (Rome, 1923), 444.

anti-Nicene and first known bishop of that see, whose eventual deposition was the subject of protest by fellow Homoians at the council of Aquileia (381).[27] Gryson and Pietri have identified this same Urbanus with the Urbanus who was present at Niké in 359 when that assembly drafted the formula that became the basis of the Ariminum creed.[28]

Scattered references are available about the case of Epictetus, who, according to Athanasius, was brought from the east by agents of Constantius and installed as the bishop of Centumcellae.[29] He was certainly well known to the Italian bishop Lucifer of Cagliari, who freely characterizes Epictetus as a breeder of impiety, and associates him with the company of Valens, Ursacius, and Saturninus as wholly supportive of the religious policies of 'the king'.[30] After Constantius' death, we do not hear of Epictetus in any of our ancient sources. One of his acts as a bishop, however, along with several other anti-Nicenes, left a legacy that would trouble the bishopric of Rome for the next ten years: his participation in the joint consecration of Felix as bishop. Once Liberius had been exiled by Constantius to Thrace, the Roman cleric Felix was appointed bishop in his absence. And despite the attempts of the *Liber Pontificalis* to rehabilitate Felix and portray him as orthodox, that is, an anti-Constantian,[31] the circumstances of his appointment continued to taint him in the eyes of pro-Nicenes with the sin of the Arian heretics. He seems to have quietly left the city upon Liberius' return from exile, thus avoiding an inevitable conflict. At the time of Liberius' death in 366, however, control over the see of Rome became fiercely contested by two parties which had formed in the wake of Felix's appointment. The one party put forward its

---

[27] *Scholia*, 344'. 125–6 (Gryson, *Scolies*, 308).

[28] Gryson, *Le Prêtre selon saint Ambroise* (Louvain, 1968), 175, and Pietri, *Roma Christiana*, i. 731 n. 3. 'Eusebio et Ypatio conss. VI Idus Octobris' in Hilary, *CAP* A V. 3 (*CSEL* lxv. 85–6).

[29] *Ad Aeg.* 7 (*PG* xxv. 553B); *Hist. Ar.* 75 (*PG* xxv. 784C). His stigmatization as a 'tool' of the emperor's is supported by the fact that Epictetus was sent by Constantius as an emissary to Julian in order to announce the rejection of the latter's elevation to Augustus. Of course it was not uncommon for bishops in the 4th century to function in this capacity. H. Chadwick, 'The Role of the Christian Bishop in Ancient Society', in *The Center for Hermeneutical Studies in Hellenistic and Modern Culture: Protocol of the 35th Colloquy* (Berkeley, Calif., 1979), 9–10.

[30] *Moriendum esse pro dei filio*, VII (*CCSL* viii. 281); *De non conveniendo cum haereticis*, VII (*CCSL* viii. 175–6).

[31] L. Duchesne, *Liber Pontificalis*, vol. i (Paris, 1886), 211. Later demonstrations of Felix's orthodoxy come from the time of the Nestorian controversy, when supposed texts of Athanasius, Julius, Felix, and other 'Fathers' of the Church were utilized in anti-heretical florilegia. These texts were in fact Apollinarian forgeries, but nevertheless cited as sources of orthodox authority. P. Gray, ' "The Select Fathers": Canonizing the Patristic Past', *Studia Patristica*, 23 (1989), 23–4.

candidate, Damasus, who had served as a deacon under Liberius and had powerful familial connections in the Roman clergy. A minority group accused Damasus of compromise with Felix and supported Ursinus, another deacon of Liberius, for the bishopric.[32] After much bloody violence, including an assault on the basilica Sicinini (or basilica Liberii) during which at least 137 persons were killed (Ammianus, XXVII. 3. 13), Damasus was ultimately recognized as the successor to the see. He was not able to enjoy unrivalled authority as bishop until 369/70.

2. OPPOSITION TO AUXENTIUS OF MILAN

Along with these appointments to Italian sees, the metropolitan seat of northern Italy had become vacant with the banishment of Dionysius at the synod of Milan (355). This was a great strategic loss to the adversaries of Valens, Ursacius, and their allies. Not only did Milan enjoy the distinction of housing one of the western imperial residences, but its bishop had episcopal jurisdiction effective over the whole of the political diocese of Italia Annonaria, which included Aemilia, Liguria, Venetia, the two Rhaetias, the Cottian Alps, Flaminia and Picenum, and part of Tuscia. To this powerful bishopric, which was second only to Rome in religious political influence, Auxentius from Cappadocia was immediately installed in 355.[33] Of all episcopal successions in Italy, this one would prove to be the most able and enduring for the cause of anti-Nicene interests in the west.

Like Valens, Ursacius, and their immediate circle, Auxentius had been condemned at Paris, just as he and the others had been anathematized at Ariminum by the first session of that council.[34] There was no mistaking the anti-Nicene sentiments in his subsequent conduct. In the *Vita Martini*, Sulpicius Severus records the harsh treatment his hero Martin received at the hands of the Arians in both Illyricum and Milan. After being

---

[32] C. Pietri, 'Damase', in *Dictionnaire encyclopédique du Christianisme ancien*, i. 621; M Norton, 'Prosopography of Pope Damasus', *Folia*, 4 (1950), 13–31; 5 (1951), 30–55; 6 (1952), 16–39.

[33] For a full dossier on the background and career of Auxentius see Cesare Alzati, 'Aussenzio (sec. IV)', *Dizionario della chiesa ambrosiana*, i. 302–4; J. Zeiller, 'Auxence, évêque arien de Milan', *DHGE* v. 935; Meslin, *Les Ariens*, 41–4; 291–3.

[34] Athanasius reports that he was condemned by the council along with Valens, Ursacius, Germinius, Gaius, and Demophilus (*De syn.* 9 (*PG* xxvi. 696B)). Strangely, Auxentius' name does not appear in the council's *damnatio* ('Eusebio et Ypatio Conss. XII Kal. August.' (*CSEL* lxv. 96–7)).

scourged and chased out of his home town of Sabaria for opposing the 'treachery of the priests', this former disciple of Hilary of Poitiers proceeded to Italy, where he attempted to establish a 'monasterium' within the city limits of Milan. Whether Martin's main motive stems from an 'anti-Arian campaign' inspired by Hilary, as N. Chadwick suggests,[35] cannot be positively determined. The idea tends to assume that Hilary would have been already a staunch opponent of Arian doctrine before his exile in 356—a view which is open to question. Auxentius took steps quickly to suppress Martin, as Sulpicius notes: 'There Auxentius, supporter and leader of the Arians, persecuted him [Martin] with intensity and having inflicted many injuries, Auxentius drove him out of the city.'[36] Auxentius would have been bishop of Milan only a short time when Martin arrived. He could ill afford trouble this soon in his episcopate, such as an untimely campaign against the oppressive measures which the emperor and his partisans were using on the churches in Gaul and north Italy.

If Auxentius had serious difficulties with supporters loyal to the exiled and former bishop of Milan, Dionysius, or any other anti-Ariminum activities under Julian, we do not hear about them. Dionysius died in exile (c.361) and, by the time Julian had finally secured Italy (which might have allowed the Gallic condemnations to have some effect in Milan), the new Augustus was no longer favouring Christianity, much less its Nicene form. By the mid-360s Athanasius could report in his letter to the bishop of Corinth that synods in Gaul, Spain, and Italy had unanimously anathematized Auxentius and the heretical Illyrian bishops,[37] but these condemnations had no noticeable impact on Auxentius' hold on the church at Milan, as he continued to maintain what had become the western capital for Homoian interests.

Once Valentinian became emperor of the west, two serious attempts to undermine Auxentius' position were tried, both ending in failure. The first was an internal operation led by Filastrius, future bishop of Brixia, who tried to organize dissident catholics in Milan to rise up against their

---

[35] Nora K. Chadwick, *Poetry and Letters in Early Christian Gaul* (London, 1955), 116.

[36] *Vita Mart.* 6. 4 (*CSEL* i. 116. 24–6).

[37] *Ad Epict.* 1 (*PG* lvi. 1051A). The epistle of the Italian bishops to pro-Nicene Illyrian bishops (*CSEL* lxv. 158) is derived from a synod that met perhaps in north Italy and may be one of the councils that sat in condemnation of the bishop of Milan. Given the Illyrian destination of the epistle, only Valens and Ursacius are mentioned. But if Feder is correct to date the letter to 363, we might readily expect action against Auxentius as partly inspired by Liberius' short pro-Nicene revival after Constantius' death (cf. Liberius' letter to all Italian bishops, *CSEL* lxv. 157. 10–22).

bishop. We will have more to say about Filastrius' part in anti-Arian polemics later in this chapter. For the present, we need only observe that Filastrius, once discovered, was beaten and chased out of Milan—a pattern strikingly similar to that of Martin.[38] A Milanese deacon, Sabinus, was also found alienated from his church for his pro-Nicene sympathies. We cannot say exactly when this took place or whether it had any relation to Filastrius' situation, but Sabinus was present at the Roman council *c*.370/1 which condemned Auxentius. The deacon was then sent as a representative of that assembly with a letter to the eastern bishops, presumably as a living witness to underscore the seriousness of the situation in northern Italy. In any case, both episodes—those of Filastrius and Sabinus—further illustrate the degree of acceptance which Auxentius must have gained with his Milanese congregation by the mid-360s. It is a fact which becomes particularly noticeable at Auxentius' death, when the church is locked in conflict in 374 over the choice of a successor. As long as Auxentius was in office, the catholics remained a beleaguered minority in Milan.

The other attempt to dislodge Auxentius is the oft-cited confrontation between the bishop of Milan and Hilary of Poitiers in 364. As we suggested in the last chapter, this kind of aggression against an avowed Homoian bishop should be interpreted as an isolated episode and not indicative of the main task of the post-Ariminum reconstruction by pro-Nicenes. In brief,[39] we are told from a written refutation which Hilary penned afterwards against Auxentius, the *Contra Auxentium*, that Hilary had accused the bishop of Milan of heresy and the latter was called to answer to the charges at an inquest (*in foro*, not a council). The inquest, which was heard by a panel of ten unnamed bishops and in the presence of the Quaestor and Magister of Valentinian's court,[40] was ecclesiastical, not civil; the type organized to deal with the situation when public charges were laid against bishops. There Auxentius professed an ambiguous confession that was meant to disarm any fears about his orthodoxy, although he later issued a written statement which was nothing less than a carefully

---

[38] Interestingly, both accounts originate from commemorative *vitae*; Sulpicius' *Vita Martini* and *De vita et obitu beati Filastrii* by Gaudentius (*CSEL* lxviii. 186). Gaudentius would have surely known Sulpicius' work and may have followed its model, just as Paulinus of Milan, a contemporary of Gaudentius, claims to have modelled his *Vita Ambrosii* on Sulpicius.

[39] A more detailed chronicle of this episode in Hilary's career can be found in D. H. Williams, 'The Anti-Arian Campaigns of Hilary of Poitiers and the *Liber contra Auxentium*', *Church History*, 61 (1992), 7–22.

[40] There is no evidence to support the assumption that these ten bishops were predisposed towards Hilary's position (as Simonetti, *La crisi ariana*, 381).

worded version of the Homoian creed, described by Hilary as that 'impiety which was resolved by all at Niké in Thrace'.[41] Hilary's attempt to persuade the inquest that Auxentius was in fact cunningly deceiving them with his responses was not convincing. To raise the population of Milan against its bishop for reasons this vague was a serious mistake in the eyes of the new administration under Valentinian. Hilary seemed well aware of the gravity of the situation since he repeatedly depicts the Milanese people as fully orthodox and therefore publicly disquieted by Auxentius and his kind.[42] The ploy did not work, however. In his own appeal to the emperor, Auxentius portrayed himself as the conservative and injured party, sensitive to the need for public order as well as to the peace of the Church. There was no reason why Auxentius should not be maintained as the legitimate bishop of Milan in the eyes of the authorities, and Hilary was ordered to leave the city immediately for attempting to incite a public disturbance.

We are still left with the question why Hilary, a Gallic bishop, had come to Milan, especially since such confrontations had not been part of the general strategy of pro-Nicenes after Ariminum. The question becomes more perplexing once we realize it is all but certain that Eusebius of Vercelli had not accompanied him in this action;[43] Hilary had undertaken this campaign against Auxentius single-handedly. But we do not have to

---

[41] *Contra Aux.* 8 (*PL* x. 614C). Hilary appended Auxentius' written confession to the end of his treatise, 'Exemplum Blasphemiae Auxenti' (*PL* x. 617–18).

[42] *Contra Aux.* 5 (*PL* x. 612A); 6 (613A and B); 9 (615A).

[43] Despite the all but universal assertion that Eusebius was present (i.e. Meslin, *Les Ariens*, 43; Duval, 'Vrais et faux problèmes', 268 and *passim*; Simonetti, *La crisi ariana*, 381; *Patrology*, iv. 46; Hanson, *The Search*, 507), the evidence strongly leans to the contrary. First, the *Contra Auxentium* is addressed to the readers only in Hilary's name. Second, Hilary never mentions that Eusebius is with him, or indeed mentions him at all, and throughout the letter Hilary always writes in the first person. Third, Hilary claims (ch. 9) that he alone was ordered by the emperor to leave Milan. Fourth, Auxentius mentions Eusebius twice (chs. 13 (617B); 15 (618C)), both times in relation to Hilary. The second reference clearly pertains to their itinerary throughout the west 'Hilarius et Eusebius, contendunt ubique schismata facere'). It is the first passage which has convinced so many that Eusebius was in Milan: 'nec his qui ante me fuerunt episcopis, nunc amplius excitati ab Hilario et Eusebio, perturbantes quosdam, haereticum me vocaverunt.' Yet it can be argued that the interpretation of this second passage is no different from the first. According to Auxentius, Hilary's and Eusebius' campaign against him has had an impact on certain people in Milan. This need not imply that Eusebius or, for that matter, Hilary was ever in Milan. The two pro-Nicene bishops had acquired a widespread reputation for their work against heresy in the west as Rufinus' account attests (*HE* i. 31). We can see in this first passage confirmation that Hilary and Eusebius were well known for their joint enterprise, and, as far as Auxentius was concerned, their efforts brought nothing but schism and disharmony among the churches. But this passage is far too weak in isolation to substantiate Eusebius' presence in Milan.

look any further than Hilary's own defence to see the reason. It appears that Auxentius had been inciting Hilary and others by accusing them publicly of heresy: 'You are accustomed . . . to labelling me as a heretic', says Hilary, justifying his attack on Auxentius.[44] The charge is not the mere blustering of a frustrated man, for the bishop of Milan on his part did not hesitate to declare at the inquest that 'all heresies which arose against the catholic faith' were rightly condemned at Ariminum, including the doctrine of the *homoousios*. Hilary's complaint that Auxentius was using tactics of aggression against pro-Nicenes is entirely plausible and coheres with the remaining pieces of evidence pertaining to Auxentius' activities before his death.

Hilary's failure at Milan was not the end of pro-Nicene attempts to have Auxentius deposed. Nor does it seem that Auxentius curtailed his anti-Nicene activities, the effects of which can be detected in several synodical letters dated to the late 360s. From Alexandria, a synodical letter written *c*.369/70 by the African bishops expressed its gratitude to Damasus for the decision of a recent assembly held at Rome which 'expelled Ursacius and Valens and those who hold with them'.[45] Concern, however, was registered over the fact that Auxentius had not yet been deposed and expelled from the Church. Since the Alexandrian synod had received word about the condemnations from Rome while it was still in session, it also wrote in return, as the letter declares, informing its western colleagues about the close association which Auxentius had had with George of Cappadocia and about the 'many offences which he committed with Gregory'. From the perspective of the Alexandrian synod, any disciple of Gregory, arch-Arian and rival of Athanasius 355–61, should have been cut off long ago. Besides, the African Nicenes were having their own problems with certain individuals who were still opposing Nicaea by citing the authority of Ariminum and 'eagerly striving that it should prevail'.[46]

The Roman assembly to which the Alexandrian letter refers is otherwise unaccounted for in our sources. Its exact date is unknown but it seems to have preceded another synod under Damasus at Rome which condemned Auxentius in 370/1.[47] Our knowledge of this latter assembly comes from its synodical letter, 'Confidimus quidem', addressed to the eastern

---

[44] *Contra Aux.* 11(*PL* x. 616A).   [45] *Ad Afros*, 10 (*PG* lvi. 1046D).

[46] *Ad Afros*, 1 (*PG* lvi. (1030B) (trans. from *NPNF* iv. 489).

[47] Mansi, iii. 447; Zeiller, *Origines chrétiennes*, 307 n. 2; Cf. Pietri, *Roma Christiana*, i. 734 n. 3, for discussion of the different dates attributed to the synod (ranging from 368 to 372).

bishops, which is extant in Latin and Greek versions.[48] There has been some question whether the Latin versions are really translations from the Greek which themselves stem from an earlier Latin exemplar, although M. Richard (following E. Schwartz) has shown conclusively that the version from the Verona LX manuscript preserves a Latin original and that there is no need to question its authenticity.[49] In the same study, Richard offers a new edition of the synodical letter according to the Verona text.[50] According to the salutation of the letter, over ninety bishops met at Rome 'for the purpose of hearing the case of Auxentius and setting forth the faith'. Lines 12–19 state precisely the occasion of the synod.

We have learned from some of our brothers of Gaul and Venice of unstable persons holding to perverse interpretations, not out of a zeal for heresy (nor are such priests of God able to fall into this evil), but out of ignorance or a certain *naïveté*. Not knowing how to distinguish sufficiently, the views of our fathers ought to be retained because different ideas are introduced to their minds. Moreover, they proscribed Auxentius of Milan, being condemned especially over this matter.

This passage summarizes a report which was sent from a synod composed of Gallic and Venetian bishops who had already condemned Auxentius of Milan. It appears that Auxentius had been provoking dissension and doctrinal discord outside the jurisdiction of his own see. The authority of other councils, almost certainly a reference to Ariminum, was being introduced and having influence on the simple-minded. Further action on the matter had now become necessary, but on a wider scale. Sozomen (and Theodoret), who is depending on an unknown source, provides valuable details of these circumstances and is worth quoting at length.

Auxentius and his followers differed from the others in opinion; he was then president of the church in Milan, and, in conjunction with a few partisans, was intent upon the introduction of innovations, and the maintenance of the Arian

---

[48] In Latin: in the collection of the deacon Theodosius, which is preserved in codex LX of the Chapter Library of Verona (printed in *PL* lvi. 143–8 and also in *PL* xiii. 347–9), and in the *Historia ecclesiastica* vocata *Tripartita*, v. 29 of Cassiodorus (*PL* lxix. 1006–7). In Greek: Sozomen, *HE* vi. 23. 7–15 (*GCS* l. 266–8) and Theodoret, *HE* ii. 22. 3–12 (*GCS* xliv. 147–50).

[49] 'La Lettre "Confidimus quidem" du Pape Damase', *Annuaire de l'Institut de Philologie et d'Histoire Orientales et Slaves*, 11 (1951), 323–40.

[50] 'Exemplum synodi habitae Rome episcoporum XCIII: ex rescripto imperiali' (pp. 326–7).

dogma of the dissimilarity of the Son and of the Holy Spirit . . . The bishops of Gaul and Venetia having reported that similar attempts to disturb the peace of the church were being made by others among them, the bishops of several provinces not long after assembled at Rome, and decreed that Auxentius and those who held his views should be removed from their communion. They confirmed the traditional faith established by the council of Nicaea, and annulled all the decrees that had been issued at Ariminum contrary to that faith, under the plea that these decrees had not received the assent of the bishop of Rome, nor of other bishops who agreed with them, and that many who had been present at the synod had disapproved of the enactments there made by them.[51]

Protected by the political policies of the Emperor Valentinian, Auxentius had little to fear from a council which attacked him for doctrinal reasons alone. There was virtually nothing Damasus and other anti-Arian bishops could do since they could not hope to expel the offending Milanese bishop from his see.

We have seen from the above passages that Auxentius was not completely isolated in his position as an outspoken adherent to the Ariminum creed. Not only did he have partisans outside Milan but he was able to wage his own campaigns against the pro-Nicenes. If the actual danger which these campaigns presented to the Nicene movement was perhaps not as great as that which existed in Illyricum, it was sufficient to warrant the convoking of several synods in Italy, raise concern in an Alexandrian synod, and maintain continued vigilance against Homoian propaganda, which was still attracting new members. Pietri nicely sums up the seriousness of the situation: 'D'Italie jusqu'à l'Illyricum, ou siègent Valens, Ursace, Germinius, une grande communauté arienne résistait . . . L'épiscopat orthodoxe d'Italie septentrionale, celui de Vénétie et même celui de la Gaule voisine, prit très sérieux la menace.'[52] Jerome might boast (c.370) that Evagrius, who came west with Eusebius of Vercelli, practically 'buried' Auxentius of Milan before his death,[53] but it is completely incongruous with all the evidence we have seen. Such a comment may have been more an attempt on the part of Jerome, who greatly revered Damasus, to cover the embarrassment which Auxentius was causing to Rome's increasing authority. Perhaps the significance of the religious legacy left by Auxentius in Milan becomes most apparent at his death, which finally resulted in the election and imperial approval of a

---

[51] *HE* vi. 23 (*GCS* 1. 266–7) (trans. from *NPNF* ii. 360).
[52] *Roma Christiana*, i. 734.
[53] *Ep.* 1. 15. The context is Evagrius' activities at Rome and his multifold assistance to Damasus.

candidate whose political standing on the issues would appease disputing Homoian and pro-Nicene factions in the city. This matter will be considered shortly.

3. NEO-NICENES AND THEIR OPPONENTS

Once it was certain that the new western emperor was not going to elevate the interests of one ecclesiastical party over those of another, the political strategies of the Neo-Nicenes had little effect against the Homoian bishops and their churches. We have already examined how Hilary of Poitiers and several western synods failed in their attempts to remove Auxentius from Milan. The conflict was now relegated to a war of words for both sides. In the last quarter of the fourth century an abundance of literature begins to pour forth from Nicene and Homoian communities; a literature that was extremely diversified and written, so it seems, mostly for the benefit of the writers' own communities.

A sizeable body of Latin Arian documents survived the imperial proscriptions of the later fourth and fifth centuries and has come down to the present. This literature can be broken roughly into two categories: (1) credal formulas[54] and (2) homiletical, exegetical, and polemical treatises and fragments (some of them very large fragments). The bulk of Latin Arian literature which remains has been preserved in three collections: the Arian *scholia* from the Codex Parisinus MS Lat. 8907, an ensemble of short and complete texts from MS Verona LI,[55] and a series of fragmented palimpsests originally discovered in the library of Bobbio, now partly preserved in the Vatican library (MS Lat. 5750) and partly in the Ambrosian library (SP 9/1–2; 9/9).[56] Outside these three groups of texts

---

[54] See App. IV.

[55] Parts of this collection were edited by C. H. Turner and B. Capelle in a series of articles between 1911 and 1928, but not until 1982 did Gryson edit the first complete text (*CCSL* lxxxvii). The collection consists of the following: an explanation of the names of the apostles (fos. 2ʳ–5ᵛ), a series of twenty-four homilies on the Gospels (fos. 5ᵛ–39ᵛ), fifteen sermons on the principal feast days of the year (fos. 1ʳ–1ᵛ; 40ʳ–77ᵛ), a treatise against the Jews (fos. 77ᵛ–98ᵛ), a treatise against the pagans, in two somewhat different recensions (fos. 98ᵛ–119ʳ; 119ᵛ–132ᵛ), a short polemical sermon directed against the doctrine that the 'Pater et Filius aequales sunt' (fos. 133ʳ–136ʳ). Fos. 119ʳ–ᵛ and 136ʳ–157ᵛ include several fragments from writings of Jerome, Augustine, and the *Apostolic Constitutions*.

[56] Roger Gryson has provided extensive codicological and palaeographical analysis of each of these collections with photographic plates of the original manuscripts. See R. Gryson and L. Gilissen, *Les Scolies ariennes du Parisinus Latinus 8907*; R. Gryson, *Le Recueil de Vérone*; and R. Gryson, *Les Palimpsests ariens latins de Bobbio* (Turnhout, 1983). Besides these texts, there is also the badly corrupted Latin MS Clm. 6329 of Munich which contains

there is also extant a very lengthy and fragmented commentary on the Gospel of Matthew which was attributed to John Chrysostom throughout the Middle Ages, but is now known simply as the *Opus imperfectum in Mattheum*,[57] an anonymous commentary on Job,[58] and an exposition or catechism of Homoian doctrine known as the *Sermo Arrianorum*.[59] Among the Augustinian corpus there exists the edited version of a debate, held in 427/8, between Augustine and a certain Maximinus[60] over the divine natures of the Son and Holy Spirit.

To claim that the above documents are representative Homoian theology assumes that there were certain common denominators in this very diverse literature. Whatever doctrinal relationships can be established, they must be made with the awareness that these writings range over a potential period of more than sixty years, and that some of the documents may originate from Arian communities which lived under Gothic or Vandal occupation. With good reason therefore has Gryson warned about overly synthetic attempts to force the literature into common moulds; a mistake which Hanson tends to make in his chapter on 'Homoian Arianism' in *The Search for the Christian Doctrine of God*. Nor need we entertain theories of artificial distinctions such as Meslin's thesis that Arian literature after AD 380 represents the thought of a 'second generation' of Homoians who were far more subordinationist, and closer to Anomoian theology, than their predecessors. His proposition of erecting a radical disjuncture between the more thoroughgoing Arianism of Palladius (whom

twenty-eight homilies, twelve of which may be composed or edited by an unknown Arian of the 4th century, as proposed by R. Était, 'Sermons ariens inédits', *Recherches augustiniennes*, 26 (1992), 143–79.

[57] *PG* lvi. 611–948. A much needed critical edition will be published by J. van Banning in the series *Corpus Christianorum*, and a status report of his progress is available in *Studia Patristica*, 20 (1989), 70–5. The manuscript tradition is extremely complex, hampered no less because of the text's diffusion under the name of Chrysostom, and in some manuscripts there was a weeding out of passages with a recognizable Arian content. Van Banning makes the fascinating suggestion that the great popularity of the *Opus* during the Middle Ages was because it provided a kind of theological antidote to Augustine's strong anti-Pelagianism. The *Opus* presents a view of free will that placed greater value on the human initiative to respond to God.

[58] *Anonymus in Iob*. For brief description, see Simonetti, *Patrology*, iv. 103; Meslin, *Les Ariens*, 222 f.

[59] It has been preserved in the works of Augustine (*PL* xlii. 677–84), sent to him by a correspondent; against it he composed the *Contra sermonem Arrianorum* (*PL* xlii. 683–708). B. Daley, 'The Giant's Twin Substances', in R. Teske and J. Lienhard (eds.), *Collectanea Augustiniana* (Villanova, forthcoming).

[60] The debate is found in the so-called *Collatio Augustini cum Maximino Arrianorum* (*PL* lvii. 709–42) along with Augustine's reply in two books to Maximinus, *Contra Maximinum Haereticum* (*PL* lxii. 743–814).

Meslin considers a second-generation Homoian!)[61] and of Valens of Mursa or Ursacius of Singidunum, who are characterized as mere 'political theologians' but less heretical, is built upon a much criticized view that these early Homoians were unjustly upbraided by their opponents for teaching doctrines which they never admitted. Both Duval and Burkhardt have rightly remarked that Meslin did not take adequate account of the strong subordinationist declaration presented by Valens and his colleagues at Sirmium in 357.[62] Indeed, one can detect points of doctrinal continuity between the Sirmium declaration and the Ariminum creed, and the thought of later western Arianism as found in the *Scholia* or in Maximinus' debate with Augustine.[63] This allows the historian to identify Homoian Arianism, despite its own evolution, as a faith possessing a discernible set of beliefs[64] and ecclesiastical communities which subscribed to these beliefs.

An even greater amount of literature, not surprisingly, produced by the pro-Nicenes from this same period is in our possession today. Pamphlets and professions of faith proliferated throughout the Latin-speaking world seeking to affirm the Nicene creed and/or its precepts, usually in contradistinction to one or more dissenting 'heretical' groups. Similar to the existing Homoian documents, the remains of anti-Arian literature are not polemical in form only, but are distributed among polemical, homiletical, or catechetical and confessional categories. This should warn us that the conflict between pro-Nicenes and anti-Nicenes was not purely a debate between intellectuals and cannot, therefore, be fully understood by evaluating the conflict in terms of *dogmengeschichte* alone. One is able to measure the intensity between 'Arian' or anti-'Arian'

[61] Palladius, bishop of Ratiaria since 346, is an elderly man by the time he writes against Ambrose in 378. Theologically, Meslin is anxious to associate Palladius with Ulfila, Auxentius of Durostorum, and Maximinus, forcing a superficial break with Valens, Ursacius, and their circle (see *Les Ariens*, 301 f.). The problem is that this level of discontinuity between first- and second-generation Homoians is not nearly as radical as Meslin thinks. Palladius (and Secundianus) are in close connection and agreement with their fellow Illyrians Valens, Paulus, and others, as the correspondence with Germinius shows (*CSEL* lxv. 159–63). Palladius is equally intent on ascertaining whether Germinius has abandoned the tenets of the Ariminum creed which Palladius obviously favoured and which were decidedly not Anomoian. Despite Meslin's insistence that Palladius is much more heavily indebted to Eunomian theology than his predecessors, we have seen that Palladius expressly denies any doctrine of *dissimilis*, referring to Demophilus (then of Constantinople) as 'the master' (*Scholia*, 349ʳ. 140).

[62] Duval, 'Sur l'Arianisme des Ariens d'Occident', 147; J. D. Burkhardt, 'Les Ariens d'Occident', *Revue d'histoire et de philosophie religieuse*, 51 (1971), 172 f.

[63] Gryson, *Scolies*, 191; Duval, 'Sur l'Arianisme des Ariens d'Occident', 148; Burkhardt, 'Les Ariens', 173–4.

[64] For a more detailed analysis of Homoian theology, see Hanson, *The Search*, 562–72; and for the theology of the *Scholia*, Gryson, *Scolies*, 173–200.

forces by comparing differing types of literary expression, and ask what these sources tell us about the nature of the conflict. For example, we learn something about the diffusion of Nicene/anti-Nicene tensions in Sirmium from the *Altercatio Heracliani laici cum Germinio*, where the articulate resistance of the pro-Nicene Heraclianus provoked a violent reaction from the spectators present, who would have attacked the layman if the Bishop Germinius had not intervened at the last moment. The hostilities which other anti-Arians encountered at Milan due to their opposition to Bishop Auxentius (*above*) may stem from similar circumstances. And yet perhaps no one was more aware and more adept than Ambrose when it came to marshalling the forces of popular feeling for anti-Arian purposes. An important part of his strategy against the Homoians in the mid-380s included teaching his Milanese congregation Trinitarian hymns whose substance was in accord with the Nicene tradition.[65] And when the relics of Gervasius and Protasius were discovered in the foundations of a new basilica, Ambrose utilized their perceived heavenly patronage for a renewed anti-Homoian campaign—a move which may have decisively determined the outcome of pro-Nicene sentiments at Milan.[66] For Ambrose, as for many other personalities on both sides of the issues, the controversy was waged in an arena much wider than that of theological exchange. We must be prepared in our present evaluation therefore to grapple with a conflict which was disseminated at different levels and consider how this was expressed in the variety of literature available to us today.

Looking at the anti-Arian reaction in the Latin west, and particularly the literature from north Italy, we will need to judge whether there exists sufficient cumulative force in the evidence to underwrite our thesis that the Homoians presented a greater threat to Nicene supremacy than is commonly supposed. Earlier in this chapter we examined the conciliar activity in the 360s and 370s against the Homoians in the west. We now wish to review several different examples of anti-Arian documents from less celebrated but important sources which will contribute to the overall picture of the period.

(a) *Filastrius of Brixia*

One of the lesser-known figures from this era is Filastrius (or Philaster), an anti-heretical activist and writer who eventually became bishop of

---

[65] *Sermo contra Auxentium*, 34 (*CSEL* lxxxii. 3. 105. 422–5) Cf. Augustine, *Conf.* IX. 7.
[66] A more detailed analysis of Ambrose's use of the relics for polemical purposes will be presented in Ch. 7.

Brixia. His appointment to this see must have been before 381 since Filastrius was one of the signatories at the council of Aquileia which condemned the Homoian bishops Palladius and Secundianus.[67] Filastrius' obscurity is partly due to the fact that he does not figure in Jerome's or Gennadius' *De viris illustribus*, nor does Filastrius himself offer any personal details in his lengthy catalogue on diverse heresies, his only known work. There is a vague reminiscence by Augustine, who saw him at Milan in the company of Ambrose, but no context is given for the event.[68] Whatever substantial information we possess about Filastrius comes from a dedicatory sermon, *De vita et obitu beati Filastrii episcopi*, delivered at Brixia by his episcopal successor Gaudentius.[69]

Filastrius did not originate from Brixia and was not even a native of Italy. According to Gaudentius, Filastrius, like the patriarch Abraham, left his own land and his father's house in order to follow the *verbum Dei*, having cast aside everything. No other reliable information is available to pinpoint his place of origin. We are told only that he practised continence and lived a solitary existence before coming to north Italy.[70] It seems also that Filastrius, in imitation of the apostle Paul, was an itinerant preacher: 'he preached the words of the Lord going about almost all the regions of the Roman world.'[71] What gave Filastrius a certain notoriety was his mission as an apologist for catholic Christianity. With a certain pride and admiration Gaudentius says that not only did he vigorously contend with Pagans, Jews, and every heresy for the sake of the faith, but he especially fought against 'the mad Arian perfidy'. His campaign against Arianism led him, not unexpectedly, to Milan, where he is said to have resisted the 'Arian Auxentius'. During this time in Milan, Filastrius is described as a 'capable guardian (*custos*) of the Lord's flock',[72] which raises interesting questions about his role in the city. Did he assume leadership over the catholic community in Milan after his arrival? And, if so, did he attempt to organize any opposition against Auxentius? It is not known how long he remained in the city, but his self-appointed mission was successful enough to produce a severe reaction. Filastrius is subjected to stripes

[67] *Gesta*, 1 (Gryson, *Scolies*, 330).

[68] *Ep.* 222 to Quodvultdeus. Augustine was in Milan 384–7.

[69] *Tractatus*, 21 (*CSEL* lxviii. 184–9). The sermon was delivered on the day of his death, XV Kal. Aug. (18 July). The authenticity of this work was disputed by F. Marx but his arguments have been decisively refuted. See A. Gluck, *CSEL* lxviii, pp. xv–xvii; H. Koch, 'Philastrius', *PWK* xix. 2. 2125; J. Wittig, 'Filastrius, Gaudentius und Ambrosiaster: eine literarhistorische Studie', in *Kirchengeschichtliche Abhandlungen*, viii (Breslau, 1909), 4–5.

[70] Marx's contention that Filastrius came from Alexandria or Egypt lacks any concrete evidence and has not been taken seriously by later scholars. See Wittig, 'Filastrius', 5.

[71] *De vita et obitu*, 6 (*CSEL* lxviii. 186. 34–6).

[72] *De vita et obitu*, 7 (*CSEL* lxviii. 186. 43–4).

(*verberibus subderetur*) and is forced to retire from Milan, since we find him next at Rome continuing his disputations with heretics. Unless Gaudentius' account at this point should be treated as a purely hagiographic reflection of the *Vita Martini*, it appears that Auxentius was successful in accusing Filastrius of creating a public disturbance and so brought the civil authorities down upon his head.[73] The scenario has become an all too familiar pattern which confronted prophets of anti-Arianism who strove to stir up opposition in Milan against its bishop.

Following a period in Rome and another stint of crusading throughout Italy, Filastrius settled at Brixia, where he was made bishop. It is rather unexpected that someone like Filastrius should suddenly terminate his itinerant activities and remain at Brixia; a town described by Gaudentius as a farming community (*rudis*) and wholly unworthy of such a celebrated man. There may have been reasons for this arrangement that Gaudentius never mentions. One is tempted to suppose that there was some connection in the geographical proximity between the two cities: Brixia being only 60 miles east of Milan. Might Filastrius have decided to settle there given the ongoing tensions between him and Auxentius, and knowing that the latter's anti-Nicene influence was still able to produce doctrinal unrest in that area? Gaudentius never says so directly, but passages from two other sermons of his imply that Filastrius was anxious to introduce a stabilizing effect to the small church at Brixia. The first reference comes from the *De vita et obitu* (*Sermo* 21), in which Gaudentius states that the church at Brixia was 'ignorant of spiritual knowledge' but eager to be taught by the 'praiseworthy man who was happy to condescend'.[74] No elaboration is offered on the church's lack of 'spiritual knowledge' but a second passage, from *Sermo* 16, supplies further information: 'through the grace generously poured out by the Holy Spirit, he established this church in the faith of the worshipful Trinity, he grounded this church in true hope and a perfected love, he incited it to fortitude, he died in peace.'[75] We are led to understand then that the church of Brixia was established in the Nicene form of faith following Filastrius' arrival. There is no mention that Filastrius was confronted with any heresy within the church, Arian or otherwise, simply that he was responsible for bringing sound teaching into their midst.

---

[73] Even if Gaudentius is patterning his hero after Martin, there is nothing overly fanciful about Gaudentius' report at this point. Auxentius used the same strategy in order to have Hilary removed in 364. The difference may lie in the simple fact that, when Hilary was ordered to leave the city, he obeyed; Filastrius, not yet a bishop, ignored the order and was punished.

[74] 21. 8 (*CSEL* lxviii. 186–76. 49–51).   [75] 16. 8 (*CSEL* lxviii. 139).

Filastrius' endeavours against heretical teaching took a written form once he became bishop. His only known work, *Diversarum hereseon liber,*[76] is a compendium of over 150 heretical groups and doctrines, many of them having obscure names or of a dubious origin, which have sprung up since the origin of the world. Of course the compilation of different heresies was no new literary form. Justin Martyr's (no longer extant) *Syntagma*, Irenaeus' *Adversus haereses*, Hippolytus' *Refutatio omnium haeresium*, Pseudo-Tertullian's *Adversus omnes haereses* and Epiphanius' *Panarion* all preceded Filastrius, and could have provided a model(s) for his work. Already by the early fifth century the *Diversarum hereseon liber* had taken its place among the better-known anti-heretical encyclopedias of the west. Augustine refers his pupil Quodvultdeus to it, along with Epiphanius' *Panarion*, though he makes it clear that Epiphanius is to be preferred.[77] Gregory I is also known to have resorted to Filastrius' catalogue on more than one occasion to check the identity of certain heretics with which he was not familiar.[78]

For all the conflict and debate which Filastrius is reputed to have had with the Arians, his work against diverse heresies says surprisingly little about them, besides being ill-informed on many details. In chapter 66, the 'Arriani' are said to have originated from Arius, a presbyter of Alexandria, who taught that the Son of God was *similis* (like) to God. In the brief description which follows, one realizes that the Arriani for Filastrius are not those who were labelled 'Arians' in the early part of the fourth century, but the Homoians of his own day: 'When he [Arius] uttered the term "like" not pertaining to the divine substance of the Father, he introduced a dangerous heresy. For a creature is also said to be "like" God, just as the Scripture says, "Let us make man after our image and likeness." '[79]

[76] Editions in *PL* xii. 1111–302; *CSEL* xxxviii. 1–137; *CCSL* ix. 217–324. I will be using Heylen's edition in *CCSL*. Wittig (pp. 8 ff.) has argued that Filastrius' work has been slightly altered and expanded in some chapters, especially chs. 128–56, by a later editor around the year 430. This should not dissuade us, however, from interpreting the heretical catalogue as a work of Filastrius. Wittig admits that any differences between the first and second hand are matters of small details. The catalogue is generally dated between 380 and 390, though closer to 380 than 390; Koch, 'Philastrius', 2127; Rimoldi, 'Filastre', *DHGE* xvi. 1474; Heylen, *CCSL* ix. 210.

[77] *Ep.* 222 (written 427/8).

[78] *Ep. ad Cyriacum episcopum Constantinopolitanum* (*MGHAA Epistolae* 1. 448. 22). On the subject of anti-heretical catalogues in general, see J. McClure, 'Handbooks against Heresy', *JTS* 30 (1979), 186–97.

[79] 66. 2 (*CCSL* ix. 244. 4–8). A. H. B. Logan has suggested that Filastrius took detailed information from a heresiological catalogue written by Marcellus of Ancyra which is no longer extant but shares parallel views with a work also authored by Marcellus, *De sancta*

A brief refutation of the 'Arriani' provided by Filastrius consists simply of what had become the stock-in-trade answers to the major Homoian propositions. The Son does share in the divine substance, for the 'Begotten one' (*genitus*) must be distinguished from men and angels in that the 'unicus filius' is eternally begotten from the Father and thus cannot be made out of nothing (*ex nihilo*) as they claim. In fact, he argues, the Son is able to be 'truly God' in no other way 'unless he is begotten peculiarly from the divine substance of the Father'. Any discussion about the likeness of the Son to the Father in terms of activity alone is also challenged by Filastrius, who argues somewhat awkwardly that the *similitudo* of the Son is according to eternal works because 'just as the Father acts so the Son acts similarly in all things'.

It is obvious that Filastrius has reduced the arguments of his enemies to their simplest form for the purpose of a quick refutation. To what extent he really understood the Homoian position is difficult to assess, but it should have been more extensively than his summary reveals. To his credit he was one of the few anti-Arian polemicists that do not attribute the doctrine of dissimiliarity to his opponents. He distinguishes the 'Arriani' from the 'Eunomiani', who teach that the Father, Son, and Holy Spirit are three qualitatively different substances ('just like gold, silver, and bronze'), and from the 'Semiarriani' (a term he probable took from Epiphanius), who believe in the consubstantiality of Father and Son, but not of the Holy Spirit.[80] However, his glib caricature of these groups demonstrates limited first-hand knowledge.

(b) *Zeno of Verona*

Another north Italian bishop of this period, Zeno of Verona, was not a controversialist like Filastrius, but he was nevertheless concerned to protect his flock from certain errors of doctrine, particularly from those of the Homoians and Photinians. Very few details remain about Zeno's background, complicating any reconstruction about his career. What little can be gleaned from the collection of homilies generally attributed to him has led scholars earlier in this century to postulate an African origin for

ecclesia. The latter had been transmitted under the name of Anthimus of Nicomedia (martyred under Diocletian) until it was recognized as a part of the disputed Marcellan corpus. 'Marcellus of Ancyra and Anti-Arian Polemic', *Studia Patristica*, 20 (1989), 194–6.

[80] Ch. 67. See Epiphanius, *Pan. haer.* LXXIII. 1 ff. (*GCS* lxxviii. 367 ff.); LXXIII. 23. (388–90) for the misguided application of the term 'Semi-Arians'.

Zeno, principally because one of the bishop's sermons is dedicated to the memory of an obscure Mauretanian martyr, St Arcadius.[81] This connection has been discounted by F. E. Vokes, who argued in a short essay in 1966 that there is no compelling literary proof to suppose Zeno came from Africa; a view which more recent analyses of Zeno's background have confirmed.[82] Not only is the question of Zeno's origins problematic, the dates of his bishopric also cannot be ascertained with any precision. Neither its beginning nor end can be definitively established. Most scholars have placed Zeno's episcopate *circa* the years 362–80.[83] All we can say for certain is that Zeno could not have been bishop any earlier than 356, since Lucillus is mentioned as holder of that see in the year Athanasius wrote his *Apologia contra Constantium*. A date of 380 is generally considered the *terminus ad quem* of Zeno's ministry for the reason that a letter of Ambrose commonly dated to *c*.380 is written to Syagrius, who is called the bishop of Verona, and reference is made to Zeno as being deceased.[84] But this too must remain in the realm of likelihood only since we have no other means of determining the beginning of Syagrius' episcopate, which presumably immediately followed that of Zeno. Nor does the roll-call of pro-Nicene bishops at the council of Aquileia (381) offer any corroborating evidence since Verona is not represented at that assembly. The most that can be concluded is that Zeno was bishop of Verona well before Ambrose became the bishop of Milan in 374, and began perhaps soon after the council of Ariminum, since no aspersion is ever cast on Zeno compromising himself with a heretical creed.

Despite the many lacunae surrounding the bishop's life, we are able to speak more definitively on the subject of Zeno's extant writings, since it is virtually certain that he is the author of ninety-two, perhaps ninety-three,

---

[81] Notably Andreas Bigelmair, *Zeno von Verona* (Münster, 1904). Cf. G. Bardy, 'Zénon de Vérone', *DTC* xv. 3686. In addition to multiple references to Tertullian, Cyprian, and Lactantius, Zeno delivered a sermon on the feast-day (12 Jan.) of St Arcadius (*Tract.* i. 39).

[82] Vokes, 'Zeno of Verona, Apuleius and Africa', *Studia Patristica*, 8/2 (= Text und Untersuchungen 93) (1966), 130–4. With regard to the sermon on Arcadius, Vokes points to the interchange of liturgical calendars between various geographical parts of the Church which was occurring with greater frequency by the end of the 4th century. Thus, Arcadius may not have been an obscure martyr to the people of Verona, who could have had some special reason to honour him (p. 133). B. Löfstedt, 'Der Verfasser', *CCSL* xxii. 6–7.

[83] Bigelmair, *Zeno von Verona*, 47 ff.; Bardy, 'Zénon de Vérone', 3687; K. Wegenast, 'Z. von Verona', *PWK* x A. 148; F. Martroye, 'L'Affaire Indicia: une sentence de Saint Ambroise', in *Mélanges Paul Fournier* (Paris, 1929), 503; Löfstedt, 'Der Verfasser', 8, See the arguments of M. Stepanich in *The Christology of Zeno of Verona* (Washington, DC, 1948), 11, which fix Zeno's consecration in the year 362.

[84] *Ep.* 56. 1: 'Zenonis sanctae memoriae judicio.' Even this date is an approximation since Ambrose's letter to Syagrius is not firmly dated.

of the 103 tractates which have been attributed to him.[85] The collection is not the work of Zeno, however, but of a later editor in the fifth century,[86] who seems to have assembled everything which remained of the bishop's literary activity. Probably for this reason the collection is an assortment of homilies, only thirty of which are complete, and shorter notices or fragments, addressing a variety of themes. The majority of the tractates are exegetical in nature, and a large number treat the subject of baptism and of Easter (Passover). Some homilies are concerned with Christian ethics, treating such matters as chastity (I. 1) or continence (II. 7) and virtues such as patience (I. 4), humility (II. 9), and justice (II. 1). Only in a few instances does Zeno address doctrinal matters, which may be indicative of the bishop's pastoral concerns or may equally well reflect the interests of the editor. When Zeno does address matters of faith his overarching concern is to expound on the correct teaching of the relationship between the Father and Son. His method is not polemical, at least not directly, but didactic, and his style of presentation on doctrinal issues follows accordingly.

Two important themes for Zeno, which occur repeatedly in his discussions on Trinitarian doctrine, are that the Son is equal in all things to the Father, and that the begottenness of the Son in no way separates him from the Father or diminishes his status of equality. For the sake of creation (*ordinem rerum*), the Word (*verbum*) is said to have burst forth directly from the 'heart' (*cor*) of the Father, the process being described as 'omnipotence propagating itself'. Thus, Zeno can echo the traditional formula 'de deo nascitur deus', for the Son possesses everything of the Father, yet, at the same time, the Father is diminished in nothing by the procession of the Son.[87] An expansion of these emphases can be found in the tractate entitled *De Genesi* (I. 17), which, despite its title, is Zeno's defence of the language of the Nicene creed, and how the begotten Son, as was postulated in Tractate I. 56, 'possessed everything of the Father's, subtracting nothing from the Father'.[88]

It is obvious that Zeno is reacting to any error which divides the Son from the Father on account of a difference in substance as well as any teaching which dates the existence of the Son from his nativity. Regarding this latter view, Zeno is well aware of those who assert, 'Jesus Christ assumed his beginning (*principium*) from the womb of the virgin Mary, and was made, not born, God on account of his righteousness' (II. 8);

[85] See Löfstedt, 'Der Verfasser', 5 ff.; Wegenast, 'Z. von Verona', 148–9.
[86] Bardy, 'Zénon de Vérone', 3687–8.   [87] I. 56. 1 (*CCSL* xxii. 131. 2–6).
[88] I. 17. 2 (*CCSL* xxii. 64. 7–10).

surely the teaching of the Photinians. But Zeno is most concerned with those who try to demean the person of the Christ because of his work as the incarnate Son. His references are umistakably anti-Arian in content and recogizably an emphasis of Homoian theology.

We can see this most clearly in Tractatus II. 5, which is a rebuttal against what seems to be an Arian interpretation of 1 Corinthians 15: 24. Apparently there were those in Verona who claimed that the inferiority of the Son is established because Christ will deliver his kingdom in the end to God the Father. To this Zeno responds that we must take account of the different scriptural passages which speak of the Son as God alone (*purum deum*) and God incarnate (*hominem mixtum*). Here he touches on what is perhaps the exegetical point in Homoian theology most frequently attacked by pro-Nicene writers. Zeno states that, when the Scriptures speak of the Son of God, they distinguish him as God and man. As a man he was born according to the flesh, son of a virgin, tasted death and conquered it, descended into Hades, and then ascended into heaven; thus we speak of him as the 'only-begotten proceeding from the Father before the beginning of all things, first-begotten from the dead'.[89] This is also the same one who glorified God in the work which he was given, and was so glorified by the Father with the glory which they shared before the world was created (John 17: 4). When Zeno turns to address directly the interpretation of 1 Corinthians 15: 24, the conclusion is easily anticipated. We cannot say that the Son was lacking what he gave to the Father (i.e., his kingdom), for 'all the Father possesses [is] all the Son possesses; what belongs to one belongs to both' (II. 5. 9).

Zeno's insistence on the absolute equality of the Father and Son leads him to minimize, almost to the point of complete silence, that the Son is other than the Father. He uses the terms 'only-begotten' and 'Unbegotten', and recognizes that they are two *personae*,[90] but he never expounds on these implications. His reaction to subordinationist Christology brings Zeno to identify the Son with the Father as closely theologically as possible without slipping into the Photinian problem of confusing the two. No room is given for his listeners to interpret the begotenness of the Son as anything but an exact duplication of nature when he says: 'the Father in Himself begets another self from Himself' (*pater in ipsum alium se genuit ex se*) (I. 17. 2). Thus it can be said that the Father has

---

[89] II. 5. 3 (*CCSL* xxii. 165).
[90] II. 8. 4: 'duplex persona, duplex vocabulum, sed originalis perpetuitatis ac deitatis est una substantia' (*CCSL* xxii. 177. 37–8).

communicated his own substance to the Son so perfectly that he has begotten another self in the Son.

The consubstantiality of the Holy Spirit is an unimportant issue for Zeno, not untypically for a western writer during this time, though he has no hesitation in affirming that the Spirit shares in the fullness of the divine nature of the Son and the Father.[91] He freely uses the term *trinitas* throughout his writings (e.g. I. 74; 53; II. 3; 19). On the whole, Zeno eschews philosophical reasoning when it comes to grappling with the mysteries of God. In a manner like that of his theological predecessor Hilary of Poitiers, he is very critical of human abilities to perceive rightly the nature of God, especially those attempts which result in dividing the Son from the Father.

In sum, the indications from Zeno's writings are of one thoroughly steeped in western theological tradition and who wrote during a time when the Neo-Nicene restoration had regained its supremacy throughout most of the west, though still struggled with Homoian resistance. This collection of homilies and fragments does not tell us anything directly about the polemical activity which was waged between Neo-Nicenes and Homoians; indeed, the implication may be drawn that Verona was not seriously troubled by that conflict. Such a conclusion should not be over-stressed however. For whenever Zeno turns to theology, his writings do reflect the kind of opposition endemic in Nicene arguments which opposed the Homoians' ontological non-distinction between the humanity and the divinity of the Son.[92]

(c) *Commentarius in symbolum Nicaeanum*

Another document which is thought to originate from north Italy[93] is an anonymous commentary on the Nicene creed.[94] This work is polemical in

---

[91] I. 7. 4 (*CCSL* xxii. 44–5); I. 45. 3; II. 5. 10 and I. 36. 32, where Zeno refers to the Father, Son, and Holy Spirit 'in tribus una sis' (*CCSL* xxii. 99–100).

[92] Stepanich notes that Zeno does not employ the terms *homoousios* or *consubstantialis* but *una substantia* (*Christology of Zeno of Verona*, 60), which may be another reflection of the anti-Photinian element present in the homilies.

[93] C. Turner, *EOMIA* i. 2. 1, 353; Dekkers, *Clavis Patrum Latinorum*, 1745; Pietri, *Roma Christiana*, i. 731 n. 3. It was Turner who first suggested that the *Commentarius* was written against Urbanus of Parma, since the work is directed against one who propagated the Arian heresy *urbanitate* (16. 16; *urbane* 17. 5); a unique designation that may also be playing on the name of the adversary. Urbanus was eventually deposed by the north Italian bishops, and is mentioned by Palladius in the *Scholia*, 344ᵛ. 25–6, among the opponents of the pro-Nicenes. See pp. 74–75 above.

[94] *PLS* i. 220–40.

style and tone, commenting on each clause of the creed with a view to refuting heretical opinion on the relation of the Son to the Father. The overwhelming concern of the commentator is the 'perverse doctrines of the Arians', who assert that the Son is 'made' or a 'creature' (based on Proverbs 8: 22), or deny that the Son is in the Father.[95] Upon reading the *Commentarius* one learns almost nothing new about contemporary anti-Arian polemics for the reason that the author does little more than present stock Arian objections to Homoousian theology with conventional refutations. For instance, the Commentator is most adamant that Arians still claim 'there was once when the Son was not', and in response to the anathema at the end of the creed, 'those who say there was a time when he was not', the writer states, 'the Arians usually say these things because they deny he was always the Son'.[96]

The writer similarly employs customary arguments and terminology in defence of each tenet of the creed. The Son, as 'only-begotten' (*unigenitus*) and 'first-begotten' (*primogenitus*), is said to be from the substance of the Father being eternally generated.[97] He is called a *persona secunda*, and, like Zeno, the writer is quick to stress that the Father lost nothing in begetting the Son.[98] As the begotten one, the Son cannot possibily be a product (*opificem*) of the Father, for just as the Father is eternal so the Son is eternal. Regarding the Nicene clause 'begotten not made', the writer employs the standard anti-Arian refutation that a distinction must be made in the scriptural language between those subordinationist descriptions which apply to the Son of man 'in his passions' and those which apply to the Son of God. Thus, the Commentator accuses his opponents of failing to distinguish the nature of the Son of God from 'being made man' by classifying the Son among all created things (*universa*).[99]

Several times the Commentator expresses concern over the subtlety of Arian doctrines in deceiving or deluding the more inexperienced members of the faithful. This is said to be especially problematic when the heretics oppose Homoousian theology by arguing that the co-eternality of the Son and the Father produces two eternal *principia*.[100] It was an argument that was apparently still used against the pro–Nicenes with a modicum of success. But just as troublesome to the writer and of interest to us is the problem that his opponents deny some of the arguments which are commonly attributed to Arians: 'Ashamed to propose such things now it is cunningly asserted that these elude the truth . . . and it is said not that

[95] *Comm.* 7 (*PLS* i. 224).
[96] *Comm.* 15 (*PLS* i. 236).
[97] *Comm.* 2 (*PLS* i. 222).
[98] *Comm.* 8 (*PLS* i. 228).
[99] *Comm.* 7 (*PLS* i. 227).
[100] *Comm.* 1 (*PLS* i. 221–2).

he was made or a creature, or that he once was not, or that he was made out of nothing.'[101] As far as the Commentator is concerned these denials stem not from any genuine differences with previous Arian doctrine, but are concocted by his opponents purely for the purpose of deceiving the unlearned and deluding the faithful. From our perspective, these denials are perhaps the closest point of intersection between the theological realities of the author's day and the Arian 'straw-men' who are demolished with facile interpretations of a creed nearly half a century old. The grounds for the Arian denial that the Son is made *ex nihilo* is explained by their confession, which asserts the Son proceeded from the will of God—yet another means (according to the *Commentarius*) by which the Arians deceive the unsuspecting.[102] Because the Commentator believes that all such redefinition on the part of the Arians is a sham, he makes no serious attempt to counter whatever new formulations he may have read or heard. All of this suggests the possibility that the *Commentarius* was not a polemic but written for fellow catholics who also assume the complete veracity of the Nicene creed. It may be that the document served as a type of catechism for the indoctrination of new believers in a climate which perceived the 'Arriani' as a defeated enemy, but not fully eradicated.

The assumed efficaciousness of the Nicene creed in treating contemporary theological issues is further demonstrated by the author's firm belief that the consubstantiality of the Holy Spirit, whom he calls the 'third person' (ch. 14) is found in the creed. Along with the doctrine of the Son which he has presented above, the belief in the 'third person of the Spirit who is sent from the Father' comprises the 'fides catholica', and whoever does not hold to the confession of the Nicene creed 'is sent into Gehenna to undergo perpetual punishments'.[103]

(d) *The* De trinitate *of Eusebius of Vercelli*

Since the seventeenth century, the work commonly known as the *De trinitate libri XII* had been attributed to either Vigilius of Thapsus[104] or Athanasius of Alexandria, since the latter's name appears as the author in the earliest and majority of manuscripts. Just before the turn of this

---

[101] *Comm.* 16 (*PLS* i. 236).   [102] *Comm.* 17 (*PLS* i. 238).
[103] *Comm.* 19 (*PLS* i. 240).
[104] P. F. Chifflet edited the work as part of the extant writings of the early 5th-century bishop; it was reprinted by Migne, *PL* lxii. 237–334, under the title 'Vigilii Tapsensis De Trinitate libri duodecim, quos edidit sub nomine S. Athanasii, episcopi Alexandrini'.

century, careful manuscript studies by G. Ficker and G. Morin, showed that neither Vigilius nor Athanasius could have been the author, and that the most ancient and numerous manuscripts contain only seven books, not the twelve which Chifflet had compiled.[105] While there does exist a longer recension which includes an eighth book, it is generally agreed that the first seven form a cohesive ensemble attributable to a single author. The latter five books are a comparatively recent agglomeration of treatises, noticeably different from the first seven in style and terminology. This consensus is reflected in the recent critical edition of the *De trinitate* (*CCSL* ix. 3–99), in which V. Bulhart treats books I–VII as a literary whole and prints the first (or shorter) and second recensions in parallel columns. But here the consensus ends. Regarding the questions of authorship and chronology for the *De trinitate*, scholarly opinion has been and continues to be sharply divided. With the publication of the *CCSL* edition (1957), Bulhart revived the view that Eusebius of Vercelli was the author of the first seven books (the first recension).[106] Even more controversial was Bulhart's adoption of Schepens's proposed chronology for the work, which assigned the first recension to AD 345–7 and the second to a date soon after the Sirmium Manifesto of 357.[107] These conclusions have attracted much justifiable criticism by M. Simonetti and A. Dattrino, who have also rejected Eusebian authorship of the *De trinitate*, dating the first recension to the last decade of the fourth century. Nonetheless, their own proposal that the *De trinitate* was the product of a Spanish Luciferian

[105] Ficker, *Studien zu Vigilius von Thapsus* (Leipzig, 1897) and Morin, 'Les Douze Livres sur la Trinité attribués à Vigile de Thapse', *RB* 15 (1898), 1–10. Essentially, Morin's article was an expansion of Ficker's conclusions.

[106] 'Praefatio', p. xxix. This view has been supported by Turner, 'On Eusebius of Vercelli', 126–8; A. E. Burns, 'On Eusebius of Vercelli', *JTS* 1 (1900), 592–9; Schepens, 'L'Ambrosiastre et saint Eusèbe de Verceil', 295–9; V. de Clercq, s.v. 'Eusebius of Vercelli, St.', *New Catholic Encyclopedia*, v. 637. Morin first agreed with Eusebian authorship, 'Les Douze Livres', 5–6, but later retracted his opinion and proposed Gregory of Elvira ('Les Nouveaux "Tractatus Origenis" et l'héritage littéraire de l'évêque espagnol Grégoire d'Illiberis', *Revue d'histoire et de littérature religieuse* (1900), 145–61). Two years later he rejected Gregory as the author and emphasized that the *De trinitate* was of Spanish provenance and perhaps could be identified with a certain Syagrius, who is said (Gennadius, *De viris illus.* 65) to have written 'septem de fide et regulis fidei libros' ('Autour des "Tractatus Origenis" ', *RB* 19 (1902), 225–45).

[107] 'Praefatio', p. vii. Schepens's argument for these dates is derived solely from a passage in the second recension (*De trin.* I. 60) which mentions Ossius (of Cordoba) as the *auctor* of a heretical document written at Sirmium that condemned the Nicene faith; an obvious reference, if not a virtual citation, to the title of the Sirmium 'blasphemia' preserved in Hilary, *De syn.* 11: 'Exemplum Blasphemiae Apud Sirmium per Osium et Potamium conscriptae' (*PL* x. 487). The first recension, Schepens reasons, must therefore have been earlier. For reasons not given, he fixes it to 345–7 ('L'Ambrosiastre et Saint Eusèbe', 299).

is unfounded and can be dismissed, as discussed in Appendix III of this volume. It is much more defensible to locate the *De trinitate* towards the end of Valentinian I's reign, and thereby include it among the anti-Homoian works as characteristic of the pro-Nicene literature of this period. Eusebian authorship is just as likely.[108]

Because of the imposing difficulties with the chronology and authorship of *De trinitate*, the contents of the treatise have been left virtually untreated by modern scholarship. Dattrino's Italian translation offers some introductory notes,[109] but his is the only discussion of the doctrine of the work, apart from other minor patrological notices. This state of affairs has served to handicap our knowledge about Homoian–Nicene tensions before the anti-Arian legislation of the 380s. As we shall see, the *De trinitate* provides one of the most informative glimpses into the evolution of Latin pro-Nicene literature, with the exception of those writings from Hilary and Ambrose.

It would appear that the treatise is not purely a polemical tract against the Arians, since its primary justification is found in setting forth the truth with regard to the relationship that exists within the Trinity. Dattrino has proposed that the underlying motive of the work stems from the fact that its original inspiration was for catechetical purposes. The constant repetition of doctrinal points already established, frequent exhortations, and accumulation of biblical citations which one encounters in the first seven books easily lends itself to this interpretation. There are also passing references to other heretical groups besides the Arians who continue to adhere to a faulty Christology. In traditional fashion, the errors of the Marcionites, Manichees, Photinians, and Jews are upbraided as heretical.[110] Furthermore, the writer makes mention of a little-known group called the Homuncionites, who appear to have taught a Photinian-like Christology by denying the pre-existent sonship of Christ.[111]

At the same time the *De trinitate* reads like a dialogue, originally oral in presentation, directed at refuting the arguments of the 'Arriani'. One finds frequent provocations such as 'tell me, heretic' (III. 78; VI. 11), 'You

---

[108] Eusebian authorship is quite plausible in this time frame. Ancient sources agree that Eusebius died during the joint reigns of Valentinian and Valens (Jerome, *De viris illus.* 96; Prosper, *Chronicon*, 1141 (*MGHAA* ix. 458)). His death, therefore, could have been no later than Nov. 375 (death of Valentinian). The first recension of *De trinitate*, if written by Eusebius, would have been produced after Eusebius returned to north Italy (late 362/early 363) and before his death, perhaps *c.*370/1.

[109] *Pseudo-Atanasio: La Trinità*, Collana di testi patristica 23 (Rome, 1980), 15 ff.

[110] *De trin.* III. 43–8 (*CCSL* ix. 41–3).

[111] III. 47; Filastrius, *De div. haer.* 97; Prudentius, *Apotheosis*, 552–7.

do not understand, Arian' (v. 23), or direct questions such as 'I ask you, respond to me' (v. 34; VI. 1). Yet, as Bulhart has observed, it is a very inconsistent dialogue, since the writer will move without warning out of the dialogical mode in order to offer a lengthy exhortation to evidently friendly readers (III. 22 ff.), or to invoke a prayer to God (VII. 1–2), or, more dramatically towards the end of the treatise, to present a general catalogue of theological blessings and cursings (VI. 5–17) in what seems to be closely emulating the terse form of a creed. The work has obviously undergone some editing. Whatever literary form we decide that the author is using, it is clear that the main object of his attack is the doctrines of the Arians, who are said to confess one God in name (*in titulo*), and by this refer to the person of the Father only, since they disallow the Son and the Holy Spirit to share in the fullness of deity. In sharp distinction, the writer sets forth the teaching of the true faith at the very outset of the treatise (I. 1): 'One God, Father, Son, and Holy Spirit who are an undivided divine unity . . . of a holy, single nature.'

Throughout the *De trinitate*, Arian dogma is arraigned and repudiated in the severest of terms. In chapter 2 the author seems especially concerned with his opponents' use of Trinitarian nomenclature and their argument that a distinction of names implies a distinction of nature. 'You, Arian, ought to distinguish the names of the Persons, but you distinguish natures on account of the names so that you claim the names of the Persons are because of three natures.'[112] To hold three different natures, the author says, inevitably leads to teaching three different and unequal (*dispar*) Gods. This is said despite the denial of the Arians themselves that they construed the Trinity as three separate substances or Gods.[113] Ambrose of Milan makes the same taunt in a context nearly identical to the arguments of the *De trinitate*: 'They who separate the divinity of the Trinity speak of three Gods' (*De fide*, I. 1. 10). Such counter-accusations of polytheism were quite common to the polemical rhetoric on both sides.

Against heretical dogma, the *De trinitate* repeatedly emphasizes that a distinction of names is not grounds for a division of the unity or divine *communia* which the Father, Son, and Holy Spirit share. Indeed, the writer is so intent to stress sufficiently the unity of the Godhead against his opponents that he typically has little to say about the interrelated distinctiveness of its members. He does describe the Trinity as containing three separate persons (II. 3) who have designated roles, 'Genitor', 'natus',

---

[112] II. 9 (*CCSL* ix. 22).

[113] Cf. I. 62 (*CCSL* ix. 17); in the Sirmium Manifesto of 357 a plurality of gods is strictly ruled out: 'duos autem deos nec posse nec debere praedicari' (*PL* x. 487–8).

and 'Spirit' (VI. 2). Yet, as we saw in the homilies of Zeno, the *De trinitate* makes such distinctions more for the purpose of avoiding the error of confusing the divine persons,[114] and has almost nothing to say about their respective roles in relation to each other. At one point in the discussion about the indivisibility of the Godhead, the writer declares that it can allow no number nor any differences at all;[115] a rather extreme if not confusing statement which served to confirm the worst fears of the Homoians.

With regard to the generation of the Son, the *De trinitate* freely admits that such an effluence of the divine substance is indescribable, quoting Isaiah 53: 8 ('Who shall declare his generation?'); a passage often associated with the credal language of Homoian theology as found in the formulas of Sirmium (357), the Dated Creed (359), and Constantinople (360). Contrary to the Homoians' apophatic use of this passage, which introduces a desired ambiguity into the question of the nature of the Son, this pro-Nicene writer is quick to argue that the indescribability of the Son's nativity is the result of a wholly divine act which is reason enough for the human mind to be incapable of grasping the matter. One must be careful to distinguish the nativity of the incarnate Son from the nature of the Son, who, being begotten of the Father, has eternally shared the same nature with the Father. And the writer is fully aware how his opponents use the Isaiah passage to divide the nature of the Son from the Father by introducing the factor of time into the Son's pre-incarnate existence. 'You do not understand Arian . . . because you speak of a Father who had not yet generated and descriptions (*nomines*) of the Son who had not yet been born' (V. 23). Since the Son was always in the Father (*in utero*), never was the Father without the Son or vice versa (V. 26). Accordingly the writer is very critical of the Homoian view that the Son of God was born from the will of God (IV. 15), or that the unity between the Father and Son exists purely in a unity of will or *concordia*, and not in a *communis naturae* (I. 19).

Throughout the *De trinitate* the Holy Spirit is rigorously and repeatedly defended as partaking in the fullness of deity.[116] This emphasis on the role of the Holy Spirit in a relation of absolute equality with the other two divine persons represents a marked difference from most other Latin Trinitarians of the Neo-Nicene period. For in the work of Hilary of

---

[114] See IV. 25 (*CCSL* ix. 62–3).

[115] 'nullus nec numerus, sed nec aliqua differentia in unita deitate patris et fili et spiritus sancti invenitur' II. 40 (*CCSL* ix. 30).

[116] I. 14. 63; II. 11. 30; IV. 11–12; V. 31; VII. 11–13.

Poitiers, as in that of Phoebadius of Agen, Gregory of Elvira, and the *Commentarius in symbolum Nicaeanum*, the doctrine of the Holy Spirit receives only marginal attention. Simonetti has argued therefore that this treatment of the Holy Spirit in *De trinitate* demands a date after 380 since in the west 'only the *De Spiritu Sancto* of Ambrose, which is from 381, shows interest in this aspect of Trinitarian polemic'.[117] Such issues of the relation of the Holy Spirit to the Father and Son were articulated in the east much earlier, as Simonetti observes in Athanasius' letter to Serapion (dated *c*.370). Surely this letter is symptomatic of an interest already current though not articulated with the precision of later years. One can venture back almost a decade to the 'Epistola Catholica' and the *Tomus* of Alexandria (362) and find the early stages of an intentional language which was used apologetically to substantiate the equality of the Spirit with the Father and Son. In chapter 5 of the *Tomus*, the readers are asked to acknowledge that the Holy Spirit subsists along with the Father and the Son, making a 'Holy Trinity, one Godhead, and one beginning, and that the Son is co-essential with the Father, as the fathers said; while the Holy Spirit is not a creature, nor external, but proper to and inseparable from the essence of the Father and the Son'.[118] If the writer of the *De trinitate* had had previous exposure to eastern Trinitarian theology of this type, which is certain in the case of Eusebius of Vercelli, there are equally good grounds for believing that *De trinitate* was written not as late as Simonetti claims, but perhaps shared the responsibility for introducing the terminology of a full Trinitarianism to the west.

Even if we were to draw such hard and fast lines between the exchange of eastern and western theologies, we must amend Simonetti's assessment about the presence of a burgeoning doctrine of the Holy Spirit in the west. Already by 366, fierce debate had begun in the Illyrian provinces over the relation of the Holy Spirit to the Father and Son. This is seen in the minutes of the *Altercatio* between Germinius and Heraclianus, during which the first third of the dialogue concerns the full divinity of the Holy Spirit. Against Germinius' insistence that the Spirit is created, the Nicene layman Heraclianus argues that the Scriptures teach a divine Trinity.[119] From this passage it does not naturally follow that the debates over the consubstantiality of the Holy Spirit were already in full swing by 366. It does sufficiently demonstrate, along with the documents of 362, that the pro-Nicenes were being compelled to articulate a doctrine of the

---

[117] 'Qualche osservazione sul *De trinitate* attribuito a Eusebio di Vercelli', *Rivista di cultura classica e medioevale*, 5 (1963), 389.

[118] *Tomus*, 5 (*PG* xxvi. 801B) (trans. from *NPNF* iv. 484).   [119] Caspari, 135.

Spirit by the later 360s that answered their opponents' hierarchical form of Trinitarianism and which was consistent with their own arguments for the nature of the Father and Son. The *De trinitate* does not offer theologically sophisticated arguments for the consubstantiality of the Spirit with the Father and Son. Indeed, the treatise assumes the full divinity of the Holy Spirit in the course of its argumentation just like the writer of the *Commentarius*. But here the writer is acutely aware that the doctrine continues to have its detractors and must be affirmed if one intends to be faithful to the full teaching of Nicaea.

In the preceding two chapters we have examined the evidence for the religious and political state of tensions which existed in the west between the Homoians and the Neo-Nicenes largely during the *imperium* of Valentinian I. The many gaps in the extant literature make any reconstruction especially difficult and require that we draw our conclusions with caution. Perhaps one of the most remarkable phenomena of the 360s is the degree and speed with which the Nicene creed became the accepted standard of orthodoxy for the majority of western bishops and churches. As we suggested in the previous chapter, the provocations of the councils of Ariminum and Constantinople had a galvanizing effect on the west theologically, producing convictions which were anti-Constantinian, and more directly anti-Arian. At the same time we cannot accept the one-sided and facile interpretation which depicts the Nicene 'triumph' as an undeviating and inexorable movement that vanquished Arianism following the death of Constantius II. To take seriously the political realities and ecclesiastical complexities of the time demands that we also evaluate the way in which imperial policies effectively stultified religious zeal on all sides. Even if the momentum of the post-Ariminum rehabilitation in the west for the Nicene faith placed supporters of Homoianism in the minority, Neo-Nicenes were never successful in replacing bishops in churches where strong devotion to the Ariminum creed persisted. Indeed, the strongest centres of such devotion, Illyricum and north Italy, continued the propagation of anti-Nicene opinions in the west. Homoianism may have become increasingly isolated, but it was not dying, as modern histories are wont to assert. Gibbon's influential and misguided verdict that Arianism died quickly in the west as Christians 'happily relapsed into the slumber of orthodoxy'[120] has nothing to recommend it.

---

[120] *Decline and Fall of the Roman Empire*, vol. ii (London, 1781), 505–6. Cf. J. G. Davies, *The Early Church* (New York, 1965), 179–82, who incorporates this kind of perspective.

The theological works which we examined in the last part of this chapter are quite diverse: a catalogue of heresies, a scattered collection of homilies, a commentary on the Nicene creed, and a doctrinal/catechetical treatise which is concerned to offer sound Trinitarian teaching in light of competing theologies. These precious remnants of Latin literature, all sharing anti-Arian motives to one degree or another, demonstrate the scope and depth to which the conflict had permeated ecclesiastical life. As was mentioned earlier, any interpretation of the Arian controversy in the late fourth century which relegates the Nicene–Homoian conflict to a kind of academic exchange between intellectuals, such as Marius Victorinus' dialogues against his literary foil Candidus, risks overlooking less dramatic but no less important evidence that bears witness to the multiple levels of participation and intensity at which the conflict was experienced.

There is a remaining reservoir of pro-Nicene writings which we have yet to tap. With the election of Aurelius Ambrosius to the see of Milan, we are introduced to a multitude of documents pertaining to the Nicene–Homoian controversy. In this 'last battle' for the Homoian stronghold of Milan, these writings throw new and important light on the relative strengths and weaknesses of both sides of the debate, and so reveal that the line of Nicene ascendancy over its opponents was anything but smooth.

4

Ambrose's Election and Early Years in Milan

IN the autumn of 374, the *doyen* of western Homoianism, Auxentius of Milan, died. It was a portentous event for the fortunes of both Homoians and pro-Nicenes throughout northern Italy. Now the critical choice had to be made of a successor on whose shoulders would fall the responsibility of continuing or stemming the present hegemony of anti-Nicenism. Through the lens of historical hindsight we know that the election of Ambrose led to the eventual eclipse of Arianism in Italy, although the link between these two events became greatly amplified in the years subsequent to Ambrose's bishopric, producing an almost heroic figure, whose career uniformly manifested an unwavering attitude of opposition toward the Arians.

According to one modern historian, when 'that foxy old Arian, Auxentius, died at Milan, the ultimate triumph of orthodoxy in this region was assured'.[1] This assessment is little more than a paraphrase of Jerome's oft-cited observation in his *Chronicle*: 'After the long-awaited death of Auxentius of Milan, Ambrose was made bishop and he converted all of Italy to a sound faith.'[2] Little confidence, however, should be placed in Jerome's opinion about the state of affairs in Italy at this moment. Not only did he compose the *Chronicle* in Constantinople (*c.*381), not having been to the west since 372/3, but his historical judgement about individuals and movements in the document is 'entirely uncritical, being coloured by violent prejudices'.[3] Accordingly, the above observation in the *Chronicle* was grounded more on Jerome's intense hatred for the Arian heresy than on the weight of historical evidence. But the modern concept of an irresistible link between Ambrose and the 'triumph of orthodoxy' is fuelled from other sources that extend beyond Jerome. The most common perceptions reflect the post-mortem *testimonia* which have served to influence

---

[1] F. Homes Dudden, *The Life and Times of Saint Ambrose* (Oxford, 1935), i. 187.

[2] *Chronicon*, AD 374 (*GCS* xxiv. 247. 16–18). Homes Dudden, *Life and Times*, i. 187 n. 4, also follows the inaccurate dating of the *Chronicle* in *PL* xxvii. 697–8 and places this citation under AD 378.

[3] Kelly, *Jerome*, 75.

subsequent perceptions of Ambrose. After the bishop's death in 397, we begin to encounter a steady stream of honorific *memoriae* and traditions which accumulated during the fifth century.[4] Among these, Paulinus of Nola, in *Carmen* XIX, enlists Ambrose among the ranks of the west's most prestigious martyrs.

> Carthage waxes strong through the martyr Cyprian . . .
> From that time onward Africa has long been a fertile ground
> for God in Chirst.
> From this seed it multiplies its abundant harvest
> and brings forth teachers outstanding in word and faith.
> No less has grace shone on the lands of the west.
> Ambrose is pre-eminent in Italy, Vincent in Spain,
> Gaul has adopted Martin, Aquitania Delphinus.[5]

Ambrose was a vehicle, *inter alia*, by which divine beneficence was bestowed upon the west. Far beyond the walls of Milan the salutary effects of his presence are said to have extended. Barely five years after Ambrose's death, the Latin church historian Rufinus was able to write in Aquileia of the bishop as 'a man worthy of all admiration, who was like a column or impregnable fortress, not only of the church of Milan but even of all churches'.[6]

Without doubt the most influential witness for subsequent historical opinion has been a 'Life of Ambrose' composed probably in 422 by Ambrose's *notarius* Paulinus.[7] Writing at the personal request of Augustine, Paulinus presents us with a figure whose divinely endowed *virtutes*

---

[4] For a comprehensive listing of ancient *testimonia*, see *PL* xiv. 121 ff.

[5] *Carmen* XIX. 141; 149–54 (*CSEL* xxx. 123).

[6] *Apologia contra Hieronymum* II. 26 (*CCSL* xx. 102. 18–21).

[7] There are few chronological hints in the *Vita Ambrosii* (hereafter *VA*) which makes its dating problematic. *VA* 31 speaks of 'Iohannes tunc tribunus et notarius, qui nunc praefectus est', but the 'Iohannes' mentioned here was praetorian prefect of Italy on two occasions, in 412–13 and 422 (*PLRE* i. 459, 'Iohannes 2'). Because there are problems in dating the statutes directed to John during his second prefecture, E. Lamirande has argued that the earlier date should be preferred (*Paulin de Milan et la 'Vita Ambrosii': aspects de la religion sous le Bas-Empire* (Montreal, 1982), 21–2). There are, however, other arguments which favour a later date for the *Vita Ambrosii*. M. Pellegrino (*Vita di S. Ambrogio: introduzione, testo critico e note* (Rome, 1961), 6) has observed that Paulinus refers to Jerome as 'beatus' in *VA* 1, which would seem to place the *Vita* after Jerome's death (419/20). The fact that Jerome is called 'beatus' is not in itself decisive, since *beatus* or *beatissimus* can be used of the living (C. H. Turner, 'II. Makarios as a Technical Term', *JTS* 23 (1921–2), 31–5). For this reason, Pellegrino notes that it is the link between Jerome and Athanasius, 'beati viri', which clinches the argument. For further evidence in favour of the later date see A. Paredi, 'Paulinus of Milan', *Sacris erudiri*, 14 (1963), 213.

established his authority over heretics, demons, disease, and even recalcitrant emperors. In effect, Ambrose is depicted as nothing less than a 'holy man',[8] the *Vita* being intentionally patterned after the literary styles of previous 'Lives' of the *viri sancti*: Paul, Anthony, and Martin. Paulinus makes this clear in the introduction:

You have urged, venerable father Augustine, that just as those blessed men, Bishop Athanasius and the Presbyter Jerome, have described with their pens the lives of the holy Paul and Anthony in their desert retreats, and also as Severus, a servant of God, has composed with refined language the life of Martin, Bishop of the church of Tours, so I also should describe with my pen the life of the blessed Ambrose, Bishop of the church of Milan.[9]

Paulinus never tells us why Augustine commissioned him to write a *vita* of the highly esteemed bishop, although Pellegrino is undoubtedly correct in observing that 'Augustine had wanted to learn more and become better acquainted with that man whose indelible memory he carried in his heart, by whose example he loved to be inspired.'[10] This does not explain, however, why the *Vita Ambrosii* was written at the height of the Pelagian controversy and what connection may have existed between the two. We know that Paulinus had come to Carthage after Ambrose's death as overseer of the commercial interests of the Milanese church,[11] and had become deeply embroiled in the struggle against Coelestius and Pelagius. Following the council of Carthage (411), Augustine entered the fray but was soon attacked by supporters of Pelagius who declared that he alone was the inventor of his view of original sin. Augustine was compelled to find support for his position from the authoritative writings of the 'venerable doctors of the catholic church'. In 412 he would quote a few lines from Cyprian and Jerome in the third book of *De peccatorum meritis*, but three years later, in *De natura et gratia*, Augustine is forced to respond to Pelagius' use of several passages from Ambrose in order to prove that

---

[8] This is especially evident in ch. 49, when Ambrose appeared, after his physical death, to 'certain holy men' in the east, praying with them and placing his hands on them (Pellegrino, *Vita*, 122). It is a scene of certification: Ambrose is identified now as one of them. In chs. 53 and 54 Ambrose is actually referred to as a *vir sanctus* against his detractors (Pellegrino, *Vita*, 126).

[9] *VA* 1. 1–5 (Pellegrino, *Vita*, 50).   [10] *Vita*, 5.

[11] The unknown author of the *Praedestinatus* (*c*.440), when recounting the anti-Pelagian activities of 411 in Africa (ch. 88), describes Paulinus as *diaconus* and 'defensor et procurator ecclesia Mediolanensis' (*PL* liii. 617D). G. Bonner errs in saying Paulinus was visiting Africa in order to collect material for his biography of Ambrose, *St Augustine of Hippo: Life and Controversies* (1963; Norwich, 1986), 320–1.

man cannot live without sin in this life and that the human will is severely limited in its capacity to choose the good apart from divine grace.[12] By the time Augustine writes in reply to his severest critic, Julian of Eclanum, references from Ambrosian treatises are used unsparingly.[13] It is most likely therefore that the impetus for Augustine's request to Paulinus was derived from a need for identification with and doctrinal sanction from an authoritative figure of the Church. Through Paulinus' pen, Ambrose became the sole 'property' of the catholics (i.e., Augustine and his friends), as against reputed schismatics, such as Pelagius, who were also claiming his authority.

Yet another reason for Paulinus' composition may be found in chapter 54 of the *Vita*. There were those who openly criticized Ambrose and 'dared to detract from the holy man', although we are never told the content of these criticisms. A certain Milanese presbyter named Donatus and, in the city of Carthage, the visiting Bishop Muranus from the town of Bol (or Vol)[14] expressed unfavourable opinions about Ambrose and so provoked Paulinus to alarm, since it 'detracted from the memory of the bishop'. For their improprieties we are told that both men were visited by an early death. Nevertheless their poisonous attitudes were shared by others, which is undoubtedly the writer's major cause for concern. Thus Paulinus concludes the *Vita* by exhorting his readers to imitate the life of Ambrose and avoid the 'tongues of detractors', unless they wish to undergo, along with the critics, the punishment of eternal damnation.[15] There are several possible reasons then for the publication of the *Vita Ambrosii*, none of which has to do with the Nicene–Homoian struggles of the 370s and 380s, but which do partially explain Paulinus' motive in composing a blatantly propagandizing work.

A large part of the difficulty in accurately determining the state of relations which existed between Nicene and Homoian parties after Auxentius' death is the larger-than-life role which the figure of Ambrose has played in most historical evaluations of the period. The fact that the *Vita Ambrosii* has continued to exercise influence on modern critical opinion has much to do with this problem. Earlier in this century Delehaye warned against placing excessive confidence in hagiographic literature

---

[12] *De natura et gratia*, LXIII. 74–5 (*CSEL* lx. 289–91). Cf. *De gratia Christi et de peccato originali* I. xxxxiii. 47 (*CSEL* xlii. 159–60), where Augustine preserves a quotation from Pelagius using Ambrose to show that man is able to live without sin.
[13] *Contra Iulianum*, I. 3. 10 (*PL* xliv. 645); I. 10. 35–7.
[14] *DHGE* ix. 614.   [15] *VA* 55. 4–5 (Pellegrino, *Vita*, 128).

since the history of a saint is too often obscured by the legends which have grown up around it.[16] Despite this general recognition Paulinus' *Vita* has been utilized, often uncritically, as a biographical source for the reconstruction of the historical Ambrose. This is not to say that the *Vita* is devoid of any material that is historically trustworthy. Paulinus relied on some sources which were concerned to provide an accurate accounting of events pertaining to the fortunes of the Church. Of course such sources were themselves ordered according to a triumphalist view of the Church in history and to how the power of God had vindicated the Church by overwhelming her enemies. For example, Paulinus is dependent on the additional two books which Rufinus wrote in continuation of Eusebius' *Historia ecclesiastica*.[17] The *Vita* also gives evidence of being acquainted with book 5 of Augustine's *De civitate dei*,[18] with the *Historiarum adversum paganos* of Orosius, and with a great number of Ambrose's letters and treatises. To this must be added Paulinus' promise to the reader that he did not knowingly include any false information, despite his 'loving devotion' for the great bishop.[19]

Notwithstanding, we must not overlook the crucial fact that Paulinus was not intending to write narrative history, as Gryson once observed: 'il ajoute de nombreux détails, qu'il a puisés vraisemblablement dans la tradition milanaise, et dont beaucoup ont déjà une saveur nettement légendaire.'[20] We have not understood the *Vita Ambrosii* if we do not come to grips with the literary nature of *vitae*; that is, literature whose internal agenda is to reveal divine manifestations in a chosen human being, whether for purposes of edification or apology. The selection of material in the Ambrosian *Vita* does not conform to historical or biographical accuracy, at least in the modern sense of the words, but rather contains those things which serve further to demonstrate its literary goals.

Closely following the precedent established in previous 'Lives', the subject of Paulinus' *Vita* is a chosen vessel whose ordination is announced by various signs. The episode of the bees flying in and out of the mouth of Ambrose when he was a baby is said to be an indication of the 'heavenly gift' already bestowed upon him.[21] As a boy Ambrose once told his older sister that someday she would kiss his hand as bishop. Scolded for

---

[16] *Les Légendes hagiographiques* (3rd edn. Brussels, 1927), 202 ff.

[17] Pellegrino, *Vita*, 16–18; Y.-M. Duval, 'Ambroise, de son élection à sa consécration', in G. Lazzati (ed.), *Ambrosius episcopus: Atti del congresso internazionale di studi ambrosiana nel XVI centenario della elevazione di sant'Ambrogio alla cattedra episcopale*, vol. ii (Milan, 1976), 243.

[18] A. Paredi, 'Paulinus of Milan', 216.   [19] *VA* 2. 1–3 (Pellegrino, *Vita*, 52).

[20] Gryson, *Le Prêtre*, 221.   [21] *VA* 3. 12–14 (Pellegrino, *Vita*, 54).

impudence, his words were nevertheless prophetic because 'it was the Holy Spirit who spoke to him'.[22] The primary goal for these and other *signa* was the fact that God had raised up Ambrose in order to preserve his Church from heresy. This plan of Deity, as Paulinus unveils, was also the reason behind the unusual circumstances of Ambrose's election.

The above observations about the literary genre and historical context of the *Vita Ambrosii* assume particular importance when we recognize that few other sources are available for the reconstruction of Ambrose's early career: Rufinus offers only a chequered account of the bishop's experiences at Milan,[23] and Ambrose himself says relatively little about his early years in the episcopate; the bulk of his surviving works are dated after 378.[24] Those treatises which were written prior to 378 are mainly exegetical in character and throw little light on the larger issues with which Ambrose struggled during this time. One is left with the sole testimony of Paulinus' *Vita* at several critical junctures in Ambrose's career. In such cases careful judgement must be exercised as to how much weight should be placed on these supports in our interpretation even if this threatens to introduce more lacunae into our knowledge of the bishop's activities.

Without pretending to offer an exhaustive survey on previously published biographies of Ambrose, it can be shown with sufficient force how the hagiographic traditions and perspectives cited above are discernible in the more major treatments of Ambrose. Homes Dudden's two-volume work *The Life and Times of Saint Ambrose* (1935), still the most widely consulted biography on Ambrose in English, recounts Ambrose's strange

---

[22] *VA* 4. 6–8 (Pellegrino, *Vita*, 56).

[23] Rufinus discusses events pertaining to Ambrose in two sections. Book II. 11 renders valuable details about his election (*PL* xxi. 521B–522A), then the narrative jumps over a decade to the events of AD 386 concerning the dispute over the use of a basilica between the bishop and the civil authorities. (II. 15–16 (*PL* xxi. 523B–525A)). The accounts in Socrates, *HE* IV. 30 (*PG* lxvii. 544A–C), and Sozomen, *HE* VI. 24. 2–5 (*GCS* 1. 268–9), which are concerned with Ambrose's election only, are closely modelled on Rufinus' *HE* II. 11. Theodoret's treatment of the sequence of events which followed Auxentius' death (IV. 7. 1– 6 (*GCS* xliv. 218–19)) contains documents of dubious historical value and will be treated in a separate discussion below.

[24] Autumn of 378 marks the publication of *De fide*, I–II which is Ambrose's first attack on Arianism. Chronologies of Ambrose's treatises and letters can be found in Gryson, *Le Prêtre*, 35–42 (cf. Homes Dudden, *Life and Times*, ii. 678–709, and J.-R. Palanque, *Saint Ambroise et l'Empire Romain: contribution à l'histoire des rapports de l'Église et de l'État à la fin du quatrième siècle* (Paris, 1933), 578–81). See the *caveat* by H. Savon, 'Aussi ne doit-on s'étonner ni des nombreuses tentatives qui ont été faites pour résoudre ce problème, ni des obscurités et des incertitudes qui subsistent malgré tant d'efforts' ('Quelques remarques sur la chronologie des œuvres de saint Ambroise', *Studia Patristica*, 10 (1970) (= Text und Untersuchungen 107), 156).

election to the bishopric and ensuing opposition to the Arians in almost
perfect accord with Paulinus' caricature of these events.[25] Ambrose is
presented by Homes Dudden as a staunch anti-Arian from the very
beginning of his episcopate, and, well before the publication of his *De
fide*, the bishop is said to have 'acquired a reputation as a defender and
restorer of orthodoxy' (i. 119). Western Arianism, on the other hand, was
little more than a religious 'shell' which 'still clung desperately to a creed
which all sensible people recognized to be effete and lifeless' (i. 222). By
the year 381 Ambrose is said to have achieved 'isolated victories over
the Arians', but the time had now come 'to strike a blow which would
effectively crush the lingering remnants of the heresy in North Italy and
Illyricum' (i. 199). This last reference pertains to the council of Aquileia,
which met in the late summer of that year. Ambrose's obvious manipulation
of Gratian's favouritism toward the Nicene faith in order to assure the
condemnation and deposition of the Homoian bishops Palladius and
Secundianus[26] is described by Homes Dudden in the most benevolent of
terms. The results achieved by the council marked a signal victory and
sounded the demise of Arianism in the west. After the council, '[o]nly
Justina, with her supple courtiers and barbarian mercenaries', continued
to patronize a religion which had almost totally fallen under the triumphant feet of the Neo-Nicenes.[27] One can find instances in *The Life and
Times of Saint Ambrose* where the author checks his own biases, but it
does little to modify the overall impression of the book.

The other standard work on Ambrose's life and literature, *Saint Ambrose
et l'Empire Romain* by Jean-Remy Palanque, was published two years
before Homes Dudden. Palanque gives evidence of being more cautious
than his English counterpart in the degree to which he incorporates
Paulinus' account prima facie into his own.[28] Noticeably absent in Palanque
is the tendency to glorify his main subject that is so obvious in Homes
Dudden. At the same time, however, Palanque has portrayed Paulinus as
a critical historian in an earlier study on the *Vita Ambrosii*,[29] which later

[25] i. 66 ff. for his election (*VA* 6–9); i. 195 ff. for the Arian opposition which Ambrose
encountered at Sirmium and the sudden death of the Arian virgin who threatened him (*VA*
11); 198 ff. for the story of the challenge by the two Arian chamberlains and how they were
accidently killed the following day (*VA* 18).
[26] Treated in Ch. 6 below.   [27] *Life and Times*, i. 206.
[28] Palanque speaks more of the 'traditions' which Paulinus was drawing upon when he
describes Ambrose's election (p. 3) or Ambrose's attempts to evade his nomination to the
episcopate (p. 28).
[29] 'La *Vita Ambrosii* de Paulin de Milan: étude critique', *Revue des sciences religieuses*, 4
(1924), 26–42; 401–20.

incurred justified criticism by Lamirande, who thought Palanque 'too indulgent' when it came to his use of the ancient biography.[30] Palanque does rely heavily on these 'traditions' as historical evidence even if he, like de Labriolle before him, is aware that Paulinus' main motive in composing his work was to edify the reader before all else.

Turning to the most recent major biographical study by A. Paredi,[31] we find that virtually all the historical assumptions held in the 1930s are intact. In an unabashedly confessional treatment of Ambrose, Paredi explains in the preface that the purpose of his book is to 'spread the fame of one who strove strenuously for the good'.[32] It is hardly surprising therefore that his caricature of the early Ambrose could result in nothing less than a committed catholic. Regarding the *Vita Ambrosii*, we receive no discussion about how this source ought to be handled, and, with one exception, Paulinus' accounts are integrated wholesale into Paredi's historical biography.[33] The Neo-Nicenes are those who hold to the 'true faith' and 'orthodoxy', whereas the 'Arians' (no other term is ever used) are heretical, troublemakers, and promote scandal by incessantly looking to assume wealthier sees. Strikingly similar to the scenario provided by Homes Dudden, Paredi attributes to the Milanese Homoians in the late 370s and 380s only a superficial existence, radically dependent on 'Justina and her children and retinue' for their continued viability.[34]

Beyond the biographical treatments discussed above, surprisingly few inquiries have been made into Ambrose's conflict with the Homoians in Milan. Duval does not exaggerate when he states, 'It is Ambrose himself . . . to whom historians have not paid sufficient attention.'[35] The reason for this neglect is hard to understand since these difficulties absorbed so much of Ambrose's early career, though one can discern some relation

---

[30] *Paulin de Milan et la 'Vita Ambrosii'*, 9.

[31] *Saint Ambrose: His Life and Times*, trans. M. J. Costelloe (Notre Dame, Ind., 1964). Trans. from *S. Ambrogio, e la sua età* (Milan, 1960). The English edition can be considered a second edition, since certain revisions and clarifications have been added to the body of the text (see p. vii).

[32] Ibid., p. vi.

[33] See pp. 122, 177, and 197. In a separate study of Paulinus, in the form of a review of M. Pellegrino's edition of the *Vita*, Paredi wholly endorses Palanque's conclusions in 'La *Vita Ambrosii* de Paulin' (n. 22), stating that 'Paulinus possessed a real critical mind' even if he is often too credulous and relates too many miracles ('Paulinus of Milan', 213).

[34] *Saint Ambrose*, 183 ff.

[35] *Latomus* 28. 2 (1969), 239. Studies devoted to *De fide* or Ambrose's early career are also very scarce, the foremost of these being P. Nautin, 'Les Premières relations d' Ambroise avec l'Empereur Gratien: le *De fide* (livres I et II)', in Y.-M. Duval (ed.), *Ambroise de Milan* (Paris, 1974), 229–44, and G. Gottlieb, *Ambrosius von Mailand und Kaiser Gratian* (Göttingen, 1973).

to the perceived uniformity which has traditionally typified Ambrose's position with regards to the Homoians.

Suffice to say that there exists a tremendous need to rediscover the 'historical Ambrose', in order to gain a more accurate picture of Ambrose's relations with Homoians at Milan and of when his conflict with them began. We must appreciate the fact that 'orthodoxy' in Milan was defined by the Ariminum creed when Ambrose received the episcopate. And although we must avoid violating the literary function of Paulinus' account with a crude demythologization, it is at least desirable to re-examine its value for biographical reconstruction and question the level of scholarly dependency on what is manifestly a hagiographical work. In so doing, we are able to make a first step at clearing away some of the mystique which has surrounded the bishop of Milan.[36]

I. AMBROSE S ELECTION TO THE EPISCOPATE

The failure of Hilary, Filastrius, and at least two Roman synods to dislodge Auxentius from the bishopric at Milan provides us with strong testimony about the tight embrace which Homoianism had on that city. Auxentius had remained in continuous possession of that see for nineteen years until his death in 374.[37] Considering the unabated commitment of Auxentius to the Ariminum creed and the zeal with which he worked for its diffusion, we should expect that most of the Milanese clergy were Homoian, or at least did not openly oppose it. Whether the same may be said for a majority of the population is more difficult to determine. In *La religione a Milano nell'età di sant'Ambrogio*, E. Cattaneo has argued that, at the time of Dionysius' exile and Auxentius' installation as bishop in 355, the greater part of the Milanese Christians were 'catholic', by which he means pro-Nicene.[38] Even if this is the case, Cattaneo fails to recognize any distinction between popular devotion to an anti-Arian bishop (Dionysius) and devotion to that bishop's theological platform. We have no concrete means of gauging the reception of Auxentius' episcopate on the Milanese Christians except by implication. Surely there existed in

---

[36] For initial work in this direction, Gryson, *Le Prêtre*, 164 ff.; id., *Scolies*, 105 ff.; Simonetti, *La crisi ariana*, 436 ff.

[37] O. Faller, 'La data della consacrazione vescovile di Sant'Ambrogio', in A. Faccioli (ed.), *Ambrosiana: scritti di storia archeologia ed arte* (Milan, 1942), 93–110. Only Palanque (*Saint Ambroise*, 484–5) has contested the date, placing it (and Ambrose's election) a year earlier.

[38] *La religione a Milano nell'età di Sant'Ambrogio* (Milan, 1974), 34–5.

Milan a sizeable enough anti-Arian faction composed of followers loyal to the memory of Dionysius to cause the 'severe dissension and dangerous upheaval' which was racking the city over the choosing of a successor.[39] Cattaneo's claim that 'the population had remained catholic and certainly rejoiced at the proper end of Auxentius' is too inflated.

As tensions continued to climb with no apparent resolution, the praetorian prefect had no desire to see a repeat of the bloody conflict which had broken out in Rome eight years earlier over a contested episcopal election.[40] Ambrose, a protégé of the prefect Probus and serving at that time as the administrative governor of the province Aemilia-Liguria, was sent to quell the disturbances. His success in doing so ironically resulted in his election to the bishopric.

Ambrose at that time possessed the consular authority (*fasces gerebat*) of this province. Upon seeing the calamity threatening the city in that place and under his jurisdiction, he hurried immediately into the church to quell the disruptions among the people. And while he pleaded with the many gathered there for peace and calmness according to the law and public decorum, there arose suddenly among the warring factions of people themselves a single shout and cry, 'Ambrose for bishop . . .'[41]

We do not know who first had the idea of proposing Ambrose as the solution by nominating him bishop. Rufinus and Paulinus are somewhat confused and too simplified hagiographically to be taken literally. Both accounts stress the immediate and sudden unanimity which grippped the divided populace when Ambrose was put forth for the office. Dramatically heightened, Paulinus slightly differs from Rufinus in that the voice of a child ('vox fertur infantis in populo sonuisse') crying 'Ambrosius episcopus' marks the moment when the factions of 'Arians' and 'Catholics' were united.[42] Paulinus seems to be utilizing here what had become by his time a known literary device symbolizing the expressed will of divinity. Augustine's conversion to Christianity, for example, was punctuated by the hearing of a child's voice which he interpreted 'to be none other than

---

[39] Rufinus, *HE* II. 11 (*PL* xxi. 521B).

[40] Between Damasus and Ursinus. The memory of this conflict and its continued reverberations would have been only too fresh in Petronius Probus' mind; he entered the prefecture of Illyricum, Italy, and Africa in 368 (*PLRE* i. 736–40).

[41] Rufinus, *HE* II. 11 (*PL* xxi. 521C).

[42] *VA* 6. 5–10 (Pellegrino, *Vita*, 58). Several leading manuscripts omit 1. 6–7: 'Ad cuius vocis sonum totius populi ora conversa sunt Ambrosium episcopum.' For emendations to Pellegrino's text, see R. M. McClure, 'Studies in the Text of the *Vita Ambrosii* of Paulinus of Milan' (Ph.D. dissertation, University of California, 1971).

a command from God'.[43] In the case of Martin's election to the episcopate of Tours, as described in Sulpicius' influential *Vita Martini* (IX), there was great division among the congregation. During the tumultuous proceedings, the appointed lector had been prevented from arriving, so a bystander, laying hold of the Psalter, read the first verse which came to him: 'out of the mouths of infants and nursing babes you have perfected praise by means of your enemies so that you might destroy the enemy and the avenger' (Psalm 8: 3). Thus, out of a child's mouth a certain bishop opposing Martin's election (whose name happened to be 'Avenger') was indicted and the people, now completely unified and in harmony, elected Martin.[44] In Paulinus' description of the election of Ambrose, Psalm 8: 3 is invoked again, but this time the actual *vox infantis* is heard!

Since Ambrose makes several allusions in later works to his election, we are given some means for the verification of our sources. Twice reference is made to the fact that he was hurried from the 'judgement seat and insignia of office' to enter into the priesthood. Mention is made also that he had not been 'brought up in the bosom of the church, nor trained from childhood', and that he had devoted himself to the vanities of the world.[45] We can understand these to mean simply that Ambrose, on the eve of his election, was not yet baptized and was pursuing a secular career. Like his older brother Satyrus, he had delayed baptism and remained a catechumen,[46] a state which was not at all uncommon among Christian nobility.[47]

Ambrose divulges further personal information in his lengthy letter to the church at Vercelli (*c*.396), claiming that, when he was nominated for bishop, he resisted the idea until compelled, and, once compelled, he attempted to stave off his actual consecration by appealing to a well-known *praescriptio* which forbade the ordination of novices.[48] While

---

[43] A fact about Augustine which Paulinus probably knew. *Confessions*, VIII. 12. 29 (*CSEL* xxxiii. 1. 194).

[44] *Vita Mart.* IX. 4–7 (*CSEL* i. 119).

[45] Respectively, *De officiis ministrorum*, I. 1. 4 (*PL* xvi. 27C); *De paenitentia*, II. 8. 72 (*CSEL* lxxiii. 192–3); *De paenitentia*, II. 8. 73 (*CSEL* lxxiii. 193. 57–60).

[46] *De excessu fratris*, I. 43 (*CSEL* lxxiii. 232–3).

[47] P. Brown, *The Body and Society: Men, Women and Sexual Renunciation in Early Christianity* (New York, 1988), 342.

[48] *Ep.* 14. 65 (*CSEL* lxxxii. 3. 269). The *praescriptio* could be an allusion to the second canon of Nicaea which forbade the elevation to presbyter or episcopus of one recently baptized ('in brevi tempore postquam baptismum'). C. H. Turner, *EOMIA* i. 114. The fact that Ambrose was said to have fulfilled 'omnia ecclesiastica officia' during the eight-day period which followed his baptism (*VA* 9. 9) may have represented a highly superficial attempt to stay within the limitations outlined in the tenth canon of the western council of Sardica (343). It states that no one should be ordained bishop without having first passed

Ambrose offers no further details on the nature of his 'resistance', the *Vita Ambrosii* supplies five subterfuges in which the recalcitrant governor attempted to discredit his nomination or even tried to escape.[49] Whether these episodes are indeed historical occurrences, as most scholars think, is besides the point. Paulinus wanted to reinforce the notion that Ambrose, whom God had raised 'as a bulwark for His catholic church against its enemies' (i.e., the Arians), was divinely chosen for the episcopate at Milan. The issue of resistance is an important literary theme which one finds in biographies of holy men.[50] Paulinus was well acquainted with Sulpicius' hero Martin, who had to be deceived in order to extract him from his monastery. Even then the people of Tours were forced to take further steps to prevent him from escaping before his consecration.[51]

Why was Ambrose chosen to be the new bishop? Part of the answer must surely lie in the compromise situation which such an election afforded. As an official of Valentinian's administration, Ambrose would have ostensibly shared Valentinian's policies of non-intervention in religious matters except where the public peace was being threatened. His brief but successful public career up to this point bears witness to the conscientious performance of duty in accordance with imperial policies and his family traditions.[52] This seems to find confirmation in that Ambrose is portrayed as enjoying the emperor's full endorsement in his unexpected election, as well as the warm approval of Probus.[53] Those political endorsements which Ambrose is said to have received are so strong that they are somewhat suspect. They may be simply another reflection of the universal unanimity found in our ancient sources surrounding the bishop's election. A different scenario is proposed by C. Corbellini, who has advanced the provocative thesis that Ambrose's election was actually the result of imperial action rising from the volatile situation at Milan. 'Probus decided on the choice of Ambrose as governor and ordered him to Milan pronouncing the well-known phrase, "Vade, age non ut iudex sed ut

through the grades of reader, deacon, and presbyter, and that one should remain in each grade for 'no brief time'.

[49] Application of torture to criminals (*VA* 7. 1–8); the dedication of his life to philosophy (7. 9–13); being visited by prostitutes (7. 14–16); attempt to flee the city by night (8. 1–11); and hiding on the estate of Leontius (9. 1–6).

[50] P. Courcelle, *Recherches sur saint Ambroise: vies anciennes, culture, iconographie* (Paris, 1973), 10 ff.

[51] *Vita Mart.* IX. 1–2 (*CSEL* i. 118–19).

[52] For his *cursus*, *PLRE* i. 52, 'Ambrosius 3'. See A. Piganiol, *L'Empire chrétien (325–395)* (2nd edn., Paris, 1972), 210–11, for a good summary of Valentinian's policies regarding religion (Pagan, Christian, and Jewish).

[53] Rufinus, *HE* II. 11 (*PL* xxi. 522A); *VA* 8. 9–11 (Pellegrino, *Vita*, 60).

episcopus" ' ('Go, act not as a governor but as a bishop').[54] Perhaps the strongest argument in Corbellini's favour is that her proposal makes the best sense of a remark which Ambrose years later utters to Valentinian II about his election:

I will not mention the fact that the people themselves already passed judgement; I am silent about how they demanded from the father of Your Clemency him whom they [now] have; I am silent that the father of Your Piety promised a peaceful future if the one elected (namely Ambrose) would assume the bishopric. I have kept faith in these promises.[55]

The passage does provide tacit confirmation of Valentinian I's approval of Ambrose's nomination and offer of assistance to restore public order in Milan as a means of prevailing upon him to accept his election. It does not neccessitate however that Valentinian had a direct role in the election as Corbellini insists. Nor does Corbellini explain sufficiently the predominant place which the ancient histories and Ambrose himself attribute to the people of Milan in electing him to the episcopate.[56] Even more problematic is the admission made by Ambrose that he strenuously resisted his nomination, which seems to contradict the idea that Ambrose had made an agreement with the emperor or Probus before accepting the office.

2. AMBROSE'S EARLY YEARS AS BISHOP

Whatever the exact circumstances, there is substantial evidence that Ambrose became bishop of Milan with imperial recognition and that the anticipated outcome of his election was a 'peaceful future' for the city of Milan. After his consecration there are yet other historical problems to confront. Did Ambrose immediately array himself 'as the new champion of Nicene orthodoxy' as Gryson and others[57] contend? It is a question

---

[54] 'Sesto Petronio Probo e l'elezione episcopale di Ambrogio', *Rendiconti: Istituto Lombardo di Scienze e Lettre*, 109 (1975), 185. The quotation of Probus is taken from *VA* 8. 11 (Pellegrino, *Vita*, 60).

[55] *Ep.* 75. 7 (*CSEL* lxxxii. 3. 77).

[56] *Expositio evangelii secundum Lucam*, VIII. 73 (*CCSL* xiv. 325–6. 882–7); See F. L. Ganshoff, 'Note sur l'élection des évêques dans l'Empire Romain au IVe et pendant la première moitié du Ve siècle', *Revue internationale des droits de l'antiquité: mélanges Fernand de Visscher*, 3/4 (1950), 476–98. The popular acclamation (including people and clerics) of a candidate as at Milan is very similar to the African model exemplifed in the popular election of Cyprian. A judgement of bishops subsequently ratified the election effected by the church community.

[57] *Scolies*, 106; Homes Dudden, *Life and Times*, i. 69.

which we will consider for the rest of this chapter. For it will be proposed that Ambrose sought to apply the religious policies which he brought from his previous secular office until he was forced to do otherwise. This view takes seriously the idea that the clergy in Milan were preponderantly Homoian, and that Ambrose more consistently fulfilled the mandate for which he was elected than is commonly supposed. Let us begin by examining the principal arguments for Ambrose's swift action against the Homoians in Milan.

(a) *Baptism by a pro-Nicene bishop*

Paulinus is our only ancient source which claims that Ambrose was baptized by a catholic bishop. The rationale given for this action is worth noting: 'when he understood the will of God concerning himself, not able to resist any longer, he demanded that he must be baptized by none other than a catholic bishop; for he carefully guarded against the perfidy of the Arians'.[58] We would hardly expect Paulinus to say anything else. If it is true, as a number of scholars agree,[59] the passage provides important evidence that Ambrose was openly committed to a pro-Nicene position from the very beginning of his episcopate. And there is good reason to think that part of what Paulinus says is accurate.

Ambrose says nothing about his baptism. He states only that the western bishops approved his ordination 'by their decision', which merely confirms established canonical procedure requiring the presence of no less than three bishops for a valid episcopal ordination.[60] It is curious that Ambrose is utterly silent about his baptism since the baptizing bishop is often named. Of course Ambrose need not have been baptized by a bishop since the baptism of a catechumen could be accomplished by a presbyter in the absence of a bishop. Given the rapidity of events that followed Ambrose's nomination, there is a strong possibility that he was baptized not by a bishop but by one of the Milanese clergy: Simplicianus. The evidence for this choice is meagre but provocative. In the *Confessions*, when Augustine first consults Simplicianus at Milan the latter is identified as the 'father

---

[58] *VA* 9. 6–8 (Pellegrino. *Vita*, 62).

[59] e.g., Paredi, *Saint Ambrose*, 124; Duval, 'Ambroise, de son élection à sa consécration', 250.

[60] According to the fourth canon of Nicaea, all bishops of the province ideally should attend the ordination of a bishop. But in cases of 'urgent necessity or because of distance', no less than three bishops are required, along with the written consent of those absent (*EOMIA* i. 116–17). There is evidence (Theodoret, *HE* v. 9. 14–15 (*GCS* xliv. 293. 9–17)) that this canon was still being adhered to in the later 4th century.

of Ambrose (then bishop) in receiving grace and whom Ambrose truly esteemed as a father'.[61] To what could Augustine be referring in his words, 'in the receiving of grace', if he is not alluding to the impartation of a sacrament such as baptism? Such a view casts new light on the way in which Ambrose spoke of Simplicianus as a 'parent' in his letters: 'love us, as you do, with the affection of a parent'.[62] Elsewhere Ambrose responds to Simplicianus' request for sermons on the writings of the Apostle Paul, 'I realize in this complaint the result of our old friendship and, what is more, a tenderly fatherly love'.[63] These passages, especially the one from the *Confessions*, develop the conclusion that Simplicianus was not only Ambrose's spiritual preceptor, but also his baptizer in that hurried aftermath of his election to the episcopate. All of this raises another question about the choice of Simplicianus. Was he chosen to baptize Ambrose because the latter was a professed Nicene?

The catholic and ascetic elements in Ambrose's family background have been well noted.[64] His sister Marcellina had taken the veil at Rome from Liberius, who delivered a sermon on that occasion punctuated with Trinitarian doctrine unmistakably Nicene. The principal inducement for Marcellina's vow was, according to Ambrose, the example of a martyr relative, Sotheris: 'the inspiration of hereditary chastity has taught descent from a martyred ancestor'.[65] Ambrose's brother Satyrus was hastily baptized after his shipwreck, though with the stipulation that the rite be performed by a bishop who was in agreement with the catholic bishops.[66] At his election, Ambrose had not yet been baptized, but it is reasonable to suppose that, when such a ceremony was performed, it was in accord with the dictates of his family tradition. It is unfortunate that Ambrose never makes mention of this event, but neither do we ever hear the charge later in his episcopate that his baptism was invalid or that it compromised his situation as a proponent of Nicaea. By the last third of the fourth century, Neo-Nicenes, Homoians, and Eunomians were all too aware of their different baptisms and believed in the invalidation of baptism if one had converted to the other's theology.[67]

---

[61] *Conf.* VIII. 2.3 (*CSEL* xxxiii. 1. 171).   [62] *Ep.* 2. 10 (*CSEL* lxxxii. 1. 19. 96).
[63] *Ep.* 7. 2 (*CSEL* lxxxii. 1. 44. 12–13).
[64] A thorough discussion can be found in Homes Dudden, *Life and Times*, i. 3 ff.
[65] *De virginibus*, III. 7. 37 (*Florilegium patristicum*, xxxi. 78. 1–2).
[66] *De excessu fratris*, i. 47. 1–5 (*CSEL* lxxiii. 235).
[67] Eusebius of Vercelli, *De trinitate*, VII. 16–17 (*CCSL* ix. 96); Ambrose, *De fide*, v. 10. 118 (*CSEL* lxxiii. 260–1); *De spiritu sancto*, I. 3. 42 (*CSEL* lxxix. 32; Socrates, *HE* v. 24 (*PG* lxvii. 649A); Sozomen, *HE* vi. 26. 9 (*GCS* l. 273).

We would like to know more about Simplicianus. His close relation-ship with Marius Victorinus, who was an avowed defender of *homoousios* doctrine after his conversion, and who wrote his anti-Arian treatises probably before 360, leads us to believe that Simplicianus had been a pro-Nicene, or at least a supporter of the exiled bishop of Milan, Dionysius, as early as Victorinus' conversion to Christianity (*c*.355).[68] We observe too that Simplicianus' fidelity to the Nicene faith is never doubted or questioned by Ambrose or Augustine in their later correspondence. It seems then that this aged presbyter fitted into that category of clergy at Milan during the later 350s and 360s who ceremoniously indulged the convictions of their Homoian bishop Auxentius while he was alive, but personally adhered to another creed.

This almost total lack of documentation for Ambrose's baptism and yet the absence of any question about its efficacy in the ensuing years leads to the conclusion that his baptism was a wholly unspectacular event. It was administered quickly and quietly by a presbyter of the Church in order to hurry the candidate on to the fulfilment of the requisite offices before the episcopate could legally begin. It was not, in other words, a de-clarative act designed to demonstrate Ambrose's public fealty to the Nicene 'party' regardless of the religiously explosive situation which existed in the Milanese church.

(b) *The translation of Dionysius' relics to Milan*

A second general token of Ambrose's unveiled commitment to the Neo-Nicenes after his consecration is his alleged request to Basil of Caesarea for the remains of Dionysius. The latter had been exiled at the council of Milan in 355, and, having died in exile, was now classed among the highly esteemed martyrs for the true faith. Of Ambrose's request, Palanque writes, 'Le nouvel évêque donne d'abord satisfaction aux catholiques de Milan, en faisant revenir triomphalement de Cappadoce la dépouille de l'évêque Denys.'[69] The idea has been recently restated by Mara, who hinges Ambrose's early opposition to the Arians on this reputed transac-tion.[70] Mara does a disservice however by not informing the reader about the questionable nature of the evidence as well as the increasing scepticism which has characterized scholarship on this matter since Palanque.

---

[68] *Conf.* VIII. 2. 3–4 (*CSEL* xxxiii. 1. 171–2).
[69] *Saint Ambroise*, 33–4.   [70] *Patrology*, iv. 145.

The sum total of direct evidence for Ambrose's request rests upon a letter of Basil (*Ep.* 197) written to Ambrose in reply to a previous communication (now lost). The letter falls into two parts. The first half is an acknowledgement of Ambrose's recent elevation to the episcopate and Basil takes this opportunity to exhort his new colleague to 'fight the good fight; correct the infirmities of the people . . . renew the ancient footsteps of the fathers'.[71] As a type of salutary greeting, this first section corresponds to Ambrose's recollection about how the western bishops sanctioned his ordination by their decision whereas the eastern bishops 'also gave their approval'.[72] The second part of the letter immediately takes up the issue of Ambrose's desire to acquire the relics of the most blessed Bishop Dionysius, which, Basil notes, 'bears witness to your complete love of the Lord, your respect for your predecessors, and your zeal for the faith'.[73] Then Basil explains how he sent one of his presbyters, Therasius, to assist Ambrose's agents in securing the remains. He gives reassurance that no one need fear any deceit in their acquisition, for the relics are indeed genuine.

The chief difficulty in adopting this letter of Basil's as proof for the attitudes of the early Ambrose is the dubious authenticity of its second half. Articles by A. Cavallin and A. Paredi testify to the fact that this second part is missing in most, and the earliest, manuscripts, appearing only in a tenth-century manuscript (Codex Parisinus Graecus, Suppl. 1020) of an unknown origin.[74] Apart from the merits of their arguments, it is instructive to point out the remarkable absence of corroborating evidence that might favour the authenticity of the letter's second half.

Only twice does Ambrose speak of his predecessor. In both cases Dionysius is described as having died for the faith in exile.[75] Ambrose never specifies the city or region where Dionysius died, nor the year of his death. More importantly, Ambrose never even hints at the translation *ad patriam* of the relics in his own writings. This lack of information is compounded by the silence in Paulinus. It is hard to imagine that the translation of Dionysius' relics to Milan would find no place in the *Vita*

---

[71] *Ep.* 197. 1. 36–40 (Deferrari, 92).

[72] *Ep.* 14. (extra coll.) 65. 667 (*CSEL* lxxxii. 3. 269).

[73] *Ep.* 197. 2. 1–4 (Deferrai, 94).

[74] A. Cavallin, 'Die Legendenbildung um den Mailander Bischof Dionysius', *Eranos*, 43 (1945), 136–49; A. Paredi, 'L'esilio in oriente del vescovo Milanese Dionisio e il problematico ritorno del suo corpo a Milano', in *Atti del convegno di studi su la Lombardia e l'Oriente* (1963), 229–44.

[75] *Contra Auxentium* (*Ep.* LXXVa) 18. 210–12 (*CSEL* lxxxii. 3. 93); *Ep.* 14. (extra coll.) 70. 733–5 (*CSEL* lxxxii. 3. 273).

Ambrosii given Ambrose's own abiding commitment to the restoration and employment of saints' remains.[76] And lastly, when Ambrose wrote to his sister Marcellina in 386 about the invention of the relics of Protasius and Gervasius, he stated that Milan was 'barren of martyrs' before their discovery.[77] Obviously Ambrose could not have made such a remark if the remains of Dionysius had already been returned to the city since Dionysius ranked among the martyrs. Ambrose himself claimed that the deceased bishop was crowned 'with an honour higher than the martyrs'.

While there is good evidence to suppose that there was in Milan by AD 475 a *memoria* or perhaps a tomb of Dionysius on the outskirts of the city, there is no trace archaeologically, according to Paredi, that a new sarcophagus or receptacle of any kind was provided during Ambrose's time for the remains of Dionysius.[78] If the latter's relics were ever brought to Milan, it would have been after Ambrose's lifetime.

Given the problems associated with the second half of Basil's letter (197) and the lack of early corroborating evidence, the authenticity of this document has been justifiably questioned. Certainly one is ill-advised to establish a case for the early attitudes of Ambrose from this text alone.

(c) *Ambrose's dismissal of a Homoian priest*

Among the newer researches which address the aftermath of Ambrose's elevation to the episcopate, it is agreed that Ambrose did not immediately alienate himself from the Milanese clergy by openly displaying a pro-Nicene bias. Rather, he preserved the numbers of clergy which had been loyal to Auxentius in order to maintain peace in the church.[79] Simonetti and Duval believe that there was one exception to this continued policy of neutrality. From a passage in *De officiis ministrorum*, they argue that a single priest had to be removed because he deserted the faith at the time of the *Ariana perfidia*, that is, for professing radical Arian ideas.[80] The passage in question deserves to be quoted in full:

---

[76] *VA* 14. 1–10; 29. 1–9; 32–3. 1–9. See also A. Bastiaensen, 'Paulin de Milan et le culte des martyrs chez saint Ambroise', in Lazzati (ed.), *Ambrosius episcopus*, ii. 143–50.

[77] *Ep.* 77. 7 (*CSEL* lxxxii. 3. 131. 72–3).

[78] 'L'Esilio', 235–6. See Cavallin, 'Die Legendenbildung', 141, for the inscription of Aurelius, bishop of Rider in Dalmatia (*ILCV* i. 1043), who was buried beside Dionysius' tomb in Milan in 475. My thanks to Professor Chadwick for drawing my attention to this inscription.

[79] Meslin, *Les Ariens*, 45; Simonetti, *La crisi ariana*, 438.

[80] Simonetti, *La crisi ariana*, 438 n. 6; Duval, 'Ambroise, de son élection à sa consécration', 254.

You remember, my children, a certain friend who seemed to commend himself by the earnestness of his duties, yet this individual was not accepted by me into the clergy because of his very shameful behaviour. Moreover, I ordered that another one whom I encountered [already] in the clergy never precede me because his insolent bearing brought a kind of scourging to my eyes; which is what I said after he returned to his duty following an offence committed. I mention this one instance, for the outcome was not surprising: both of them left the church. Just as they were betrayed by their walk, so the treachery of their souls was made known. For the one deserted his faith at the time of the Arian troubles (*Arianae infestations*); the other through the love of money.[81]

It is generally assumed that the passage applies to the period just following Ambrose's consecration. But this is surely a mistaken interpretation. One must ask when were the 'Arian troubles' which Ambrose mentions here. Of the two men who left the Church, our concern is with the first. Ambrose tells his listeners that he never ordained this one because of some questionable behaviour. Not only was the individual in question not a priest, his rejection for ordination had nothing to do with doctrinal matters. The other individual was already a member of the Milanese clergy when Ambrose arrived, and his later apostasy was linked to the love of money. The first man, due to his continued disaffection with Ambrose, is said to have deserted the faith 'at the time of the Arian troubles'. Since the *De officiis ministrorum* was probably written in the second half of 389,[82] we must ask how Ambrose's audience would react toward the reference to 'Arian troubles'. Doubtless the designation would conjure up images of the most intense series of public attacks sustained by Ambrose and the pro-Nicene community during the basilica controversy in 385–6.[83] We are left to conclude that the layman was rejected by Ambrose not simply because he absorbed a form of Arian theology, but because he 'deserted the faith' in 385/6 when a number of people in Milan defected to the Homoian camp. It appears then that this passage does not support the contention that Ambrose took early steps against any member of his clergy or other individuals in the congregation because of their doctrinal orientation.

(d) *Ambrose's role in the election of a Nicene bishop in Sirmium and the opposition from Justina and the Homoians*

Paulinus is again the only ancient source which describes for us how Ambrose, soon after he received the episcopate, went to Sirmium in order

---

[81] *De officiis*, I. 18. 72 (*PL* xvi. 49A–B).
[82] Gryson, *Le Prêtre*, 37; Palanque, *Saint Ambroise*, 526–7.   [83] As described in Ch. 6.

to consecrate Anemius bishop.[84] Almost certainly this is the same Anemius who was present at the council of Aquileia in 381 and who subscribed against the Homoian bishops Palladius and Secundianus.[85] The context of Ambrose's visit is grounded upon the assertion that pro-Nicene gatherings in the church at Sirmium, presumably assembled to elect Anemius, had been thwarted by the Arian Empress Justina, using imperial authority, in order to ensure that an Arian bishop might be consecrated instead. Upon arriving at the church, Ambrose immediately assumed the bishop's chair, giving visible support to the Nicene cause. The stalemate between the two parties was suddenly broken when an Arian virgin who had laid violent hands on Ambrose died suddenly the following day. Paulinus explains that this event 'threw no little fear in his opponents and brought great peace to the church allowing the consecration of the bishop'.

There are a great many problems with the fragmentary evidence about whether Ambrose went to Sirmium and the date(s) of his alleged journey(s). If we accept Paulinus' account at face value, it insinuates that Ambrose went to Sirmium early in his episcopate, perhaps a year or two after his consecration. Immediately there arises a difficulty, in that separate evidence exists for Ambrose meeting with Gratian in Sirmium at the end of 378, which leads to the problematic conclusion that Ambrose was twice present in the Pannonian city between 375 and 378.[86] Since the complexities involved in this issue open a 'Pandora's Box' of problems that we cannot definitively solve here, we must confine ourselves to a simple review of the data and their relevance to our stated inquiry.

Modern scholarship on the whole has tended to accept Paulinus' account of Ambrose going to Sirmium as a historical reality for the reason that such a visit can be adapted to coincide with Theodoret's account of an Illyrian council held about the same time. The three documents in Theodoret which describe this council consist of (1) an imperial edict in the name of Valentinian [I], Valens, and Gratianus to the bishops in four provinces of Asia Minor endorsing the Nicene Trinitarianism that had been received by a synod of bishops in Illyricum; (2) the decrees of the synod confessing the doctrine of consubstantiality and condemning Arian views about the Son's generation; (3) a synodical letter addressed to the churches of the same four provinces telling them of the condemnation of six unknown 'Ariomaniacs' and urging them to teach no other doctrine than that which the Fathers confirmed at Nicaea.[87]

---

[84] *VA* 11. 1–2 (Pellegrino, *Vita*, 64). The former bishop, Germinius, is reckoned to have died soon after Valentinian's death (17 Nov. 375).

[85] *Gesta concilii Aquileiensis*, 1. 4 (*CSEL* lxxxii. 327).

[86] As per Gryson, *Le Prêtre*, 158; Hanson, *The Search*, 667.

[87] Theodoret, *HE* IV. 8. 1–7; 8. 8–11; 9. 1–9 (*GCS* xliv. 220–7).

These three documents are suspiciously out of context on many counts, and some scholars have rejected them completely as spurious.[88] The overarching problem with the supposed edict is the obvious conflict between Valentinian's attested neutral political policies with regard to religious matters and his proclamation and public endorsement of a council favouring Nicene doctrine. Zeiller's hypothesis[89] of amending the imperial titles to read Valens, Gratianus, and Valentinian II, thereby identifying the imperial edict and the council with the name of Gratian, does not alleviate the political problem, since Gratian is not known to have legislated any action against Arians in 378 and would not have endorsed a synodical decree condemning the same. It is true that Gratian resided in Sirmium after Valens' defeat at the battle of Hadrianople from August 378 to February of the following year,[90] and is thought to have met with Ambrose during this time, in either the summer or autumn of 378. If Ambrose met with Gratian it is reasonable to think he did so while the council was in session. The council has been located therefore in the summer or autumn of 378 in conjunction with Gratian's presence in Sirmium.[91] An advantage of this view is that it unifies Ambrose's two journeys to Sirmium—one for the election of Anemius and one for the council—into a single trip.

Further confirmation for the existence of this council and Ambrose's participation is thought to come from the so-called 'Dissertatio Maximini', specifically the *scholia ariana* in defence of those who were condemned at the council of Aquileia (381). In this apology for the orthodoxy of the Homoian faith, Palladius lashes out against his opponents for having confirmed 'that blasphemy at Sirmium' which teaches belief in 'three omnipotent Gods . . . three eternals, three equals, three veritables (*veros*), three who labour together (*cooperarios*), three enthroned together (*consessores*), three who have no difference (*indifferentes*), three indistincts (*inresolutos*), three for whom nothing is impossible'.[92] Damasus is mentioned in correlation with this teaching and Gryson has proposed that Palladius is citing a passage from the *Tome* of Damasus which was used by the Sirmium council of 378.[93] The difficulty with this suggestion is that the words of Palladius' complaint do not replicate the content of the synodical letter in Theodoret, which Gryson acknowledges. A recent

[88] G. Bardy, 'Sur un synode de l'Illyricum (375)', *Bulletin d'ancienne littérature et d'archéologie chrétienne*, 2 (1912), 259–74; L. Duchesne, *Histoire ancienne de l'Église*, vol. ii (Paris, 1908), 398 n. l.

[89] *Origines chrétiennes*, 313.   [90] *Regesten*, 250.

[91] Palanque, *Saint Ambroise*, 498; Gryson, *Scolies*, 112; Y.-M. Duval, 'Le Concile d'Aquilée vu par les Homoéens', *RHE* 76 (1981), 326–7.

[92] *Scholia*, 345ᵛ. 128 (Gryson, *Scolies*, 310–12).   [93] Gryson, *Scolies*, 115 ff.

article by N. McLynn has convincingly shown that neither does the terminology of Damasus' *Tome* match with that of Palladius' remarks, and that the 'blasphemy of Sirmium' is not referring to an event or dogma which was propounded by a council in Sirmium. Instead, McLynn argues that the 'blasphemy' which Palladius has in mind is none other than the *De fide* of Ambrose which was sent to Gratian in Sirmium.[94] Thus, further supports for the existence of this elusive council are removed.

There are obviously serious problems with the idea that Ambrose was present at an Illyrian council in 378 which elected Anemius bishop, condemned six Arian bishops, and issued a pro-Nicene formula of faith to churches in Asia Minor. Such a view is attempting to connect three totally disparate pieces of evidence: chapter 11 of the *Vita*, Theodoret, and Palladius' 'blasphemy of Sirmium'.

Looking more closely at the documents in Theodoret, we are told vaguely that the council took place in Illyricum and was composed of bishops from Illyricum; one must simply assume that Sirmium was the location. There is nothing whatsoever in the synodical decrees or letter about the election or consecration of a new bishop of Sirmium, nor is there a reference to Ambrose or any other non-Pannonian bishop present at the council, which we would expect to see in the preface of the conciliar letter (*HE* IV. 9. 1), especially if one present was a metropolitan. Likewise, Ambrose never makes mention of such a council, nor makes use in his own writings of the theological terminology employed by the Illyrian council, such as the formula 'one essence, three hypostases'.[95]

The synodical letter itself seems to be responding to issues completely different from those in the first two documents in Theodoret, since it is concerned with the Macedonian tendencies of its readers in Asia Minor. Indeed, the whole tone of the letter assumes the existence of a thorough-going Nicene trinitarianism in the eastern half of the empire—a very questionable assumption for the year 378. Even more questionable is the legal basis for the synod's deposition of six unknown Arian bishops in Illyricum: Gratian maintained his father's stance toward ecclesiastical politics at least until August of 379 and probably longer, after which heretical assemblies could be prosecuted by law.[96] If in fact six Arian

---

[94] 'The "Apology" of Palladius: Nature and Purpose', *JTS* 42 (1991), 57–66.

[95] M. Simonetti, 'La politica antiariana di Ambrogio', in Lazzati (ed.), *Ambrosius episcopus*, 273.

[96] *C. Th.* XVI. 5. 5 (3 Aug.). The clause 'Denique antiquato rescripto, quod apud Sirmium nuper emersit' lends itself to the interpretation that Gratian passed a law of toleration while he resided at Sirmium during the l2atter half of 378 and early 379. For the preferred date of *C. Th.* XVI. 5. 4, see pages 134–5 above.

bishops were condemned and deposed in Sirmium, it is strange that we do not hear about this from ~~the~~ Palladius, who was quick to charge his opponents with such injustices.[97]

For the lack of any connection between the council in Theodoret and the presence of Ambrose in Sirmium, we come back to the *Vita Ambrosii* as our sole source of information. Despite the fact that Ambrose never says he was in Sirmium, there is some reason to think he visited Gratian there, perhaps in late 378 or early 379, as we will discuss later. But for this, we would have no satisfactory explanation for the presence of a Milanese bishop in Sirmium.[98] The all-too-common conclusion that Ambrose was motivated above all 'to crush the Arians in their last stronghold of Illyricum'[99] caters to a Paulinian view of Ambrose that has little to undergird it.

Paulinus attributes the successes of the Arians in Sirmium to the *potentia* of Justina, which brings us to a final point. The role of the second wife of Valentinian and mother of Valentinian II[100] as a heretical *femina monstruosa* is essentially a literary creation of the *Vita Ambrosii*. Her shadow looms large in the anti-Nicene affairs at Sirmium, as it does later in Milan, her presence acting as the primary source of vitality and ambition for the western Arians in these communities. Justina rightfully won herself the reputation as a pushy 'mother regent', and also as a political patroness dedicated to the defence of the Homoian party at Milan. Both Rufinus and Augustine report on Justina's vicious attacks against Ambrose and the pro-Nicenes during the middle 380s.[101] Rufinus in particular freely elaborates on her impieties: agitating discord among the people, threatening the priests, and attempting to have Ambrose exiled; a true 'alumna of the Arian heresy'. By the early fifth century, Paulinus saw fit to expand Justina's notorious reputation by including her active opposition towards Ambrose when the latter came to Sirmium towards the end of 378. The model is consistent with Paulinus' caricatures. Just as Ambrose was chosen to defend the true faith from the very beginning of his career, so Justina is depicted as a persistent combatant and patroness of heresy; an antithetical pair which cannot fail to remind the reader of Elijah and Jezebel.

[97] *Scholia*, 344ᵛ. 125 (Gryson, *Scolies*, 308).

[98] On the problems with metropolitan organization and jurisdiction of this region during Ambrose's time, see J. Gaudemet, *L'Église dans l'Empire Romain (IVᵉ–Vᵉ)* (Paris, 1958), 384 ff.

[99] *La crisi ariana*, 438.

[100] Zosimus, IV. 9. 1 (*Zosime: Histoire nouvelle*, ed. and trans. F. Paschoud, vol. ii (Paris, 1979), 279); Socrates, *HE* IV. 31 (*PG* lxvii. 548B).

[101] Rufinus, *HE* II. 15 (*PL* xxi. 523C–524A); *Conf.* IX. 7. 15 (*CSEL* xxx. 1. 208).

Once we examine the strengths and weaknesses of the arguments which reveal Ambrose's anti-Arian policies in the early years of his episcopate, there is no doubt about his attachment, familial and personal, to the Nicene form of Christianity. But this viewpoint must be carefully distinguished from Ambrose's non-aggressive religious-political agenda which he established in Milan at the time of his becoming bishop. The standard assessment of Ambrose as one who openly opposed Arianism from the beginning is seriously flawed for the lack of evidence in its support. It is far more reasonable to postulate an Ambrose who maintained the religious-political policies he defended as governor of the province. After all, the upholding of these policies was the ostensible reason for his election.

Our findings above allow us to think of Ambrose's first years as bishop with a different nuance: one whose administrative and legal abilities far outweighed his grasp of theological and ecclesiastical matters. Pietri is surely correct in saying, 'the new bishop Ambrose is too young, his position too uncertain, to have become so soon the champion of orthodoxy'.[102] It is a much more realistic assessment with which to begin our understanding of the historical Ambrose.

---

[102] *Roma Christiana*, i. 736.

5

The Publication of and Reaction to
Ambrose's De fide, *I–II*

F o r the first three years of Ambrose's episcopate there is a virtual black-out of information. Not until 377 did the bishop venture forth a publication which took the form of an encomium written to his sister Marcellina on the 'birthday' of the martyr-virgin St Agnes. 'Although distrustful in my ability, but provoked by the examples of divine mercy, I venture to compose an address . . . O that Jesus should look upon me in any way still lying under that fruitful fig-tree, and also that our fig-tree would bear fruit after three years.'[1] Ambrose was acutely aware of his own deficiencies upon assuming the reins of ministry at Milan, referring to himself as 'indoctus' (unlearned) and an 'initiate in religious matters'.[2] In the years which followed his consecration, he furthered his theological education amidst the pressing duties of performing his office as bishop. If Ambrose was occupied with controversial affairs during this time,[3] he does not tell us about them. Nor do his earliest treatises, which were probably written sometime during 377–8,[4] indicate that Ambrose was struggling with the Homoians at Milan, since there is a complete absence of polemic against anti-Nicenes. To be sure, these documents provide clear evidence of

---

[1] *De virginibus*, I. 1. 2; I. 4 (*PL* xvi. 229C).

[2] *De officiis*, I. 1. 4 (*PL* xvi. 27C); *De paenitentia*, II. 8. 73 (*CSEL* lxxiii. 193).

[3] We have already ruled out the likelihood that Ambrose went to Sirmium in 376–7 to participate in the election of Anemius against the Homoians (Ch. 4, s. 2 (*d*).).

[4] Given the relative uncertainty about which of Ambrose's works are earliest, it is risky to make an absolutely definitive statement with regard to the bishop's early attitudes and practices. There is general agreement among modern chronologies that the following works can be dated to or before 378: *De virginibus*, *De viduis*, *De virginitate*, *De paradiso*, *De Cain et Abel*, *De Noe*, and *De excessu fratris* (O. Faller, *S. Ambrosii 'De virginibus'* (Bonn, 1933), 8–9); Palanque, *Saint Ambroise*, 493–5; Gryson, *Le Prêtre*, 36–8; *Patrology*, iv. 153–6, 167–8. It is unfortunate that Schenkl offers no discussion on dating in the critical edition of Ambrose's exegetical writings in *CSEL* xxxii. Very few of Ambrose's ninety-two letters can be dated with confidence. Those which are datable come from the bishop's later career (Gryson, *Le Prêtre*, 38–42). For the question of the authenticity and organization of Ambrose's letters, see J. P. Mazières, 'Un principe d'organization', in Duval (ed.), *Ambroise de Milan*, 199 n. 1.

Ambrose's own doctrinal orientation toward Nicene catholicism, as G. Corti has shown in his exegesis of Ambrose's *De paradiso* and *De Cain et Abel*.[5] In the sermon *De excessu fratris*, delivered in the winter of 377/8, Ambrose tells his listeners that he will avoid a tangent by not elaborating at length on the doctrine of Christ, but he warns, 'The treatment of this topic demands more arguments from which we could demonstrate the authority of the Father, the property of the Son and the unity of the whole Trinity.'[6]

The absence of polemic or any concrete references to a conflict with the Homoians in these early writings do not lend support to the 'Paulinian' picture which depicts the new bishop of Milan as an aggressive and relentless anti-Arian. There is no reason to dispute the conclusion that Ambrose took no hostile action against Homoians during his early years at Milan. Administratively, at least, Ambrose continued to maintain a careful balance between dissenting religious opinion, which, as we recall, was the primary reason for his unexpected election in 374. He would not be able to maintain this posture for much longer however.

Despite his usual dependence on the Paulinian perspective, Paredi has rightly observed that Ambrose said virtually nothing about the Arians until he wrote *De fide*, books I and II.[7] If we are correct in our preceding analysis of Ambrose's ecclesiastical tactics, the publication of *De fide* represents a sudden and dramatic reversal in his policies toward the Homoians in Milan. Probably written in late autumn of 378,[8] the document is

---

[5] 'Lo sfondo Ambrosiano del concilio di Aquileia', in *Atti del colloquio internazionale sul concilio di Aquileia del 381*, Antichità Altoadriatiche 16 (Udine, 1981), 55–6. Cf. *De virginibus*, I. 8. 46, 48; III. 1. 4.

[6] *De excessu fratris*, I. 14 (*NPNF* x. 163 (altered)) (*CSEL* lxxiii. 216).

[7] *Saint Ambrose*, 176.

[8] Palanque (*Saint Ambroise*, 498), Homes Dudden (*Life and Times*, i. 189), Paredi (*Saint Ambrose*, 180), and Faller (*CSEL* lxxviii. 5*–7*) place *De fide*, I–II, between the death of Valens (9 Aug. 378) and the elevation of Theodosius at Sirmium (19 Jan. 379), based on the phrase in *De fide*, I. 1, where Ambrose addresses Gratian: 'and you are not Augustus of a single people but of the whole world' (*CSEL* lxxviii. 4. 5–6). The implication drawn from this passage is that books I–II must have been written sometime while Gratian was sole emperor. H. Savon has shown, however, that Gratian was never sole Augustus of the empire since Valentinian II was elevated in Sirmium six days after his father's death, and that the title 'totius orbis Augustus' reflects not a state of actual affairs, but a theory according to which the empire remains a 'patrimonium indivisum' ('Quelques remarques sur la chronologie des œuvres de Saint Ambroise', 159–60). A wholly different approach is taken by Gottlieb, who argues that the writing of books I–II did not take place until 380, following Gratian's (second) meeting with Ambrose at Milan in Apr. (*Ambrosius von Mailand*, 49). The argument hinges on his interpretation of *De fide*, II. 142 ('Italy . . . which you formerly defended from barbarian enemies, now you have liberated again' (*CSEL* lxxviii. 107. 43–4)), in which Gottlieb sees a distinction between two times: 'formerly' and 'now'.

nothing less than a full-scale attack against western Arianism, denigrating it as the worst of heresies and as an enemy to the truth. Such a transformation indicates that the carefully balanced scales of Ambrosian administration had been tipped. In reality, however, this polemical manifesto by Ambrose is not so surprising. As we shall see below, much had transpired at Milan to vitiate Valentinian's promise to Ambrose that his episcopate would be characterized by a 'peaceful future'. The composition of *De fide* is itself a reaction to these events and must be considered in light of the political and religious circumstances which gave rise to it.

I. GRATIAN S RELIGIOUS POLITICS

At 9 years of age Gratian had been invested by his father as an Augustus and co-regent of the western half of the empire,[9] though in practice he exercised no real power until Valentinian's death on 17 November 375. Gratian was at Trier at the time and immediately assumed full command with seemingly little fanfare. But the political situation was not so simple. With Valentinian's passing in the midst of a campaign on the Pannonian frontier, high officials at the Danubian court were prompted to take other steps in order to ward off a political crisis. There was fear that, if the Gallic troops were not quickly presented with an emperor from the family of Valentinian, they might acclaim Sebastianus, a popular military

The earlier period is a reference to how a successful military check was administered to the Goths on the frontier of Italy; the *nunc* signifies how the Roman armies had recently gone on the offensive and been victorious over the Goths. According to Gottlieb, Ambrose is referring here to the 'important victories' achieved by Gratian and Theodosius in 379, so that the 'successful' Gratian and his chief military officers, Bauto and Arbogast, returned to Illyricum in 380 (pp. 18–19). The degree of military success which Gottlieb claims for Theodosius' campaigns in 379 and 380 is open to question. In fact, Zosimus, IV. 31. 2–32. 1; 33. 1 (which Gottlieb cites as evidence) tells how successful the barbarians were in stalling Theodosius' advance. This did not stop Theodosius from entering Constantinople in Nov. 380 'in splendour and celebrat[ing] a triumph as if he had won a great victory' (IV. 33. 1). Furthermore, Nautin has criticized Gottlieb's interpretation of 'now you have liberated again' since the rest of *De fide*, I–II (see I. praef. 3; II. 136–7), demonstrates that Ambrose was speaking of a *future* victory over the Goths ('Les Premières Relations', 233). Nautin convincingly argues that the context of II. 141–3 is not political in significance, so that 'vindicasti' refers not to a military victory (Gottlieb) but to Gratian's recent vindication of the truth (namely asking Ambrose for an explanation of the Nicene faith) (pp. 234–5). We return, therefore, to traditional dating of *De fide*, I–II, of sometime after the battle of Hadrianople but before Theodosius' accession in Jan. Further precision for the date will be offered below.

[9] AD 367 (Ammianus, XXVII. 6. 4–16 (Seyfarth, 42–5)).

commander and rival of the *magister militum* Merobaudes.[10] Merobaudes personally saw to it that Sebastianus was transferred to a remote outpost. Six days after Valentinian's death his second son, Valentinian II (from his second marriage to Justina), was summoned to Bregetio near Sirmium and was hailed by the army as Augustus.[11]

Gratian ratified the the transaction grudgingly, and the result of this new arrangement was that the province Illyricum was attributed to Valentinian II as a specially created prefecture.[12] The relationship between Gratian and the new emperor, who was just 4 years old, seems to have been more a reflection of the way in which Gratian had reigned when his father was living. Cast in the most benevolent light possible, Ausonius writes of Gratian's reception of the young Valentinian with the words, 'just as a son, your brother was received into the imperium'.[13] Far more illuminating of Gratian's attitude is the evidence found on all coins struck by the mint of Trier between 375 and 378 (Valens' death): Gratian and Valentinian II never appear together as co-emperors until after 378. At Lugdunum and Arles, Valentinian is ignored altogether in the currency produced at this time.[14] All other western mints, with exception of Sirmium, which struck coins for Valentinian, included IVN (= iunior) in his legend in order to establish his position of dependence on Gratian. It is worth noting that the signification of a junior Augustus is never found on the currency after Gratian's accession to the throne as a child (AD 367).

Even though Valentinian II did share the consulship with the eastern Emperor Valens for the years 376 and 378, no independent imperial directives, legal or otherwise, are known to have been issued from Sirmium. Because of these circumstances the role of Valentinian II until Gratian's death has been aptly described as 'un empereur fictif'.[15]

Reliable information about Gratian's religious background is difficult

---

[10] J. Matthews, *Western Aristocracies and Imperial Court AD 364–425* (Oxford, 1975), 64; J. M. O'Flynn, *Generalissimos of the Western Roman Empire* (Edmonton, 1983), 2.

[11] Ammianus, XXX. 10. 4 (Seyfarth, 157–8); Zosimus, IV. 19. 1 (Paschoud, 279); Socrates, *HE* IV. 31 (*PG* lxvii. 546B).

[12] Deduced by V. Grumel, 'L'Illyricum de la mort de Valentinien I (375) à la mort de Stilicon (408)', *Revue des études byzantines*, 9 (1952), 7; Piganiol, *L'Empire chrétien*, 224. Contrary to Zosimus' claim that Valentinian received not only Illyricum but the entire prefecture (IV. 19. 2), Gratian continued to exercise his power over the other two territories of the prefecture, Italy and Africa. This political arrangement was temporary. After the court of Valentinian came to Milan in the autumn of 378, Gratian must have resumed jurisdiction over Illyricum, since he independently conceded the eastern part of the province to Theodosius when the latter was elevated to the purple on 19 Jan. 379 (see n. 49).

[13] *Decimi Ausonii Burdigalensis opuscula*, ed. S. Prete (Leipzig, 1978), 216.

[14] *RIC* ix. 6.

[15] H. Glaesener, 'L'Empereur Gratien et saint Ambroise', *RHE* 52 (1957), 468.

to obtain. Great care must be exercised in drawing from our two most valuable sources for the life of Gratian: the writings of his tutor Ausonius and those of Ambrose. From the former, there is extant a panegyric of Gratian written in gratitude by Ausonius for his being named to the consulship in 379—a work which Gibbon once characterized as 'a servile and insipid piece of flattery'. This appraisal is not far from the mark. Gratian is arrayed as a model of humility, charity, piety, and temperance, even possessing all the ascetic virtues of a fourth-century saint. There are subtle, but unmistakable, references to Gratian's Christian beliefs, and he is said from boyhood to have always worshipped God.[16] Significantly Ambrose too speaks of Gratian's 'faith which from earliest childhood you have always cherished with pious affection'.[17] Indeed all of Ambrose's recollections of Gratian are of an emperor who was pious and 'faithful to the Lord' (i.e. a pro-Nicene),[18] although it must be remembered that Ambrose's reflections were written well after Gratian had committed himself publicly to favour the Nicene faith, and most of these references were given in the context of eulogies delivered years after Gratian's death.

From the combination of Gratian's tender years and the assumption that he appears to have come under the sway of Ambrose rather quickly after 378 (following the publication of *De fide*) in support of the Neo-Nicene cause against the Homoians, it is commonly supposed that the young emperor was docile and pliable in the hands of his mentors, particularly in matters of religious politics. De Labriolle, for instance, speaks of the 'close relations' which Ambrose and Gratian shared even before the summer of 378, when the emperor marched through north Italy on the way to assist Valens against the Goths. It was a relationship of master and pupil: how was Gratian 'to know the proper course to pursue in the midst of the theological disputes let loose by Arianism'?[19]

A radically different interpretation is articulated in a short study by Gottlieb on the relations between Ambrose and Gratian which denies that Gratian had any experience with or any bias toward the ecclesiastical politics of the Nicene–Homoian conflict prior to 380. Gottlieb points out that during Gratian's stay in Illyricum and north Italy from June 378 to August 379 both Nicenes and Homoians attempted to influence him. The

---

[16] *Actio ad Gratianum imperatorem pro consulatu*, XIV. 63–7 (Prete, 227).

[17] *De fide*, I. prol. 2 (*CSEL* lxxiii. 4–5).

[18] *De obitu Valentiniani*, 74 (*CSEL* lxxiii. 364. 10–11); 79b (*CSEL* lxxiii. 366. 18); *De obitu Theodosiani*, 51 (*CSEL* lxxiii. 398. 12–15); *Ep*. 73. 34 (*CSEL* lxxxii. 3. 51. 334).

[19] *The Life and Times of Saint Ambrose* (New York, 1928), I. 2–3.

emperor did not meet with Ambrose until the former had entered Milan in August of 379, and then again in the spring of 380.[20] Even then Ambrose enjoyed no special dominance over the good wishes of Gratian. Of greater importance to the young emperor, according to Gottlieb, was the maintaining of the carefully balanced model of religious tradition and political prudence which his father had bequeathed to him: 'His legislation in the affairs of church and faith complemented the issues dealt with by his predecessor, and he followed the principles of equality laid down by his father.'[21] An important component in this argument is that Trier was far removed from the Trinitarian wranglings of the southern provinces. The bishop of Trier, Britto, has no record of personal collaboration with pro-Nicene bishops who sought to oppose the Illyrian Homoians. And it is unlikely that Ausonius introduced his pupil to the dogmatic controversies of the Nicenes and Homoians in any depth, if at all. Whatever influence the tutor had on the young emperor in religious matters, it would have been to urge Gratian toward a 'liberale Religionspolitik'.[22]

Nautin takes a similar position to Gottlieb, at least with regard to the practical outcome of Gratian's religious and legal position. Because Valentinian I was known to have favoured Nicene catholicism, it follows, though not necessarily, that Gratian would think accordingly. Nautin insists that such a religious orientation did not cloud Gratian's political policies, at least before 379. For Gratian sought above all the interests of the empire and, from the example of his father, to maintain an equal balance between the religious parties of the Nicenes and the Homoians.[23]

At least three laws attributed to Gratian before 379 are commonly cited to underscore the above portrait of the western emperor. The first is an edict dated 17 May 376 in which Gratian confirmed a previous decision of his father by making a distinction and separation of civil and ecclesiastical jurisdiction.[24] Dissensions over religious matters are to be heard by a synod of that diocese, criminal actions are to be tried in civil courts. Of course this also meant that the decisions of ecclesiastical tribunals were not enforced by the power of the State. Only once it was proven that a religious offender posed a threat to the public welfare could the matter be treated as a civil offence. Apart from such exceptions, Valentinian I was

---

[20] *Ambrosius von Mailand*, 48. Where and when Ambrose met with Gratian is a much disputed point and Gottlieb's arguments are not especially convincing.

[21] *Ibid.* 28.

[22] The fact that Gratian retained the Pagan Altar of Victory on the senate steps in Rome and the imperial title 'Pontifex Maximus' until 383 seems to reinforce the idea of Ausonius' influence on his pupil's views of religious tolerance. Cf. Piganiol, *L'Empire chrétien*, 277.

[23] 'Les Premières Relations', 244.   [24] *C. Th.* XVI. 2. 23 (cf. XVI. 2. 12).

content, as was Gratian, to believe that priestly affairs were beyond his jurisdiction.

Another edict which was issued from Trier is more problematic. It is catalogued in the *Codex Theodosianus*, XVI. 5. 4, classified under the category of 'De haereticis'. Addressed to Hesperius p[raefectus] p[raetori]o, it orders that the practice of heretical assemblies should cease and that offending parties should have their meeting places and cultic objects confiscated. The major difficulty with our interpretation of this statute lies in its date, 22 April 376, and that Hesperius is named as praetorian prefect.[25] If in fact this edict was sent to the praetorian prefect of Italy and Gaul, then it would have to be redated to 378 at the earliest, since Decimius Hilarianus Hesperius did not fill this office until 378–9.[26] Our concept of Gratian's attitude toward religious tolerance would also have to be radically altered. Since it is certain that Hesperius was proconsul of Africa from spring of 376 to September 377,[27] Seeck has tried to solve the prosopographical problem by emending the law to read 'ad Hesperium proconsulem Africae'.[28] This solution allows us to maintain the date of 376. There is however the additional problem that the content of the law does not fit with the prevailing understanding of Gratian's religious attitudes in 376 or 378. Nor is Palanque's complicated emendation of relocating the edict to a later year satisfactory.[29] It seems best to accept Seeck's revision, conceding that Gratian issued a law ordering the confiscation of cultic places of heretics. 'But', says Piganiol, 'as it was addressed to Hesperius as proconsul of Africa, it is likely that it was concerned solely with the Donatists.'[30] Gottlieb convincingly defends this interpretation by noting that Valentinian had already promulgated such a law against the Donatists (*C. Th.* XVI. 6. 1), as he had against the Photinians and the Manichees.[31] Gratian's law of 376 seems to reflect this previous legislation: 'Previously on behalf of the religion of catholic sanctity and so

---

[25] *C. Th.* VIII. 5. 34 makes the same error.

[26] *PLRE* i. 428, 'Hesperius 2'; *C. Th.* XVI. 5. 5.

[27] T. Barnes, 'Proconsuls of Africa, 337–392', *Phoenix*, 39 (1985), 151, 153. Cf. A. H. M. Jones, 'Collegiate Prefectures', *JRS* 54 (1964), 78, who observes that a common cause of error in the Theodosian Code is that men who were subsequently praetorian prefects are given this title in laws addressed to them when holding lower offices earlier in their career. *C. Th.* XVI. 5. 4 is cited as a primary instance of this error.

[28] *Regesten*, 246. Cf. *C. Th.* XV. 7. 3.

[29] 'Sur la date d'une loi de Gratien contre l'hérésie', *Revue historique*, 168 (1931), 87–90, criticized by E. Stein, 'La Liste des préfets du Prétoire', *Byzantion*, 9 (1934), 341; M. J. Higgins, 'Reliability of Titles and Dates in Codex Theodosianus', *Byzantion*, 10 (1935), 635–6.

[30] Piganiol, *L'Empire chrétien*, 227–8, n. 7.   [31] *Ambrosius von Mailand*, 77.

that encroaching assemblies of heretics should cease, we order . . .' It is reasonable to believe that schismatics such as the Donatists would have counted as 'heretics' to Gratian in 376 as they did to Valentinian; both emperors maintaining, nevertheless, relative policies of religious tolerance in the west.

A third ruling of Gratian's is known to us purely by implication. In an edict issued from Milan on 3 August 379 reference is made to a former rescript 'which was recently issued from Sirmium' (*C. Th.* XVI. 5. 5) that the new legislation now nullified. The implication is that the previous rescript allowed a degree of religious toleration in the west which Gratian no longer approved. The vast majority of historians, such as Homes Dudden, Piganiol, and Hanson, link this so-called 'edict of toleration' from Sirmium with a description found in Socrates and Sozomen detailing Gratian's rulings immediately after the battle of Hadrianople (9 August 378).[32] It is not absolutely certain that the implied rescript and the legislation mentioned by the ancient historians are identical. Socrates (upon whom Sozomen is dependent here) states that Gratian first recalled all bishops who had been exiled under Valens, and that he gave the legal right to all religious sects freedom of assembly—except of course those groups already outlawed, namely, the Eunomians, Photinians, and Manichaeans. If the 'rescript' issued from Sirmium is a reference to these enactments, then it must pertain only to the second part of the ruling since Gratian never nullified his recall of exiled bishops. For now it suffices to show that both the 'rescript' and the accounts from the ancient histories confirm a continued policy of neutrality by Gratian toward the majority of religious groups at least as late as August 379, and that he did not favour the Nicenes by public policy over the Homoians. We will return to the question of the legal status of religious toleration when we examine the edict of 3 August 379 in greater detail in the next chapter.

2. RELIGIOUS POLITICS AT MILAN BEFORE *DE FIDE*, I–II

The policy of religious tolerance advocated by the western emperors had practical consequences not all of which were seen. Its net effect for Neo-Nicenes and Homoians over the last decade had been to create something like a 'demilitarized zone' between these identity groups. Arius and Arianism had long achieved the status of topoi in the theological literature

---

[32] Socrates, *HE* V. 2 (*PG* lxvii. 568A–B); Sozomen, *HE* VII. 1. 3 (*GCS* l. 302).

of Neo-Nicenes as the quintessential heretic and his heresy, whereas the doctrine of the *homoousios* in the minds of its opponents remained a 'hated and detestable, distorted and perverse profession which is scorned and rejected as a diabolical instrument and doctrine of demons'.[33] There was no constructive dialogue between these groups in the later fourth century, only literary bombardments, aimed at the enemy though written for the edification of one's own peers. The ordained absence of imperial recognition of any one religious persuasion effectively expropriated the power of ecclesiastical condemnations by not reinforcing their depositions. As we saw in Chapter 2, this state of affairs probably saved the post-Ariminum Homoians from an early extinction. But policies of religious tolerance could also serve as cloaks for limited mobility in the fortification of one's position. Auxentius of Milan had certainly taken advantage of this unofficial flexibilty in Italy and Gaul. Others would do the same in later years.

Ambrose had tried initially to mirror the prevailing imperial attitudes toward his clergy and people at Milan, but this eventually worked against him. We know no more than fragments about a period of time on which Ambrose provides only scant comment years afterwards when he is more self-confident and secure. The chronology of events is almost impossible to determine with any certainty, but it seems that, sometime between 376 and 378, a certain Julian Valens arrived in Milan having come from Illyricum. In one of the synodical letters of the council of Aquileia, he is said to have formerly held the see of Pettau (Poetovio), replacing an 'orthodox' bishop, but was afterwards rejected by the people: 'he was not able to remain in Pettau, now he agitates in Milan after the overthrow of his country, or should we say betrayal of his country.'[34] It is not clear what is meant by Valens' 'betrayal of his country', which is probably related to an earlier statement that Valens 'was desecrated by the impiety of the Goths'.[35] A reference in *De fide*, II, suggests that Valens received the bishopric of Pettau as a kind of reward (*munus*) when it was overrun by the Goths on the grounds that he evidently shared their Arian perspective.[36] On account of his heterodox theology, which was tantamount

---

[33] 'Letter of Auxentius' describing Ulfila's opinion of heretics in *Scholia* 305ʳ. 45 (Gryson, *Scolies*, 238).

[34] *Ep.* 2. 10 (*CSEL* lxxxii. 3. 323. 122–6).

[35] *Ep.* 2. 9 (*CSEL* lxxxii. 3. 322. 108–10).

[36] In the conclusion of *De fide*, II. 16. 140, Ambrose is perorating against the Gothic invasions which have brought both insecurities of state and blasphemy of religion: 'It is not pleasant to remember the murders, tortures, and exiles of confessors, priesthoods given to the impious, or rewards to traitors' (*munera proditorum*). Since Julian Valens is declared to

to his alignment with the invaders, he was not accepted by the congregation. Thus Valens became a twofold traitor, with regard to his *patria* and to the true faith; both themes being closely related to each other by Ambrose in *De fide*, I–II.

Shortly after Julian Valens had been installed at Pettau, he was forced to leave the city by the factions within it. He then came to Italy and Milan, where 'he now, by means of illicit ordinations, associates himself with those like himself and seeks to implant seeds of his impiety and treachery into any degenerate person'.[37] We are probably correct in supposing that Valens had established himself at the head of the Homoian community at Milan, carrying on a kind of clandestine operation which began to trouble the peace of the churches throughout north Italy. Through ordinations and spreading the perfidious 'seeds' of Homoian doctrine, Valens presented a threat to Ambrose sufficient that the latter besought the emperor in 381 to take legal action against Valens by banning him from the city.[38] Some of his seeds had indeed taken root among those who once had been proponents of the Nicene faith: the *gesta* of the council of Aquileia tell of the presbyter Attalus who was condemned for not professing the Nicene creed along with Palladius, despite the fact that he had once subscribed in writing to that faith. He is further described by that council as a disciple of Julian Valens.[39]

Julian Valens was not without supplemental assistance in his efforts at Milan. Sometime after his arrival in Milan, Ursinus, arch-rival of Damasus for the Roman see, appeared in the metropolitan city and joined with Valens in the task of covertly nurturing anti-Nicene sentiments. Another synodical letter from the council of Aquileia accounts for Ursinus' activities at Milan as follows: 'he was in league and joined with the Arians at this time with who, along with Valens, he tried to throw the church of Milan into confusion; holding detestable assemblies sometimes before the doors of the synagogue, sometimes in the homes of the Arians, hatching secret schemes and uniting their followers.'[40] Ursinus himself was not a Homoian,[41] and his motivation was different from that of Valens in that he was utilizing the factious situation at Milan for his own ends. He had

---

have aligned himself with the Gothic invaders, the latter part of the description 'impiorum sacerdotia, munera proditionum' could easily be a passing reference to him.

[37] *Ep.* 2. 10 (*CSEL* lxxxii. 3. 323. 119–21). [38] *CSEL* lxxxii. 3. 323. 117–19.

[39] *Ep.* 2. 9 (*CSEL* lxxxii. 3. 322. 105–6).

[40] *Ep.* 5 (extra coll.). 3 (*CSEL* lxxxii. 3. 183–4. 33–7).

[41] *Ep.* 5 (extra coll.). 3 (*CSEL* lxxxii. 3. 184. 37–40). Given Ursinus' activities at Milan, it is hardly likely that Ursinus was once a Luciferian as M. R. Green argues in 'Supporters of the Anti-pope Ursinus', *JTS* 22 (1971), 531–8.

already been banished from the city limits of Rome on two occasions, and was then finally exiled to Gaul under Valentinian I.[42] Gratian reiterated his father's decrees against Ursinus at the request of the Roman synod of 378,[43] but the legislation was only partially enforced. Ursinus was wise enough not to try to return to Rome. Instead it seems that he left Gaul and went to Milan. Even then he hoped to overthrow Damasus, so it is possible that he wanted to take advantage of the undercurrent of strife in Ambrose's city as a means of unsettling the Nicene stability upon which Damasus had maintained his power. But we can only make conjectures about why the former deacon of Liberius enmeshed himself in this alien alliance. From the synodical letter of the council of Aquileia addressed to Gratian, Ursinus was reported to be still sowing discord at Rome, presumably through the instigation of his followers there, and doing the same at Milan. The emperor was urged by the council to expel him once and for all.

There is no proof for us to accept Palanque's reconstruction of this period, namely that after 375 there was a 'changement d'atmosphère' in which Valens (and Ursinus) stayed their opposition, only to resume once Justina arrived in Milan.[44] Valens could not have arrived before 375, nor is there any indication in our fragmented evidence to suggest a hiatus in his activity once he began. It is certain that Justina's arrival in the city and her immediate political patronage of the Homoians contributed, more than any other factor, to stirring up anti-Nicene sentiments against the bishop.

By late spring of 378, Gratian was on his way to assist the eastern Emperor Valens in his campaign against the Goths who were ravaging the countryside in Thrace and Moesia. Two years earlier Valens had agreed to allow these peoples to inhabit certain parts of Thrace.[45] Now, after a winter of starvation exacerbated by the cruel exploitation of their Roman overseers, and the assassination of the imperially disposed Gothic

---

[42] 'Quae gesta sunt inter Liberium et Felicem episcopos', 10–12 (*CSEL* xxxv. 4. 7–18); (*Ep.* 12) 'Idem Augg. Maximino Vicario Urbis Romae' (*CSEL* xxxv. 53. 19–23). A law issued under Honorius on 4 Feb. 400 (*C. Th.* XVI. 2. 35) makes reference to Gratian's actions against Ursinus, who was expelled 100 miles outside the Roman city limits.

[43] In the rescript, Aquilinus is ordered: 'Ursinum quidem Gallia cohercet' (*CSEl* xxxv. 55. 14–15).

[44] *Saint Ambroise*, 73.

[45] Ammianus, XXXI. 12. 8 (Seyfarth, 188–9); Socrates, *HE* IV. 34 (*PG* lxvii. 554B); Jordanes, *Getica*, XXV. 131–2 (C. C. Mierow, 'Jordanes: The Origin and Deeds of the Goths' (Ph.D. diss., Princeton University, 1908), 41). According to Ammianus, the Gothic general Fritigern had sent a Christian presbyter as an envoy to Valens at Hadrianople requesting Thrace as a permanent habitation for his people.

chieftain Fritigern, the Goths revolted *en masse*. Gratian was still at Sirmium when Valens decided to attack at Hadrianople for reasons that are still not completely understood.[46] The results were catastrophic: the Roman forces suffered a stunning defeat on 9 August in which Valens and a large portion of the army perished.[47]

In the perilous aftermath of Hadrianople, the barbarians completely overran Thrace and came to the very walls of Constantinople.[48] Gratian, remaining in Sirmium for the winter, realized that he could not manage the entire empire alone; in addition to the Gothic uprising he was forced to contend with new incursions by the Alemanni along the Rhine. To cope with the situation in Thrace, he recalled Theodosius, the son of Valentinian I's *magister equitum*, who had retired prematurely to his estates in Spain, and on 19 January 379 proclaimed him Augustus at Sirmium.[49]

As panic spread through Pannonia many fled west across the Alps. Among the refugees was the court of Valentinian II and his mother Justina, arriving in Milan probably during the early autumn of 378. It is quite possible that Gratian himself ordered their transfer from Sirmium to the imperial residence in Milan until tensions abated. As the influx of refugees streamed in from the besieged Illyrian provinces, the number of Homoians in Milan was considerably augmented, creating new needs for religious accommodation in the Homoian community. These needs were soon expressed in a request to Gratian for the use of a basilica in the city. Gratian responded by ordering a church to be sequestered:[50] a decision which conformed to his political policy of toleration, although it demonstrates that a policy of tolerance is not the same as non-interference. Homes Dudden allows his zeal for orthodoxy to override his historical judgement when he declares that the Homoians 'had the audacity to occupy a Catholic basilica'.[51] It seems, rather, that Gratian willingly gave

---

[46] For a thorough and concise treatment of these issues, see T. A. Burns, 'The Battle of Adrianople: A Reconsideration', *Historia*, 22 (1973), 336–45.

[47] Ammianus, XXXI. 13. 12–17 (Seyfarth, 193–4); Zosimus, IV. 24. 1–2 (Paschoud, 286).

[48] Socrates, *HE* v. 2 (*PG* lxvii. 565C); Sozomen, *HE* VII. 2. 1 (*GCS* l. 302).

[49] Socrates, *HE* v. 2 (*PG* lxvii. 568B); Sozomen, *HE* VII. 2. 1 (*GCS* l. 302–3); Zosimus, IV. 24. 4 (Paschoud, 286); *LRE* l. 156. Theodosius was given charge not only of the regions which Valens had ruled, but also of the dioceses of Macedonia and Dacia (see *LRG* ii. 1099 n. 44). The sudden retreat of Theodosius from political and military life had occurred in 376, when his father the elder Theodosius was executed in Africa, the victim of influential rivals once Valentinan I was dead (Jerome, *Chron.* 379 (*PL* xxvii. 507–8); Orosius, *Historiarum adversum paganos*, VII. 33. 7 (*PL* xxxi. 1145–6); Theodoret, *HE* v. 5. 1 (*GCS* xliv. 284)). Cf. Ch. 7 n. 48.

[50] *De spiritu sancto*, I. 1. 19–21 (*CSEL* lxxxix. 24–5).   [51] *Life and Times*, i. 190.

the building over to the Homoians, perhaps at the personal request of Justina. As portrayed by Rufinus, Justina had begun to manifest her Arian sentiments openly once her husband (Valentinian I) was dead and by the time she had come to Milan.[52] There is no doubt that her patronage was enthusiastically received by the Milanese Homoians, who, it will be recalled, were relegated to meeting in their own homes. When Ambrose reflected about the loss of the basilica two years later, Gratian's actions were portrayed as euphemistically as possible, blame for the emperor's decision to sequester the basilica being laid on the influence of others.[53] This was partially true.

The entire episode must have been an affront to the bishop of Milan. The court, now residing in the city, was openly hostile to Ambrose, since he was an avowed adherent of the heretical Homoousian teaching. Concurrent with the issue of the basilica, a campaign of hostility developed against Ambrose in which the bishop was accused of breaking apart and selling the church's sacred vessels (*vasa mystica*) in order to ransom captives from the barbarians. It seems Ambrose's motives were being impugned by his opponents,[54] perhaps because this act of charity was conveniently being used as a subtle means of erasing the Arian past in Milan. The melting down of the church plate destroyed the memory of those Christian families (supporters of Ambrose's Arian predecessor) whose names would have been engraved on the edges of the revered patens and along the rims of the Eucharistic chalices.[55] Whatever the exact reason for the Homoian backlash, it was successful in creating further pressure on the bishop. Ambrose was forced to justify his actions before the congregation on more than one occasion.[56]

In the midst of these mounting hostilities, the Emperor Gratian wrote to Ambrose requesting a *libellum* explaining his faith: 'You also, holy emperor Gratian . . . wish to hear about my faith.'[57] By the end of 378 Ambrose had replied with a volume in two books which was the first of his dogmatic treatises and which marked his entry into the polemical contest between Nicenes and Homoians.

---

[52] Rufinus, *HE* II. 15 (*PL* xxi. 523C). Cf. Socrates, *HE* v. 11.

[53] *De spir. sanc.* (*CSEL* lxxxix. 25. 18–27).

[54] *De officiis*, II. 28. 136 (*PL* xvi. 148A–B).

[55] Brown, *Power and Persuasion in Late Antiquity*, 96.

[56] *De officiis*, II. 28. 137 (*PL* xvi. 148B); II. 15. 70–1 (*PL* xvi. 129A–B).

[57] *De fide*, I. praef. 1 (*CSEL* lxxviii. 3–4); III. 1. 1 (*CSEL* lxxviii. 108). The actual letter of Gratian is not extant.

3. THE PUBLICATION OF *DE FIDE*, I–II

Why did Gratian ask Ambrose for an explanation *de fide* when he did? Solutions to this question have generally been based on an assumed prior relationship between the emperor and the bishop. Homes Dudden, for instance, declared that Gratian sought a treatise from Ambrose since the latter 'had already acquired a reputation as defender and restorer of orthodoxy'.[58] Paredi suggested that Gratian contacted Ambrose 'because at Sirmium everyone remembered Ambrose's resolute intervention in 376 for the election of a Nicene bishop'.[59] Both hypotheses can be quickly discounted. As the results of our preceding analysis have shown, there is no reason to suppose that Gratian would have sought a relatively unknown bishop who was over 500 miles distant from Sirmium. Nautin rightly observes that Ambrose had written no dogmatic works to distinguish himself as a defender of Nicaea, nor had he yet become the celebrated doctor of later years.[60] If Gratian had wanted instruction on the faith, he would surely have had clerics closer to him in Trier capable of fulfilling such a request. Or, if Gratian desired an exposition from an important figure of Nicene orthodoxy, why did he not seek out Damasus at Rome, whose views would have been well known to him by 378?

We cannot say that Gratian was devoid of any knowledge of the Milanese bishop. As we ascertained earlier, Ambrose had some personal contact with the emperor, probably before *De fide*, I–II, was written. But the only reference to an actual meeting between the two is found in *De fide*, III. 1. 1: 'Since, most clement emperor, you ordered for your guidance some occasion of describing my faith, and you yourself had encouraged my timidity in person so that I wrote the two books just as one ready for combat, in which I might show the certain ways and paths of faith.'[61] There is no scholarly consensus on where and when the meeting took place; whether Gratian received Ambrose in 378 either *en route* to Sirmium before the battle of Hadrianople, which is the traditional rendering of events, or while Gratian wintered at Sirmium, or that Ambrose never went to Sirmium and his rendezvous with the emperor for the first time

[58] *Life and Times*, i. 189.
[59] *Saint Ambrose*, 180. Cf. Mara (*Patrology*, iv. 146), who comes to a similar conclusion.
[60] 'Les Premières Relations', 237.
[61] *CSEL* lxxviii. 108. 1–5. Reinforcement for a face-to-face meeting between the two comes from the opening line of Gratian's letter to Ambrose, 'Cupio valde, quam recordor absentem, ut cum quo mente sum, cum eo etiam corpore sim praesenti' (*CSEL* lxxix. 3. 3–4).

was not until the latter passed through Milan in the summer of 379. None of these views is free from problems. If the *De fide*, I–II, is properly dated to the autumn of 378 then the above passage makes it plain that Ambrose saw the emperor in person (*coram*) some time before he published his work. This hardly provides an answer, however, to the question why Gratian requested an explanation of Ambrose's faith.

According to Nautin's theory, the reason Ambrose was asked to give an acount of his faith is because he was being attacked by the Illyrian Homoians, Palladius in particular, who were charging the Milanese bishop with heresy. 'Or il n'était à cette époque qu'un seul moyen pour se défaire d'un évêque gênant, c'était d'attaquer sa doctrine, car . . . un évêque qui tombe dans l'hérésie n'est plus évêque.'[62] Gratian would have been concerned to investigate such charges on the grounds that he was seeking to conciliate the Illyrian Homoians now that the Emperor Valens was dead and because of their influence on the population and on account of their link with the bishop of Constantinople, Demophilus, who was a Homoian. Gratian was therefore assuming the role of a diplomat by attempting to reconcile ecclesiastical differences which existed between Homoians and Nicenes. When the emperor requested from Ambrose a profession of his faith, he was taking the charges of heresy seriously, but also he hoped to secure an opportunity 'd'un accord doctrinal qui rétablirait la paix religieuse dans la région'.[63]

Nautin's article is successful in that we are able to renounce completely the image of Gratian as a pliable young man seeking in the person of Ambrose a master of theology and spiritual counsellor. The engaging interpretation of Ambrose's plea in *De fide*, I. 20. 134, prods us to recognize just how tolerant Gratian was in listening to the viewpoints of the Homoians while he resided at Sirmium.[64] But Nautin's overall explanation of the circumstances surrounding the publication of *De fide*, I–II, is not adequate for at least two reasons. First, Nautin is in danger of contradicting himself when he asserts that Ambrose had no reputation as a defender of the Nicene faith yet attracted the attention of the Homoian bishops in Illyricum to such an extent that they felt compelled to denounce him to the emperor. What would Ambrose have done to warrant such

---

[62] 'Les Premières Relations', 40. Cf. Meslin, *Les Ariens*, 46 n. 82.

[63] Meslin, *Les Ariens*, 239–40.

[64] Ibid. 241; *De fide*, I. 20. 134: 'And now Lord, leaving behind those who slander you and your enemies, grant yourself to us and purge (*sanctifica*) the ears of our ruler Gratian, and also all into whose hands this book should come. Keep my ears free from the filth of treacherous talk that it may never lodge in them' (CSEL lxxviii. 56).

attention in the Pannonian provinces, excluding his reputed nomination of the pro-Nicene Anemius at Sirmium in 375, before the writing of *De fide*? A second difficulty, which is connected to the first, is the central role which Nautin attributes to the attacks on Palladius of Ratiaria, such that Palladius is said to be the primary target in *De fide*, I–II.

Undoubtedly Ambrose was acutely aware of his (unnamed) critics when he first wrote *De fide*,[65] and he fully realized that his work would be read by them. Nevertheless, the *De fide* is not written in the style of an apology as if the author were fending off explicit attacks, nor does it seem to be directed at any one individual.

> Grant forbearance, holy emperor, if I turn attention to the words of those men for a short while. But who in particular shall I mention—Eunomius, or Arius, or Aetius, or their teachers?
> And so they are divided into many forms: some follow Eunomius or Aetius, others after Palladius, or Demophilus or Auxentius and his sort of heresy, or other types as well.[66]

As we will see below, Palladius was responsible for mobilizing a Homoian reaction to *De fide*, I–II, but there is a lack of evidence to infer that the same situation existed before books I and II were written.

If the driving force behind Gratian did not stem from accusations in Illyricum, then what accounts for his request in the autumn of 378 that Ambrose prepare a statement of faith? The most obvious alternative is to consider the situation in Milan. Since Gratian's request and Ambrose's composition of the *De fide* occurred at the same time as, or just after, the heated basilica affair in Milan, then it is reasonable to suppose that this was the context for a series of accusations made against the bishop. Glaesener has proposed that Justina, following the controversy and ultimate sequestering of the basilica, was responsible for flooding Gratian with a series of objections to the Homoousian theology of the bishop.[67] A charge of heresy against the metropolitan of north Italy would certainly draw the attention of the emperor; just as Hilary of Poitiers had done against Auxentius during Valentinian I's reign. Of course we must beware of the historical tendency to inflate the role of Justina before the early 380s. This does not rule out that such complaints could have been articulated by the expanding anti-Nicene presence in Milan: there was present at least one Homoian bishop (Julian Valens), and there were those loyal to

---

[65] *De fide*, I. 1. 4 (*CSEL* lxxviii. 6. 26–31); 2. 14 (9. 24); 9. 58 (25. 1–3).
[66] *De fide*, I. 6. 44 (*CSEL* lxxviii. 18. 10–12); 6. 45 (19. 19–22).
[67] 'L'Empereur Gratien et saint Ambroise', 472.

the memory of Auxentius who had been recently bolstered by the influx of Illyrian refugees. The fact that Gratian had recently sequestered the basilica would have provided further encouragement to these Milanese Homoians in their ongoing campaign against Ambrose.

The result was that the emperor was prompted to demand from Ambrose a clarification of his views. Even if Gratian was personally disposed to the Nicene form of faith, as hinted by Ambrose several times,[68] accusations of gross heresy could not be ignored. It is quite likely that Gratian had been saddled with similar criticisms of the Nicene position in Sirmium, where he had been located since June. The most persistent of these charges had been to accuse the Homoousians of tritheism because of their insistence that God was three equal and eternal *ousiai*. To the Homoians, this was a kind of idolatry that was tantamount to contemporary Paganism,[69] or else it produced a confusion in the Godhead reminiscent of the theology of Marcellus or Photinus, both of whom had been condemned.

Ambrose responded to Gratian's demand with a treatise in two books which was written, according to the author, not for the emperor's instruction, but for his approval.[70] In a brief summary of his faith, Ambrose stresses the unity of the divine essence, distinguishing his Trinitarianism from the commonly known errors of the day. He is acutely aware of the accusations of tritheism against Homoousian theology and attempts to undercut the argument, in one instance, by charging the Arians with tritheism because they divide the *divinitas* of the Trinity.[71] Ambrose's own position for the indivisibility of the Godhead is built upon the well-worn argument in western theology that the divine nature is common to the Father, Son, and Holy Spirit. The plurality inherent to the Trinity is declared to be one in name and power (*potestas*). Christ commanded the disciples to go and baptize the nations in the name, not names, of the Father, Son, and Holy Spirit (Matthew 28: 19). Less common in Latin anti-Arian polemics, with the exception of Marius Victorinus, is the emphasis on the one *potestas* of the Trinity:[72] 'We confess Father and Son and Holy Spirit with the result that the fullness of divinity and unity of power exist in perfect Trinity.' *Potestas*, like *perfectus*, is used here to refer to the whole of Trinitarian relations, but it applies more directly to the

---

[68] *De fide*, I. 18. 121 (*CSEL* lxxviii. 51. 17–18); II. 16. 139 (106. 23–5).

[69] *Scholia*, 345ʳ. 128–9 (Gryson, *Scolies*, 310–12); 303ʳ. 36 (Gryson, *Scolies*, 230–2).

[70] *De fide*, I. prol. 1 (*CSEL* lxxviii. 4. 6–7).   [71] *De fide*, I. 1. 10 (8. 25–9).

[72] *Potestas*, or the scriptural term *virtus* (1 Cor. 1: 24), is used quite liberally in *De fide* and elsewhere as a means of defining the essentially shared nature of Father and Son, or the entire Trinity. See *De virginibus*, III. 1. 2 (*PL* xvi. 232B–C); *De excessu fratris*, I. 13 (*PL* xvi. 1351A); *De fide*, I. 4. 33 (*CSEL* lxxviii. 16. 23); I. 17. 112 (48. 37–8); II. 10. 87 (88. 24).

Son, who is called in 1 Corinthians 1: 24 the 'power and wisdom of God'. Thus Ambrose writes in defence of the divine nature of Christ that shares all the attributes of the Father: 'He is called "word", he is called "Son", he is called "power", he is called "Son of God", "wisdom of God". He is the "word" undefiled, he is called "power" because he is perfect, "Son" because he is begotten of the Father, "wisdom" because he is "one with the Father", one in eternity, one in divinity.'[73] Like the Latin writers we reviewed in a previous chapter, the *unum* of the Father and Son is affirmed to its utmost extent in which there is no multiplicity (*multiplex*) because they are *indifferens*. Nor is the term *persona* used as a means of distinguishing Father and Son in books I–II, despite its inclusion in de Romestin's English translation (*NPNF* x).[74] The sole task of the *De fide* is to defend and substantiate the absolutely essential unity of the Father and Son so that no possible wedge of inequality can be driven between them. Given the primacy of this objective, Ambrose says little about the internal operations of Trinitarian relations, and even less about the Holy Spirit, treating the third member of the Trinity only in a later work specially requested by Gratian.[75]

Having defined the content of his faith, Ambrose then turns to consider the disputations of the Arians. The rest of *De fide*, I–II, deals with six propositions which his opponents are said to teach. They are as follows:

1. They affirm that the Son of God is unlike the Father (6. 43–8. 57).
2. They affirm that the Son of God had a beginning in time (9. 58–13. 85).
3. They affirm that he was created (14. 86–19. 131).
4. They deny that he is good (II. 1. 15–3. 33).
5. They deny that he is the true Son of God; they deny his omnipotence (4. 34–6. 51).
6. They deny that he is one in divinity with the Father (7. 52–12. 107).

Ambrose acknowledges that there are different sects of Arians and that there exists disagreement between them. Even so, the bishop betrays a lack of acquaintance with the theology of differing sects, even with the Homoians to whom the above propositions refer. He is reduced to using a rhetorical strategy of attacking his opponents that was already common in the fourth century; that of classifying opposing opinions and persons

---

[73] *De fide*, I. 2. 16 (*CSEL* lxxviii. 10. 32–4).   [74] Compare *De fide*, II. 1. 18; 3. 33.
[75] 'Cupio valde' (*CSEL* lxxix. 3–4).

in relation to previously condemned positions. This method is well exemplified in the writings of Athanasius and Gregory of Nyssa.[76] Thus the *De fide* construes the various denominations of Arianism as a theological whole: Arians are Arians no matter how diverse their historical backgrounds. They have many names, yet they share a common unbelief as well as a common enterprise in breeding dissent and attacking the church: 'I shall call those whom I have to answer by the common name of heretic.'[77] Their heresy is like the fabled Hydra whose head, when cut off, always sprouted a new one. Or, like the monstrous Scylla, heresy has divided itself into many shapes of unbelief while pretending to be a Christian sect.

Using this kind of procedure, Ambrose asserts that Arius (and all Arians therefore) is responsible for teaching that Christ is *dissimilis* (unlike) the Father.

The Apostle says that Christ is the image of the Father, though Arius says that he is unlike (the Father). Why is the term 'image' used if likeness is not meant? People do not prefer to be unlike their portraits, and Arius contends that the Father is unlike the Son, insisting that the Father begot one unlike himself, as if he were impotent, unable to generate one like him.[78]

Predictably the Homoians were outraged by such a charge, as Palladius' *contra Ambrosium* shows. The bishop was clearly not informed about their theology. But Ambrose had at least two reasons for his accusation of *dissimilis* that went beyond the polemical device of amalgamating competing beliefs as a heretical whole. First, he was utterly opposed to their idea that the concept of *generatio* could be modelled after human generation, which meant that the one who generates was temporally prior to the one generated.[79] To impose such an analogy on the generation of the Son was to subject divine generation to the limits of time and physical bodies. Anything begotten, including the Son, must have had a beginning and came into existence from non-existence. Ambrose argued that the *genitus* of the Son was incomprehensible and was begotten impassibly from the Father; both concepts finding equal favour with the Homoians. Where Ambrose diverged from his opponents is that the incomprehensibility of the divine process provided assurance that the generation of the Son was wholly other than human production. Only 'very God from very God'

[76] J. R. Lyman, 'A Topography of Heresy: Mapping the Rhetorical Creation of Arianism', in Barnes and Williams, *Arianism after Arius*, 45–62.
[77] *De fide*, I. 6. 46 (*NPNF* x. 208). 　　　[78] *De fide*, I. 7. 48 (*CSEL* lxxviii. 21. 7–12).
[79] *De fide*, I. 11. 70 (*CSEL* lxxviii. 30–1).

was appropriate to that unique and inviolate transaction which took place 'before all understanding'. *Generatio*, therefore, is nothing less than an extension of nature.[80] These are standard arguments in the anti-Arian arsenal of Latin writers. Ambrose had yet to develop a more contemporary theological sophistication as he shows in *De fide*, III–V, and *De incarnationis domenicae sacramento*, where he is familiar with and refutes the Homoian application of *ingenitus / genitus* as a means to define the separate essences of Father and Son.

Secondly, there is the possibility that Ambrose's characterization of his opponents as those who teach the unlikeness of the Son was to associate them with the adherents of Eunomian theology, which would have had serious political repercussions. Socrates and Sozomen indicate that while Gratian was in Sirmium he had excluded Eunomians, along with the Photinians and Manichees, from the privilege of free assembly in his 'edict of toleration' of 378.[81] This legislation was meant as a provision for the eastern half of the empire now that the Emperor Valens was dead. Anomoianism was not an issue in the west and we do not find any legal enforcement against it from Valentinian I to Theodosius. This should not prevent us from assuming that this form of Arianism shared the same heretical reputation in the west as it had, albeit for different reasons, in the east.[82] Gratian's exclusion of the Eunomians, Photinians, and Manichees from the toleration edict was a perfunctory piece of legislation, offering no surprises since these groups had been condemned before. The new eastern Emperor Theodosius followed suit by condemning Eunomianism on two occasions in 381[83] and periodically throughout his reign.[84] By associating his Homoian opponents, in name and theology, with Aetius and Eunomius, Ambrose sought to make their position as contemptible as possible in the emperor's eyes. Accusations of heresy from a group which ascribed to the same principles as Eunomian theology would lose their credibility and easily be dismissed.

Even though *De fide*, I–II, has little theological originality, it is a tour de force depicting all anti-Nicenes as enemies of the Church and State. Arians are called 'antichrists' (II. 15. 135), compared to Jews (II. 15. 130) and Pagans (I. 13. 85; I. 16. 103), and are blamed for the present troubles

---

[80] *De fide*, I. 17. 110 (47. 21–5).

[81] Socrates, *HE* v. 2 (*PG* lxvii. 568B); Sozomen, *HE* VII. 1. 3 (*GCS* l. 302. 13–15).

[82] The Emperor Valens publicly favoured Homoianism above all other sects (Socrates, *HE* IV. 1 (*PG* lxvii. 465A)), including Anomoianism, which had already been condemned in 360 at the council of Constantinople (Philostorgius, *HE* IV. 12 (*GCS* xxi. 65. 11–22)).

[83] *C. Th.* XVI. 5. 6 (10 Jan. 381), reaffirmed on 19 July 381 in *C. Th.* XVI. 5. 8.

[84] *C. Th.* XVI. 5. 11 (25 July 383); 5. 12 (3 Dec. 383); 5. 13 (21 Jan. 384).

afflicting the Roman Empire. The Gothic invasions, which were predicted in Ezekiel 38: 14 ff. ('That Gog is the Goth'), are the direct result of divine judgement on doctrinal unfaithfulness and persecution of the defenders of Nicaea: 'Enough already and even more have we atoned, Omnipotent God, by our destruction and by our blood for the deaths of confessors, the exiles of priests and wickedness of such impiety. It is clear that those who violate the faith cannot be safe. Turn to us, Lord, and raise up the banners of your faith.'[85] In this closing prayer of Ambrose, God is invoked to grant Gratian military victory because the emperor too believes that the Son is the 'true power and wisdom of God, not confined to time nor created'. For only through the establishment of the true faith will the empire be rescued from the barbarian.

4. THE HOMOIAN REACTION TO *DE FIDE*, I–II

Ambrose's frontal assault against contemporary Arianism did not go unchallenged. Less than two years later[86] the bishop found it necessary to defend and expand upon his earlier arguments with three more books.[87] Ambrose had been relieved to learn that Gratian was favourably impressed with the arguments in *De fide*, I–II,[88] the latter strongly hinting at his own agreement with Homoousian theology in a letter written from Sirmium in the first half of 379.[89] But now Ambrose felt the need to defend himself again, evidently aware of the passionate response which the *De fide* had invoked. The emperor also had asked for further elaboration, but specifically about the Holy Spirit. In the preface to book III of *De fide*, Ambrose explains the necessity for his further labours.

Because certain depraved minds, fixed on the sowing of disputes with their pen, are arousing even further labours to be done, and also the pious concern of Your

---

[85] *De fide*, II. 16. 141 (106). Cf. *Ep.* 36. 28, 'Ad Constantium'.

[86] Faller, *CSEL* lxxviii. 8*–9*.

[87] Despite Ambrose's allusion to the literary unity of the five books (v . prol. 7 (*CSEL* lxxviii. 218. 43–5)), *De fide*, III–V, were never part of Ambrose's original intention. Indeed, he had not yet decided to compose them when he responded to Gratian's letter ('Cupio valde') in his 'Non mihi affectus' (*CSEL* lxxxii. 3. 219–21), roughly datable to 379/80. For the problems in dating both letters, see n. 104.

[88] 'I sent two books and, because they were approved by your Clemency, I am not fearful of the danger' (*Ep.* 12 (extra coll.). 7 (*CSEL* lxxxii. 3. 221. 61–2)).

[89] 'Cupio valde', 2: 'He will teach me when I do not deny whom I trust to be my God and Lord, not imposing on Him—namely, being a creature—as I see in myself; whereby I confess that I am able to add nothing to Christ' (*CSEL* lxxix. 3. 8–11).

Clemency invokes other matters wishing for demonstration in many things which you approved in a few, it is necessary for me to describe somewhat more fully those issues which I only lightly touched upon earlier so that we do not seem to have abandoned these views as if carelessly asserted, but rather proposed them in the assurance of fidelity.[90]

Although the mention of 'depraved minds' is not identified, it is almost certainly a reference to Palladius of Ratiaria, whose position, *inter alia*, Ambrose had attacked in *De fide*, I–II.

We know practically nothing about this Illyrian bishop[91] prior to 379, when he appears suddenly as a spokesman for western Homoianism and as the arch-opponent of Ambrose. His leadership role would seem to indicate that the great figures of his generation, such as Valens of Mursa and Ursacius of Singidunum, had disappeared.[92] Palladius moved to the centre of the theological stage when he published a withering polemic against *De fide*, I–II. Only a fragment of this polemic is extant among the corpus of the *scholia* found in the Paris MS Latinus 8907 (336[r]. 1–337[r]. 49).[93] This portion consists of a response or rebuttal to two extracts from the *De fide* (I. 5. 41–2; I. 6. 43–7). It is virtually certain that this fragment was written by the bishop of Ratiaria (not Maximinus) and represents a separate and earlier work than the longer *apologia* which the same author wrote in response to the disgraceful treatment of the Homoian bishops at the council of Aquileia (337[r]. 50–349[r]. 4).[94]

In response to the first extract from *De fide*, Palladius utterly rejects Ambrose's argument that the Homoians teach the doctrine of *dissimilis*. 'If we believe that the Son said, "Whatever the Father does the Son also does similarly" [John 5: 19], how can we claim he is "unlike"?'[95] Ambrose is said to accuse them of teaching *dissimilis* for the simple reason that they say the Son is not co-existent and co-eternal with the unbegotten Father. And yet, says Palladius, even Ambrose admits that the Son is begotten and thereby differs from the Father. Palladius' problem with Ambrose's

---

[90] *De fide*, III. prol. 2 (*CSEL* lxxviii. 108).

[91] With confidence, he can be identified with the Palladius who assisted in 366 in the investigation of Germinius of Sirmium, who was being questioned for teaching doctrine contrary to the Ariminum creed ('Incipit Rescriptum Germini ad Rufianum, Palladium et Ceteros' in Hilary, *CAP* B VI (*CSEL* lxv. 160 ff.)).

[92] Gryson, *Scolies*, 83.

[93] Kauffmann, *Aus der Schule des Wulfila*, p. xxxvi; C. P. Hammond-Bammel, 'From the School of Maximinus: The Arian Material in Paris MS. Lat. 8907', *JTS* 31 (1980), 394–5.

[94] McLynn has shown how the two documents were published together after 381, which is how they were preserved in the *Scholia*. 'The "Apology" of Palladius', 54–7.

[95] *Scholia*, 336[r]. 7–10 (Gryson, *Scolies*, 264).

hermeneutics—a problem endemic to the majority of western anti-Arian writers—is that virtually no ontological distinction is allowed to exist between the Father and the Son. Ambrose is asked at one point, 'why do you calumniate that we divide Christ from the Father just because we say he is never one with the Father?'[96] In his comments on the second extract (*De fide*, I. 6. 43–7), Palladius accuses the doctrine of *homoousios* of obviating the personal qualities (*propriaetates*) of the Father and Son which results in the denial of both, since the properties peculiar to Father and Son are run together and lost. Such a view also does violence to the integrity of the Father–Son relationship. If the Son is pleased to be subject to the Father in all things, why does Ambrose insist that the Father must beget him as an equal? For this 'monstrous blasphemy' Ambrose is urged to beg favour from God 'against whom you sinned by impiously denying the character of both. For you acknowledge neither the Father nor the Son.'[97]

In both extracts, Palladius takes great offence at his opponent's characterization of Homoian doctrine since, although he does not really know them or their writings, he nevertheless condemns their views and attaches stigmas to them which are not true. Even worse is that the emperor has been deceived by Ambrose and now favours his position: 'Why, moreover, do you seek favour from the emperor when, by his command, you are not convicted of impiety, nor is a catholic and doctor of the truth [Palladius?] able to be heard against you?'[98] Only by 'sinning against religion' is Ambrose said to have secured the emperor's patronage for his heresy. Palladius' admission is especially significant for it acknowledges a deterioration of Gratian's stance of religious neutrality sometime before the council of Aquileia (381). This should not however be construed to mean that Gratian had changed political policy in order to favour the Nicenes, at least not yet.

Towards the end of the fragment, Palladius sternly admonishes Ambrose with a series of imperative verbs to put away any 'unconstructive and superfluous report of a subtle deceit',[99] and to cease from 'monstrous comparisons'; a reference to Ambrose's offensive analogy between his

---

[96] *Scholia*, 337[r]. 10–14 (Gryson, *Scolies*, 272).

[97] *Scholia*, 337[v]. 48*b*–49 (Gryson, *Scolies*, 270).

[98] *Scholia*, 336[v]. 44–6 (Gryson, *Scolies*, 270). Faller (*CSEL* lxxix. 13*) has noted a parallel between Palladius' words here and *De fide*, I. 6. 44: 'Da veniam, sancte imperator' (*CSEL* lxxviii. 18. 10).

[99] *Scholia*, 337[r]. 32–4 (Gryson, *Scolies*, 272).

opponents and the mythical Hydra and Scylla. Another fragment of an apology on behalf of those condemned at Aquileia (381)[100] likewise upbraids Ambrose for calling Palladius, Demophilus, and Auxentius (of Milan) 'Arians' as in *De fide*, I. 6. 45. Rather, Ambrose is told to 'wake up' (*resipisce*) to an understanding of the truth, for only by changing his course can he hope to escape the fire of Gehenna to which he is being ineluctably drawn.

The significance of Palladius' work should not be underestimated. The western Homoians had produced almost no known polemical literature prior to this time, and Palladius' *contra Ambrosium* offered a formidable offensive, not only in attacking the Homoousian theological platform, but in asserting the distinctiveness of post-Ariminum theology. A strong testimony to the polemical value of the treatise in Homoian circles is that it was still circulating at the end of the fifth century, when Vigilius of Thapsus felt compelled to write a short refutation of it.[101]

Following the publication of *De fide*, I–II, Ambrose now preached a regular diet of anti-Arianism to his congregation. Many of these sermons form the content of the next three books of *De fide*,[102] which he compiled in his response to Palladius. The bishop was obviously concerned with the Homoian counter-arguments. Despite the fact that Gratian originally had asked for further elaboration on books I–II with particular reference to the role of the Holy Spirit,[103] Ambrose chose only to defend and re-inforce the same arguments he had advanced in *De fide*, I–II. Not until the beginning of book V of *De fide* does Ambrose acknowledge Gratian's request and promises 'a fuller disputation on the Spirit' (V. prol. 7) in a future publication.

In his only known letter ('Cupio valde') to Ambrose, which can best be

[100] *Scholia*, 337ʳ. 50–1 (Gryson, *Scolies*, 274).

[101] *Contra Arianos*, II. 50 (*PL* lxii. 230A).

[102] Cf. III. 17. 142: 'ferias hodierni sermonis habeamus' (*CSEL* lxxviii. 158. 37–8); IV. 10. 119: 'Considerate, quid lectum sit hodie' (199. 15–16); V. prol. 8: 'Date ergo veniam, si quos prolixioris huiusce sermonis offendit audacia' (219. 51–2); V. prol. 9: 'Vos nobis estis omnia, qui haec auditis aut legitis' (219. 62).

[103] 'Cupio valde', 3: 'I ask that you devote to this matter, just as you gave me that treatise, faithful disputation by enlarging in particular on the Holy Spirit; show from Scripture and reasoning that he is God' (*CSEL* lxxix. 4). The meaning of 'des ipsum tractatum' is not completely clear. De Labriolle (*The Life and Times of Saint Ambrose*, 273) and Glaesener ('L'Empereur Gratien et saint Ambroise', 376) believe the passage, when taken prima facie, indicates that Ambrose wrote *De fide* twice. But a more likely interpretation of the passage incorporating the rest of the sentence 'augendo illic de sancto spiritu' implies that Gratian wants an expansion or second version of books I–II with additional material on the Holy Spirit. Ambrose fulfilled the first part of the request but not the second.

dated to the early months of 379,[104] Gratian had also requested the bishop to meet him at an undisclosed location as he was returning from the east: 'Hurry to me, religious priest of God so that you may teach true doctrine to one who believes.'[105] Curiously, Ambrose delicately declines the invitation in his reply, offering no other reason than personal timidity. Considering the potential of Gratian's patronage of the Nicene faith, Ambrose's refusal to join him is very perplexing. One is tempted to suppose that Ambrose could not afford to leave his see because of the Homoian unrest now aggravated by the controversy which *De fide*, I–II, had sparked. Certainly the struggle with Arians occupied much of his time and energies, as a pastoral letter from early 379 reveals. At the close of his instructions to the recently installed bishop Constantius (of Siscia), Ambrose sternly warns him about the 'madness' of the Arians which has spread false seeds of doctrine among the faithful. Catholics are admonished not even to go near the Arians since the poisons of infidelity can be extracted only with great difficulty. Even those who willingly convert from Arianism to the Nicene faith are to be received gradually and with the utmost caution.[106] Ambrose was speaking from first-hand experience. Many of these 'Illyrians imbued with the false teaching of the Arians' now dwelt in Milan, and he could see the impact they were having on his own congregation.

Whatever moderation and political tact Ambrose had shown to the religiously diverse community in Milan during his early episcopate had been permanently erased through the events of 378/9. The writing of *De fide*,

---

[104] The dating of Gratian's letter presents a difficult dilemma. Did Gratian write to Ambrose before he left Sirmium, or *en route*, which would place the letter in the first half of 379 (Faller, *CSEL* lxxix. 9 ff.), or was Gratian inviting Ambrose to come to Trier, putting the letter after Sept. 379 (Palanque, *Saint Ambroise*, 501–2)? There are more problems for the second view. First, Ambrose refers to the emperor in his reply letter as 'returning' ('Revertenti tamen si non occurri vestigio'), presumably from his campaigns in the east. Palanque has rejected 'reverterenti' as proof that Ambrose wrote to Gratian as the latter was returning from Sirmium on the grounds that Ambrose would not say 'returning' if Gratian were coming to Milan for the first time (Un épisode des rapports entre Gratien et saint Ambroise: à propos de la Lettre 1 de saint Ambroise', *Revue des études anciennes*, 30 (1928), 296). But 'reverterenti' could just as easily, and probably does, refer to Gratian's returning to the imperial residence in Trier. Secondly, there is no mention that Gratian has been in Milan (before he arrived at end of July 379) and it is clear from Ambrose's reply that the two have not communicated since Gratian's letter. Thirdly, Ambrose's reply is still formal and unassuming, differing from his only other and later correspondence to Gratian, *De evangelio tractatus* (L. Machielsen, 'Fragments patristiques non-identifiés du ms. Vat. Pal. 577', *Sacris erudiri*, 12 (1961), 530), which was also written in response to an inquiry made by Gratian—this time on a purely exegetical matter.

[105] *CSEL* lxxix. 3, 4–5.   [106] *Ep.* 36. 28–9 (*CSEL* lxxxii. 2. 18–19).

I–II, marked a turning-point in Ambrose's career, both in the circumstances which provoked it and in the reaction it provoked from the Homoians. Contrary to the hagiographically inspired picture of Ambrose's dealing with the Arians, the *De fide* did not represent a major polemical victory over its opponents. As we have seen, events subsequent to its publication revealed an increase in opposition which required Ambrose to restate his case in three additional books. The city of Milan had witnessed a tremendous surge within the Homoian community numerically, on account of the Gothic invasions, and politically, on account of the arrival of the court of Valentinian II. Emboldened by recent events, the Homoians had asked the emperor for one of the basilicas used by the Nicene Christians and received it. Gratian had shown himself hospitable to the theological views of Ambrose, but this had had no practical significance in political support of the Nicene Christians since he continued to maintain the Valentinian distinction between personal religion and political policy.

All of these facts present a strikingly different picture of Ambrose's earliest opposition to the Arians from that of the victorious and self-assured Ambrose we see several years later. The Paulinian tendency towards biographical conflation must be resisted. In order to apprehend the historical Ambrose, we must read our sources with an appreciation of the theological and political evolution of the bishop; an obvious methodology but one rarely applied in a consistent fashion within modern Ambrosian literature. Such an understanding will affect our perception of the western Homoians, who in 378/9 enjoyed a boom situation in their quest for theological and ecclesiastical survival. It is hardly surprising that Ambrose seized an opportunity when it presented itself to take more drastic measures against his opponents. This opportunity was none other than the council of Aquileia.

6

The Achievements of the Council of Aquileia

GRATIAN'S favourable acceptance of *De fide*, I–II, provided a welcome relief to Ambrose. Not only did the emperor show himself sympathetic to Nicene theology, but he was personally supportive of Ambrose's authority as one who teaches 'true doctrine'. In his only extant letter to the bishop of Milan, which he reportedly wrote with his own hand, Gratian designates Ambrose as his 'father', 'religious priest of God', and 'labourer of the Eternal God'.[1] The timing could not have been better. During 377–8 Ambrose had been under increasing attack by hostile forces in Milan which had promoted anti-Nicene sentiments. As we saw in the last chapter, opposition organized by Julian Valens along with Ursinus, antagonism from the pro-Homoian court of Valentinian II, and the loss of a basilica to Arian hands had upset the carefully balanced tranquillity that had characterized the Milanese church since Ambrose's election in 374. When Ambrose wrote back to Gratian a short time later, he expressed the significance of Gratian's warm reception: 'You have returned to me the tranquillity of the church (*quies ecclesiae*), for you have shut the mouths of the heretics (*perfidiorum*); how I wish you would have shut their hearts also. This you did no less as an act of faith than as by the authority of your power.'[2] It is almost universally agreed among scholars that this passage refers to the returning of the sequestered basilica to Ambrose which Gratian is said to have ordered when he returned to Milan at the end of July 379.[3] Such an interpretation depends upon an anachronistic reading of three chapters in *De spiritu sancto*,[4] a work which Ambrose did

---

[1] 'Cupio valde', 1–2 (*CSEL* lxxix. 3. 5; 4. 19–20).

[2] *Ep.* 12 (extra coll.). 2 (*CSEL* lxxxii. 3. 219. 22–5).

[3] e.g. Homes Dudden, *Life and Times*, i. 191; Faller, *CSEL* lxxix. 13*; Mara, *Patrology*, iv. 147; Hanson, *The Search*, 795.

[4] I. I. 19–21: 'Since you, most merciful emperor, are so fully instructed concerning the Son of God . . . especially when you recently showed yourself to be delighted by an argument (*adsertione*) of this nature, that you commanded the basilica of the church to be restored without any urging. So then we have received the grace of your faith and the reward of our own; for we cannot say otherwise than that it was of the grace of the Holy Spirit that, when we were all unconscious of it, you suddenly restored the basilica. And I do not regret the losses of the previous time, since the sequestration of that basilica resulted

not write until early 381.[5] Compared to the description of Gratian's returning the basilica in *De spiritu sancto*, the supposed allusion in Ambrose's letter is cryptic indeed. More problematic is the complete absence of any such reference by Ambrose in *De fide*, III–V, which preceded *De spiritu sancto* and whose polemical purposes provided an excellent context to signal such an event had it occurred. On the contrary, the passage in *De spiritu sancto*, I. 1. 19–21, suggests that Gratian's action, attributed by Ambrose to the inspired operation of the Holy Spirit, had happened only recently: 'You lately (*proxime*) showed yourself to be delighted so that you commanded the restoration (*reformari*) of the church's basilica without any urging.'

Once we jettison the faulty interpretation, we are allowed to consider the passage in context. What is Ambrose alluding to when he observes that the 'tranquillity of the church' has been returned to him now that the emperor 'has shut the mouths of the heretics'? We know of no antiheretical legislation in the west prior to 379 which would have altered Ambrose's present situation, nor is it likely that the anti-heretical law which Gratian issued from Milan on 3 August 379 was applicable to the Homoians. More will be said about this law in a moment.

Gottlieb has pointed out that one of Palladius' criticisms in his *contra Ambrosium* (*Scholia*, 336^r–337^r. 49) is directly parallel to the comments in Ambrose's letter to Gratian.[6] As we have already seen, Palladius blamed Ambrose for having obtained immunity from charges of impiety through a 'special order' of the emperor, so that 'no catholic or doctor of the truth is heard if they speak against you'. If the connection between this criticism of Palladius and Ambrose's letter as suggested by Gottlieb is correct, we may deduce that Gratian's approval of *De fide*, I–II, resulted in the dropping of heresy charges which had been plaguing the bishop and were the reason for the composition of *De fide* in the first place. This makes better sense of the statement in Ambrose's letter of the effect which the emperor's approval of his two books has had: 'I am not fearful of the danger.'

---

in a sort of gain in usury. For you sequestered the basilica that you might give proof of your faith. And so your piety fulfilled its intention, having sequestered that it might give proof, and so gave proof in restoring. I did not lose the fruit, and I have your judgement, having been made clear to all that, with a certain diversity of action, there was in you no diversity of opinion. It was made clear to all, I say, that it was not of yourself that you sequestered, but it was of yourself when you restored it' (*NPNF* x. 96 (altered); *CSEL* lxxix. 24–5. 11–27).

[5] Internal factors allow a fairly accurate dating of this treatise; see n. 49 below.

[6] *Ambrosius von Mailand*, 44 ff. Cf. H. von Campenhausen, *Ambrosius von Mailand als Kirchenpolitiker* (Berlin, 1929), 43.

With regard to Ambrose's words, 'You have returned to me the tranquillity of the church', could this not be a direct allusion to Valentinian's promise to Ambrose in 374: 'he promised a tranquil future (*quietem futuram*) if I, now elected, would accept the bishopric'?[7] It stands to reason that this promise was meant to secure the maintenance of order in the city of Milan, including religious affairs, preserving the new bishop from unjust attacks. Now in 378–9 the bishop was under attack by hostile forces in the city. The *quies ecclesiae*, which was once secured by Valentinian and now restored by Valentinian's son, is not in reference to a particular church or basilica, but to a state of affairs which Ambrose once enjoyed and has regained. Such a scenario fully accounts for the jubilant tone which permeates his letter to Gratian.

Of course Ambrose's declaration that the peace of the church had been restored to him had its limitations. In September of 381, following the council of Aquileia, he would still complain to Gratian, via a synodical letter,[8] that Milan was troubled by Julian Valens and his kind. But the fact that Ambrose had been exonerated, and his theology approved by the western emperor, held great promise for the bishop's career. His own position was now secure. With the continuation of imperial approbation Ambrose was eventually given licence to drive his enemies from their sees; something which pro-Nicene bishops had been unable to do for two decades.

From 379 to 381 we can trace what Palanque called a 'intimité définitive' that grew between Gratian and the bishop of Milan. Without question, the successes of the council of Aquileia (381) represent the summit of this relationship: '[I]e pouvoir impérial est étroitement mêlé aux origines et aux suites de ce concile'.[9] It can be argued that the 'triumph' of the Nicene faith over the Arians at Aquileia was significant in that it was symbolic of the changing political climate of the west. Such climactic changes provided Ambrose with an opportunity to turn the tables on his opponents by accusing them of heresy; it being no longer necessary to cloak such charges under the legal prohibition of inciting a public disturbance, as the Roman synod of 378 was forced to do against certain Arian bishops. The bishop of Milan was quite capable of exploiting these new advantages and did so by convincing Gratian to alter his original plans for a more general council by limiting the number of attending bishops. This

---

[7] *Ep.* 75. 7 (*CSEL* lxxxii. 3. 77). See D. H. Williams, 'When did the Emperor Gratian Return the Basilica to the Pro-Nicenes in Milan?', *Studia Patristica*, 24 (1994), 208–15.

[8] *Ep.* 2 ('Agimus gratias sanctae'). 9–10 (*CSEL* lxxxii. 3. 322–3).

[9] *Saint Ambroise*, 78–9.

amounted to what was manifestly a heresy trial leading to the anticipated condemnation of two Homoian bishops, Palladius of Ratiaria and Secundianus of Singidunum, as well as the deportation of Julian Valens from Milan.

Before we can appreciate the events of the council at Aquileia and their significance for the history of the Nicene–Homoian conflict, it is necessary to understand the evolution in Gratian and Ambrose's relations and examine under what circumstances the emperor dissolved the Valentinian distinction between imperial preference and political religious policy. Of course the observation that the political situation turned against the Homoians under Gratian is hardly novel. But the question of when and how this happened is open to dispute and merits a fresh survey of the available data. It will be argued below that Gratian did not modify his ecclesiastical political position toward the Homoians until after Theodosius issued his general anti-heretical edict of 10 January 381 (*C. Th.* XVI. 5. 6).

I. GRATIAN AND AMBROSE 379–381

We know little of Theodosius' military exploits against the Goths in the year following his elevation to Augustus and ensuing victories over the Sarmatians at the end of 378 and early 379.[10] The first season of his campaigns must have been successful enough for Gratian to feel that he could return to the west, especially since recent incursions of the Alemanni into Rhaetia required his attention.[11] By the beginning of September Gratian was back in Trier.

En route to Gaul, the emperor passed through north Italy, stopping at Aquileia, and by the end of July he was in Milan. Ambrose would have been informed of his coming and it is very likely, though not certain, that the two men met. While the emperor was in the city, we have a record of an edict which he issued on 3 August 379. The interpretation of this particular edict is critical for ascertaining the degree to which Gratian's own pro-Nicene bias and his relationship with Ambrose had determined his political policies by this date. The legislation, directed to Hesperius, now praetorian prefect (of Italy, Illyricum, and Africa), is as follows:

Let all heresies, forbidden by divine and imperial laws, cease forever. If any profane person with punishable audacity subverts the concept of God, let him

---

[10] Matthews, *Western Aristocracies*, 91–2.
[11] Ausonius, *Grat. Actio*, 18. 82; Socrates, *HE* v. 6 (*PG* lxvii. 572C).

think of such harmful matters only to himself and not spread them to others. If any person having been redeemed through the venerable baptismal font corrupts his body with a renewed death, so that its benefit is taken away by being repeated, he shall keep such things to himself alone, not ruining others with his nefarious custom. And let all teachers and ministers alike of that perverse superstition abstain from the assemblies of an already condemned view, whether by assuming that priestly office and so defaming the title of bishop, or, which is more recent, by feigning religion in the name of presbyter, or calling themselves deacons, although they are not even Christians.[12]

No group is identified by name, rather, the first line gives the appearance of being a general anti-heretical statement. Given such an interpretation, the edict represents a dramatic departure from Gratian's political policies concerning religion, for a blanket condemnation such as this would certainly have included the Arians, who constituted the largest potential threat against the Nicene faith in the west and who had been sorely harassing Ambrose. Older scholarship has typically deduced from this interpretation that Ambrose prevailed on the emperor to take such drastic action while the latter was in Milan. Ehrhardt, for instance, draws the conclusion that Gratian 'had fallen under the spell of Ambrose', which can only explain the emperor's sudden abandonment of the policy of religious neutrality.[13] There is good reason however to doubt this exegesis of the above legislation. A. R. Birley has rightly questioned whether the edict of 3 August 379 was intended to revoke the position of toleration which had been maintained in the west.[14] The basis for his scepticism rests on the conclusions of Gottlieb, who argued quite convincingly that this edict, like the one issued in 376 (*C. Th.* XVI. 5. 4 above), was directed solely at the Donatists and is not, therefore, a general anti-heretical law. Assuming Gottlieb to be correct, such a reinterpretation has wide-reaching implications for how we are to understand Gratian's political decisions and his relationship to Ambrose. We are obliged therefore to consider his main arguments.

The case which Gottlieb builds rests principally on the observation that the above statute is being directed against those who practice rebaptism:

---

[12] *C. Th.* XVI. 5. 5.
[13] 'The First Two Years of the Emperor Theodosius I', *JEH* 15 (1964), 4. Cf. Meslin, *Les Ariens*, 46; Homes Dudden, *Life and Times*, i. 191–2; Piganiol, *L'Empire chrétien*, 246–7. Piganiol differs only in that he attributes the inspiration of the edict to Damasus, not Ambrose, who sought and obtained support from the secular arm to enforce the decisions of the Roman synod of 378.
[14] 'Magnus Maximus and the Persecution of Heresy', *Bulletin of the John Rylands University Library*, 66 (1983–4), 16 n. 19; cf. Hanson, *The Search*, 795.

'If any person corrupts his body with a renewed death (*reparata morte*), having been through the venerable baptismal font, its benefit is taken away by being repeated.' According to Gottlieb, it is an unmistakable reference to the Donatists.[15] The terminology employed in the statute closely parallels previous anti-Donatist legislation. Gratian's rescript to the *vicarius* Aquilinus states, concerning the Donatist Bishop Claudianus, 'because repetition does not add to the rule (*disciplinam*) of most holy religion, but overturns it . . . destroys souls whose bodies are redeemed'.[16] That rescript was issued in response to the Roman synodical letter of 378 which sought imperial action, *inter alia*, against Claudianus, one of the 'sacrilegious rebaptizers from Africa'. In both pieces of legislation, there is the striking similarity of the phrase 'redeemed bodies', applying to Donatist practice. Elsewhere in the edict of 3 August 379, the doctrine of rebaptism is called a 'superstitio', which, as Gottlieb correctly points out, is used of Donatist teaching in two later edicts found in the *Theodosian Code*.[17] Moreover, Gratian accuses the 'teachers and ministers of this perverse superstition' of having abused the priestly office by using the appellations of 'episcopus', 'presbyter', or 'diaconus', since they are titles unique to Christians. A similar type of accusation against the Donatists was made by Valentinian in 373 in his edict to the proconsul of Africa: 'We judge the priesthood of any bishop unworthy who repeats the holiness of baptism with an illicit practice and against the teaching of all, contaminates the act of grace by repeating it.'[18]

The fact that Gratian issued an anti-Donatist law to a praetorian prefect was not at all unusual. Praetorian prefects of Italy, whose administrative jurisdiction included Africa, were the designated recipients of many such edicts against the Donatists. Even so, the Donatist problem addressed by the 379 edict was not confined to Africa. The rescript to Aquilinus shows that Donatists were in Rome and that Gratian had been forced to expel the 'rebaptizers' from Rome on an earlier occasion. Still the Roman church continued to be disturbed by the Donatist Bishop Claudianus, so much so that, at the request of the synod of 378, Gratian ordered the bishop to be sought out and severely punished.

A major, even near fatal, weakness in Gottlieb's argument is his insistence that only Donatists practised rebaptism at the end of the fourth century: 'The Donatists were the only ones at that time who were concerned

---

[15] *Ambrosius von Mailand*, 60.   [16] *Coll. Avell.* 13. 8 (*CSEL* xxxv. 56. 17–23).
[17] *C. Th.* XVI. 5. 39 (by Honorius, 8 Dec. 405) and *C. Th.* XVI. 5. 54 (by Honorius, 17 June 414).
[18] *C. Th.* XVI. 6. 1 (20 Feb. 373).

to renew baptism'.[19] He claims that only after AD 400 were there other groups, such as the Novatians and Eunomians, accused of renewing baptism. But Gottlieb is too dependent on the evidence of the *Theodosian Code* alone. There exists clear testimony that Eunomians and Homoians practised rebaptism in the 380s on those who converted to their sects from the Nicene Church. Philostorgius and Sozomen similarly point out that the Eunomians were so repelled by the doctrine of their opponents that they would not recognize their baptism (or their ordination), requiring initiates to be rebaptized in conformity with their tradition.[20] At Milan in the mid-380s, Ambrose tells us how the Homoians, under the leadership of Auxentius (from Durostorum), received ex-Nicenes into their fellowship by annulling the baptism of Christ: 'Why does Auxentius insist that persons faithfully baptized in the name of the Trinity must be re-baptized, since the Apostle says, "One faith, one baptism . . ."?'[21] The subject of Arian rebaptism has been discussed in greater detail by Meslin, who points to further evidence of the practice in a sermon of Quodvultdeus, bishop of Carthage from 440,[22] and in the *Opus imperfectum*, which justifies rebaptism scripturally by the example of John the Baptist, whose baptism was not 'complete' (*plenum*) but superseded by the Church.

It is not impossible then that *C. Th.* XVI. 5. 5 could be referring to the rebaptism of Arians, not just that of the Donatists. There is however a line from the edict which clinches the argument that the Donatists are alone the object of this imperial condemnation: 'And all teachers and ministers alike of that perverse superstition . . . let these abstain from assemblies of an already condemned view.' Only one sect fits the above description of rebaptizers who had an 'already condemned view' in the west. Throughout the 360s and 370s, most religious expressions were permitted, with the exception of the Manichees, Photinians, and Donatists. The last-named group had been condemned by Valentinian in 373 and again, as we saw in the last chapter, in 376 by Gratian. Interestingly, the Donatists are not mentioned among the outlawed groups (Eunomians, Photinians, and Manichees) in Gratian's so-called 'toleration edict' at Sirmium (378).[23] Part of the reason for this oversight may lie in the fact

---

[19] *Ambrosius von Mailand*, 61.

[20] Sozomen, *HE* VI. 26. 7 (*GCS* l. 273. 17–20); 26. 9 (l. 273–4); Philostorgius, *HE* X. 4 (*GCS* xxi. 127)

[21] *Contra Aux.* (*Ep.* LXXVa), 37 (*CSEL* lxxxii. 3. 107. 458–61).

[22] The sermon describes one of the rites of Arian rebaptism: the minister blows, in the rite of exorcism, on the baptized orthodox after which he proceeds to a new baptism (*Adversus quinque haereses*, VII. 9 (*PL* xlii. 1115 ff.)). Cf. *Liber promissionum et praedictorum dei*, IV. 8. *Les Ariens*, 388. Meslin implausibly dates the sermon to 374.

[23] Socrates, *HE* V. 2 (*PG* lxvii. 568B); Sozomen, *HE* VII. 1. 3 (*GCS* l. 302).

that the edict was issued primarily for the eastern empire, since it was connected to Gratian's recall of all bishops exiled under the Emperor Valens. Gottlieb is probably correct to discern in the 379 edict an attempt on Gratian's part to correct his earlier oversight with the words which come at the end of the edict: 'that former rescript which was recently issued at Sirmium.'[24] Any hopes of toleration for the Donatists which the omission in the 378 edict might have raised would have been quenched by this new edict.

We must conclude that Gratian was not committing a political volte-face under Ambrose's influence by issuing this new law of 3 August 379. The law was not a general anti-heretical declaration and it was not, consequently, a blast directed at the Homoians of the west.

(a) *Theodosius' anti-Arian legislation*

By the end of 380 Ambrose had expanded his arguments in *De fide* I–II with three more books[25] which he sent dutifully to the emperor. As previously noted, these books formed a response to the severe criticism which *De fide* I–II had provoked, especially from the pen of Palladius of Ratiaria. *De fide* III–V contains frequent appeals to the emperor[26] and is just as vindictive in tone as the two previous books. The essential thrust of Ambrose's argumentation against his opponents also remains the same: 'above all other points', the Arians 'say that Christ is distinct from the one and true God'.[27] Ambrose's insistence that the Son, like the Father in every way, is 'truly God' (*verus deus*) anticipates the line of argument he will use against Palladius at the council of Aquileia. At the same time, books III–V give evidence that Ambrose has studied the writings of his opponents, taking more seriously the large number of exegetical arguments in their arsenal which defend the many distinctions between the Father and the Son. Interestingly, we hear no more mention of Eunomius,

---

[24] *Ambrosius von Mailand*, 78.

[25] No precise dating of these books is possible from internal indications. The discussion of Faller (*CSEL* lxxiii. 10*), *De fide*, V. prol. 7, makes it clear that III–V were written before *De spiritu sancto*, which can be dated to early 381. Ambrose's letter to Gratian provides a *terminus ante quem* since there is no indication that Ambrose has yet written three more books or is considering them. Faller places III–V at the end of 380, although there is no reason why they could not be earlier. It can be reasonably conjectured that Gratian's return to Sirmium and in particular his audience with leading Homoians was the ostensible motivation for the publication of *De fide*, III–V. Gratian was in Sirmium at the end of Aug. and early Sept. of 380.

[26] III. 1. 1; 14. 108; IV. 1. 1; 8. 78; V. prol. 6; 7. 88; 13. 153.

[27] V. 1. 16 (*CSEL* lxxviii. 222. 6–8).

nor that the Arians teach the doctrine of *dissimilis*, except to say that it is an implication of their theology.[28]

Another noteworthy difference in *De fide*, III–V, is that the author manifests no hesitation about the imperial reception of this work; an apology is offered only about its unexpected length. Gratian had not sought further elaboration of the arguments in books I–II, yet Ambrose felt justified in that the indivisible Godhead of the Father and Son merits such detailed treatment in order to answer 'the impiety of the heretics'. Still he recognizes that he has yet to fulfil the emperor's original request by treating the doctrine of the Holy Spirit which had to be omitted in the present exercise.[29]

Whether Ambrose met with Gratian again when the latter sojourned at Milan on his way to Sirmium in the spring of 380 is unknown. One should not attribute too much importance to Gratian's stops in Milan since, like the city of Aquileia, it housed an imperial residence. Gratian would ordinarily stay at these locations on his eastward or westward journeys. In any case, the emperor would have been deeply preoccupied with military affairs on this trip. At Theodosius' urgent request, Gratian was bringing his army, commanded by Bauto and Arbogast, into the Balkans in order to help free Thessaly from invading Goths.[30] After a summer campaign of only minimal success, the two emperors are known to have convened in Sirmium early in September,[31] though there is no record of the exchange between them.

While at Sirmium, Gratian received a delegation from the Illyrian Homoians led by the bishop of Ratiaria, Palladius. Evidence for this visit is derived from Palladius' own remarks in the recorded proceedings of the council of Aquileia that 'the emperor himself spoke to us' when he was at Sirmium.[32] According to Zeiller and Palanque,[33] the purpose of the delegation was to propose the idea of a council to the emperor, but this is far from certain. Palladius never takes such credit, nor does the imperial rescript which authorized the council of Aquileia (and was read at its opening) attribute the initial concept of the council to the Illyrians.[34] The only part of the dialogue with the emperor which Palladius relates pertains to the emperor's assurance that the eastern bishops had been invited to attend the forthcoming council: 'we asked, "have the easterners been

---

[28] v. 1. 27 (226. 81–2).   [29] v. prol. 7 (218. 40–2).
[30] Zosimus, IV. 33. 1 (Paschoud, 296).   [31] *L'Empire chrétien*, 244; *Regesten*, 254–5.
[32] *Gesta concili Aquil.* 8 (*CSEL* lxxxii. 3. 330. 70–1); 10 (331–2. 99–105).
[33] *Origines chrétiennes*, 324; *Saint Ambroise*, 78–9.
[34] *Gesta*, 3–4 (*CSEL* lxxxii. 3. 328–9).

convoked to come?" He [the emperor] said, "They have".[35] In a defence of Palladius and his fellow Homoians which was written over twenty-five years later, the commentator Maximinus has no new light to shed on the convening of the council, except to quote Palladius' own words.[36]

Judging from this limited information, Gryson believes that the decision to hold a council had already been made before Palladius met with Gratian and that the Homoian bishop came to Sirmium in order to ensure that the council was not a trap by receiving assurance from the emperor of its ecumenicity.[37] If this view is correct then it throws open the question of who initiated the idea of holding a council. The fact that Ambrose took reactive measures by convincing Gratian to reduce the size and scope of the projected council[38]—the only act of tampering with the council of which Palladius accuses him—indicates that the initial concept did not lie with him. Only the emperors are mentioned at the commencement of the council as the ones who ordered (*iusseramus*) the convening of the assembly for the purpose that doctrinal discord and controversy between bishops should be resolved. Gryson has argued therefore that the decision to convoke a general council at Aquileia was conceived by Gratian and Theodosius, probably when they met at Sirmium. This too is fraught with problems. The use of *iusseramus* or *constituissemus* in the imperial rescript read at the council provides no substantial proof that the conception of the council originated with the emperors. Such language is the terminology of convention and proves nothing in itself. There is further indication that the two emperors would not have collaborated in such a manner in any case. Relations between them had been strained from the beginning. Even though Gratian was responsible for Theodosius' recall from Spain, it is possible that the latter forced Gratian's hand to grant him almost immediate recognition as an Augustus by consolidating his support in the brief period between his military successes in 378 and his accession in 379.[39] The existence of disharmonious relations is well exemplified by the panegyrist Themistius, who pleads with Theodosius to maintain harmony with Gratian.[40] We should not read into the silence that surrounds the nature of the imperial rendezvous at Sirmium (beyond

---

[35] *Gesta*, 10 (*CSEL* lxxxii. 3. 331. 102–3). Cf. *Gesta*, 8: 'Imperator noster Gratianus iussit orientales venire; negas tu iussisse eum? Ipse imperator nobis dixit se orientales iussisse venire' (*CSEL* lxxxii. 3. 330).

[36] Quoting *Gesta*, 8, *Scholia*, 299ʳ. 1–2 (Gryson, *Scolies*, 208).

[37] *Scolies*, 129. [38] *Gesta*, 6 (*CSEL* lxxxii. 3. 329. 53–5).

[39] J. Vanderspoel, 'Themistius and the Imperial Court', (Ph.D. diss., Toronto, 1989), 193.

[40] Ibid. 184 ff.

the likelihood of some joint military strategizing) by assuming a co-operative effort in planning eastern and western councils. It is more probable that such decisions were made irrespective of each other, although Theodosius' strong commitment toward setting a course of imperial direction through ecclesiastical politics makes it easy to imagine that Gratian's decision to hold a council was in tacit emulation, if not competition, of his junior Augustus. The upshot of this interpretation makes for a significant, albeit preliminary, finding: that there is nothing in the summoning of the councils of Constantinople and Aquileia to demonstrate that they were initially intended to mirror or be in harmony with one another. The proceedings of the councils will underline this hypothesis.

To return to Palladius and Secundianus at Sirmium. We do not know the precise content of their interview with Gratian over the announced council, although it appears that they went away satisfied with the emperor's projected method of handling it. His later decision to place new restrictions on the attendance of the council, which was so strongly protested by Palladius, would indicate that the original arrangement of the council was at least conceived in accordance with Palladius' designs. This was an important concession for the ongoing existence of religious tolerance in the west. Palladius was undoubtedly aware of the changing political winds against Homoian Christianity in the east.

Momentous events were already underfoot in the eastern half of the empire concerning religious matters. On 27 February 380 Theodosius had published an imperial declaration, the 'Cunctos populos' edict, which spelled out with meticulous clarity that the standards of religious orthodoxy were henceforth to be measured by the faith of Damasus of Rome and Peter of Alexandria.[41] Within these two leading bishops, the 'religion which the holy Peter transmitted to the Romans' is said to be preserved; that is, the religion which is defined by impeccable fidelity to Nicene Trinitarianism: 'We believe in one God, under an equal majesty and under a pious Trinity of Father, and Son, and Holy Spirit.'

Later that year, after the conference in Sirmium with Gratian, Theodosius fell dangerously ill at Thessalonica, and, under the threat of death, he was baptized by the bishop of the city, Acholius—a stalwart

---

[41] *C. Th.* XVI. I. I. Cf. Sozomen, *HE* VII. 4. 5–7, for a near accurate citation of the edict. *C. Th.* XVI. 2. 25, which is dated 28 Feb. 380, may be part of the same law. Ehrhardt's argument ('The First Two Years', 11), that this edict was designed to preserve Theodosius' religious/political loyalties to the catholics since he was employing Arian Goths for military purposes, seems unnecessary to explain Theodosius' motivation.

advocate of the Nicene faith.[42] Acholius' reputation as a long-time defender of 'orthodoxy' was well known in the west. At the time of the bishop's death (383), Ambrose wrote to the church at Thessalonica and spoke of their recently deceased bishop with great respect and affection, characterizing his meritorious life as a 'wall of faith, of grace, and of sanctity'.[43]

Once Theodosius recovered from his illness, he entered Constantinople in full ceremony on 24 November,[44] now as a baptized catholic. Upon his arrival in the city, he wasted no time in settling the Nicene–Homoian tensions present there. The bishop of Constantinople and patriarch of eastern Homoianism, Demophilus, was immediately deposed and replaced. In his stead, the leader of the pro-Nicene minority, Gregory of Nazianzus, was installed as bishop on 27 November; only three days after Theodosius' official entry into the city.[45] Within weeks (10 January 381) Theodosius had published a strongly worded edict which mandated Nicene catholicism as the official religion of the Roman (eastern) Empire.[46] Photinians, Arians, and Eunomians were condemned by name and forbidden to hold assembly on threat of banishment. Only the Nicene faith, as 'previously transmitted by our ancestors', was to be maintained and observed as 'divine religion'. Whoever would be accepted as a true adherent of catholic religion was obliged to confess that 'Almighty God and the Son of God are one in name, God from God, light from light' does not deny (*negando non violat*) the Holy Spirit, nor 'the undivided substance of the incorrupt Trinity'.

Such aggressive tactics on the part of Theodosius against 'Arian heretics' provide a striking contrast to the ecclesiastical politics of Gratian that we have seen up to this point. The fact that Palladius of Ratiaria, a notable spokesman for the anti-Nicenes, was able to receive an audience with Gratian in Sirmium to discuss ecclesiastical matters without the fear of reprisal or confessional coercion indicates that the Valentinian distinction between imperial religious preference and public policy had not yet been

---

[42] N. Q. King, *The Emperor Theodosius and the Establishment of Christianity* (London, 1961), 30; Ehrhardt, 'The First Two Years', 10–11. Seeck's sequence of events, illness–baptism–legislation (*Geschichte des Untergangs der antiken Welt*, vol. v (Stuttgart, 1923), 484), has been definitively refuted by W. Ensslin, *Die Religionspolitik des Kaiser Theodosius der Grosse* (Munich, 1953), 17 ff., and is no longer followed by historians (see King, *The Emperor Theodosius*, 30 n. 3; Matthews, *Western Aristocracies*, 122 n. 2).

[43] *Ep.* 51. 5 (*CSEL* lxxxii. 62).

[44] Socrates, *HE* v. 6 (*PG* lxvii. 572C–573A); *Regesten*, 255.

[45] King, *The Emperor Theodosius*, 31; Matthews, *Western Aristocracies*, 122–3.

[46] *C. Th.* XVI. 5. 6.

annulled, despite the growing influence of Ambrose over Gratian. This state of affairs in the west, however, was not to last much longer. By the time Ambrose fulfilled his obligation of writing a treatise on the doctrine of the Holy Spirit in the spring of 381, it appears that Gratian was openly favouring the western Nicenes.

(b) *Gratian's new ecclesiastical politics*

Easter of 381 (28 March) brought special tidings for Ambrose. After spending the winter in Trier, Gratian appears to have moved his residence to north Italy;[47] perhaps out of 'affection for the great bishop' as Palanque suggests, although the imperial itinerary was by no means confined to Milan. Whatever the reason, it is noteworthy that the emperor was present in Milan for the Easter season. And it is at this time that Ambrose chose to publish his work *De spiritu sancto* in three books. Faller has shown that the prologue, delivered at Eastertide (*ipso paschatis die*), was written last,[48] and that the rest of the treatise had been completed sometime after Athanaric's death and burial in Constantinople (February 381).[49] *De spiritu sancto* tells us a great deal about Gratian's overt political patronage of Ambrose. The terse polemical tone which characterized *De fide*, III–V, is absent in much of the work on the Holy Spirit.[50] Most significant of all, Ambrose recounts the recent event of Gratian's being led by the Holy Spirit to return the basilica which he had sequestered on behalf of the Homoians three years ago: 'You ordered the basilica of the church to be restored without any urging.'

We have already demonstrated in the beginning of this chapter that the return of the basilica could not have occurred in 379, but must have taken place just before the writing of *De spiritu sancto*. It may be that the

---

[47] Seeck, *Regesten*, 256. There is no record of Gratian returning to Trier again.

[48] *CSEL* lxxix. 16*–17*.

[49] *De spiritu sancto*, I. prol. 17 provides several pieces of valuable information which allow the work to be precisely dated: 'After she [the church] renounced those alien to the faith, the enemy himself, the judge of kings, whom she was always wont to fear, saw him captured, received as a suppliant, and buried him in death . . .' (*CSEL* lxxix. 23. 167–9). The reference to 'the enemy himself' undoubtedly pertains to the feared Gothic king Athanaric who, having made peace with Theodosius, entered Constantinople on 11 Jan. and died exactly two weeks later (Zosimus, IV. 34. 4; Jordanes, *Get.* 28; Socrates, *HE* V. 10 (conflated)).

[50] Palanque, *Saint Ambroise*, 75. This does not mean that it is not a polemical work, since the essence of the treatise is to refute those who believe the Holy Spirit is a creature (I. 5. 75), being made by the Son (I. 2. 27), and thereby denying the full Godhead of the Holy Spirit (I. 10. 112).

transaction took place when Gratian arrived that March in Milan. One cannot fail to notice the triumphal note which Ambrose sounds in his treatise, not only over these events, but over the radical change of fortune for the Nicene faith across the entire empire.

This is the special prerogative of your goodness by which you have redeemed the entire world one portion at a time. Elijah was sent to one widow, Elisha cleansed one; yet You, Lord Jesus, have cleansed today these thousands for us. How many in the city of Rome, how many in Alexandria, how many in Antioch, how many also in Constantinople! For now Constantinople has received the word of God and has earned clear evidence of Your judgement. For a long time she cherished the poison of the Arians nestled within her midst, troubled by neighbouring wars, 'hostile forces echoed around her walls'.[51]

Faller insists that this passage makes reference only to the Paschal day (*hodie*) of baptism in which Christ 'has cleansed today these thousands'. Certainly this is the context of Christ's 'cleansing', which is confirmed in the following paragraph beginning with the words: 'Damasus has not cleansed, Peter [of Alexandria] has not cleansed, Ambrose has not cleansed, Gregory [of Constantinople] has not cleansed, nor our servitude, but your sacraments have.'[52] The meaning of the passage cannot be restricted to this interpretation, however. In typical Ambrosian fashion, the baptismal motif has been expanded to reveal a deeper implication. Ambrose employs a similar technique of dual meaning in his exhortation to Gratian in *De fide*, II. 142,[53] where the necessity of military conquest and avenging the orthodox faith become synonymous in order to illustrate the point that God's wrath had come upon the empire (namely the barbarian invasions) because of heresy. Christ is said to have cleansed thousands at Rome, Alexandria, Antioch, and even at Constantinople, now that that city 'has received the word of God', that is, the Nicene faith. As long as she cherished (*fovebat*) the Arian heresy, hostile arms echoed around her walls. But as soon as she rejected those who are 'alien to the faith'—a probable allusion to the deposition of Demophilus—divine favour manifested itself through the self-imposed submission of the barbarian king (Athanaric). Ambrose concludes the paragraph with a different nuance attached to the meaning of 'cleansed': 'How many therefore have you cleansed at Constantinople, how many at last you have cleansed today all over the world!'

Such 'cleansing' has become symptomatic in the west also, now that

---

[51] *De spiritu sancto*, I. prol. 17 (*CSEL* lxxix. 23. 158–67).
[52] I. 1. 18 (*CSEL* lxxix. 23. 171–3).   [53] See *De fide*, II. 16. 140–1.

the basilica has been restored and that, through this action, the emperor has given full proof of his orthodox faith. One is left to wonder about the political implications of this obviously aggressive act against the Milanese Homoians. It suggests a marked change in Gratian's ecclesiastical policies. In effect, the restoration of the basilica to the Nicenes annuls the principles of religious tolerance which were the technical grounds for sequestering the basilica in the first place. There are yet further indications that a drastic political change has taken place. At the outcome of the council of Aquileia, five months later, we discover that two Homoian bishops are convicted on charges of *impietas*,[54] and for this reason alone Gratian is requested by the council to arrange for their deposition.[55] Not for two decades had the west witnessed state-enforced deposition of bishops on purely theological grounds. Another synodical letter to Gratian infers the political provision that has made such enforcement possible: 'Preparation has been made, most clement Rulers, by the enactments of your Tranquillity so that the treachery of the Arians may not be concealed or spread about any further; thus we are confident that the decisions of the council will not lack its effect.'[56] It is hard to imagine what provision had been made by the emperors so that the 'Arian *perfidia* could no longer hide or spread about' unless this is a reference to some recent anti-heretical legislation, the existence of which gave confidence to the Aquileian council that their condemnations would be enforced. Despite the fact that Gratian was the senior Augustus, it must be conceded that Theodosius' more militant orthodoxy had influenced him, being further bolstered by the persuasive Ambrose. The conditions which *C. Th.* XVI. 5. 6 (10 January 381) had laid down against heretics in the east appear to have been applied also in the west.[57] There was nothing to forbid Theodosius' influence on Gratian in such matters; indeed, it is likely that Gratian was encouraged in his refusal of the traditional title of Pontifex Maximus in 383[58] by the knowledge that Theodosius had already rejected this Pagan

---

[54] *Ep.* 1 (synodical). 2 (*CSEL* lxxxii. 3. 316. 14–18); *Ep.* (Ad Gratianum), 2. 5 (320. 66–7).

[55] *Ep.* 2. 8 (*CSEL* lxxxii. 3. 92–102). The only reason offered for their guilt is that they are 'impietatis assertores et adulteros veritatis'. There is no attempt to depict the accused as disturbers of the public peace, which had been the usual pretence offered to convict doctrinal opponents.

[56] *Ep.* 5 (extra coll.). 1 (*CSEL* lxxxii. 3. 182.5–8).

[57] It was typical that laws were issued in the names of all the Augusti. *C. Th.* XVI. 5. 6 was no exception ('Imppp. Gratianus, Val[entini]anus et Theod[osius] AAA'), which meant that the conditions stated therein were, in principle, applicable to the entire empire.

[58] I am following Cameron's chronology in 'Gratian's Repudiation of the Pontifical Robe', *JRS* 58 (1968), 96–102.

office in 379 upon assuming the purple.[59] We are left to surmise therefore that Gratian began to patronize Ambrose and the Nicenes politically, at the expense of the Homoians, sometime after Theodosius' anti-heretical edict in January. This would indicate that Gratian was also enforcing *C. Th.* XVI. 5. 6 in the western provinces, or issued a very similiar statute which does not survive.

Almost certainly before Gratian departed in April for Aquileia, he and Ambrose convened to discuss the matter of the proposed council. Ambrose took the opportunity to convince Gratian that the original plans caused unnecessary hardship on aged or infirm bishops who would be forced to undertake a long journey. What is the need of convoking a large number of bishops, Ambrose argued, if the truth is equally present in a few? Gratian was persuaded by the seeming rationality of such reasons, citing them in his rescript which was read at the commencement of the council.[60] Yet the rescript does not mention what was probably Ambrose's most-pressing argument against the necessity of a full council. Only in the synodical letter (*Ep.* 2. 3) do we learn how Palladius and Secundianus were depicted as isolated cases of heterodoxy opposing the uniform fidelity to the Nicene faith which characterized the Church world-wide. They are described as 'two men stinking with heresy' and a source of trouble to be dealt with, not placated through the calling of a large assembly. But, in fact, Ambrose may have been concerned that a large number of eastern bishops were still favourable to Arian theology,[61] and their attendance at the upcoming council would hardly permit him to strike a decisive blow against anti-Nicenes as he now hoped to do.

2. THE COUNCIL OF AQUILEIA

Patristic scholarship in the 1980s was witness to a veritable explosion in the study of the council of Aquileia (381) and the polemical literature related to it. Before we look at the events which transpired at the council, it is necessary to review some of the major strides that have been made.

For the acts of the council, a new critical edition has been prepared by M. Zelzer, published (1982) in the third volume of Ambrose's works in the *CSEL* lxxxii series.[62] The value of this edition for Ambrosian research

---

[59] Piganiol, *L'Empire chrétien*, 237. Cf. Augustine, *De civitate dei*, v. 26, which speaks of Theodosius opposing Paganism or heresy 'ex ipso initio imperii sui' (*CCSL* xlvii. 162. 44).

[60] *Gesta*, 3–4 (*CSEL* lxxxii. 3. 328–9).

[61] Simonetti, 'La politica antiariana di Ambrogio', 274.

[62] 'Gesta Episcoporum Aquileiae adversus Haereticos Arrianos', *CSEL* lxxx.3. 326–68.

cannot be overstated, since no other version has been available since the Maurist edition of 1690, which was based on the twelfth-century Paris MS Lat. 1758 (reproduced in *PL* xvi. 955–79). In the *CSEL* text, Zelzer has employed the recently restored Parisinus Latinus 8907 of the Bibliothèque Nationale, a fifth-century uncial text[63] which contains, besides the *gesta* of Aquileia, Hilary of Poitiers's *De trinitate, Contra Auxentium, De synodis,* and Ambrose's *De fide,* I–II. This collection of anti-Arian writings was probably compiled not long after the council of Aquileia for polemical purposes, but then fell into the hands of an Arian enthusiast[64] who filled the margins of the Paris manuscript in two places with a unique set of pro-Homoian material directed at Ambrose and the proceedings of the council of Aquileia: in the margins of *De fide* (fos. 298ʳ–311ᵛ) and in the margin of the conciliar *gesta* (fos. 336ʳ–349ʳ).

These marginalia or *scholia* have been the subject of new critical editions by R. Gryson along with historical background and textual commentary.[65] *Contra* F. Kauffmann's thesis, which held that all the *scholia* were the work of a single author,[66] Gryson's reconstruction has led him to the conclusion that only the first block of marginalia belong to the pen of Maximinus. This is considered to be the same Maximinus who debated with Augustine in 427/8 over the doctrine of the Trinity.[67] The first block of material, entitled by Gryson, 'Commentaires de Maximinus', includes an attack on the decisions of the council of Aquileia in defence of Palladius, a quotation of a post-mortem panegyric of the Gothic Bishop Ulfila by his disciple Auxentius of Durostorum, and a citation of Ulfila's profession of faith. A second block in the margins of the conciliar acts of Aquileia consists of two fragments from a polemical work against Ambrose's *De fide,* I–II, written by Palladius of Ratiaria (336ʳ. 1–337ʳ. 49), followed

---

[63] For a complete description of the manuscript, its history, and present state, see Gryson and Gilissen, *Les Scolies ariennes du Parisinus latinus 8907.* Gryson has also provided a critical version of the conciliar *gesta* in Gryson, *Scolies,* with a French translation. Zelzer's text is to be preferred, for not only is her apparatus criticus more comprehensive, but it seems that the *Scolies* of Gryson is based on a preliminary reconstruction sent to him by Zelzer. See Zelzer's accusations in the 'Praefatio', *CSEL* lxxxii. 3. ix.

[64] C. P. Hammond-Bammel has argued that the editor of the Paris manuscript, himself an Arian and perhaps a disciple of Maximinus, copied the material into the margins from Maximinus' own edition and commentary. Maximinus is believed to have edited the collection of texts soon after the council of Aquileia, but a later Arian editor is responsible for the marginalia ('From the School of Maximinus', 396).

[65] Gryson and Gilissen, *Scolies ariennes,* and in *CCSL* lxxxvii. 147–96.

[66] *Aus der Schule des Wulfila.* Kauffmann's edition of the marginalia, which was the first complete edition, was reproduced in *PLS* i. 693–728.

[67] A new edition of the *collationes* between Augustine and Maximinus is expected to appear in the *CCSL* series.

by a long *apologia* also written by Palladius[68] in defence of those who were condemned at Aquileia (337[r]. 50–349[r]. 4*a*). A short note by Maximinus (349[r]. 4b–349[r]. 43) marks the end of the collection which can be dated roughly to AD 429–38, the time of the compilation of the *Theodosian Code*.[69]

Proper attention to these unique documents is long overdue since they shed valuable light on the events at Aquileia from the perspective of those who were excommunicated and deposed by the council. This material informs us that the decisions made by the council did not occur without a reaction on the part of the leaders of the Homoian community. Historical analyses of Ambrose's anti-Arian efforts previous to Gryson's work have made little or no attempt to integrate the *scholia* into our picture of the Nicene–Homoian conflicts. One of the many insights which the *scholia* provide, as we will see below, is that the decisions of the council of Aquileia by no means brought an end to the Homoians' theological presence in the west, thus continuing the tensions between Arians and pro-Nicenes.

In addition to the new critical editions of the *gesta* and the Arian *scholia* which are now available, an international colloquium on the council of Aquileia was held in 1981, the proceedings of which were published in the Antichità Altoadriatiche series, volume 21 (1981).[70] A year later the same series published another volume, *Aquileia nel IV secolo*, in which several articles dealt with the Aquileian council or events surrounding it. Among the contributions, G. Cuscito provides a lengthy review of Gryson's *Scolies*, appending to his article an Italian translation of the *gesta*.[71] No small attention has been paid, mostly by Italian scholars, to the doctrinal arguments of the combatants present at the council. Studies by C. Corti, Y.-M. Duval, A. de Nicola, and Cuscito[72] have greatly enlarged our

---

[68] Y.-M. Duval, 'La Présentation arienne du concile d'Aquilée de 381', *RHE* 76 (1981), 319. This section was written before 384 since it mentions Damasus as still living (fo. 344[r]. 5–6). Gryson (*Scolies*, 91 f.) proposes a date of 383, whereas A. d'Haeneus ('De la trace hétérodoxe', *Revue théologique de Louvain*, 12 (1981), 86) thinks it is closer to 381.

[69] Maximinus quotes two laws in consecutive fashion, though in reverse order (*C. Th.* XVI. 4. 2 and 4. 1), evidently drawing upon the collection of laws later codified in the form known as the *Theodosian Code*.

[70] *Atti del colloquio internazionale sul concilio di Aquileia del 381* (Udine, 1981).

[71] 'Il concilio di Aquileia del 381 e le sue fonti', in *Aquileia nel IV secolo* (Udine, 1982), 189–223; 'Atti del concilio di Aquileia', ibid., 224–54.

[72] Respectively, 'Le posizione dottrinali nel dibattito conciliare', in *Il concilio di Aquileia del 381 nel XVI centenario* (Udine, 1981), 42–9; 'Le Sens des débats d'Aquilée pour les Nicéens: Nicée Rimini Aquilée', in *Atti di colloquio internazionale*, 81 ff.; 'Il dibattito teologico negli atti del concilio di Aquileia del 381', in *Ricerche religiose del Friuli e dell'Istria*, 2 (1983), 47–93; *Fede e politica ad Aquileia: dibattito teologico e centri di potere (secolo IV–VI)* (Udine, 1987), 64 ff.

understanding of the Nicene–Homoian conflict as reflected in the wealth
of polemical documents which survive from this period.

(a) *The convocation and commencement of the council*

Despite this abundance of new material, certain problems continue to
plague scholarly attempts to explicate fully the commencement of the
council and the details which surround its convocation. It is universally
admitted by modern-day analyses that the circumstances which led to the
convoking of the council of Aquileia are not altogether clear. Part of the
difficulty lies in the obscure origins of the council's conception.

We considered earlier in this chapter the problems pertaining to the
imperial initiation of the council, but perhaps a word should be said in
response to the text in the *gesta* where Palladius exclaims that he was
expecting a 'generale et plenum concilium' upon his arrival in Aquileia,[73]
from which Gryson has theorized that the original intent of the emperors
was to convoke an ecumenical council. A joint imperial operation of this
type has already been ruled out. To this can be added several difficulties
with the case put forward by Gryson, despite Cuscito's enthusiastic acceptance.[74] In the first place, Gryson does not explain satisfactorily why
Palladius required an assurance from Gratian that the eastern bishops
were invited if an ecumenical council had indeed been proclaimed. Perhaps Palladius' interview had more to do with establishing just how
ecumenical the council would be. But secondly, Palladius' demand for a
'generale et plenum concilium' before the bishops at Aquileia may mean
that he was demanding an ecumenical council, though it need not.
'Ecumenicity' is a term that did not yet carry the sense so commonly
attributed to it in later eras. The closest definition of a 'full' council for
Palladius can be found in *Gesta*, 11, when he asserts that the absence of
his episcopal 'associates' (*consortes*) nullified the legitimacy of the council.
Unfortunately this piece of text is largely corrupted. Its reconstructed
form (by Zelzer) in translation is as follows: 'I had come as one expecting
a complete council (*Qui quasi ad concilium plenum veneram*), but I saw that
none of my associates were present so that I am coming and speaking
according to the [emperor's] order.'[75] In other words, Palladius' interest
was not in the council's ecumenicity as much as it was in the attendance
of fellow Homoian bishops—and most of these were in the 'east', that is,
the eastern part of the province under Gratian's jurisdiction. When

---

[73] *Gesta*, 6 (*CSEL* lxxxii. 3. 329. 54).
[74] 'Il concilio di Aquileia del 381 e le sue fonti', 204 ff.
[75] *Gesta*, 11 (*CSEL* lxxxii. 3. 332. 122–4).

Palladius approached Gratian about the council in September 380, Theodosius' overt patronage of Nicene catholicism had clearly begun to manifest itself. The bishop of Ratiaria would have heard about the deposition of Demophilus from the Constantinopolitan see and of the new anti-Arian statutes issued by Theodosius. Under these political conditions in the eastern empire, it is not at all clear what benefit Palladius would have gained by requesting an ecumenical council.[76] In September of 380 Gratian's ecclesiastical policies of waning religious tolerance for Arians were still less threatening than those of Theodosius'.

Less problematic is the date for the commencement of the council. The date for its official opening (3 September) is established at the beginning of the *gesta* and appears to be straightforward: 'Syagrio et Eucherio viris clarissimis consulibus III Nonas Septembres Aquileia in ecclesia.' This is little over a month after the closing of the council of Constantinople, which convened from May to the middle of July.[77] In older Ambrosian scholarship, scepticism was voiced about the veracity of the date given in *Gesta* 1 for the opening of the Aquileian council. If the western council is subsequent to the eastern, it becomes difficult to explain why the council of Aquileia in its synodical letters appears to be ignorant of certain decisions made in Constantinople; namely, the consecration of Flavian as bishop of Antioch after Meletius' death.[78] Palanque claims it is inconceivable that the Aquileian council proposed an alternative solution to the Antiochene schism (namely the acceptance of Paulinus) after the election of Flavian, which had taken place shortly after the eastern council had begun. He has thus proposed amending the date given in *Gesta* 1 and placing the start of the western council in May/June.[79]

There has been little acceptance of Palanque's conclusions by later studies on the council of Aquileia. Just four years after the publication of

---

[76] Indeed, no Arian bishops are known to have been present at the council of Constantinople because of Theodosius' recent proscription. For a discussion of the episcopal lists, see E. Schwartz, *Über die Bischofslisten der Synoden von Chalkedon, Nicaea und Konstantinopel* (Munich, 1937), 83 ff.

[77] King presents a useful summary and chronology of the council in *The Emperor Theodosius*, 36 ff. No official *acta* of this council are available but the essential facts are contained in Socrates, *HE* v. 8 (*PG* lxvii. 576–81); Sozomen, *HE* vii. 7–9 (*GSC* l. 308–13); and Theodoret, *HE* v. 6. 3; 8. 1–8 (*GCS* xix. 285; 287–8).

[78] 'Quamlibet' *Ep.* (extra coll.) 6. 4 (*CSEL* lxxxii. 3 188–9). When Ambrose and several north Italian bishops write to Theodosius after the conclusion of the council, they are aware that 'someone' has been appointed in Meletius' place, though not Paulinus ('Sanctum' *Ep.* (extra coll.) 9. 2 (*CSEL* lxxxii. 3. 201–2).

[79] Palanque (*Saint Ambroise*, 504 ff.) has been followed in this regard by Homes Dudden, *Life and Times*, i. 200–1, and by M. Beyenka in her English translation of Ambrose's letters (*FC* xxvi), who dates all the synodical correspondence in the letter headings to May or June of 381.

Saint Ambroise, Zeiller wrote a refutation which definitively undercut Palanque's arguments. Zeiller showed that the bishops at Aquileia must have had some knowledge of the decisions rendered at Constantinople about the Antiochene affair. The concern which they register in the synodical letter 'Quamlibet' gives indication that the news of Meletius' death has reached them as well as 'the noise of the ill-will toward Paulinus'. While Flavian was chosen for the Antiochene episcopate, probably in June, Zeiller points out that he was not consecrated to the see until after the funeral of Meletius, and after the closing of the council of Constantinople.[80] The bishops at Aquileia at least knew of the issues and made their appeal for Paulinus in September. They became better informed, as the letter to Theodosius ('Sanctum') shows, that a replacement had been designated by the eastern council, but even then they appealed for Paulinus as the appropriate successor to Meletius. Zeiller concludes that there is nothing to prevent a prima-facie acceptance of the date as given in *Gesta* 1. His arguments have not been contested and the issue is regarded closed by most modern scholars.

As a result of the new directives which Gratian issued for the council, only about two dozen bishops had assembled in Aquileia by the beginning of September. If one goes by the number of subscriptions found in the minutes of the *gesta* which followed the interrogation of Palladius (*Gesta* 54–64),[81] twenty-five bishops were on hand for the official beginning of the council on 3 September. Most of these were from north Italy, conforming to the suggestion which Ambrose had made to the emperor. Besides Ambrose and Valerian, the latter presiding over the council as the host bishop, there were bishops from the following Italian sees: Ticinum, Tridentum, Bononia, Placentia, Vercelli, Emona, Dertona, Laus, Brixia, Altinum, and Genua. This is the group ('conspiracy') which Palladius has in mind when he denounces the council for not having more than 'twelve of your neighbours'.[82] Also present were two episcopal legates from North Africa, Felix and Numidius, whose sees are not mentioned. Gaul was officially represented by bishops from Lugdunum (Lyons), Massalia (Marseilles), Arausio (Orange), Gratianopolis (Grenoble), Octodurum (Martigny), and Ioviensius (or Iova).[83] From Illyricum came Anemius of

---

[80] 'La Date du concile d'Aquilée (3 septembre 381)', *RHE* 33 (1937), 39–45.

[81] As stated in the imperial rescript (*Gesta* 4) (*CSEL* lxxxii. 3. 328. 32–7).

[82] *Scholia*, 343ᵛ. 42–3 (Gryson, *Scolies*, 304); 338ᵛ. 47: 'eo quod et vos duodecim vel tredecim vix essetis' (Gryson, *Scolies*, 282).

[83] The last-named city reads 'ioviensium' in Paris MS Lat. 8907 and in two 9th-century MSS, which is the reading Gryson employs in his text, Amantius episcopus Ioviensium' (*Gesta* 64 (*Scolies*, 376)), and is listed as one of the sees in Illyricum (*Scolies*, 131). Despite

Sirmium (Mitrovica) and the bishops of Diader (Zadar) and Siscia (Sisak). The last-named bishop in the conciliar roll-call to subscribe to Palladius' condemnation was a certain Ianuarius,[84] whose see is not listed in the *gesta* and is otherwise unknown.

Judging from the sees represented, the gathering of bishops resembled a north Italian synod more than a general western council. No one from Spain or Britain was present. Nor were any delegates from the bishop of Rome sent. And, much to Palladius' chagrin, no representative from the east attended, except perhaps for Evagrius, 'presbyter et legatus', who participated in the deliberations of 3 September on the side of the Nicenes.[85]

The *gesta* taken at the council are concerned with events of 3 September only. After the condemnation of Palladius and Secundianus had been pronounced on that day, it appears that several more bishops joined the assembly. One finds that the list of subscribing bishops affixed to the end of the synodical letter 'Benedictus' totals thirty-four signatures.[86] This is an additional nine bishops to the number which actually subscribed at the close of the *gesta*. This number also differs from the thirty-two bishops which are listed in the beginning of the minutes taken on 3 September. One may assume that the names of the late-comers were added to both subscription lists after the events of 3 September.[87] But we do not know when these other bishops arrived, nor are their sees identified in the two episcopal lists.

(b) *Tactics employed on 3 September*

As bishops assembled in Aquileia in the beginning of September, Palladius must have realized that the original intention for the council had been waylaid and that he had fallen into a trap. Perhaps still hoping that reinforcements would come, he had invited his adversaries to meet him on the morning of 3 September for a full debate of the issues. Unofficial

Zelzer's emendation of 'ioviensium' to 'Lotevensium', a city in Gallia Narbonensi (*CSEL* lxxxii. 3. clxii–clxiii), there is the town 'Iovia' in Pannonia inferior (*PWK* Suppl. ix. 104) which would confirm Gryson.

About Bishop Amantius almost nothing else is known, with the possible exception of a verse epitaph, recommended to me by H. Chadwick, of a bishop with this name found not far from Aquileia (*Corpus inscriptionum Latinarum*, v. 1. 1623). The epitaph, which can only roughly be dated to the end of the 4th century, celebrates Amantius' qualities as one who presided over two peoples, presumably Romans and Goths, for twenty years until his death. No town is named.

[84] *Gesta* 64 (*CSEL* lxxxii. 3. 363. 809–11).
[85] *Gesta* 11 (*CSEL* lxxxii. 3. 332. 117). Cf. *Scholia*, 338ᵛ. 49 (Gryson, *Scolies*, 282).
[86] *Ep.* 2. 12 (*CSEL* lxxxii. 3. 325). [87] Gryson, *Scolies*, 132.

deliberations had already been going on for three or four days. Upon hearing the reading of the imperial rescript, Palladius realized the truth: the council had been radically changed into a type of tribunal in which he and his fellow bishop Secundianus, along with a presbyter named Attalus, were being tried for heresy. Immediately Palladius accused Ambrose of rigging the council by having pressured the emperor to alter the conditions which provided for the eastern bishops to attend.

Palladius said: 'Our emperor Gratian ordered the eastern bishops to come; do you deny he ordered this? The emperor himself said to us that he had ordered the eastern bishops to come.'
Ambrose said: 'In any case, he ordered whoever he did not prohibit to come to this place.'
Palladius said: 'But your petition made it so that they did not come; by an appearance of false intention you obtained this and narrowed the council.'[88]

Gratian had assured Palladius at Sirmium that he had also convoked the easterners, but no mention of this fact is made in the rescript. Only a passing acknowledgement can be detected over this unannounced alteration, that is, between the invitation first offered to all bishops and the way it became limited to those in the vicinity of Aquileia and Milan.[89] Palladius makes it clear that had he known of this change in plans he would not have come. For this reason, he repeatedly insists that the present gathering cannot be considered a genuine or full council, but, rather, a preliminary hearing (*praeiudicium*) void of any recognized authority.[90]

Palladius had good reason to think that he was before a tribunal rather than a council. The physical arrangement of the assembly on the morning of 3 September easily lent itself to this interpretation. According to Palladius' *Apologia* (written soon after the close of the council), the meeting took place, not in the basilica proper, but in a small room annexed to the church, which could contain a limited number of people: 'privately he [Ambrose] saw you inside one *secretarium* of the church in accord with your wishes' ('privatim vos intra eclesiam aput [unum] secretarium pro vestra vidisset voluntate').[91] One would have never learned of this from the nondescript language of the *gesta* which states only that the council

---

[88]   *Gesta*, 8 (*CSEL* lxxxii. 3. 330. 69–76).
[89]   Hanssens, 'Il concilio di Aquileia del 381 alla luce dei documenti contemporanei', *La scuola cattolica*, 103 (1975), 562–3.
[90]   *Gesta*, 12 (*CSEL* lxxxii. 3. 333. 139–40). Cf. *Gesta*, 14; 29; 32; 41; 44; 48.
[91]   *Scholia*, 337ᵛ. 1–2 (using the reconstructed reading in S. Tavano, 'Una pagina degli scolia ariana la sede e il clima del concilio', *Atti del colloquio internazionale*, 151).

was held 'in the church at Aquileia'. Palladius characterizes the *secretarium* where the assembly met as 'narrow', purposely chosen by Ambrose and his colleagues, and so designed to be a private meeting and not a general council. The overall effect was heightened by the fact that the presiding bishop, Valerian, was seated on a dais. At his side a special chair was reserved for Ambrose.[92] Such a setting made it clear to Palladius that this was not a council chamber where debate could take place between equals, but a 'room of audience' where his case was being judged.

In the *Apologia* Palladius further accuses Ambrose of having placed clerics who knew stenography (*exceptores*) behind the backs of the two bishops during the deliberations of 3 September in order to 'eavesdrop' and take down words uttered in passing without mental caution.[93] His charges, in this case, are exaggerated. When one looks at the *gesta* of the council, Ambrose openly announced that stenographers were being used to record the proceedings of the assembly, to which the entire assembly responded in the affirmative. But the substance of Palladius' complaint in the *gesta* was that the clerics were pro-Nicene in sentiment and, therefore, would produce a biased report of the proceedings. In several instances, Palladius refused to answer any questions on the grounds that his answers were not being accurately recorded.[94] This is the complaint which Maximinus draws upon and expands in his attack on the council's proceedings a generation later. He accuses Ambrose's *exceptores* of writing down only 'that which pleased them', and he believes that they deliberately attributed incoherent words to Palladius in order to make him look ridiculous.[95] While it is impossible fully to determine the veracity of Palladius' complaints about biased reporting during the council, his fear of further deceit or tampering seems fully justified in light of what he had experienced thus far in Aquileia. Evidently he was unable to supply his own stenographers, which he had been invited to do.

The strong-arm tactics which were employed by Ambrose and his north Italian circle of supporters are nowhere more apparent than in their method of interrogation of the two Homoian bishops. In the ensuing examination, Homes Dudden gleefully notes, 'the ex-magistrate was in his element' playing the double role of public prosecutor and judge.[96] As

---

[92] *Scholia*, 337ᵛ. 6–7 (Gryson, *Scolies*, 274; 276).

[93] *Scholia*, 339ʳ. 5–9 (Gryson, *Scolies*, 282).

[94] *Gesta*, 43: 'Non tibi respondeo, quia quaecumque ego dixi non sunt scripta; vestra tantummodo scribuntur verba, non vobis respondeo' (*CSEL* lxxxii. 3. 352. 572–4). Cf. *Gesta*, 34; 46; 51; 52; and 69 (by Secundianus).

[95] *Scholia*, 301ᵛ. 37–8; 302ʳ. 29–35 (Gryson, *Scolies*, 222; 224).

[96] *Life and Times*, i. 201. Hanson refers to him simply as 'a bully' (*The Search*, 667).

soon as the imperial rescript was read, Ambrose revealed a letter of Arius, which he introduced with the words: 'it contains blasphemies from the beginning' because it says that the Father alone is eternal. Palladius is asked either to deny the doctrine contained in the letter or confirm it.

The letter in question is Arius' letter to Alexander, which by this time was widely diffused in the west as a symbol of the official doctrine of Arianism.[97] By *c*.360, a Latin translation had appeared in Hilary of Poitiers's *De trinitate*, IV. 12–13. Like Marius Victorinus, who employs Arius' letter to Eusebius of Nicomedia as a foil to refute his opponents,[98] so Ambrose exhumes this text of Arius, making it a watershed of orthodoxy or heresy. The fact that Ambrose did not resort to Palladius' own writings for discussion, writings with which he was surely familiar by now, reveals that he had no intention of debating theology at all. Strategy, not theology, was the need of the moment, and Ambrose wanted simply a damning pretext which would serve to condemn the Homoian bishops. Palladius recognized the ploy, as he later protested in his defence: 'You put forward an unknown letter of Arius, one dead for a long time, not for the purpose of holding a disputation . . .'[99] Even the letter of Arius was reduced to a few token propositions in the course of Ambrose's presentation. We can accept Palladius' complaint then that the Nicenes did not want to debate the issues but rather wished to arrive at the decision which was made before the start of the council. 'A decision (*sermo*) was approved', he says, 'although one party was shut out as an enemy by the dominating party.'

At first Palladius steadfastly refused to succumb to the mode of questioning being used by his inquisitors (*Gesta*, 3–16). He did deny that he knew Arius,[100] but declined to enter into any doctrinal debates on the grounds that the council was not legitimate. When it became apparent that he was about to be condemned for refusing to condemn Arius, Palladius was forced to acquiesce and participate in the proceedings.

Arius was condemned by the Nicenes because he denied that 'the Son was truly God'; a conclusion drawn from his letter to Alexander (of Alexandria) that the Father was 'only eternal, only without beginning, only true, only immortal'. Palladius had no difficulty in saying Christ was 'the true Son of God', basing his acceptance on the language of Romans

---

[97] On the influence of this letter of Arius, see G. Bardy, 'L'Occident et les documents de la controverse arienne', *RSR* 20 (1940), 30–1; P. Nautin, 'Candidus l'Arien', in *L'Homme devant Dieu: mélanges offerts à Henri de Lubac*, vol. i (Lyons, 1963), 312–14.

[98] *Candidi epistola*, II. 1 (*CSEL* lxxxii. 49–50).

[99] *Scholia*, 337ᵛ. 45–6 (Gryson, *Scolies*, 76). Cf. 337ᵛ. 47 ff.

[100] *Gesta*, 14: 'Arrium nec vidi nec scio qui sit' (*CSEL* lxxxii. 3. 334. 158). Cf. Secundianus, 'Qui fuerit Arrius ignoro' (*Gesta*, 66 (365. 834)).

9: 5 (*Gesta*, 17). Secundianus was likewise prepared to confess 'true God only-begotten Son of God' (*Gesta* 70). But both resisted using their opponents' language of 'deum verum dei filium' ('true God, Son of God'), arguing that it was unscriptural; only the Father is described (by the Son) as 'solum verum deum' ('only true God'), according to John 17: 3. This did not mean that Palladius denied the divinity of Christ. To be 'verum filium' was a clear indication that his ontological status was wholly different from the rest of creation. The uniqueness of the Son made it possible for Palladius to agree that Christ's divinity did not die on the cross, since 'he is incorruptible according to his divine generation' (*Gesta*, 24).

In Ambrose's mind, there was 'deceit' (*fraus*) in these assertions. He had been warned by reading Hilary that the Arian confession of 'one true God' was nothing less than a detachment of the Son from the name and nature of God.[101] He was aware how the fathers at Ariminum had been deceived by the language taken from Arius' letter, that the Son of God was a perfect created being, but not as the rest of creation. And he already knew that the Arians referred to Christ as God, but not in the sense that the Son possessed the fullness of the Father's *divinitas*.[102] The fact that Palladius would not commit himself to confessing 'filium deum verum' was just another instance of deceit in the history of the Arians. Among the ultra-conservatives at Aquileia, there was now no longer any room for theological ambiguity. One notes throughout the conciliar proceedings how Palladius is repeatedly asked to speak 'clearly' or 'without cunning' (*Gesta* 12), or that he has 'vacillated' (*refugio*) or 'quibbled' (*cavillor*) in his answers (*Gesta* 47).

When it became clear to Palladius that his condemnation was inevitable, he abandoned any attempt to find a compromise. It was the break Ambrose and his colleagues had been waiting for. Regarding the proper interpretation of Philippians 2: 6–8, Palladius rejected his opponents' Christology, which established a radical distinction between 'the form of a servant' and the 'form of God' in the incarnate Son of God (*Gesta* 35–40). While he did recognize a difference between the divine and human natures in that the Son was immortal and so died 'in the flesh', the entire process of Christ's humiliation implied that the Son's divinity could not be wholly severed from the passions of the flesh. As far as Palladius was concerned the incarnation demonstrated that the Father was greater than the Son, for 'verum deum' could not assume flesh. The Son was 'sent' by the

---

[101] *De trinitate*, v. 3 (*CCSL* lxii. 153).   [102] *De fide*, III. 16. 133 (*CSEL* lxxviii. 155).

Father by becoming incarnate and, therefore, unequal to him. All objections by Ambrose to the effect that the Son was less by reason of his humanity were rebuffed.

Sensing the circular motion of the arguments, Ambrose returned for a final time to his earlier question whether Palladius claimed Christ was created or not. Again, the latter declined to answer and he was at that juncture condemned by each of the pro-Nicene bishops present. Along with Palladius, a presbyter named Attalus was condemned. He had once subscribed to the Nicene faith but was now numbered 'inter Arrianos'.[103]

Once the case of Palladius had been resolved, Secundianus was then examined in like manner. He too avoided confessing that the Son of God was 'verum deum', and, in one instance, outrightly denied it (*Gesta* 68). Like Palladius, the 'true God is he who is unbegotten; and who begot the true only-begotten Son'. Here the *gesta* suddenly break off, ending in the middle of a dialogue between Secundianus and Ambrose (line 916).[104] Our knowledge of Secundianus' fate is derived through the synodical letters which couple the condemnation of Secundianus with that of Palladius. In one of these letters to Gratian, the emperor is asked to depose both bishops and allow replacements as designated by the council.[105]

Before dismissing, the council dealt with several other matters which are revealed in two synodical letters addressed to Gratian. In the first, concern is registered over the continued activities of Julian Valens in Milan, where he operates in collusion with the presbyter Attalus, sowing 'seeds of impiety and treachery'. Despite the fact that Valens refused to appear before the council and so be formally examined, the council sought his expulsion from north Italy. The same letter requests the enforcement of previous legislation against the Photinians who were still holding assemblies in Sirmium. In the second letter, attention is once more directed to Milan over the disturbances caused by Ursinus in conjunction with Julian Valens and his followers. Judging from the description of the disturbances,[106] even if we assume it is somewhat exaggerated, and from the fact that this situation merited a synodical letter alone, we can conclude that Ambrose was still much troubled by ecclesiastical strife in his see. At the close of the letter, the emperor is entreated to eject this 'most

---

[103] *Gesta*, 44 (*CSEL* lxxxii. 3. 353. 591).

[104] Gryson doubts that the break is due to lost folios since the text is completed in the penultimate line of the last column with the word *amen* (*Scolies*, 57 n. 2). Nor do the later *scholia* reproduce any of the lost parts of the *gesta*.

[105] *Ep.* ('Benedictus') 2. 8 (*CSEL* lxxxii. 3. 320. 97–102).

[106] *Ep.* 5 (extra coll.). 3 (*CSEL* lxxxii. 3. 183–4. 30–40).

troublesome man' and restore peace to the bishops (i.e., Ambrose) and to the city of Rome also being agitated by Ursinus' disciples.

It is clear that the authority of a council, not to mention the expectation of imperial ratification, gave Ambrose an unparalleled opportunity to deal decisively with his antagonists. The only constructive act of the council was the initiation of an inquiry into the reasons for Paulinus' rejection by the council of Constantinople for the bishopric of Antioch.[107]

3. THE ACHIEVEMENT OF THE COUNCIL OF AQUILEIA

How do we measure the achievement of the council of Aquileia in the history of the late fourth-century conflict between Nicenes and Homoians? Is Simonetti correct when he ends his massive survey of the Arian controversy with the conclusion that the council represents 'the definitive defeat of Arianism in the west, just as in the east the council of Constantinople effectively marked the definitive defeat of the same heresy'?[108] Modern scholarly opinion has generally flowed along these lines. Like Simonetti, W. H. C. Frend presents the meetings at Aquileia and Constantinople as dual councils which 'mark[ed] the end of Arianism in the Roman empire',[109] and Cuscito has simply re-echoed this view in his recent studies of the period.[110]

If we are to accept such a generalization it must not be without certain necessary qualifications. These qualifications are intended to avoid the sweeping conclusion that (1) the council of Aquileia was a political and ecclesiastical convocation parallel to the council in the east and (2) the council of Aquileia was responsible for erasing the last vestiges of Homoianism in the west.

There is very little similarity between the eastern and western councils given the information at our disposal. Once we have dismissed the notion that Gratian and Theodosius originally intended to hold either an ecumenical or collaborative conciliar gathering, there is no need to presume that the circumstances which gave rise to these assemblies have a

---

[107] This issue is raised in the synod's only known letter to Theodosius ('Quamlibet'). Theodosius is asked to convene a synod of bishops in Alexandria in order to deal with the dissension produced by the episcopal elections (*Ep.* 6 (extra coll.). 5 (*CSEL* lxxxii. 3. 189)).

[108] *La crisi ariana*, 547.

[109] See W. H. C. Frend, *The Early Church* (Philadelphia, 1965), 177.

[110] 'Il concilio di Aquileia', 189; *Fede e politica*, 75. Cf. Homes Dudden, who concludes, 'The Council of Aquileia marks the victory of Catholicism over Arianism so far as the Western Empire was concerned' (*Life and Times*, i. 205–6).

common denominator. The convocation and the results produced from each council show the differences clearly enough.

At Constantinople Theodosius was directly responsible for assembling a council together in order to ordain his choice of Gregory (of Nazianzus) as the new bishop of that city and to confirm the establishment of the Nicene faith which had recently been mandated by law.[111] About 150 bishops supportive of the Nicene confession arrived from various parts of the eastern empire. An additional thirty-six Macedonian bishops (followers of the views of Macedonius, once bishop of Constantinople, who denied the consubstantiality of the Holy Spirit) were present for part of the council. The main objectives of the convocation were fulfilled: a pro-Nicene bishop (Nectarius) was elected to the episcopate, and the Nicene faith was affirmed.[112] Four canons,[113] which can be considered genuine from the council of 381, were also passed. On 30 July, after the final proceedings of the council were over, Theodosius issued an edict enforcing the decisions of the assembly commanding that all churches be turned over to Nicene bishops and that whoever was not in communion with the bishop of Constantinople, as well as with other leading bishops named in the edict, should be expelled from their churches as heretics.[114]

The much smaller synod which gathered at Aquileia in September was fundamentally different in its origins and produced no symbol nor is known to have formally reaffirmed an existing one. It is obvious that the Nicene faith was the touchstone of orthodoxy in the deliberations with Palladius, but nowhere in the *gesta* or in the synodical letter is there found a credal statement. Tavano overstates the case therefore when he says that the 'purpose of Ambrose was solely that of reaffirming the Nicene faith'.[115] It seems rather that the major purpose of Aquileia was to

---

[111] Socrates, *HE* v. 8 (*PG* lxvii. 576B); Sozomen, *HE* vii. 7. 1 (*GSC* l. 308). Both historians claim that the council was assembled to elect a bishop, but Gregory withdrew when the arriving bishops began to dispute over his election (Sozomen, *HE* vii. 7. 8 (*GSC* l. 309–10)).

[112] Mansi, iv. 567–8. There are many problems about whether this council officially affirmed any other creed than that of Nicaea, or accepted an expanded version of the same creed elaborating the consubstantiality of the Holy Spirit, or did both. Kelly's overview of the issues is still unsurpassed. *Early Christian Creeds*, 296–331.

[113] These pertained to the anathematization of all heresies, the forbidding of bishops of one diocese to interfere with the affairs of another diocese, the establishment of Constantinople as the 'new Rome' and its bishop as the primate of the east, and the rejection of Maximus' claim to episcopal ordination (in Alexandria), which effectively annulled his efforts to seize the bishopric of Constantinople. Full text in Hefele with translation and commentary, *History of the Church Councils*, vol. ii, trans. H. N. Oxenham (Edinburgh, 1896), 353–9.

[114] *C. Th.* xvi. 1. 3. Cf. Sozomen, *HE* vii. 9. 5–7 (*GCS* l. 312–23).

[115] Quoted in Cuscito, 'Il concilio di Aquileia', 222.

dispose of the leaders of western Homoianism and other local pockets of resistance, which *de facto* confirmed the state's recent wedding to Nicene Christianity. The theological perspective exhibited by the Nicenes at Aquileia is reactive, almost regressive, in the sense that the assembly is concerned with attacking the Christological theses exemplified at Ariminum by means of Arius' letter. One is equally struck by the complete absence of any mention of the Holy Spirit in all documentation stemming from the council, despite the fact that the Spirit's consubstantiality was being debated in the west at this time. In effect, no progress is made theologically, and that the dialogue of the *gesta* 'tourne vers le passé'[116] underlines the limited nature of the council's objectives.

To what degree was the council of Aquileia successful in eliminating Homoianism from the west? One must be cautioned against blithely accepting Ambrose's pronouncement of the death of Arianism as a result of the council's decisions. In the synodical letters Palladius and Secundianus are arraigned as doctrinal curios and anachronisms whose blasphemy had previously thrown into confusion only a small corner of eastern Dacia, whereas 'the communion of the faithful remains one and unsullied'[117] throughout all territories, districts, and villages of the west.

To a large extent the enthusiasm of the synodical reports is justified. We remember how Palladius fought so diligently for the invitation of the eastern bishops at the council of Aquileia, without whom he lacked support for his position. That episode indicates the degree to which the Homoians no longer possessed a majority party or episcopal control over any western see. This state of affairs, however, owed practically nothing to the decisions made at Aquileia. Homoians had been a party in decline throughout the west for most of the last decade. The council did not mark the 'definitive defeat' of Arianism as much as it demonstrated the latter's weakness due especially to the ascendancy of unrestrained imperial patronage of pro-Nicene bishops and churches. Understood in this way, the decisions of the council possess little significance in themselves and perhaps are part of the reason why the council is not mentioned in Latin sources where we would most expect it, such as Paulinus' *Vita Ambrosii* or Rufinus' *Historia ecclesiastica*. It is more accurate to say, rather, that the Aquileian assembly was merely symbolic of the political/religious developments that had occurred under Gratian and Theodosius.

In no way does the council of Aquileia end the conflict between Nicenes

---

[116] Duval, 'Le Sens des debats', 96.
[117] *Ep.* 6 (extra coll.). 3 (*CSEL* lxxxii. 3. 188. 30–2).

and Homoians in the west. To say otherwise completely ignores the
course of events after 381. Evidence in the synodical letters from Aquileia
shows that the Homoian minority in Milan still possessed leadership,
held assemblies, and were capable of creating major disturbances in the
city (*above*). Presumably, the action against them which the council requested from Gratian had some effect, despite the subtle but persistent
patronage from the court of Valentinian II. Now that Gratian continued
to bolster the Nicenes in their opposition against Arianism, the final
eradication of Homoianism from Milan seemed inevitable. And yet, such
hopes were guaranteed only as long as Gratian remained alive and in
power. No one, Ambrose included, could have predicted the radical shift
in religious affairs that was about to happen.

7

A Homoian Revival in Milan

THE decisions made at the council of Aquileia did not go unchallenged. Palladius had been condemned and deposed but not silenced. Sometime after the close of the council but before the end of 384, a different version of the events which had transpired at Aquileia began to circulate among ecclesiastical circles in Milan and elsewhere. This document was written as a *riposte* to those accusations formulated against Palladius and Secundianus which they were not given opportunity to answer in the council. The fragmented text is found only among the marginalia of the Paris MS Latinus 8907, a part of a larger *apologia*,[1] and divulging the existence of an embittered Homoian reaction against the heavy-handed tactics employed at Aquileia. Its object of scorn is unquestionably Ambrose of Milan, who, although he is not mentioned by name, is repeatedly accused of 'insidiousness' (*versutiae*), administratively and theologically.

While we have no exact means of gauging the effect of the anti-Aquileian document in the west at this time, one indicator of its usefulness for Homoian purposes may be seen by its preservation and interpretation a full generation later by Maximinus. His 'Dissertatio Maximini contra Ambrosium' (so-called by Kauffmann) was responsible for preserving a number of unique pro-Homoian documents from the 380s, and among these is the denunciation of the events at Aquileia by Palladius in his *apologia*. Yet another means of detecting a Homoian reaction after the council of Aquileia is from the writing of *De incarnationis dominicae sacramento* by Ambrose, *circa* 382, in which the bishop still finds it necessary to refute anti-Nicene arguments referred to him by the emperor. We cannot say for certain whether these arguments stem from more recent polemics following the council, but, if the story which Paulinus records about the two Arian chamberlains demanding a public debate with Ambrose is true, then we can most easily place this challenge, and Ambrose's response, which was later published as *De incarnatione*, in the

---

[1] So Gryson has entitled it, 'Fragment from an Apology of the Condemned of Aquileia', *Scholia*, 337ʳ. 50–349ʳ. 4 (Gryson, *Scolies*, 274–324).

context of the aftermath of Aquileia. A brief overview of these documents will reveal the suggested connections between them.

I. THE ANTI-AQUILEIAN REACTION

There is little doubt that the author of the post-Aquileian apology is none other than Palladius himself.[2] The *apologia* was obviously written by someone present at the proceedings of the council of Aquileia since the writer offers additional details not found in the *gesta* of the council, and only Palladius, Secundianus, Attalus, and perhaps some lesser clergy were present on behalf of the Homoians. Maximinus provides us with positive identification when he makes an allusion in his commentary to several passages of the apology and indicates that the author is Palladius.[3] The only problem remaining, which was the original reason the *apologia* was originally attributed to Maximinus, is that the entire work is written in the third person. But this too has a simple solution as suggested by Gryson: that Palladius was speaking not only for himself but on behalf of his colleagues as a representative of his ecclesiastical identity.[4] Indeed, one can say that the Homoian Church through Palladius' pen is making its appeal in response to the condemnations at Aquileia. This assessment is vindicated when the reader comes to the conclusion of the apology and discovers that its intent is to call for a public debate before the Roman senate where experts from Homoians and Nicenes would contend with each other before the intellectual élite of the empire.[5]

The style and tone which Palladius adopts for the *apologia* are a dramatic reversal of the conditions manifested at the council of Aquileia; now Palladius is the accuser and Ambrose is the accused. 'Tell me', states Palladius, 'you have said that Palladius, Demophilus, and Auxentius were certainly Arians because they held different opinions from you, and to whom you have promised to respond.'[6] Undoubtedly Palladius is alluding to *De fide*, I. 6. 45, where Ambrose classifies together the above-mentioned with the offensive name of Arians. His point here is one that

---

[2] Hammond-Bammel, 'From the School of Maximinus', 394; Gryson, *Scolies*, 83 ff.; A. de Halleux (review of Gryson, *Scolies*), *Revue théologique de Louvain*, 12 (1981), 85. The balance of views over the last century has favoured Maximinus as the author.

[3] *Scholia*, 308ᵛ. 13–21 (Gryson, *Scolies*, 252).   [4] Gryson, *Scolies*, 95.

[5] *Scholia*, 348ᵛ. 40–348ᵛ. 3 (Gryson, *Scolies*, 322). Composition of the work occurred sometime after the close of the council in Sept. 381, and before the death of Damasus of Rome (11 Dec. 384), who is mentioned as still living (fo. 384ʳ. 37–40).

[6] *Scholia*, 337ʳ. 50–1 (Gryson, *Scolies*, 274).

is common to the argument of the apology: any preparation for an open council at Aquileia to discuss the issues was abandoned on account of Ambrose's intervention with the result that 'it was not a council at all'. Instead, Palladius retorts, you submitted 'the unknown letter of Arius, dead for a long time' in order to prevent a debate on contemporary matters.[7] The fact that he and his colleagues were forced to deny or subscribe to this profession of faith (Arius' letter) is utterly detestable. Just as he had eschewed all association with the name of Arius at the council of Aquileia (*Gesta* 25), so Palladius rejects that association with the Homoian party. Such was a common complaint by those in Palladius' tradition as they sought to establish their identity in the face of pro-Nicene hostilities. Locked in bitter conflict with an anti-Arian majority, western Homoians were increasingly forced to assert their right to a Christian past and hence to the Christian name.[8] Later in the *apologia* Palladius will cite (from memory) the opening line of Arius' confession of faith to Alexander,[9] and prefaces the formula by saying it shows proper reverence to the Almighty Father. Like many of his episcopal predecessors who opposed Homoousian teaching in the earlier stages of the controversy, Palladius did not follow Arius even if he shared some of the same presuppositions about the nature of God the Father.

When Palladius and his colleagues refused to subscribe to Arius' letter, Ambrose is said to have tried to extort their signatures by means of intimidation, 'in the stern manner of a civil authority figure'.[10] The elevated seats of Valerian and Ambrose, the small hall in which the council was held, the placing of stenographers next to the defendants, and the staccato-like methods of interrogation, all is described and denounced. Of course one should not be surprised by the use of such tactics against holy and aged bishops, laments Palladius, by a man who received the episcopate neither in accord with the proper 'ecclesiastica disciplina' nor on account of the merits of his faith and life, but 'through the favours of friendship you were elected (*crearis*) undeservedly by means of human approbation without propriety'[11]—a taunting reference to Ambrose's sudden election to the Milanese see through political support and clout. The insinuation

---

[7] *Scholia*, 337ʳ. 45–6 (Gryson, *Scolies*, 276).
[8] R. P. Vaggione, 'A Detection of "Arians": The Opponents of Nicaea and the Problem of Classification', 3. The author was gracious enough to let me cite this paper in its typescript form which is an excerpt from his forthcoming book on Eunomius (Oxford University Press).
[9] *Scholia*, 339ʳ. 39–45 (Gryson, *Scolies*, 284).
[10] *Scholia*, 339ʳ. 14–16 (Gryson, *Scolies*, 282).
[11] *Scholia*, 343ʳ. 3–4 (Gryson, *Scolies*, 302; 304).

is that Ambrose deposes bishops from their sees as easily and as passively as he entered into one.

With unequivocal hostility and sarcasm, Palladius declares that a true hearing of his position was never provided because of Ambrose's obstructionist activities at Aquileia. Now Palladius seeks an opportunity to redress the issues unless the bishop of Milan is too afraid that his own errors will come to light. He suggests that they formally present their arguments: 'If you place any confidence in your faith, let us testify to the faith in the senate of that city [Rome] for 30 or 40 days according to the authority of the Scriptures.'[12] Palladius is well aware that Pagans and even Jews will be in the audience, but this is not a deterrent; rather, it presents at least two benefits. First, it provides an opportunity to evangelize them since both groups would be familiar with the Scriptures, especially the Jews, in that they know the Law. Second, and of greater importance, such an audience ('externi esse videntur') would be more likely to hand down an impartial decision. Palladius made a similar proposal on a much smaller scale during the council of Aquileia when he realized that his condemnation was inevitable. After repeatedly refusing to respond to Ambrose's questions, he demanded fresh *auditores*, who should come from neither side, to hear his case. Ambrose rebuffed this suggestion as testified by the *gesta* on the grounds that 'priests ought to judge the laity, not laity the priests'. Interestingly Ambrose will use the same argument in 386 during a second conflict over the basilica when faced with the Homoian insistence on lay arbitration in resolving the crisis. He may have had Palladius' *apologia* in mind when he wrote to the young Emperor Valentinian refusing to be heard by lay judges because it 'surrendered the triumph of Christ to some Pagan or Jew'.[13] The proposal which Palladius makes in his apology for impartial judgement by non-Christians does manifest desperate measures on his part, although it is hardly likely that we are seeing here the result of a convergence between the Arian minority, Pagans, and Jews during the time of Valentinian II.[14] The apparent desperation is more symptomatic of the monopoly which Nicene theology had in the churches. Ambrose was well aware of this and was not about to throw the 'triumph of Christ' (i.e., Nicene faith) away.

---

[12] *Scholia*, 348ᵛ. 1–3 (Gryson, *Scolies*, 322).

[13] *Ep.* LXXV. 13 (CSEL lxxxii. 3. 79. 91–3).

[14] L. Cracco Ruggini, 'Ambrogio e le opposizioni anticattoliche fra il 383 e il 390', *Augustinianum*, 14 (1974), 412–16. Nor is there any solid evidence that the Homoians tended to be 'softer' on Paganism than Catholics as Birley interprets the proposal of Palladius, 'Magnus Maximus and the Persecution of Heresy', 27.

When Maximinus undertook the work of collating various pro-Homoian documents half a century later, he himself appended further criticisms of the council of Aquileia and its treatment of Palladius and his colleagues. He has no first-hand knowledge of the events he is recording but he does possess the *gesta* of the council, Palladius' *apologia*, and perhaps an unknown letter of Palladius which the latter submitted to the council.[15] Maximinus rehearses the matter of Ambrose falsifying the original intention of the council (fo. 299^r. 1–35), the use of biased stenographers (301^v. 9–31; 37–8), and Palladius' (now 'sanctus Palladius') arguments that the council was not legitimate but a *praejudicium* (302^r. 1–35). Only because he was confounded by the arguments of Palladius did Ambrose turn to the letter of Arius, pressing Palladius to confess his faith before these blasphemers. The latter utterly declined to respond to the questions because of the heretics' unrestrained impiety. The episode bore similarity in Maximinus' mind to the exchange which took place between the Pagan Demetrianus and St Cyprian, who refused at first to speak to Demetrianus because he spoke 'with sacrilegious lips and impious words' and would not listen to the truth.[16] A paradigm then is erected between Demetrianus–Ambrose and St Cyprian–St Palladius; the unjust persecutor and the one persecuted on account of the truth. Demetrianus blamed the faith of the Christians for the increase in droughts, wars, etc. In the same way, 'O Ambrose, you assert that the devastation of barbarian invasions happened on account of us'—a charge made by Ambrose in the *De fide* (II 16. 140–1) in an attempt to spur Gratian on to whole-hearted support of the Nicene Church. In parallel to Cyprian, Palladius is said to have been oppressed for his faith, and the reader is meant to understand that Cyprian and Palladius held the same views regarding the 'one and only true God' who sent the Son and is recognized by him as 'solum verum Deum' (John 17: 1–3).[17] Maximinus argues that it is ridiculous to assume such views originated with Arius, as the council of Aquileia did when they resorted to his letter as a means to condemn Palladius: 'It is well known that Arius followed the bishops, not bishops following Arius.' Arius was in full accord with the doctrine of Cyprian in his letter to Alexander, and, therefore, was within the traditional teaching of the Church. Just as we saw

---

[15] This letter appears to have been read at the council but is not included in the minutes. *Gesta* 10 (*CSEL* lxxxii. 3. 331. 95–8). The letter in question was probably the correspondence which Palladius sent to the Emperor Gratian urging him to convene a council so that the Homoians could present their case against Ambrose and the Nicenes.

[16] *Scholia*, 299^v. 3–300^r. 39, citing *Ad Demetrianum*, 1–2 (*CCSL* iiiA. 35–6).

[17] *Scholia*, 300^v. 15–34 (Gryson, *Scolies*, 216).

with Palladius, Maximinus was not concerned to defend Arius, but recognized that Arius' presuppositions bore witness to the same faith of the Fathers. These presuppositions represented the principal watershed which divided the Homoians from their opponents.

(a) *The* De incarnationis dominicae sacramento

Despite his passionate pleas for justice, Palladius stood as a condemned bishop without a see and his proposals for another hearing had no effect. It stands to reason that any anti-Nicene efforts were doomed to ultimate failure, especially now that Gratian had moved to the imperial residence in the city of Milan.[18] But this did not prevent Ambrose's enemies from still trying to discredit him. Sometime after the court of Gratian had arrived in Milan, Ambrose was challenged to a public debate over the doctrine of Christ's nature with regard to the incarnation. The context is established in the opening line of *De incarnationis dominicae sacramento*,[19] which is the title of an edited version of the address Ambrose delivered before the Milanese congregation while waiting for his challengers to appear. 'I desire to pay off [my] debt, but I do not find my creditors of yesterday unless perhaps they imagine we are shaken by the unexpected encounter, but the true faith is never shaken. And so perhaps while they are coming . . .'[20] One does not learn from Ambrose's address whether his opponents finally arrived, who they were, or how the debate was concluded; in fact, very few details are provided in the text. This frustrating silence has induced scholars to admit Paulinus' account of the occasion as the historical setting for the debate. According to the *Vita Ambrosii*, two chamberlains of the Emperor Gratian, who were members 'of the Arian

---

[18] Gratian's movements for most of 381 and early 382 are poorly documented in our ancient sources, though he must have settled in Milan no later than the autumn of 382 and perhaps as early as the spring of 381 (*Regesten*, 258; 260).

[19] The title is taken from VII. 7. 63: 'Et tamen de patris et fili divinitate consummaturum responsionem in superioribus me spoponderam, hoc autem libro de incarnationis dominicae sacramento plenior . . .' (*CSEL* lix. 256. 9–11). There is general agreement about placing the date of the confrontation at end of 381. From factors internal to the work, we can say for certain that it was written after the five books of *De fide*, which are cited as a unit ('quinque illis quos scripsisti libris' (VII. 62)) and probably after *De spiritu sancto* (Faller, *CSEL* lix. 46*), which was published in the spring of 381. We know too that an edited version of the address was sent to Gratian (*De incarn.* VIII. 80), showing that the work was published before his death (Aug. 383). Paulinus' chronology, though generally not trustworthy, places his account of the confrontation (ch. 18) after the court of Gratian came to Milan, which is probably correct.

[20] *De incarn.* I. 1 (*CSEL* lix. 225). Faller reads 'cudo' instead of 'cupio'. *PL* xvi. 853A uses 'cupio' as does, interestingly, the *Vita* of Paulinus.

heresy', posed a *questio* for Bishop Ambrose to discuss in public regarding the incarnation of Christ. But the next day, instead of going to the Portian basilica where the issues were to be discussed, the two climbed into a carriage 'as if going for a drive' and quickly left the city. Unmindful of their promise and swollen with pride, the chamberlains were visited by divine judgement: the carriage lost control and they were instantly killed when thrown from their seats.[21] It is evident that Paulinus has the *De incarnatione* in part or whole in front of him because he closes his brief narrative with Ambrose beginning his sermon with the opening words, ' "Brethren, I desire to pay off [my] debt, but I do not find my creditors of yesterday" and the rest which was written in the book entitled, "On the Incarnation of the Lord".'

It is not our intent here to question Paulinus' version of the occasion for *De incarnatione*, especially since we have already discussed his literary agenda in Chapter 5. Certain elements of his account are more credible than others.[22] Ambrose never specifies the issue proposed to him in the course of the sermon, which constitutes the first part of the *De incarnatione* (chs. 1–78), though in the appendix (chs. 79–116) added afterwards he explains that the same men to whom he once addressed himself on the nature of the generated Son[23] had recently restated their views, this time with the question, 'How can the Unbegotten and the Begotten be of one nature and substance?' When the matter reached the ears of Gratian, he approached Ambrose for an answer. The bishop was not on the defensive as he was before 381; he was nevertheless obligated to answer his critics.

It is true that he had treated the subject of the incarnation in *De fide*, especially book III, where the sacrament of the incarnation is one of the major themes.[24] New challenges had arisen since then requiring careful reformulation of his understanding of the divine/human relationship in the incarnate Christ. One of these challenges came from quarters which accepted the Nicene faith but mixed the divinity of the Word with humanity such that 'the flesh and divinity of the Lord are of one nature'.

---

[21] *VA* 18. 1–12 (Pellegrino, *Vita*, 74; 76).

[22] The identification of two Arian chamberlains belonging to the retinue of Gratian is surprising, though not impossible. *Cubicularii* were a part of the emperor's personal household and so were a mobile part of the administration (*LRE* i. 49). This means that the two chamberlains could have come with the emperor to Milan from Trier, where Homoianism had little, if any, influence. Whatever anti-Nicene or anti-Ambrosian sympathies the two may have harboured, they would have found much encouragement for their views from the Homoian community at Milan. The other alternative is that the two were new appointments to the staff of Gratian after the court arrived in the city.

[23] VIII. 79 (*CSEL* lix. 264. 1–6).

[24] See *De fide*, III. 3. 15–17; 5. 35–8; 7. 46; 9. 59; 10. 65.

Ambrose is referring to the Apollinarians, with whom he had had few dealings till now. It is not clear from the *De incarnatione* whether Ambrose fully understood their doctrine, since he continually insists that they taught that the Word was changed into the nature of the body. His commentary may reflect Apollinarius' insistence that the Word was substantially one with his flesh or one nature. Accurate or not, such a position was extremely offensive to the strict dichotomy which Ambrose attributed to the incarnation:

The divinity of the Word therefore is not immolated because the divinity of the Word does not sin. And so the nature of the Word is not transmuted into the nature of the flesh because divinity, in the presence of sin, is immune to it, which it does not commit, nor committed to offer itself. Christ presented in himself that with which he was clothed, which he did not possess before . . . but he assumed flesh that he might throw off the covering of flesh.[25]

Palanque underestimates the severity of Ambrose's speech against Apollinarian teaching in the *De incarnatione* when he claims it is not until later (namely in the letter to Sabinus, *Ep.* 39) that Ambrose strenuously opposes the 'virus of Apollinaris' when a follower of this sect attacked one of his works.[26] *De incarnatione*, VI. 49, speaks of these as having 'vomited so great a sacrilege', even less tolerable than the Arians since it provides them with further support to assert that the Father and the Son are not of one substance. But nor is it correct to suppose that Ambrose's delivery of the *De incarnatione* was meant to distinguish him from Apollinarius.[27] Only chapters 49–61 are concerned with this doctrine and it does not seem to be the principal motive for the address or the appendix. The question of Christ's incarnational nature was just as intense an issue between the Nicenes and Homoians.

In *De incarnatione*, VII. 62, Ambrose observes that his enemies had raised further objections since he had written about the divinity of the Father and the Son 'in those five books' (*De fide*). Judging from the responses discussed in the *De incarnatione*, it is evident that he is speaking in part about Palladius' writings. The latter held, as did nearly all Arians, that the incarnate Word had no human soul (or mind); the Word thus experienced all that was human. Ambrose is accordingly compelled to renew his arguments for a distinction between the sufferings and death of Christ's human nature and the impassibility of his divine nature (v.

---

[25] *De incarn.* VI. 56 (*CSEL* lix. 252–3).   [26] *Saint Ambroise*, 105.
[27] So Meslin, *Les Ariens*, 47 n. 88.

37–45). In the course of his argument, he asks his opponent in rhetorical fashion, 'Why do you attribute to divinity hardships of the body and join to the divine nature infirmities of human suffering?'[28] It was a completely accurate assessment. Without blinking Palladius was glad to affirm the unmitigated sacrifice of the God-Man on humanity's behalf, and in his *apologia* there is a sustained refutation of Ambrose's radical separation of the human and divine natures of Christ just to avoid the inevitable subordinationist language applied to the Son in the Scriptures. The Scriptures say, 'Christ died for our sins' (1 Corinthians 15: 3), which Ambrose applies to the flesh (*carnem*) of Christ. But, Palladius critically observes, since Ambrose believes that 'Christ' is a human and divine appellation, such strict separation of the two natures is not possible. With compelling force he concludes: 'Therefore believe not that he suffered in the flesh alone, but as God and man, and Son of God and Son of man, that is, with both allied together; the Lord of glory was crucified.'[29]

Hanson's evaluation of Arian theology is at its best on the issue of the Son's incarnation. He writes, 'Because Arians were determined that the Son of God did genuinely, seriously undergo human experiences, within the limits of their doctrine they understood the scandal of the Cross much better than the pro-Nicenes.'[30] The scandal for Ambrose is that the Homoians could implicate the divine nature in such a fashion that debased it to the level of the human. While Ambrose never quotes the above passage or any other from Palladius' writings, it is reasonable to assume that the object of Ambrose's virulent attack in *De incarnatione*, v. 41 ff., is Palladius, or at least a circulating version of his arguments which took exception to Ambrose's view of the God-Man.

Ambrose's response to the question raised about the substantial unity of the Unbegotten and the Begotten forms the reason and substance of the appendix in the *De incarnatione*. The very wording of the question posed the necessity of articulating new theological insights, as Ambrose himself admitted. In *De fide*, iv. 8. 82–91, he had argued that 'to beget' was a function of the Father's nature, and did not pertain to a prerogative of his authority over the Son, just as the generation of the Son was an attribute of the Son, not a mark of his division from or inferiority to the Father. The query posed in the *De incarnatione*, asserting that the term *genitus* applies to essence, juxtaposes the essence of the Son, 'generated',

---

[28] v. 41 (*CSEL* lix. 244. 65–6).   [29] *Scholia*, 340ʳ. 38–41 (Gryson, *Scolies*, 292).
[30] 'The Arian Doctrine of the Incarnation', in Gregg (ed.), *Arianism: Historical and Theological Reassessments*, 203.

to the essence of the Father qualified as 'ungenerated' and so different from that of the Son.[31]

Ambrose charged that such a view demonstrates the Father and the Son are ultimately *dissimilis*; a charge that Ambrose had lodged against his oppponents once before in *De fide*, I. 5. 41–2, and found himself needing to defend it with greater tact. Palladius had taken particular exception to this charge in his refutation of *De fide*, I–II, since the Homoian intent was simply to show that the begotten Son was not co-existent and co-eternal to the unbegotten Father: 'You claim therefore that we teach unlikeness because we say he [the Son] is not co-existent with the Unbegotten and co-eternal to the Father even though, just as you also often have professed, the truth commends the Begotten from the Father.'[32] With the reintroduction of *ingenitus* and *genitus* into the debate, as we find in *De incarnatione*, greater weight is being placed on *ingenitus* as a unique quality of the Father, which Ambrose now undertakes to refute by showing that *ingenitus* is not a scriptural term (VIII. 80–8). The source of the terminology is none other than Arius, who used the titles 'the unbegotten Father and the begotten and created son'—a near quote from his infamous letter to Alexander.[33] Palladius does not deny the link between the two. Rather he is very critical of the Aquileian council in the *apologia* for detracting from Arius' profession of faith (which he quotes: 'Credo in unum solum verum Deum, auctorem omnium, solum ingenitum, solum sempiternum Deum,' etc.), and, in so doing, is defending the acceptability and traditionality of that doctrine which Arius shared. The result of Ambrose's arguments, in Palladius' view, would be to despoil the Father of his uniqueness which makes him truly God. This same criticism, therefore, is behind what is almost certainly Palladius' question, 'How can the Unbegotten and the Begotten be of one nature and substance?'

By considering the polemical roles of Palladius' *apologia* and Ambrose's *De incarnatione*, we have been able to glimpse something of the exchange which took place after the council of Aquileia between the Nicenes and Homoians, and the desperate situation which the enemies of Ambrose faced. It was a losing battle for the Homoians. Whatever effect Palladius' writings had on the Milanese community, it was a moot point as long as the western emperor remained pro-Nicene and engaged his imperial power to undergird the position of his favoured constituents.

---

[31] *De incarn.* IX. 95 (*CSEL* lix. 270).   [32] *Scholia*, 336[r]. 11–20 (Gryson, *Scolies*, 264).
[33] *De incarn.* IX. 91 (*CSEL* lix. 268. 17–18).

2. MAXIMUS' USURPATION

There was no longer any doubt about Gratian's firm loyalty to the bishop of Milan and to the bishop's theological convictions. Just as he had taken steps to ban all forms of Christian heresy, so now, a year after the council of Aquileia, Gratian sought to diminish the privileges traditionally accorded to the official Pagan cults at Rome. By means of an edict which is no longer extant[34] revenues which were used to maintain ceremonial sacrifices and the priestly colleges were diverted to the imperial treasury. Public subsidies allotted to the Vestal Virgins were also confiscated.[35] An even greater blow was delivered that same year when Gratian ordered the Altar of Victory to be removed from the senate-house steps. Its removal brought great consternation to the Pagan element of the senate, since the altar was symbolic of Rome's prosperity and upon it sacrifices had inaugurated senatorial sessions ever since the days of Augustus.[36] Gratian was hardened to the ensuing reaction, refusing even to grant audience to a delegation led by the Pagan aristocrat Symmachus who had come to plead for its restoration.[37] It appears that Ambrose had already presented the emperor with a counter-petition organized by Christian senators who objected to the proposal for the altar's restoration.[38]

While Gratian was getting high marks from the Christian bishops for his religious policies, his mismanagement of political affairs was brewing unrest. Certainly his legal action against Pagan religion was not popular with large segments of the Roman nobility, though it can scarcely be

[34] The edict is attested in a law of 415 (*C. Th.* XVI. 10. 20) stating that 'in accordance with the constitution of the divine emperor Gratian we ordain that all places assigned by the false doctrine of the ancients to their rituals shall be joined to the property of our personal treasury' (C. Pharr, *The Theodosian Code* (Princeton, NJ, 1952), 475 (modified)). Cf. Ambrose's first letter to Valentinian II over the Altar of Victory controversy, which refers to the 'former rescripts' which abolished the rites of Pagan sacrifices and made them a thing of the past (*Ep.* 72. 5 (*CSEL* lxxxii. 3. 13. 36–40)).

[35] Ambrose, *Ep.* (to Valentinian) 73. 3 (*CSEL* lxxxii. 3. 35); Symmachus, *Relatio*, III (= *Ep.* 72a). 11 (*CSEL* lxxxii. 3. 27–8).

[36] Matthews, *Western Aristocracies*, 204. Only the altar was removed; the statue (of Victory) was retained.

[37] Symmachus, *Relatio*, III. 1; 20 (*CSEL* lxxxii. 3. 22. 7–8; 32. 179–81). The fact that Gratian never granted an audience to the Pagan delegation undermines Cameron's hypothesis that it was only when Gratian received the senatorial embassy that he put off his pontifical robes in protest ('Gratian's Repudiation of the Pontifical Robe', 97 ff.). Note, too, that Ambrose does not number this rejected delegation as one of the embassies sent to emperors for the repeal of the 382 law (*Ep.* 57. 2 (*CSEL* lxxxii. 3. 205)). Cameron is correct in pointing out that Gratian must have rejected his title of Pontifex Maximus around this time, although we cannot say precisely when.

[38] This counter-petition was first submitted to Damasus, who, in turn, had it sent to Ambrose (*Ep.* 72. 10 (*CSEL* lxxxii. 3. 15–16)).

blamed for Gratian's premature downfall.[39] A more pertinent factor, as Zosimus reports, was the resentment among his troops due to the excessive favouritism which he showed to the barbarian Alans employed as his personal bodyguard.[40] When news of a revolt in Britain, led by the *comes Britanniarum* Magnus Maximus, reached Gratian, the latter was in the midst of a campaign against the Alemanni in Rhaetia (June/July 383).[41] Acclaimed as Augustus by the army, Maximus crossed the channel and quickly overran Gaul and Spain. Gratian confronted the forces of the usurper at Paris, but most of his troops deserted to Maximus and he was forced to flee with 300 cavalry.[42] Pursued to Lugdunum, Gratian was captured and immediately put to death on 25 August by Maximus' *magister equitum* Andragathius.[43]

Whatever personal motives Maximus may have had for the invasion, historians are agreed that he perceived his regime, or at least wished to have it envisioned, as a restoration of the rule of Valentinian I, under whom both he and Theodosius had begun their careers. Certainly legitimization was absolutely necessary if his usurpation was to be justified.[44] Thus one can discern specific steps taken by Maximus to present himself as a legitimate successor to Valentinian. Not only was Trier immediately re-established as the capital city,[45] but Maximus' earliest gold coinage from that city's mints was a revival of Valentinian I's type of 'Restitutor reipublicae'. Its reverse shows two emperors equal in size, probably representing Maximus and Theodosius as the western and eastern Augusti.[46]

---

[39] As argued by E. Stein, *Histoire du Bas-Empire*, I, French trans. and ed., J.-R. Palanque, vol. i (Paris, 1959), 200–1.

[40] Zosimus, IV. 35. 1 ff. (Paschoud, 300). Cf. *Epitome de Caesaribus*, 47. 4–6 (F. Pichlmayr, *Sexti Aurelii Victoris liber de Caesaribus* (Leipzig, 1970), 174).

[41] Socrates, *HE* V. 11 (*PG* lxvii. 593C); Sozomen, *HE* VII. 13. 1 (*CGS* l. 316. 16–18).

[42] Based on Zosimus, IV. 35. 4–6 (Paschoud, 302). In a panegyric to Theodosius delivered after his triumph over Maximus (summer of 388), Pacatus alludes to the betrayal of Gratian at Paris, 'perfidia ducum, defectione legionum'. *Panegyricus Theodosio*, XXIII. 4 (R. A. B. Mynors, *XII panegyrici Latini* (Oxford, 1964), 100–1).

[43] Pacatus, *Paneg. Theod.* XXIV. 4 (Mynors, 102); Socrates, *HE* V. 11 (*PG* lxvii. 596B). Zosimus has Gratian flee across the Alps and be murdered in Singidunum (IV. 35. 6).

[44] A. L. Wardman, 'Usurpers and Internal Conflicts in the 4th Century A.D.', *Historia*, 33 (1984), 220–37.

[45] Palanque, 'Sur l'usurpation de Maxime', *REA* 31 (1929), 36. Palanque's argument that Maximus rode to power because of his opposition to the German element which had been overtly favoured by Gratian, making Maximus 'comme l'artisan d'une réaction nationale', seems too exaggerated. Both Maximus and Theodosius used barbarian troops in their armies. Maximus' *magister equitum* was probably of German stock (see 'Andragathius 3', *PLRE* i. 62–3).

[46] *RIC* ix. 8. Another type in silver, 'Victoria Augg.', also depicts the two emperors, ignoring Valentinian II, who is conspicuously absent, as is the case with all coins minted in Gaul (pp. 28–30).

Maximus probably anticipated a positive reaction from Theodosius, hoping for the latter's recognition of his rule since Maximus shared the 'Spanish origin and old links of friendship with the family of Theodosius'.[47] Gratian was after all directly or indirectly responsible for the elder Theodosius' death sentence in 375, which might have given Maximus further hope that Theodosius would not seriously disapprove of Gratian's assassination.[48]

Maximus was also a Christian who was anxious to win the support of the Church. Indeed, recognition from the local bishops would be one of the most effective ways to legitimize his authority as a pious emperor who was divinely appointed to rule.[49] In a letter sent to Siricius, Damasus' successor, in 386, Maximus reminds the pontiff that he was baptized by a catholic bishop: 'I ascended to the throne (*imperium*) immediately from that font of salvation.'[50] He does not say when, but Matthews's suggestion that he was baptized (by the bishop of Trier) following his seizure of power and the murder of Gratian seems most plausible.[51] Maximus' wife was also a Christian, even more devout than her husband. A dialogue detailing certain events from this period in Gaul by Sulpicius Severus tells how the queen greatly revered Martin (then bishop of Tours) and is said to have waited upon him in the manner of a lowly servant whenever the holy man visited the court at Trier.[52]

The Priscillianist controversy came at the same time when Maximus was eager to prove his piety, giving him an excellent opportunity to take stern measures against heresy. Once the new emperor arrived in Trier,[53] Bishop Ithacius of Ossonuba presented grave criminal charges against Priscillian and his followers. Letters were sent to the new prefect of Gaul and *vicarius* of Spain instructing them to summon all who were affected

---

[47] Matthews, *Western Aristocracies*, 175. Cf. Pacatus, *Paneg. Theod.* XII. 24. 1.

[48] See A. Demandt, 'Die Feldzüge des älteren Theodosius', *Hermes*, 100 (1972), 81–113; id. 'Die Tod des älteren Theodosius', *Historia*, 18 (1969), 600–7, for the probability that Gratian bore responsibility for the execution.

[49] J. Ziegler points out the necessity for Maximus to distance himself from the topoi which had usually characterized the usurper and his reign. Providing evidence of a divine 'call' and aid would serve to justify the usurpation. *Zur religiösen Haltung der Gegenkaiser im 4. Jh. n. Chr.*, Frankfurter althistorische Studien 4 (Frankfurt, 1970), 74–85.

[50] *CSEL* xxxv. 90. 28–9. For this reason, he claims to hold to the traditional faith of the Church, 'hoc me confiteor curam habere maiorem' (90. 28).

[51] *Western Aristocracies*, 165. Cf. Birley, 'Magnus Maximus and the Persecution of Heresy', 14.

[52] *Dialogus*, II. 6 (*CSEL* i. 187–8).

[53] What follows is based upon Sulpicius' *Chronicorum*, XLVI. 5–LI. 4 (*CSEL* i. 102–4); H. Chadwick, *Priscillian of Avila: The Occult and the Charismatic in the Early Church* (Oxford, 1976), 43 ff.

by the heresy before a synod in 384 at Bordeaux. The episcopal supporters
of Priscillian were obliged to attend, and they were condemned and later
exiled. But Priscillian, wishing to avoid 'being heard by the bishops',[54]
appealed to the emperor for a hearing. Under the prosecution of Ithacius,
Priscillian was found guilty in two other hearings which followed Bordeaux
on the charges of *maleficium*; that is, sorcery and adultery, and soon after
was executed with four members of his sect. Others were put to death or
exiled in an intense period of inquisition which followed. By Maximus'
ruthless suppression of heresy, he had assured the Church of his own
orthodoxy and of his divine appointment; that God had raised him up to
check the spread of heresy— an argument Maximus uses in his letter to
Siricius.[55] Quite probably Maximus' treatment of the Priscillianist affair
was also a calculated attempt to attract Theodosius' support for his regime.

The imminent threat of an invasion of north Italy in 383 spurred the
court of Valentinian into action. The experienced and dedicated Petronius
Probus was recalled to assume the prefecture for a fourth and last time,[56]
while Gratian's *magister militum*, Bauto, assumed control of all western
armies and ordered the Alpine passes blocked. Whatever religious differences had been sparked between Ambrose and the pro-Homoian court at
Milan were deferred, at least for the moment. To buy time, Ambrose was
sent as an envoy to Maximus near the end of 383 in order to learn something of the usurper's intentions and to ask for peace.[57] Religious affinities
in this regard were important and could be used. The fact that Ambrose
was chosen as legate demonstrates that the Milanese court was well informed about Maximus' Nicene tendencies as one who came out of the
same theological matrix as the radical Theodosius.

Ambrose's mission was successful only in that he stalled further action
on the part of Maximus.[58] Without explicitly making false promises,

---

[54] It is not completely clear whether Priscillian was a layman or not. Sulpicius claims that
Instantius and Salvianus appointed (*constituunt*) Priscillian as the bishop of Avila (*Chron.* ii.
47. 4) even though the two bishops were already 'damnati iudicio sacerdotum' (condemned
by the decree of bishops). It is highly untenable that Priscillian's ordination was recognized
by anyone outside the sect, and this was, therefore, the reason why Priscillian's appeal to a
secular court was accepted with no scruples. H. Chadwick has disputed this conclusion on
the grounds that theological dissensions were decided by episcopal courts but criminal
charges were heard in secular courts (*Priscillian*, 129). Priscillian's subsequent execution by
civil authorities adds further testimony against the validity of his ordination. K. Girardet,
'Trier 385: Der Prozess gegen die Priszillianer', *Chiron*, 4 (1974), 577–608.

[55] *Coll. Avell.* 40. 3–4 (*CSEL* xxxv. 91).   [56] Jones, 'Collegiate Prefectures', 85.

[57] Ambrose, *Ep.* 30. 6 (CSEL lxxxii. 2. 209–10). This letter is virtually our sole source
of information for Ambrose's first mission to Trier.

[58] Cf. *Ep.* 76. 23: 'Maximus did not say that I am a tyrant to Valentinian, he complained
about the obstruction of my embassy so that he was not able to cross into Italy' (*CSEL*
lxxxii. 3. 123. 231–3).

Ambrose deflected Maximus' demand that Valentinian should come to him in Trier with the argument that it was unreasonable to expect a young boy and his widowed mother to make such a journey in the midst of winter. A delegation which Maximus had sent to Milan at the same time as Ambrose's departure for Gaul returned with the same polite refusal. But Ambrose must have led Maximus to believe that Valentinian would arrive in the spring, which temporarily pacified the aspiring Augustus of the west. If Maximus was indeed seeking legitimization for his rule, he would have much preferred to have a scion of the house of Valentinian ally himself willingly instead of by force. It was good politics, therefore, to wait. In the mean time, Bauto engineered an attack by the barbarians on Maximus' northern frontier which was meant to occupy the energies of the latter's troops.[59]

Theodosius' own position with regard to the acceptance of Maximus as an imperial colleague is hard to read when the tensions of 383 and early 384 were at their height. The eastern emperor seems to have at first ignored the affairs in the west, offering no reply to Maximus' initial demand for either recognition or civil war.[60] Gratian's death was hardly reason enough for Theodosius to have adopted a hostile position toward Maximus. Not only was Gratian a member of the dynasty that had engineered the execution of the elder Theodosius, but we have already reviewed evidence that relations between Gratian and Theodosius after the latter's elevation in 379 were strained and disharmonious. One need not assume therefore that Theodosius was initially opposed to Maximus' seizure of power in the west. It is also debatable whether Maximus would have attributed himself the consulship in 384, thus contradicting the designation of Richomer and Clearchus made by Theodosius.[61] Such an act would have been an obviously offensive gesture on the part of Maximus toward one whose goodwill he was vitally interested to secure. Moreover, his alleged self-designation is inconsistent with what we know about Maximus' other political and religious actions to woo Theodosius' acceptance.

In 384 an official accord of some type was reached between the three emperors recognizing authority over their respective territories, that is, the Gauls to Maximus, the prefecture of Italy to Valentinian, and the Orient to Theodosius.[62] Reference is made by Pacatus to a 'treaty' which

---

[59] Ambrose finds himself in a precarious position when he returns to Trier a second time in 386 and is accused by Maximus of deceit on these very points (*Ep.* 30. 4).

[60] Zosimus, IV. 37. 10 (Paschoud, 304).

[61] As asserted in *Regesten*, 264, and R. S. Bagnall *et al.*, *Consuls of the Later Roman Empire* (Atlanta, 1987), 302–3.

[62] J.-R. Palanque, 'L'Empereur Maxime', in *Les Empereurs romains d'Espagne* (Paris, 1965), 257–8.

Maximus is said to have violated when he later invaded north Italy (in the summer of 387).[63] There is evidence that Theodosius sent a legation to Valentinian at the end of the summer of 384 perhaps in Aquileia,[64] where the terms of this agreement were reached. Thereafter, signs of Theodosius' acceptance of Maximus are manifest and unambiguous.[65] This did not mean, however, that Maximus gave up his intention of absorbing Italy, as Ambrose revealed in his letter to Valentianian after his second embassy to Trier.

(a) *Ambrose and the Milanese court*

The hazardous mission which Ambrose undertook on behalf of the court of Valentinian gave the bishop certain political advantages which he would be able to use in the future with great profit. Brief mention of this embassy to Trier in 383/4, found in Epistle 30 addressed to Valentinian after a second embassy in 386, gives the impression that Ambrose sternly confronted Maximus with the declaration that Valentinian was his equal and that the usurper was culpable for Gratian's murder. Given the precarious position which marked the embassy of 383/4, it is hardly credible that Ambrose would have conducted the interview with Maximus with such audacity. Ambrose's report is obviously written more for its readership so that there will be no room to accuse the bishop of betraying the interests of the court. The fact that he felt obliged to write a report on the events of his second embassy, whereas he had not done so for the first, reveals that the court did not fully trust his intentions. There was good reason for such suspicion after Ambrose's return from Trier. Whatever leverage Ambrose had obtained by his communication with the pro-Nicene Maximus was used as a subtle weapon against the Milanese court, it can be argued, on at least two occasions: the first being the renewed

---

[63] *Paneg. Theod.* XXX. 1 (Mynors, 105).

[64] The two emperors did not actually meet as is sometimes alleged. Chadwick has shown that the evidence from *C. Th.* XII. 1. 107 which places Theodosius in Verona ('Veronae') on 31 Aug. (as according to Palanque, 'L'Empereur Maxime', 258, and *Regesten*, 265) may result from a corruption of 'Beroeae' (*Priscillian*, 113 n. 3).

[65] In the autumn of 384 most eastern mints issued a bronze coin of the Emperor Theodosius which includes Maximus, and, for the first time, Valentinian II is given the legend of an independent Augustus (*RIC* ix. 139). Zosimus' description (IV. 37. 3) of how a portrait of Maximus was displayed in Alexandria best pertains to the period following the summer of 384 (Cf. D. Vera, 'I rapporti fra Magno Massimo, Theodosio e Valentiniano II nel 383–4', *Athenaeum*, 53 (1975), 279–82; and, the consulship of Maximus' praetorian prefect Euodius was acknowledged for the year 386 in the eastern empire along with Theodosius' son Honorius (*Regesten*, 268–9).

Altar of Victory controversy in the summer of 384, and the second in the spring of 386 as a means to dissolve the will of the pro-Homoian court in its demand for a basilica. The so-called Altar of Victory controversy of 384 has received much scholarly attention so there is little need for us to rehearse all the details apart from making some observations about its significance for the relationship between Ambrose and the Milanese court. The role of Ambrosian politics in resolving the basilica confrontation has been given, in contrast, little consideration and will shape the form of our conclusion to this chapter.

As long as the threat of an invasion of north Italy persisted, complicated by the seemingly aloof Theodosius, a guarded truce between Ambrose and the court of Valentinian was maintained. Ambrose had shown his good faith to the court by his mission; he had been held hostage in Trier by Maximus until the latter's son Victor, who led the delegation to Milan, should return safely.[66] In the summer of 384, when Symmachus again sought the restoration of public funds for ceremonial sacrifices and the Altar of Victory in a lengthy *relatio* sent to Valentinian, Ambrose lodged an impassioned protest.[67] Laying aside theological differences for the moment, Ambrose appealed to Valentinian as a Christian emperor within a tradition of Christian emperors as grounds for refusing a petition which favoured Pagan religion. Just because Justina and her son were Homoian Arians did not mean that they were more inclined to accept Pagan proposals than if they were Nicenes, as suggested by some modern historians. It should not be forgotten that the allegedly pro-Arian Constantius was the first Christian emperor to remove the Altar of Victory upon his arrival in Rome in 357, and in the preceding year he had prohibited Pagan sacrifices upon pain of death.[68] The more pressing problem for Ambrose in 384 was the precarious situation that a 13-year-old regent was almost wholly

---

[66] *Ep.* 30. 7 (CSEL lxxxii. 2. 211).

[67] This is the first of two letters which Ambrose wrote on this matter (*Epp.* 17 and 18 (*PL* xvi) or 72 and 73 in *CSEL* lxxxii. 3) not yet having seen the *relatio*. On the controversy there exists no one satisfactory treatment, though the fundamentals can be found in A. Sheridan, 'The Altar of Victory: Paganism's Last Battle', *Antiquité classique*, 35 (1966), 186–206; H. A. Pohlsander, 'Victory: The Story of a Statue', *Historia: Zeitschrift für alte Geschichte*, 18 (1969), 588–97; and A. Dihle, 'Zum Streit um den Altar der Viktoria', in W. den Boer *et al.* (eds.), *Romanitas et Christianitas* (Amsterdam, 1973), 81–97. Important corrections can be found in Matthews, *Western Aristocracies*, 175 ff., and J. J. O'Donnell, 'The Demise of Paganism', *Traditio*, 35 (1979), 74 ff.

[68] *C. Th.* xvi. 10. 6. Successive edicts by Constantius had been issued against temple sacrifice in previous years (*C. Th.* xvi. 10. 2–5). See also R. O. Edbrooke, 'The Visit of Constantius II to Rome in 357 and its Effect on the Pagan Roman Senatorial Aristocracy', *American Journal of Philology*, 97 (1976), 40–61.

dependent upon the guidance of his senior officials, Bauto and Rumoridus, who were either Pagan or of dubious religious commitment. Moreover, one of the leading lights of traditional Roman religion, Praetextatus, was presently praetorian prefect and consul designate for the coming year, and thus very influential in political circles. Having appealed to the young emperor's Christian sensibilities, Ambrose began to drop subtle threats toward the end of his letter if the court were to decide to grant Symmachus his request. First he reminds the young Valentinian that Theodosius would never approve of such a petition since, as he was well aware, matters of religion were of fundamental importance to the eastern emperor. The implication was that the court should not alienate one whose goodwill was important to their political survival. Valentinian is then threatened with excommunication: 'You may come to church but you will not find a bishop there.'[69] Since there is no reason to think that Valentinian attended a liturgical pro-Nicene assembly, this warning has a hollow ring. Finally Ambrose remarks that, if he should give way to the Pagan aristocrats, he will be abrogating his brother Gratian's edicts on religion, which even Maximus had not done when he dismantled Gratian's regime.[70] It is hard not to see in this section an implication that Maximus, as one who does keep the true faith, will become the protector of the Italian churches if Valentinian further betrays that faith through complicity with its enemies. The Milanese court was alerted to Maximus' religious sympathies, and, although Maximus perceived his regime along the former lines of Valentinian I, he did not follow the same course concerning religious toleration of Pagans or heretics. All of these considerations were good reasons for the court in the summer of 384 to refuse the Pagan petition.

3. THE ARRIVAL OF AUXENTIUS OF DUROSTORUM

After the imperial accord of the summer of 384, Justina grew more confident that the Milanese court would be upheld by Theodosius, and therefore left in peace by Maximus. As a result, she became increasingly open about her allegiance to the Homoian community and more belligerent toward Ambrose and the Nicene clergy. A somewhat conflated and embellished description in Rufinus' *Historia ecclesiastica* graphically renders this new stage in the relations between the two parties:

---

[69] *Ep.* 72. 13–14 (*CSEL* lxxxii. 3. 17–18).
[70] *Ep.* 72. 16 (*CSEL* lxxxii. 3. 18–19. 147–51).

Justina, his [Valentinian's] mother, a pupil (*alumna*) of the Arian heresy, easily deceived her son and manifested the poison of her impiety freely. Now located in Milan, she incited disturbances in the churches; bishops pushed aside were threatened with exile unless they subscribed to the decrees of the council of Ariminum by which the faith of our fathers was defiled. By this war she was attacking the wall and turret of the church, the most sturdy Ambrose. And he was fatigued no less with with threats and every manner of opposition.[71]

Now that Gratian was gone and Maximus was at bay, Justina began to oppose the intolerant Nicene Church with every political means in her power with a view to reinstating Homoian doctrine as defined by the Ariminum creed. The exact context for the actions attributed to Justina here is not disclosed but the passage most easily describes the period just before the basilica dispute in the spring of 386 which Rufinus proceeds to unfold in the ensuing lines of the same chapter. From the above description, it is evident that whatever measures Gratian had taken against the Homoians in Milan were being reversed. In little over a year[72] a new pro-Homoian statute would be issued declaring the legality of the faith which was accepted at Ariminum and Constantinople (360), granting freedom of assembly to all holders of that creed, while barring any interference from hostile parties (namely Nicenes) on the threat of capital punishment. Very wisely, no offensive steps were taken against Nicene Christians in this decree so as not to alienate Theodosius. Nor was the new law a return to the state of religious toleration as under Valentinian I, probably for the same reasons.

Other attempts were made by the Milanese court to secure adequate meeting places for Homoians, which had been denied to them since 381. In that year, Gratian had banned the Homoians from worshipping in the basilica which he had transferred to them three years before. Now they wanted it back. As we will see below, another attempt to procure the Portian basilica was made in 385 without success. As soon as the new law was passed, giving equal rights of assembly to Homoians, the legal option to seize a basilica was now available, which the court repeatedly tried to enforce in 386.

Politically, at least, circumstances were becoming more favourable for the Homoians in north Italy. There is also intriguing evidence that the Homoians themselves were undergoing something of a religious revival at this time thanks to the recent arrival of a Homoian bishop in Milan. If

---

[71] *HE* II. 15 (*PL* xxi. 523–4). Apart from the usual exaggeration Rufinus' account offers an apt summary of details, some of which can be corroborated from other sources.

[72] *C. Th.* XVI. I. 4 (23 Jan. 386). Cf. XVI. 4. I, which repeats the last part of the same law.

our knowledge about this new bishop was solely dependent upon Ambrose's highly polemicized portrait of him in the *Sermo contra Auxentium*, we would be left with the impression that this individual was just another political schemer who was in league with the Milanese court against the Church. According to Ambrose, this Auxentius came from the region of Scythia (*in Scythiae partibus*), where his name was Mercurius, but having arrived in Milan he assumed the name Auxentius because he was so ashamed of his past wickedness in Scythia, and so that people would confuse him with the former Arian bishop of Milan of the same name.[73] The *Contra Auxentium* roundly accuses Auxentius of sacrilege, public disruption (ch. 17), violence against the saints (ch. 23), and opposing God (ch. 28), all because the latter is seeking a Nicene basilica for Arian worship and claims to be a bishop. In fact, Auxentius was a very talented person and devout cleric whose leadership of the Homoian community was successful enough to convince Ambrose that a full-scale attack was necessary.

(a) *The* epistula de vita et obitu Ulfilae

Fortunately, the Arian *scholia* provide further information about this intriguing figure. A remark by Palladius of Ratiaria in the *apologia* establishes the separate identities of Auxentius of Durostorum and the episcopal predecessor of Ambrose, Auxentius of Milan: 'For although you remember both of the Auxentii, you do not indicate of which you speak, whether the one now alive, that is, of Durostorum, or of Milan.'[74] When Palladius wrote this (no later than December 384) Auxentius, still the bishop of Durostorum, had not yet come to Milan. This is the probable reason why Palladius stated that the church at Milan is presently 'without a successor' (fo. 348ᵛ. 38). In Homoian eyes, evidently, Ambrose was no longer considered the episcopal successor to the deceased Auxentius of Milan. This state of affairs has important implications for the role which the second

---

[73] *Contra Aux.* (= *Ep.* LXXVa), 22 (*CSEL* lxxxii. 3. 96). Ensslin is too quick to believe Ambrose's report; see 'Mercurius, arianischer Bischof von Mailand', *PWK* xv. 1. 974–5. Ambrose does admit that he had been a bishop before coming to Milan. Notice too the play on the name Mercurius ('the wolf') which Ambrose makes in order to illustrate his opinion of Auxentius' character. (*CSEL* lxxxii. 3. 96. 258–61).

[74] *Scholia*, 348ᵛ. 36–8 (Gryson, *Scolies*, 322). Palladius is responding to the passage in Ambrose, *De fide*, I. 6. 45, which designates Palladius, Auxentius, and Demophilus as 'Arians' but does not distinguish which Auxentius is meant here. The criticism is a misguided one. There is no cause for Ambrose to have referred to Auxentius of Durostorum at the time he wrote *De fide*, I–II.

Auxentius assumed when he came to Milan. For it is clear that in 385–6 Ambrose (rightly) perceives Auxentius as a rival bishop.

Our information about Auxentius' background is based upon a large fragment of a panegryric of the Gothic Bishop Ulfila, the so-called *epistula de vita fide et obitu Ulfilae*,[75] attributed to Auxentius of Durostorum,[76] which is preserved among Maximinus' collection of Homoian documents (fos. 304ᵛ. 1–308ʳ. 35). Because the panegyric reveals Auxentius' close relationship to one of the chief theorists of Homoian Arianism, Ulfila, it is worth pausing to consider its contents, from which we may learn something of Auxentius' own convictions.

The fragmented text can be divided into three parts: the major tenets of Ulfila's trinitarian doctrine (chs. 41–54), Ulfila's career (chs. 55–62), and a creed attributed to him (ch. 63). From the biographical data provided (chs. 41–54), we receive the bulk of our information about the Gothic bishop not obtainable from any other source and some insight into the persecution of Christians in Gothia (i.e., outside the Roman borders) during the regime of Constantius II. Ulfila's personal history has been the subject of several important studies,[77] so there is no need to chronicle all the details available in Auxentius and elsewhere. It suffices to say that a major effect of the panegyric is the emphasis on Ulfila's long-standing faithfulness to the truth which has characterized the bishop's eventful forty-year career:

During 40 years in the episcopate, gloriously flourishing with apostolic grace, he preached in Greek, Latin, and Gothic languages without intermission about the one and only church of Christ . . . he also [produced] in those three languages many homilies and commentaries for the use and edification of those wishing them, as an eternal memorial and recompense to himself after his departure.[78]

Under Auxentius' pen, the very stages of Ulfila's life are, just like his doctrine, found to be parallel to the Scriptures. Like David, who was

---

[75] The text appears in *PLS* i. 693–728 and Gryson, *Scolies*, 236–63. The title is Kauffmann's.

[76] In a commentary which follows the panegyric, Maximinus attributes the material about Ulfila's journey to Constantinople, and presumably the preceding material about the great bishop's background, to Auxentius (*Scholia*, 308ᵛ. 2–3). Capelle argued in 1922 that Maximinus is the author of the 'letter' and the ensuing commentary ('La Letter d'Auxence sur Ulfila', *RB* 34 (1922), 224–33), but the 'letter' is now universally considered by scholars to be a separate work of Auxentius. See Gryson, *Scolies*, 58 ff.; Simonetti, *Patrology*, iv. 96–7.

[77] e.g., E. A. Thompson, *The Visigoths in the Time of Ulfila* (Oxford, 1966), esp. 115 ff.; S. Teillet, *Des Goths à la nation gothique* (Paris, 1984), 43–88; H. Wolfram, *History of the Goths*, trans. T. J. Dunlap (Berkeley, Calif., 1988), 75–85.

[78] *Scholia*, 306ʳ. 27–36; 306ᵛ. 2–4 (Gryson, *Scolies*, 242; 244).

made prophet and king at 30 years old, so Ulfila was ordained bishop from a lector at the same age 'by the providence of God and mercies of Christ for the salvation of the Gothic people'.[79] We do not know exactly when this took place but there is no reason to doubt Philostorgius' report that Ulfila was sent by the Visigothic Christians and consecrated by Eusebius of Nicomedia[80] sometime before the latter's death in 341. Despite Socrates' and Sozomen's belief that Ulfila was committed to the Nicene faith until he signed the Homoian creed at Constantinople,[81] it appears that Ulfila harboured his antipathy to the doctrine of *homoousios* from the beginning of his episcopate. Like most bishops at Constantinople in 360, Ulfila subscribed to the creed more for reasons of platform unity and imperial expectations, although his own trinitarian theology was governed by a hierarchical conception slightly more subordinationist in content.[82]

Towards the end of his life, when the political climate had radically changed under Theodosius, Ulfila was compelled to go to Constantinople 'by order of the emperor' for a doctrinal debate. The text is corrupt at this point[83] but Auxentius' description best resembles the so-called 'Conference of Sects' which was convened in Constantinople in June of 383.[84] Ulfila never got the chance to debate with his adversaries for he is said to have died shortly after his arrival in the city. Just before he died he left a written confession of his faith (*Scholia*, 308ʳ. 1–35), which Auxentius appends to his description.

[79] *Scholia*, 306ᵛ. 19–34 (Gryson, *Scolies*, 244). The beginning of Ulfila's ministry is compared to Joseph, who was 'manifested' at 30 years old, and Jesus, who, after he was baptized, began to preach at 30 years old (307ʳ. 1–3). When Ulfila was forced to flee into Roman territory during a severe Gothic persecution in 347–8 (see E. A. Thompson, 'Early Visigothic Christianity', *Latomus*, 21 (1962), 507–8), Auxentius explains that that exodus was parallel to Moses leading the children of Israel out of Egypt (307ʳ. 38–307ᵛ. 4).

[80] *HE* II. 5 (*GCS* xxi. 18. 1–2). If Ulfila died, as Auxentius reports, after forty years as a bishop in June 383 (during the Conference of Sects in Constantinople), then he could not have been ordained under the regime of Constantine as Philostorgius insinuates. On the other hand, the forty-year episcopate may be simply another biblical image that Auxentius is adapting to his master's career and should not be taken literally. See T. D. Barnes, 'The Consecration of Ulfila', *JTS* (1990), 541–5, who argues that Ulfila's consecration was associated with the celebration of Constantine's *tricennalia* at the council of Constantinople in 336.

[81] Socrates, *HE* II. 41 (*PG* lxvii. 349C); Sozomen, *HE* IV. 24. 1; VI. 37. 8–10 (*GCS* l. 178. 11; 295–6). Both are completely unaware that Ulfila was ordained by Eusebius and find various reasons to explain away Ulfila's signing the creed at Constantinople (360).

[82] M. Simonetti, 'L'arianesimo di Ulfila', *Romanobarbarica*, 1 (1976), 297 ff. Simonetti's thesis that Ulfila derived his more radical theology from Eunomianism is not convincing.

[83] *Scholia*, 307ʳ. 15 ff. (Gryson, *Scolies*, 248).

[84] Socrates, *HE* V. 10 (*PG* lxvii. 584 ff.); Sozomen, *HE* VII. 12 (*GCS* l. 314–16); Gregory of Nazianzus, *Ep.* 173 (*PG* xxxvii. 281).

Auxentius received much of his knowledge of Ulfila first-hand because, as he tells us, he was a disciple of the great bishop from a very
young age (*Scholia*, 306ᵛ. 5–18): 'I am debtor to him more than anyone;
how much more will he continue to labour in me. He, who received me
at infancy from my parents and taught me the sacred letters and revealed
the truth and through the mercy of God and grace of Christ, taught me
as his son in the faith both in the flesh and in the spirit.' The last line is
especially worth noting: 'He taught me as his son in the faith', which
leaves us to believe that the doctrinal position which Auxentius attributed
to his master was also his. Assuming that Auxentius was genuinely
portraying Ulfila's views, we learn that the absolutely sole and unique
unbegotten God, by means of his will and power (*potestas*), had 'created
and begotten, made and established' the only-begotten Son.[85] The Son
also has a unique divine nature, although of a clearly secondary order, as
reflected in the appellations 'the second God' and 'God of every creature'.[86]
The Holy Spirit is not unbegotten nor begotten, but 'created on a third
level' (*in tertio gradu creatum*), and thus is not God or Lord, but from
God through the Lord as Illuminator, Sanctifier, etc.[87] This strict hier-
archy of persons is perhaps more rigorously applied than is manifested in
Palladius' writings, but their theologies are virtually the same in substance and intent.[88]

Just as importantly, the above doctrinal position included an attitude
toward heresy about which Ulfila was completely intolerant. Auxentius reports that his teacher 'deplored the error and impiety of the Homoousians';
'he scorned and rejected that hateful and execrable, depraved and perverse
profession of the Homoousians as a diabolical invention and doctrine of
demons'.[89] For this reason, it is said that Ulfila sought the destruction of
that sect, and not only the Homoousians, but also the Homoiousians and
Macedonians, along with many other perceived heresies.

Thus Ulfila was master and model for the young Auxentius. Theologically, the Gothic bishop was revered as a true imitator of the apostles,
and his pastoral role was understood, *inter alia*, as taking a strong stand
against heresy: 'he repelled the perverse doctrine of the heretics . . . as a
good pastor.'[90] We may presume that this is the kind of episcopal agendum
that Auxentius brought with him to Milan.

---

[85] *Scholia*, 304ᵛ. 30–8 (Gryson, *Scolies*, 236). Note the lengthy list of mostly apophatic
predicators which define the Father as 'Unum solum verum deum' (304ᵛ. 5–30).

[86] *Scholia*, 304ᵛ. 39; 305ʳ. 33–4.   [87] *Scholia*, 305ᵛ. 27 ff. (Gryson, *Scolies*, 240; 242).

[88] Cf. *Scholia*, 339ᵛ. 31–42; *Gesta*, 20. The editor Maximus wholly endorses the hier-
archy of persons, as witnessed in *Scholia*, 304ʳ. 36–7.

[89] *Scholia*, 305ᵛ. 3–5 (Gryson, *Scolies*, 238).

[90] *Scholia*, 305ᵛ. 9–17 (Gryson, *Scolies*, 240).

When and for whom did Auxentius write this tribute to Ulfila's memory? Unfortunately, the document is corrupted in the beginning and the end so that the salutation is missing. Other than the obvious fact that the document was written to a sympathetic, probably Homoian, audience, no other personal indicators are found in the text. Even though the end of Auxentius' panegyric is lacking, the death of Ulfila in Constantinople appears to end the narrative part of the document, which would insinuate that the death of Ulfila was the occasion for the writing, and it may have been published soon after the summer of 383. This carries the added implication that the intended audience were those faithful who knew and respected the deceased bishop.[91] It could have just as easily been intended for wider circulation, especially since a spate of anti-heretical legislation followed the Nicene 'victory' at the Conference of Sects in Constantinople,[92] and the document was written to encourage the faithful during this period of persecution.

But another scenario is just as likely and may better explain the undeniable didactic character of the panegyric and the lack of evidence that it was originally written in anything other than Latin.

(b) *Auxentius in Milan*

Exactly when Auxentius arrived in Milan is difficult to establish but close approximations are possible based upon our understanding of the political situation. As we observed above, Auxentius was still in Durostorum at the time Palladius completed his *apologia*, which could have been as late as the end of 384. With the death of his spiritual father and the increased stringency of Theodosius' measures against Arian assembly, Auxentius had good reason to leave Durostorum and seek asylum elsewhere. It was also about this time that the pro-Homoian court in Milan was beginning to go on the offensive against Ambrose and the increasing stranglehold which he had over that city. Since we do not hear anything about Auxentius from Ambrose's writings until the time of the basilica conflict, which began in the early spring of 385 (below), we may presume that Auxentius came to the north Italian city sometime in 384. As a disciple of the great Ulfila, whose reputation would have been familiar to Justina, the latter having spent so many years in Pannonia, it is quite possible that Auxentius

---

[91] Kauffmann, *Aus der Schule des Wulfila*, p. lix n. 3; Zeiller, *Origines chrétiennes*, 498 n. 1.

[92] *C. Th.* XVI. 5. 11 (25 July 383); XVI. 5. 12 (3 Dec. 383); XVI. 5. 13 (21 Jan. 383). The 'Arians' and 'Eunomians' are mentioned among the sects condemned.

was invited by the court to come to Milan in order to revive the Homoian community there. If indeed the Homoians considered the true church of Milan still 'without successor', they would be looking to make an episcopal appointment. This scenario also provides an answer to Meslin's query why Auxentius is the only Homoian bishop to come to Milan when Theodosius' legislation must have affected numerous Arian bishops.[93]

Inspired by the renowned missionary activities of Ulfila, Auxentius began to undertake the inspiration and teaching of sound doctrine in Milan. He is nothing less than an Arian evangelist, carrying on his master's work in that tradition. This was the most opportune time to disseminate the teachings of the true faith and exemplary life story of Ulfila as introduced by Auxentius in his panegyric. The document would have been well suited for propagandizing the Homoian viewpoint. Furthermore, the specific attack on *homoousios* doctrine as diabolical and as a perversity to be shunned (*Scholia*, 305^r. 3–18), almost polemical in character, is best understood in these circumstances.

While we have no direct information as to the success of Auxentius' endeavours as aided by Justina's support, one can detect from certain inferences that the sagging Homoian community in Milan was being revived—and with new blood. One of these indications comes from *De officiis*, I. 18. 72 (written *c.*389), in which Ambrose recalls how a certain layman, disgruntled over the fact that Ambrose did not admit him into the ranks of clergy, deserted the faith 'at the time of the Arian disturbances'. It was during this period that the layman apostacized, presumably to the Homoian Church (above, pp. 121–122). If such disaffections from the Nicene fold were sufficiently repeated, the need for a basilica would become acute, since the Homoians rebaptized anyone who converted from the Nicene camp. When Ambrose accused Auxentius in the *Contra Auxentium* of nullifying the grace of Christ by rebaptizing Nicene catholics, it is clear that the layman of *De officiis* was not only the convert to Homoian ranks: 'Can Auxentius dissolve the baptism of Christ? For that is a baptism from heaven not of man, as the angel announces to us great plans that we may be justified to God. Why therefore does Auxentius claim that the faithful ought to be rebaptized in the name of the Trinity?[94] Nowhere else do we see the ecclesiastical and episcopal rivalry so clearly. To the Homoians, Nicene baptisms were not baptisms at all since heretical rites had no efficacy. Only the 'true Church' introduced a valid and first cleansing from sin.

[93] *Les Ariens*, 48.   [94] *Contra Aux.* 37 (*CSEL* lxxxii. 3. 107. 456–60).

The subsequent demand by the Milanese court in 385 for one of the basilicas indicates a growing number of new converts and apostate Nicenes which set the stage for the first confrontation between Ambrose and the court. It is also true that Justina and the pro-Homoian court required a place for worship, although Homes Dudden's biased assessment, that there was no Arian congregation at this time apart from 'Arian courtiers, officials and soldiers',[95] completely ignores the new rivalry between the two churches which invested the controversy of 385–6 with such intensity. Such rivalry explains Ambrose's fears that an Arian priest would be killed when he fell into the hands of a pro-Nicene crowd. In order to avoid bloodshed, Ambrose was compelled to send members of his clergy as a rescue party.[96] While the political pressure brought to bear on Ambrose by the court is a significant element in our understanding of the dynamics of the controversy, it is, nevertheless, only a single factor in a complicated mosaic of factors which precipitated the events of 385–6. The genius of Ambrose in this situation is that he understood both forms of power, political and popular, using both to his advantage in order to overwhelm the court of Valentinian II.

4. THE CONFLICT OVER THE BASILICAS

Without question, the conflict between Ambrose and the Milanese court during 385–6 is the most celebrated period of Ambrose's career in ancient sources,[97] with the exception of the bishop's unusual election to the episcopate. These notices, however, provide very inexact references to the events as they unfolded, focusing solely on the high points of the confrontation. Ambrose provides a more meticulous description by means of four documents: three letters; Epistles 75 (to Valentinian) and 76–7 (to his sister Marcellina), and the sermon which he preached against Auxentius, which is preserved as a letter (*Ep. 75a*). The Maurists placed Epistle 76 (= *Ep. 20, PL* xvi) chronologically first since they believed that it was written in 385, while the other three were composed in the year after. Seeck has convincingly demonstrated that all four were written in 386,

---

[95] *Life and Times*, i. 271. Such a view exhibits a tacit acceptance of Ambrose's caricature of his enemies as essentially alien to Roman society which is itself identified with the kingdom of God (*De fide*, II. 16. 137–9).

[96] *Ep.* 76. 5 (*CSEL* lxxxii. 3. 110–11).

[97] Rufinus, *HE* II. 15–16; Augustine, *Conf.* IX. 7. 15; Paulinus, *VA* 13; Socrates, *HE* V. 11; Sozomen, *HE* VII. 13; Theodoret, *HE* V. 13.

and that the events which they describe took place in 386.[98] The only exception is found in *Contra Auxentium*, 29, where Ambrose narrates a series of episodes which happened, he says, 'the year before'. It is universally agreed that this chapter refers to the court's first demand for a basilica in 385. But here is where the agreement ends. Despite Ambrose's detailed information, scholars have found great diffculty in rendering a chronological account of the recorded confrontations in 386 because it is not clear from Ambrose's letters exactly when certain events occurred or even which basilica was being besieged at which time.

In a trilogy of articles, J. H. van Haeringen makes one of the only concerted attempts to solve the chronological problems,[99] a solution which has been recently reaffirmed by A. Lenox-Conyngham, who has, in turn, suggested a solution to the topographical difficulties of the controversy.[100] To unravel all the intricacies of their arguments is neither necessary nor germane to our purposes here. We are more interested in the dynamics which the controversy produced between the Nicenes and Homoians, and how the controversy was brought to a conclusion. Since a brief overview of the events of 385–6 is required, we will draw upon van Haeringen's and Lenox-Conyngham's conclusions, especially where they deviate from traditional reconstructions.

The only occasion on which Ambrose actually went before the consistory was in the spring of 385, when the emperor is said to have first threatened Ambrose with the seizure of a basilica. *Contra Auxentium* 29 is Ambrose's one and only mention of that episode and he admits that the overbearing manner of the court intimidated him: 'when the emperor wished to seize the basilica I was intimidated (*infractus*) at the sight of the royal court, not maintaining the constancy of a bishop, and I shied away from the law which was being violated.'[101] This admission presents a sharp contrast to Palanque's description of the incident; he declares that Ambrose met his opponents head on, 'pied à pied', without being daunted by the imperial pomp and power.[102] On the contrary, it is difficult to tell from Ambrose's

[98] *Geschichte des Untergangs*, v. 204 ff.

[99] 'De Valentiniano II et Ambrosio: illustrantur et digeruntur res anno 386 gestae', *Mnemosyne*, 3rd ser. 5 (1937): (1) 'Valentinianus II basilicam adornitur (de Ambrosii epistula XX)', 152–8; (2) 'De Ambrosii epistula XXI', 28–33; (3) 'De Ambrosii epistulis XX et XXI: temporum descriptio', 229–40.

[100] 'A Topography of the Basilica Conflict of AD 385/6 in Milan', *Historia*, 31 (1982), 353–63; 'Juristic and Religious Aspects of the Basilica Conflict of AD 386', in *Studia Patristica*, 18 (1985), 55–8.

[101] *Contra Aux.* 29 (*CSEL* lxxxii. 3. 101. 354–102. 356).

[102] *Saint Ambroise*, 145. Cf. Homes Dudden, who describes Ambrose's behaviour as 'inflexible' to the court's demands (*Life and Times*, i. 272); K. M. Setton, *Christian Attitude*

own words what his initial reaction was. What saved him, however, was the arrival of a mob outside the palace which demanded the release of the bishop. Palatine guards were unable to disperse the menacing crowd and finally Ambrose was asked to go out and calm the people with many dissuasions. The potential expolosiveness of the incident was quickly defused by the court's retraction of its demands.

Nowhere does Ambrose specify at what time of the year this first altercation between him and the court took place, but it is quite likely that the demands were made sometime before Easter. As we saw above, there was an unknown number of conversions to Homoianism under Auxentius' ministry which created the need for baptismal facilities. The attempt to secure a basilica was undoubtedly linked to the approach of the Paschal season, the climax at which catechumens were baptized.[103]

The Milanese court realized that there was no advantage in sequestering the desired basilica in 385 given the absence of any legal provision which gave the right for Homoian Arians to assemble. It was thus necessary to modify Gratian's religious legislation. On 23 January 386 Valentinian issued a new edict (*C. Th.* XVI. I. 4) which proclaimed liberty of worship for the adherents of that faith defined at Ariminum and confirmed at Constantinople.[104] Homoianism had now regained official recognition as the catholic faith, at least in the prefecture of Italy. Not only was Homoianism given the right to exist, its opponents were denied their former prerogatives to impede or interfere in any manner with Homoian activities. This ensured the unobstructed spread of Homoian doctrine. Ambrose exaggerates when he claims that Auxentius wrote this legislation with his own hand (*Contra Aux.* 16); however, it is quite likely that Auxentius, a frequent visitor to Valentinian's consistory, had some responsibility for the outcome. Episcopal pressure of this type was all too familiar to Ambrose, who, as we have seen in several instances, had used his influence on Gratian to effect political advantage for the Nicenes.

There was opposition to the new law. Some bishops and even senators

---

toward the Emperor in the Fourth Century (New York, 1967), 109–10: 'When the request for a church was make to Ambrose, he had straightaway refused it.'

[103] Meslin, *Les Ariens*, 49.

[104] 'We bestow the right of assembly upon those persons who believe according to the doctrines which in times of Constantius, of blessed memory, were decreed as those that would endure forever, when the priests had been called together from all over the Roman world and the faith was set forth at the council of Ariminum by these very persons who are now known to dissent, a faith which was also confirmed by the council of Constantinople . . .' (Pharr, *Theodosian Code*, 440).

may have protested to Valentinian,[105] but we have no details about the degree of this opposition. Better documented is the story of the *magister memoriae scriniorum* of the Milanese court, Benivolus, who refused to prepare the pro-Homoian statute for publication on the grounds that it violated the Nicene faith and was opposed to God.[106] He was offered a promotion by the court if he complied, but Benivolus preferred to resign his office: 'he wished to be more noble in faith than in honours', at which time he is said to have dramatically thrown his *cingulum* at the feet of Justina. Benivolus was replaced and the new edict issued, though given the minority status of Homoians throughout north Italy it is unlikely that the law much affected Nicene–Homian relations outside Milan. Even in Milan, where the court resided, full compliance was practically impossible to achieve.

Early in March, tensions began to rise again when the court renewed their demands for the Portian basilica. Ambrose flatly refused to yield and was therefore ordered to leave Milan on the grounds of having violated the new edict.[107] It seems that the order was not carried out, for shortly afterwards the *tribunus et notarius* Dalmatius was sent to Ambrose commanding the bishop to choose judges, just as Auxentius had done, for a hearing before the consistory. This time Ambrose declined even to come to the palace. In a letter to Valentinian (*Ep.* 75) written as a response to the imperial demand, Ambrose completely rejects what he knew to be Auxentius' plan for holding a debate before a panel of impartial judges for the same reason that Ambrose had earlier rejected a similar proposal by Palladius: laity are not to judge bishops 'in causa fidei'.[108] In any case, Ambrose observes, what judges, lay or otherwise, could he bring to the debate without endangering their lives because of the new edict which forbade nonconformity to the wishes of the emperor? Because the edict is an endorsement of the Ariminum creed, it is contrary to the truth of the Nicene faith and ought to be rejected. For this reason Ambrose refused to yield the basilica. He then reminded Valentinian that the Nicene faith

---

[105] *Contra Aux.* 16 (*CSEL* lxxxii. 3. 91. 182–5). Ambrose is surely exaggerating when he says that bishops were being expelled, or, if they resisted, were put to the sword, and every senator who did not obey was proscribed.

[106] Rufinus, *HE* ii. 16 (*PL* xxi. 524B); Gaudentius, *Ad Benivolum, magistrum memoriae*, 5 (*CSEL* lxviii. 3–4); Sozomen, *HE* vii. 13. 6 (*GCS* l. 317. 10).

[107] *Ep.* 75. 18 (*CSEL* lxxxii. 3. 81).

[108] *Ep.* 75. 4 (*CSEL* lxxxii. 3. 75–6). Ambrose is also critical that Auxentius planned (so he had heard) to use non-Christians as his judges (*Ep.* 75. 13; *Contra Aux.* 26), just as Palladius had once suggested as the only means of achieving impartiality.

is accepted by Theodosius as well as in the Gauls and Spain, that is, by Maximus, making a subtle but unmistakable hint that the court should not push its programme too far.

The court was not impressed with Ambrose's reaction and quickly turned to more radical solutions. On 27 March, the day on which Ambrose began his written chronicle of the ensuing conflict in the letters sent to his sister Marcellina, some 'illustrious men, officers of the imperial consistory' came to Ambrose and demanded the new basilica, being a larger building inside the walls.[109] The move may have been nothing more than a psychological manœuvre to obtain the Portian basilica, since yet another request was made for the Portian on the following day.[110] Both attempts were rebuffed. On Palm Sunday it was reported to Ambrose that imperial banners (*vela*) were being hung in the basilica (probably the Portian) to indicate its sequestration as imperial property. Many people made their way to that basilica in order to keep it from falling completely into the emperor's hands, though Ambrose states that he did not go: 'nevertheless, I remained on duty; I began to offer the mass' (*missam facere coepi*) (*Ep.* 76. 4). In fact, Ambrose never seems to have gone to the Portian during those intense days of Holy Week, and we can agree with Lenox-Conyngham that the rest of the letter sounds as if Ambrose was not there in person but learned of the events through daily reports. If this is correct, then the events which are reported in the *Contra Auxentium* must refer to a separate and second confrontation[111] from the one in Epistle 76, since there Ambrose delivered his sermon against Auxentius in a basilica which was surrounded by soldiers for several days and this is the same occasion when he taught the congregation anti-Homoian hymns as a means of relieving tension while maintaining their faithfulness.[112]

The first siege of the Portian basilica (during Holy Week) intensified when armed men were sent to enforce the imperial sequestration on Tuesday. Ambrose feared a general slaughter, although he refused to restrain the people when asked to do so by an embassy of Gothic tribunes.[113] Also during that week, heavy fines or even imprisonment were imposed upon Milanese businessmen who were known sympathizers with

---

[109] *Ep.* 76. 1 (*CSEL* lxxxii. 3. 108. 7–8).

[110] Lenox-Conyngham, 'Topography', 357.

[111] This is the most distinctive part of van Haeringen's and Lenox-Conyngham's thesis as opposed to conflating the events of the two letters, as in Meslin, *Les Ariens*, 50 ff.; Matthews, *Western Aristocracies*, 189, and Zelzer, *CSEL* lxxxii. 3. xxxvi.

[112] Augustine, *Conf.* IX. 7. 15 (*CCSL* xxvii. 141–2).

[113] *Ep.* 76. 9–10 (*CSEL* lxxxii. 3. 113).

pro-Nicenes. This action demonstrates that the court was aware of the support which Ambrose had at different social levels, and that it was necessary to intimidate these supporters in order to avoid any orchestrated efforts against their policies. A break in the deadlock occurred when those catholic soldiers guarding the basilica were threatened with excommunication.[114] The result was that these entered the church where Ambrose was presiding, having abandoned the besieged basilica, and asked for prayers, presumably prayers of forgiveness. On Maundy Thursday word came that the emperor had ordered all soldiers to withdraw from the basilica and the *signa* of sequestration had been removed.

If van Haeringen and Lenox-Conyngham are correct, a second siege of the (probably the Portian) basilica took place sometime after Easter. This occasion, for which Ambrose was personally present and which he discusses in the *Contra Auxentium*, was characterized by 'vigils all through the night and day' and 'being surrounded by soldiers rattling on account of which the church was walled in'.[115] Because the sermon which Ambrose preached during this siege was against Auxentius and his demands for the basilica, it may be that Auxentius was responsible for prodding the court to attempt a second sequestration. Throughout the sermon Ambrose chides the Homoian bishop for calling himself a bishop, and for taking advantage of the present law by which he seeks a basilica with rumours of slaughter and bloodstained hands. There is no indication in the text when this second attempt by the court was made, but it cannot have been too long after Easter, since Auxentius' plea for a basilica still has to do with the need for proper baptismal facilities.[116] We also do not know when the confrontation ended. The court evidently backed down again, but the reasons for its acquiescence are not supplied in the *Contra Auxentium*. It is unlikely that the court capitulated simply because it wished to avoid a conflict between the soldiers and the people, as Homes Dudden states. The fact that the court had laid an even tighter siege to the basilica for the second time indicates that it was prepared for extreme measures. Only extraordinary circumstances would have caused the court to call off voluntarily the siege a second time.

---

[114] *Ep.* 76. 13 (*CSEL* lxxxii. 3. 114. 87–92). This assumes that at least some of the soldiers guarding the Portian were catholic and not all Gothic/Arian, as Homes Dudden claims (*Life and Times*, i. 275), in which case the threat of excommunication from Ambrose would be meaningless.

[115] *Contra Aux.* 7 (*CSEL* lxxxii. 3. 86. 73); 4 (84. 35–6).

[116] *Contra Aux.* 37 (*CSEL* lxxxii. 3. 107).

(a) *The threat of Maximus*

There is evidence that the Milanese court had reason to fear reprisal from Maximus if they persisted in their persecution of the Nicenes. It appears that Justina's continued opposition to Ambrose and the church at Milan precipitated a letter from Maximus which expressed indignation over her behaviour.[117] The letter of Maximus survives and is preserved in the *Collectio Avellana* (39) and, while it is undated, its contents make reference to circumstances that can only pertain to the state of affairs in the spring of 386 when the basilicas were being beseiged.

these things are now said to be going on in the regions of Your Tranquillity: the overthrow and subversion of the catholic law . . . indeed I hear (for infamy cannot be kept secret, especially what is done to the people) force has been used on catholic churches according to the new edicts of Your Clemency, bishops have been besieged in basilicas, many have been threatened, there are more reasons for capital punishment and the most revered law has been overturned in the name of this unknown law.[118]

Valentinian is reproached for his anti-Nicene policy, which is directly opposed to the faith believed in all Italy, Africa, the Gauls, and Spain, for it is a very grave matter to change 'what has been established and confirmed for so many ages'. Even his father, Valentinian of blessed memory, is said to have ruled the empire 'faithfully by this profession' and did not dare to alter it.

It is not clear how Maximus was informed about the oppression of Nicene catholics in Milan. In his letter to Valentinian he says only that he had heard from a report (*fama*) which could not have been kept secret. What was the source of this information? Palanque believes that the terms used in the letter 'strangely resemble' those of Ambrose,[119] which invites the insinuation that the besieged bishop had sent word to the orthodox Maximus about the volatile situation in north Italy. While these 'resemblances' are rather ambiguous, it is wholly plausible to speculate that Ambrose made sure the present crisis situation was somehow communicated to the court in Trier. Doubtless the persecution of Nicene catholics in north Italy afforded Maximus an excellent opportunity to interfere in Valentinian's dominion. Maximus assumes the posture of a senior Augustus in the letter, addressing Valentinian as 'your Youthful Serenity', and urges his young colleague to desist from his hostilities. He assures Valentinian

---

[117] Rufinus, *HE* II. 16 (*PL* xxi. 524C).
[118] *Coll. Avell.* 39. 1 (*CSEL* xxxv. 88. 19–21); 3 (89. 4–9).
[119] Palanque, *Saint Ambroise*, 169.

that his admonishment stems from only sincere intentions, but there is an unmistakable threat cunningly conveyed in the letter.

If there did not exist a simple trust and understanding of full harmony between Your Serenity and Our Clemency, I am certain that the disturbance and upheaval of catholicism, which is reported to have occurred in your dominions, would pose an opportunity for my purposes. For what could one, if he were an enemy, desire more than that you should undertake an action against the churches of God, which is against God Himself, and so determine to commit sin where error is inexcusable?[120]

Knowing Maximus' zeal as a defender of the catholic faith as well as his continued ambition to extend his borders southward, the present harassment of Nicenes was a sufficient excuse to bring him to north Italy. The Milanese court was well aware that, if his remonstrance were disregarded, Maximus could invade with impunity, for Theodosius was no less devoted to pro-Nicene policies and might not oppose such measures if they were done in defence of the faith. We can conclude with some confidence that Maximus' veiled threat was the principal factor which brought an end to the court's aggressive action against Ambrose and the Nicene Church.

Even so, this defeat of the pro-Homoian court should not be exaggerated or considered final. The ending of the basilica blockade did not result in a legal modification of the court's pro-Homoian policies in north Italy. Nor did the court make any ideological concessions of its position to Maximus as eventually it was forced to do in 387/8, when Theodosius' military support against Maximus was being sought. Now that Maximus was looking menacingly again at north Italy, it was necessary to take steps to maintain the truce-like arrangement which had characterized the relations between the two courts since 384. Ambrose's co-operation would have to be secured—another reason to have terminated the siege of the basilica—given the successes of his first mission to Maximus. Such was only a temporary contingency to preserve peace, and not a capitulation to the Nicene faith.

---

[120] *Coll. Avell.* 1 (*CSEL* xxxv. 88. 17–24). Cf. Theodoret, *HE* v. 14 (*GCS* xliv. 304. 9–14), which states that Maximus threatened war if his advice was not heeded.

8

The Political Triumph of Nicene Catholicism in North Italy

AMBROSE was keenly aware that the recent withdrawal of imperial soldiers from the Portian basilica was a temporary measure. He feared still that the court might reverse its decision or that the collapse of popular enthusiasm would induce a commencement of new hostile initiatives. Even if there was a cessation of open aggression, the religious and political conflict between Nicenes and Homoians in north Italy was far from over. Not long after Easter (386), Ambrose wrote to his sister Marcellina that he was at that moment in need of *defensores*, for the Church required even greater protection.[1]

Two important events in 386/7 gave Ambrose the defenders he was looking for and completely reversed the political situation in north Italy. The first of these two events is well known and celebrated, namely, the discovery of the relics of the martyrs Protasius and Gervasius. It is less recognized that the significance of this *inventio*, regardless of whether it was contrived or genuine, gave Ambrose and the Nicene Church divine ratification which strengthened their opposition to the authority of the court. But the actual demise of western Homoianism as a ecclesio-political force came about with a second event; the sudden invasion of Italy by Maximus in the summer of 387. With this invasion all political patronage of Homoianism was withdrawn never to return, as the defeat of Maximus in the following summer brought the stringent enforcement of anti-heretical laws in the person of Theodosius. Despite the far-reaching implications of these political and military changes, their central significance for the resolution of the Nicene–Homoian tensions in north Italy is virtually unnoticed by modern historians. In order to see how the cumulative effect of the above events brought about the ultimate triumph of the Nicene Church, we shall briefly examine each of the stages.

---

[1] *Ep.* 77. 10 (*CSEL* lxxxii. 3. 132. 95–9).

1. THE *INVENTIO* OF GERVASIUS AND PROTASIUS

Ambrose's only report about the discovery of the relics is found in a letter to his sister Marcellina in which he describes how the bones of the martyrs were found and the salutary effects these relics produced as a demonstration of their genuineness.

Since I am accustomed to let nothing escape the notice of your Holiness regarding those events which have occurred in your absence, you should know then that we found holy martyrs. For when I had dedicated the basilica, there were many who began appealing to me with one voice, 'Dedicate the basilica just as you did the Roman basilica.' I responded, 'I will do so provided I find the remains of martyrs.' And immediately I was struck by a burning presentiment, so to speak, of some kind.

Need I say more? The Lord bestowed his grace: I ordered the ground to be cleared away in that place which is before the grating of saints Felix and Nabor even though the clergy were fearful. I found promising signs . . . We found two men of wondrous size just as were produced in ancient times. The skeletons were all intact, and there was much blood. A large throng of people remained during the entire two days. Need I say more? We preserved everything in order, and since evening was upon us, we transferred them to the basilica of Faustus; there a vigil was kept all night, with the imposition of hands. On the following day we transferred them to the basilica which is called Ambrosian. While they were being transferred a blind man was healed.[2]

The rest of the letter contains extracts from two sermons which Ambrose delivered; one on the day after the discovery of the relics (3–13), and the second on the third day of their *depositio* in the recently constructed Ambrosian basilica (15–23).

Apparently, Milan had not produced its own martyrs until this time. Ambrose characterizes the city in the same letter as 'barren of martyrs' prior to the discovery of Protasius and Gervasius. The fact that the people asked Ambrose to dedicate the new basilica in the same way as he had dedicated the Roman basilica ('Sicut in Romana basilicam dedices'), that is, with relics, indicates that there were other relics in Milan, but they originated elsewhere. Given the correct identification of the 'Roman basilica' with the basilica of the Holy Apostles,[3] Paulinus speaks of this basilica as housing relics of the apostles (from Rome): 'where the relics of the holy Apostles were deposited on the previous day with the complete

[2] *Ep.* 77. 1–2 (*CSEL* lxxxii. 3. 126–8).
[3] Also called San Nazaro. *Cinque chiese dell'antica Milano* (Milan, 1984), 44.

devotion of everyone.'[4] Nor were the saints Felix and Nabor mentioned in the above passage indigenous to Milan. According to later legend,[5] they were martyred in Laus (Lodi) under the Emperor Maximian and their remains later transferred. The relics of Dionysius, a former bishop of Milan who had been in exile in 355 and died several years later in Asia Minor, had not yet been translated to Milan,[6] or else he would have been celebrated as a Milanese martyr and Milan need not have been 'barren of martyrs'.

The miracles which allegedly accompanied the transfer of the relics to the Ambrosian basilica provided the necessary authentication that these relics were indeed those of holy martyrs. Demoniacs were cured and the blind were instantly healed.[7] Even Augustine, who tended to be very reserved on the question of contemporary miracles,[8] was impressed by these occurrences, recalling with fine detail in *Confessions*, IX. 16, the story about a blind man's sudden recovery of his sight.[9] The drama which characterized those days in Milan came to be memorialized in song. A hymn, attributed to the pen of Ambrose, was written shortly after the discovery[10] commemorating the series of wonders which followed. Two stanzas are devoted to the healing of Severus.

> A blind man after receiving his sight
> demonstrated the merits of the holy dead:
> the name of the man was Severus,
> a servant of public renown.

> As he touched the garment of the martyrs
> cloudy outlines were wiped away
> light gleamed straightaway
> and blindness fled and was banished.[11]

---

[4] *VA* 33. 11–14 (Pellegrino, *Vita*, 98; 100).

[5] *Acta sanctorum*, June, vol. iii (Paris, 1867), 268–70. Cf. H. Delehaye, 'Des publications hagiographiques', *Analecta Bollandiana*, 25 (1906), 362.

[6] As discussed in Ch. 4, s. 2 (*b*).   [7] Cf. *VA* 14. 9–14 (Pellegrino, *Vita*, 70; 72).

[8] See P. Courcelle, 'L'Invention et la translation des saints Gervais et Protais (17–19 juin)', in *Recherches sur les confessions de St Augustine* (Paris, 1968), 139–42.

[9] *CCSL* xxvii. 142. 22–7. Augustine makes mention of this story again in *De civitate Dei*, XXII. 8 (*CCSL* xlviii. 816. 37–44).

[10] Bastiaensen convincingly has shown that Paulinus used the hymn in the *Vita Ambrosii* 14, 19–20 ('Paulin de Milan et le culte des martyrs chez Saint Ambroise', in Lazzati (ed.), *Ambrosius episcopus*, 143).

[11] Hymn XII, lines 17–19, in A. S. Walpole, *Early Latin Hymns* (Cambridge, 1922), 90–1.

The possibility that Ambrose engineered the discovery of relics in order to impress his adversaries, as Seeck contends,[12] is beside the point here. Ambrose was certainly astute enough to know the potential effect which such a find would have on the masses, even though ancient writers are just as emphatic that the martyrs revealed themselves to Ambrose.[13] A more balanced and relevant outlook is offered by Aubineau, who states, 'Sans lui prêter autant de cynisme, on conviendra du moins que cette invention de reliques venait à point et que l'évêque en tira fort habilement parti contre ses adversaires ariens.'[14] The connection between the discovery and its utilization as a means of repressing anti-Nicene harassment is made absolutely clear by one who observed the process as a catechumen at the church of Milan. In *Confessions*, ix. 16, Augustine declares that the bodies of Gervasius and Protasius were found, having been stored uncorrupted for so many years: 'You revealed [them] at the right moment to repress the fury of a woman, even a queen.' And the fame which resulted from the miraculous healings served the same purpose; 'thereafter the mind of that enemy, even if not turned to healing belief, was checked nevertheless from the rage of persecution'.[15]

Once the relics had been translated to the new (Ambrosian) basilica, Ambrose delivered a sermon to an immense crowd which had grown over the last two days as pious enthusiasm swept through the city. Taking the opportunity to capitalize on the situation, Ambrose cited the *inventio* as the 'gift of God' which 'the Lord Jesus has granted in the time of my bishopric'. No time was wasted in appropriating the relics as certain signs of divine favour. Ambrose announced that the triumphant martyrs should take their place beneath the altar of the new basilica, a spot which he had originally reserved for his own burial. By this move, Gervasius and Protasius became inseparably linked to the communal liturgy in a church which had been built by the bishop and where that bishop presided.[16] In light of the present religious and political tensions which Ambrose faced, such a move had special significance. Now the presence of the martyrs was identified with the Nicene faith, and their *potentia* served as bulwarks against the Homoian persecution.

---

[12] *Geschichte des Untergangs*, v. 207.

[13] Gaudentius, *Tract.* xvii. 12 (*CSEL* lxviii. 144. 90–3); Paulinus, *VA* 14. 1–2 (Pellegrino, *Vita*, 70).

[14] 'Jean Damascène et "l'Epistula de interventione Gervasii et Protasii" attribuée à Ambroise de Milan', *Analecta Bollandiana*, 90 (1972), 2.

[15] *Conf.* ix. 16 (*CCSL* xxvii. 142. 17–18; 28–9).

[16] P. Brown, *The Cult of the Saints* (Chicago, 1981), 37.

Thanks be to You, Lord Jesus, for having roused the spirit of the martyrs at a time such as this when your church needs greater protection. Let everyone know that I require such defenders who are not accustomed to attack but are able to defend. These I have acquired for you, holy people; they who provide aid, and harm no one.[17]

So Ambrose declares with dramatic force in the midst of his sermon. The military motifs which he proceeds to draw upon, referring to the martyrs as *milites* and *defensores*, are placed in contrast with the *saeculi milites*, that is, earthly soldiers or the troops which the court used in its siege of the basilica. With these heavenly soldiers as his 'bodyguards' (*stipatores*), Ambrose says he fears no animosity from those who grudge him the use of such defenders.

The enthusiastic devotion and frenzied activity which the relics produced so effectively galvanized the Nicene community that the Homoians in Milan were anxious to deny their authenticity. In a second sermon, delivered on the day of *martyrum depositio*, Ambrose points out how 'the Arians remonstrate, "These are not martyrs, nor can they torment the devil, nor free anyone"'.[18] The Milanese court was equally incensed against Ambrose's tactics of arousing popular sentiment, and accused the bishop of staging the reputed exorcisms. In the course of the same sermon, Ambrose accurately touches upon the source of his opponents' enmity against the relics when he asks, 'Do they grudge me or the holy martyrs?' Since he is not the author of the many miracles recently accomplished, it must be that they grudge the martyrs. And if they do grudge the martyrs, Ambrose states, it must be because the martyrs are of a different faith from theirs.

They show that the martyrs are of another faith than what they believe. Nor would they begrudge their works unless they recognized that the faith of these martyrs is different from their own; that faith established by the tradition of the fathers which the demons can not deny but which the Arians do.[19]

It was not that the 'Arians' denied the possibility or significance of martyr patronage: we have seen how Maximinus claimed the teaching of the North African bishop Cyprian as a doctrinal model for Homoian theology.[20] This appeal to the authority of Cyprian was precisely because

---

[17] *EP.* 77. 10 (*CSEL* lxxxii. 3. 132. 93–8).
[18] *EP.* 77. 16 (*CSEL* lxxxii. 3. 136. 168–70). Cf. 136. 160–1.
[19] *Ep.* 77. 19 (*CSEL* lxxxii. 3. 138. 207–12).
[20] Ch. 7, s. 1. Cyprian is but one of the authorities claimed by Latin Arianism; see Y.-M. Duval, 'L' Influence des écrivains africains du IIIᵉ siècle sur les écrivains chrétiens de l'Italie du nord dans la seconde moitié du IVᵉ siècle', in *Aquileia e l'Africa*, Antichità Altoadriatiche 5 (Udine, 1974), 191–225.

he died as a martyr and thereby possessed the indisputable grounds of divine veracity. In similar fashion, Ambrose now 'claimed' the martyrs Gervasius and Protasius as witnesses to the truth of the Nicene faith (and, conversely, the falsity of Homoian doctrine).

The entire affair provides one of the best examples from the fourth century that religious polemics cannot be understood solely as an theological exchange between leading intellectuals. Popular interest and support for doctrinal issues was quite common in the later Roman Empire even if most people were not capable of explaining the subtleties of their faith.[21] Given the religious complexities at Milan, theological passions were especially intense and it is not surprising that Ambrose was able to marshal and sustain popular support against a 'heretical' government through the acquisition of martyr relics. As a result of the speedy appropriation of these *signa* of divine vindication, Ambrose forged for himself a powerful weapon which he used against the Milanese court with complete success. There is no evidence of any further acts of aggression against Ambrose or the Nicenes after the spring of 386. Of course the court was also mindful of Maximus' recent threat and the need to maintain some semblance of diplomatic relations if civil war was going to be avoided.

2. THE INVASION OF ITALY

After the second siege of the Portian basilica, Valentinian could not afford any further strain in relations with Gratian's usurper. Indeed, some appeasement of Maximus was necessary in order to assure him that all hostilities against the Nicenes had ceased. This seems to be the proper context for locating Ambrose's second embassy to Trier, a mission which Ambrose unambiguously declares he undertook,[22] and a record of which is found in Ambrose's letter (*Ep.* 30) to Valentinian. If we place the discovery of the relics sometime between the end of Easter and the middle of June,[23] then it is likely that Ambrose's embassy to Maximus occurred

---

[21] A. H. M. Jones, 'Were Ancient Heresies National or Social Movements in Disguise?', *JTS* 10 (1959). 296 ff.

[22] *De obitu Valent.* 28: 'Ego te suscepi parvulum, cum legatus ad hostem tuum pergerem . . . ego tuus iterum legatus repetivi Gallias' (*CSEL* lxxiii. 343).

[23] 17–19 June 386 is the date almost universally given for the *inventio* and translation of the relics to the Ambrosian basilica. With the exception of the Maurists, who date the translation closer to Easter, scholars assume that the date fixed by the martyrology of Gervasius and Protasius (19 June) in the *Acta sanctorum* (June, iv. 680–704) is also the day of their translation. Palanque defends the date of translation by appealing to the *Vita Ambrosii*,

in the summer or autumn of 386 once matters in Milan were somewhat stabilized. An allusion in the letter to Valentinian by Ambrose to the fact that his visit coincided with the execution of the Priscillianists provides further corroboration for the date.[24] Some modern historians have rejected the possibilty of a second co-operative effort of this type given the state of relations which must have existed between Ambrose and the court after the basilica controversy. The most common alternative is to place the second embassy at the time of the imperial concord in 384,[25] but the arguments in support of this scenario are entirely unconvincing as well as unnecessary once we recognize that the basilica conflict was not ended by a reconciliation, and that a second mission to Trier offered a favourable opportunity for both Ambrose and the Milanese court in their war against each other.

(a) *Ambrose's second embassy to Trier*

There were good reasons for the Milanese court to send their strongest adversary to Trier. In order to restrain Maximus from war, it was necessary to show that all attacks against the Nicenes had broken off. As episcopal leader of the Nicene Church, Ambrose was the most obvious choice, in addition to the fact that he had been partly responsible for alleviating tensions between the two courts once before. There was also an advantage in sending Ambrose since it legitimately removed him from Milan, where his popularity was well established, and one could hope that the nature, and perhaps failure, of this diplomatic mission would discredit him. On the other hand, if negotiations were successful, peace would be achieved between Milan and Trier and with the bishop who took this

which shows that the *inventio* occurred slightly after Easter (*Saint Ambroise*, 515). But in fact *VA* 14 places the *inventio* within the context of the basilica crisis, stating that 'per idem tempus' did Protasius and Gervasius reveal themselves to the bishop (Pellegrino, *Vita*, 70). There is also an apocryphal letter of Ambrose, circulating in Latin and Greek versions before the 6th century (John of Damascus quotes from the Greek version in *De imaginibus oratio*, II (*PG* xciv. 1316B)), in which the *inventio* is prefaced with the words, 'In diebus itaque transactae nuper Quadragesimae' (*PL* xvii. 821C). None of these early references provides exact information about the date. Unless one is prepared to accept the evidence of the martyrology prima facie, it appears that the actual day for the invention of the relics is uncertain but occurred shortly after Easter.

[24] So Palanque, 'L'Empereur Maxime', 260; Chadwick, *Priscillian*, 137; Birley, 'Magnus Maximus and the Persecution of Heresy', 33.

[25] V. Grumel, 'La Deuxiéme Mission de saint Ambroise auprès de Maxime', *Revue des études byzantines*, 9 (1951), 154–60. Paredi (*Saint Ambrose*, 237) follows Grumel's arguments; cf. Seeck, *Geschichte des Untergangs*, v. 185; Ensslin, *PWK* vii. 2. 2210.

mission on behalf of the court, thereby eliminating the public perception that Ambrose was an enemy and opponent of the pro-Homoian court.

Ambrose agreed to undertake the mission doubtless because he wished to avoid an invasion of north Italy just as much as the government in Milan. There were other motivations as well: the letter which Ambrose sent to Valentinian after his return from Trier demonstrates that the court did not trust him and the bishop knew that he had to disengage himself from any suspicions of collusion with the enemy.[26] Indeed, the protestations found throughout the letter that Ambrose struck a compromise with Maximus at the expense of the court are excessive to the point of effusiveness and should not be taken literally in our interpretation of Ambrose's true feelings toward Valentinian or Maximus as modern Ambrosian biographers are wont to do. In the first part of the letter, Ambrose explains how he defended Valentinian's interests before Maximus by asserting Valentinian's equality as a reigning Augustus (ch. 3) and that, in contrast to the 'threats' of Maximus, Valentinian is the peacekeeper (ch. 4). When the discussion turned to the matter of the return of Gratian's remains, Ambrose reports that he became even more forthright. He identifies Maximus's hesitation to part with the remains for fear of arousing sympathies among his troops as a pretence (ch. 10), and he asks Maximus how he can keep alleging that he did not give the order to slay Gratian when he does not allow him to be properly buried; the implication being extended that Maximus is the murderer of Gratian and that he is a usurper and not an emperor. Ambrose then proceeds to accuse Maximus of ordering Vallio, one of Gratian's generals, to be killed after the invasion of Gaul. Lastly, when Ambrose refused even to fraternize with the bishops of the court because they were seeking the death penalty against certain heretics (the Priscillianists), it is stated that Maximus became very angry and ordered Ambrose to leave at once. Ambrose states that he left Trier even then fearing an ambush: 'Indeed, I am free to go although some thought I would not escape treachery.'[27]

Palanque and Homes Dudden have argued on the strength of Paulinus' sole testimony that Ambrose excommunicated Maximus, although not for the murder of Gratian but for mishandling the Priscillianist affair.[28] As a consequence, both biographers assume that the tone in the epistle to Valentinian should be taken seriously, which would indicate that there was a rupture in relations between Ambrose and Maximus. Yet there is

[26] *Ep.* xxx. 1 (*CSEL* lxxxii. 1. 207–8).
[27] *Ep.* xxx. 12 (*CSEL* lxxxii. 1. 215. 144–5).
[28] Palanque, *Saint Ambroise*, 174–5; Homes Dudden, *Life and Times*, i. 349.

no sound evidence that Ambrose broke off relations with Maximus, keeping in mind that Paulinus' account is yet another instance in which the hagiographer is seeking to demonstrate the *virtutes* of the bishop over temporal political powers, so that Maximus is denied communion and ordered to do penance; he refuses, and later loses his kingdom.[29] Quite the contrary, Ambrose had every reason to preserve relations between himself and the pro-Nicene emperor who was indirectly responsible for forcing the court of Valentinian to relinquish martial law in Milan. Whatever personal feelings Ambrose had about Maximus as the assassin of Gratian, they are not allowed to interfere. A second mission to Trier gave Ambrose the opportunity to re-establish just enough tension between the two courts thus preventing further hostilities from the Milanese court which continued to pose a viable threat to the Nicene community. Maximus' intent to exert his authority beyond the Gauls was also apparent to Ambrose and the treatment which Ambrose says he experienced in Trier as an emissary of Valentinian is not unrealistic. Perhaps the most reliable statement of the letter to Valentinian is the warning with which Ambrose concludes his letter: 'Farewell emperor, and be on guard against a man who is concealing war under a cloak of peace.'

(b) *The flight of the Milanese court*

Despite the warning to Valentinian about Maximus' bellicose intentions, Ambrose was not successful in bringing calm to the situation, as the complete failure of Domninus' negotiations shows.[30] Once the ambassador from Milan was assured of a secured peace between the two courts, he accepted a large military escort for the return trip to Italy. Maximus then followed the delegation with a large force across the Alps and so entered Italy without warning or resistance. When word of the invasion reached Milan, Valentinian's government dispersed immediately; the emperor and his mother travelled to Aquileia, and from there to meet

---

[29] *VA* 19 (Pellegrino, *Vita*, 78). The entire episode reads like a tragical conflation of *VA* 24, where Theodosius is denied communion until he repents.

[30] According to Zosimus (IV. 42. 3–4), Domninus, a special confidant of Valentinian, was sent to Maximus seeking guarantees of a more secure peace. Moreover, a major barbarian uprising in Pannonia induced the government at Milan to appeal for Maximus' assistance (Piganiol, *L'Empire chrétien*, 273; cf. Stein, *Histoire du Bas-Empire*, 204–5). Maximus is reported to have received the delegation graciously, heaping many gifts upon Domninus and making promises of compliance.

Theodosius at Thessalonica.[31] There the pro-Homoian court of Milan remained in exile for a year under the eastern emperor's protection.

In the mean time, Maximus wasted no time in setting up court in Milan as the new western emperor. Coins issued from mints in Milan and Aquileia after the summer of 387, which had hitherto portrayed only Valentinian, Theodosius, and Arcadius, now exclusively carried the images of Maximus and his son Victor.[32] In celebration of Maximus' self-proclaimed consulship for the year 388, Symmachus travelled to Milan, acting on behalf of the senate, and delivered a panegyric to the new ruler.[33] Presumably, Maximus stayed in Milan for Easter (9 April), where he would have attended the church where Ambrose presided. Unfortunately there is no word from Ambrose or any other source about the relations which existed between the two men. It is significant that Ambrose did not also flee at Maximus' coming, as he did when another usurper, Eugenius, approached Milan in 393. Once we dispel the idea that Ambrose was set against Maximus, there is no reason to think that the relations between the emperor and the bishop were anything but cordial and even mutually beneficial on matters of faith. Certainly no Homoians solicited the use of the basilica that Easter and it is likely that the Homoian Church and its leaders were forced to go underground, although there is no record of any anti-heretical legislation for the year Maximus remained in Milan.

In Thessalonica, Latin Homoianism was losing its last vestiges of political patronage: Valentinian and his mother Justina were completely dependent on the good graces of Theodosius in hopes of being restored to their kingdom. Theodosius seems to have been reluctant at first to respond militarily against Maximus for reasons that are far from clear.[34] According to Zosimus' hostile caricature of the Christian emperor, Theodosius had to be seduced by Justina's offer of marriage to her beautiful daughter

[31] Zosimus, IV. 43. 1 (Paschoud, 311); Rufinus, *HE* II. 16 (*PL* xxi. 524C); Theodoret, *HE* ff. 14 (*GCS* xliv. 304. 14–17) (Theodoret says Valentinian fled to Illyricum).

[32] *RIC* ix. 56; 79–80.

[33] Matthews, *Western Aristocracies*, 229. An act for which Symmachus was forced to render a formal speech of apology before Theodosius a year later (cf. Socrates, *HE* v. 14 (*PG* lxvii. 601A–B)).

[34] Socrates, *HE* v. 12 (*PG* lxvii. 597C), and Sozomen, *HE* VII. 14. 1 (*GCS* l. 318), claim that Maximus sent an embassy to Theodosius after the invasion of north Italy, but the latter neither received nor rejected the delegation. It is very possible that they have confused this embassy with the one Maximus sent in 383 after the invasion of Gaul (Zosimus, IV. 37. 1–2). Just as dubiously, Zosimus, IV. 44. 1, reports that Theodosius initiated the idea of sending an embassy to Maximus for the purpose of avoiding war.

Galla before he decided to intervene on behalf of Valentinian.[35] Such a story hardly suffices as an explanation for Theodosius' willingness to engage in civil war. It is much more likely that the emperor's decision was motivated by the rising threat which Maximus now posed as the formidable Augustus of the west. Valentinian II had been, and would, no doubt, continue to be, much easier to contain politically than Maximus. The fact remains nevertheless that Theodosius did marry Galla toward the end of 387 and thereafter began to prepare for war against Maximus.[36] There was a decided advantage in Theodosius' marriage to Galla as a political manœuvre designed to cement a bond between the two imperial houses.[37] The arrangement would have at the very least justified the embarrassing change in policy of the action proposed against Maximus. By 387 the claims of Maximus must have seemed genuine, and important political supporters of Theodosius would not have understood how he could assist Valentinian and his Arian mother against a thoroughly Nicene Augustus or why Theodosius proclaimed himself to be an avenger of Gratian when the house of Valentinian bore the responsibility for the execution of his father. The marriage to Galla not only solved these problems but also gave Theodosius legitimate authority to oversee the affairs of Valentinian, who was technically the senior Augustus of the two.

Part of this agreement between Theodosius and the family of Valentinian included the renunciation of the latter's Arian beliefs. Valentinian, in particular, was required to make certain religious concessions before Theodosius was willing to support his right to the throne against Maximus. Prior to Valentinian's arrival in Thessalonica, Theodosius is alleged to have sent him a letter chiding the young emperor for fighting against piety, which is the reason for his recent discomfiture and his enemy's victory.[38] The letter is of doubtful authenticity but it may attest to the actual grounds of Valentinian's capitulation to the Nicene faith while he was in Thessalonica. Years later Ambrose makes it clear in his *oratio* delivered at Valentinian's funeral (in 392) that Valentinian had indeed abandoned heretical opinions, offering hope that the soul of the young emperor was accepted into heavenly fellowship with his brother Gratian. Even though Valentinian had died in the flower of his youth, 'such was the correction of his life in

---

[35] Zosimus, IV. 44. 2–4 (Paschoud, 312).

[36] S. I. Oost, *Galla Placidia Augusta* (Chicago, 1968), 47.

[37] K. Holum, *Theodosian Empresses: Women and Imperial Dominion in Late Antiquity* (Berkeley, Calif., 1982), 45 ff. Cf. W. Ensslin, *Die Religionspolitik des Kaisers Theodosius*, 56.

[38] Theodoret, *HE* v. 15. 1–2 (*GCS* xliv. 304–5). Cf. v. 15. 3 (305. 4–9), which tells of Theodosius' intent to drive out the 'intruding pestilence of impiety' from Valentinian's soul.

that critical period in the time of adolescence'.[39] Ambrose does not specify when this 'correction' occurred but we can presume it took place in Thessalonica. Whatever offence this forced conversion may have brought to the Empress Justina mattered little. Within a year after their arrival in Rome, she was dead[40] and the young Valentinian, later restored as co-emperor of the west, was placed under the smothering tuteluge of Theodosius' *magister militum* Arbogast.

3. THEODOSIUS' ARRIVAL IN THE WEST

Once Theodosius decided to take action against Maximus events moved swiftly. After a series of stunning military defeats, Maximus fled to the city of Aquileia, where he was killed on 28 August 388 by Theodosius' advance guard.[41] His son Victor suffered the same fate shortly afterwards. Andragathius, Gratian's assassin, committed suicide rather than face whatever fate awaited him. In other respects however Theodosius is reported to have shown clemency to the soldiers and nobility who had collaborated with the tyrant. The Pagan senator Symmachus, for instance, was exonerated from all charges of treason after delivering an apologetic speech before the court and was even granted the honour of a consulship for the year 391.[42] Pacatus' panegyric to Theodosius was successful in acquitting the Gallic nobility from any apparent collusion with Maximus' policies,[43] and Pacatus himself received a distinguished post as proconsul of Africa in 390.[44] Nevertheless, Theodosius took stern measures against legislation issued during the usurper's regime. By means of edicts promulgated at Aquileia and Milan, all forms of decisions and honours bestowed (or demotions) were to be abrogated immediately.[45]

Theodosius' entry on to the western political scene had momentous consequences for religious affairs in Milan, especially for the Homoian Arians. Maximus and the threat of his anti-heretical fanaticism was gone,

---

[39] *De obitu Valent.* 46 (*CSEL* lxxiii. 351–2).
[40] Just after her return, with Valentinian, to the west. Rufinus, *HE* II. 17 (*PL* xxi. 525A); Sozomen, *HE* VII. 14. 7 (*GCS* l. 319. 16).
[41] *Paneg. Theod.* 32–8. Cf. Zosimus, IV. 46. 2–3 (Paschoud, 314).
[42] Bagnall et al., *Consuls of the Later Roman Empire*, 316–17. Cf. Symmachus' letter to Flavianus (*Ep.* II. 31).
[43] Nixon, 'Introduction', in *Panegyric to the Emperor Theodosius* (Liverpool, 1987), 9.
[44] *C. Th.* IX. 2. 4 (4 Feb. 390). He was later appointed *comes rei publicae* (*C. Th.* IX. 42. 13 (12 Jan. 393)); *PLRE* i. 272. Cf. J. Matthews, 'Gallic Supporters of Theodosius', *Latomus*, 30 (1971), 1078–9.
[45] *C. Th.* XV. 14. 6 (22 Sept. 388) and XV. 14. 7 (10 Oct. 388).

but in his stead came one more pointedly pro-Nicene in his affinities and just as stringent in his legislation. We have no way of knowing whether the emperor met with Ambrose while the court was established in Milan,[46] though it is quite likely that Theodosius consulted with Ambrose, Siricius at Rome, and other leading bishops of the west[47] in that first year he acted as the western Augustus. The emperor needed little prodding to change the political policies affecting religion which had been effected under the pro-Homoian court of Valentinian. In the east, Theodosius had shown himself to be a champion of Nicene Christianity through the passage of strict anti-heretical edicts, and now that he was in the west he intended to take this opportunity of ending religious strife once and for all by legislating theological uniformity for the entire empire.

Theodosius had been in Milan for not quite two months when he took action against the Donatists, probably the main object of *C. Th.* XVI. 5. 19, which banned all subscribers of perverse teaching, lay or clerical, 'from defiling assemblies'. A more general anti-heretical edict was issued on 19 May 389 expelling all persons polluted with heresy from cities and villages, and completely forbidding conventicles, whether public or private, from assembly *C. Th.* XVI. 5. 20. In effect, whatever tolerance had been established in January 386 (*C. Th.* XVI. 1. 4) for the followers of the Ariminum creed was annulled, and the Homoians found themselves outlawed along with other 'heretical' groups. The political policies which had been mandated in 381 under Theodosius and Gratian were now restored.

The ineffectiveness of anti-heretical laws as a method of eradicating theological dissension needs little comment. We can assume that the Homoian communities in Milan and other centres throughout the west were never completely eliminated by the new religious regime. Homiletical, exegetical, and polemical literature continued to be produced by Arians for Arian congregations well into the fifth century. But the truth was that Latin Homoianism had lost its ability to have any dominating influence on the development of ecclesiastical affairs in Milan or in any other western city after 386. To be sure, popular disturbances still occurred in Nicene strongholds which were said to be the work of Arians.[48] Eunomianism also continued to have its adherents in the east during and after Theodosius' rule.[49] None the less there is virtual silence in the major

---

[46] From Oct. to the beginning of May (*Regesten*, 275).

[47] Cf. Socrates, *HE* v. 14 (*PG* lxvii. 601B).

[48] e.g., Socrates, *HE* v. 13 (at Constantinople).

[49] Philostorgius, *HE* x. 6 (GCS xxi. 127–8. 3). For legislation against, see *C. Th.* XVI. 5. 27 (24 June 395); 5. 31–2 (21/2 Apr. 396); 5. 34 (4 Mar. 398); 5. 36 (6 July 399).

chroniclers of this period with regard to the Homoian Church (referred to simply as 'Arians') or about the continued conflict between Nicenes or Homoians. As far as the career of Ambrose is concerned, neither Rufinus, Paulinus, nor Ambrose himself has anything to say about the presence of Arians in Milan after the discovery of the relics in 386 and Maximus' invasion. This silence is significant. We can interpret it to mean that Ambrose's episcopate was no longer troubled by Homoian rivals or potentially damaging accusations from politically influential anti-Nicenes. On the positive side, there is evidence that the conflict with heretics was over. In the *Hexameron*, a work probably published just after the events of 386/7,[50] a triumphant note is sounded by Ambrose, who, in commenting on Genesis 1: 6, 'Let the waters be gathered together', explains how this has been fulfilled in his day through the coming of heretics and Pagans into the fold of the Church.

Here the waters are gathered together which formerly came out of all the valleys, out of all the marshes, out of all the lakes. Heresy is in the valleys, paganism is in the valleys, because God is on the mountain not in the valley. Finally in the church there is rejoicing; in heresy and paganism there is mourning and sadness . . . for out of every valley catholics are gathered together but are one congregation, one church . . . out of the heretics and pagans the church has been filled.[51]

The conclusion is easily drawn that the 'orthodox' church in Milan now enjoys a kind of unity that includes its major opponents and thus is characterized as 'una congregatio, una ecclesia'.

From this point onwards in the history of the western Church, Arian Christology becomes almost totally associated with barbarian racism as the hegemony of the Nicene faith established under Theodosius is later challenged by the fifth-century invasions of Visigoths, Ostrogoths, Vandals, and Gepids. The close association, or 'trait d'union',[52] between the Arian heresy and barbarism represents the culmination of a trend already present in pro-Nicene literature of the later fourth century. It is especially apparent in Ambrose's *De fide*, II. 16. 137–9, where he built his case for anti-Arianism upon an assumed intricate relation between Nicene Christianity and the prosperity of the Roman Empire. The heretic and the foreigner alike are to be rejected from the sacred union of terrestrial and

---

[50] P. Courcelle, *Recherches sur les confessions de saint Augustin* (Paris, 1959), 93–106; Gryson, 'Chronologie des œuvres d'Ambroise', in *Le Pretre*, 36.

[51] *Exameron*, III. 1. 3 (*CSEL* xxxii. 1. 60. 13–22).

[52] Simonetti speaks of a ' "trait d'union" fra l'arianesimo occidentale del IV secolo e l'arianesimo importato con le grandi invasioni barbariche', 'La politica antiariana di Ambrogio', 279.

divine empire. A further example noted earlier in Chapter 6 comes from the time of the basilica controversy, when Ambrose attempted to discredit his Homoian opponents by depicting them solely as those who belonged to the imperial retinue or as Gothic soldiers.[53]

Certainly the many Romanized Goths who had been won to Arian Christianity helped bolster the ranks of Homoians in Illyricum and cities of north Italy. It is wholly unlikely however that the western Homoians could have earned political tolerance and patronage during the latter part of the fourth century if the movement had been led by or largely composed of Gothic Arians. For no matter how fully enmeshed Goths became in Roman society, they were always distinguished as essentially alien to the cultural empire. We remember how sarcastically Julian Valens, onetime organizer of Homoians in Milan, was caricatured in the council of Aquileia's letter to Gratian for his alleged collaboration with the Gothic invaders of the town of Poetovio. Not only was he Arian in his beliefs, but he had betrayed his country by complicity with barbarians. Valens was, despite the accusation, a Roman even if his behaviour was exceptional. Both Auxentii of Milan were thoroughly Roman in custom and outlook, as were all other leading Homoians from the time of Constantius. Ironically, Meslin has observed that the Latin Homoians generally shared the Nicene prejudices of equating Roman patriotism and the defence of the true faith (as opposed to the barbaric countries of Pagan belief). Consequently the Homoians do not seem to have been given to missionary endeavours among barbarian peoples, with the known exception of Ulfila, who was himself a child of captives.[54] 'Jamais les communautés ariennes d'Occident, pourtant persécutées par l'Empire, à partir du règne de Gratien, n'ont lié leur sort à celui des Barbares convertis à la même foi religieuse.'[55] We must not assume that Latin Homoians wholly identified themselves with barbarian peoples on the mere grounds of a shared Christology.

Once we have acknowledged this distinction we can speak of a Latin Homoianism which ceased to have religious influence as an ecclesiastical body after Maximus' invasion of 386; the events of 386–7 ushered in an oppressive system of pro-Nicene policy which brought the political demise of the remaining elements of Homoianism in the west.

---

[53] *Ep.* 76. 12: 'Prodire de Arrianis nullus audebat, quia nec quisquam de civibus erat, pauci de familia regia, nonnulli etiam Gothi' (*CSEL* lxxxii. 3. 114. 78–80).

[54] M. Meslin, 'Nationalisme, état et religions à la fin IVe siècle', *Archives de sociologie des religions*, 9/18 (1964), 7.

[55] Ibid. 11.

CONCLUSION

THE 'triumph' of the Christian Church over its enemies is a skilful construct about the nature of conflict, first erected by fifth-century historians, that has endured in its ability to influence subsequent historical opinion. Heretics, no less than Pagans, were subdued by a series of 'memorable victories'[1] as chronicled for later generations. When Sozomen dedicates his ecclesiastical history to the Emperor Theodosius II, God's aid is invoked to assist the emperor and the 'holy empire' in conquering all their foes. It is fitting that, as his history draws to a close, the final gasp of Pagans and Arians is recorded as Attalus' usurpation of the Emperor Honorius fails.[2]

In the preceding historical reconstruction of the years 360–87, we have attempted to challenge assumptions which are a result of the 'triumphalist' model, namely, that the west had always been sympathetic to Nicene Christianity and that its complete subjugation of Homoian Arianism was accomplished soon after the loss of its political support under the Emperor Constantius. In the first place, Nicene or Homoian 'parties', that is, as conscious theological and ecclesiastical identities, did not fully crystallize until after the councils of Ariminum and Constantinople — events which marked the beginning of the Nicene–Homoian conflict in the west. One is able to chart an 'awakening' of the west to the distinct forms of eastern theology, Homoian leadership, and potential allies, such as the Homoiousians, as western bishops began to return from their exiles in the east. Among this group, the 'confessors' Hilary of Poitiers and Eusebius of Vercelli played seminal roles among those involved in the restoration of bishops who had capitulated at the council of Ariminum.

---

[1] Brown, *Power and Persuasion in Late Antiquity*, 128.
[2] HE IX. 9: 'The failure which had attended the designs of Attalus was a source of deep displeasure to the pagans and Christians of the Arian heresy. The pagans had inferred from the known predilections and early education of Attalus, that he would openly maintain their superstitions, and restore their ancient temples, their festivals, and their altars. The Arians imagined that, as soon as he found his reign firmly established, Attalus would reinstate them in the supremacy over the churches which they enjoyed during the reigns of Constantius and Valens' (*NPNF* ii. 424).

The result was a general acknowledgement of the Nicene faith through-out the Gauls and north Italy.

In the second place, it is surely an exaggeration to call Arianism a dying religion after 360, or theologically unable to sustain enduring devotion without political support, any more than was the Nicene form of faith. Homoianism became increasingly isolated in western communities after Constantius, but the ostensibly neutral political policies toward religion under Valentinian I and Gratian's early reign quelled any serious aggression by Neo-Nicenes or disgruntled Homoians. We charted a surge in Homoian and pro-Nicene texts during this time which provided insights into the ecclesiastical-doctrinal dynamics of the period. In certain sees the struggle between the two groups became very intense. Most notably at Milan, the Nicene–Homoian conflict continued into the mid-380s, producing several crisis situations.

We have also construed the early career of Ambrose in a way that radically diverges from the heroic caricature exhibited in presentations overly dependent on hagiographic literature. One perception, which has been so instrumental in modern biographical treatments of Ambrose, is the matter of Ambrose's control in the midst of controversy. The bishop is always able to manage the current situation and prevails against his opponents, whether they be emperors, Arians, or malcontents of any kind. This view has had a profound effect on historical interpretations of Ambrose's role in the Nicene–Homoian conflict. Ambrose himself does little to correct this glorified misconception. Almost never does he admit or even mention in his large corpus of surviving treatises that he is hard pressed by an adversary. Nevertheless, we have been able to show that Ambrose was under attack in 378 by Homoians in Milan and that he was accused of heresy before the emperor. He was able to clear himself of this charge and soon began to enjoy Gratian's confidence. He was not, however, able to reap any tangible political benefits from Gratian's favouritism until 381 with the returning of the sequestered basilica to the Nicene community.

Nor did the synod of Aquileia (381), organized by Ambrose and composed mainly of fellow north Italian bishops, put an end to the conflict with the Homoians as he had certainly hoped. On the contrary, the synod seems to have acted as a lightning rod, charging renewed Homoian efforts against Ambrose. During the years 381–6 Milan witnessed a short-lived revival of anti-Nicene literature and activities: Palladius of Ratiaria published his own account of the synod of Aquileia and its deceptive measures, Auxentius of Durostorum arrived in Milan as the new bishop of the

Homoian Church, and new attempts were made by the pro-Homoian administration of Valentinian II and his mother Justina to restore to Homoian hands the basilica which Gratian had removed.

The picture which emerges from this new reconstruction is that Ambrose was not the master of the situation as much as the traditional scenarios depict. He was, none the less, an astute politician and a passionate orator. The personal ties which Ambrose had made with Gratian's usurper, Maximus, on his two embassies to Trier proved invaluable for preventing Valentinian II from taking any direct action against the pro-Nicenes in Milan. It is very likely that the threat of an invasion by Maximus ultimately caused Valentinian to back down from enforcing the sequestration of a Nicene basilica. And the 'finding' of the relics of Gervasius and Protasius in 386 was utilized by Ambrose to the fullest extent for securing the Nicene position to Milanese society.

An event which marks the political demise of Homoianism in the west, we have argued, is Maximus' invasion in the summer of 387 and Theodosius' subsequent occupation of the western provinces after his defeat of Maximus. The absence of any further political or conciliar activities against Arians, with the exception of perfunctory laws issued against all heretics,[3] allows us to make the deduction that Homoianism no longer presented any threat to Neo-Nicene bishops. This is the most effective barometer for placing an end to what is called the 'Nicene controversy'.

To call the final result of this process the 'triumph of Nicaea' is seriously flawed. One cannot presume upon a line of continuity stretching from the council of Nicaea to the age of Ambrose, as later historiographers were wont to do, casting an almost Romantic tinge over their retrospective glance at the Nicene–Arian conflicts. We have shown rather that no such historical continuity existed in the west before the 350s. This does not mean there were no fundamental agreements about what constituted acceptable Trinitarian expression, but simply that there existed no uniform articulation which faith communities were prepared to acknowledge as universally orthodox. Moreover, it must be admitted that the faith of the Neo-Nicenes in the 370s and 380s represented a considerable accretion to the doctrines articulated in the creed of Nicaea as in the case of the consubstantiality of the Holy Spirit, as insisted by the 'Epistola Catholica' of the Alexandrian synod of 362, or in the precarious but necessary balance between the human/divine natures of Christ as

---

[3] *C. Th.* XVI. 5. 19–22, 24, 26, 28–30, and *passim*.

passionately argued by Ambrose in *De fide*, I–II. Nicene 'orthodoxy' towards the end of the fourth century meant something different and
expanded from what it had meant in AD 325. If such augmentation was
not foreign to the earlier intent of doctrinal definition, it does show the
result of polemical demands and theological practicality as orthodoxy was
continually forged in the ecclesiastical furnace of dissenting opinions. At
least from a historical perspective, the final hegemony of the Neo-Nicene
faith should be presented, not as a triumph, but as an outcome from the
struggle between theological traditions, each clinging to the conviction
that they alone possessed the *fides vera et sola*.

APPENDIX I

A Chronology of Letters Attributed to Liberius of Rome

1. *Ep. ad Constantium imperatorem per Luciferium episcopum* (AD 353/4), in *CAP* A VII (*CSEL* lxv. 89–93).
2. Fragment from *Ad Caecilianum episcopum Spolitinum* (AD 353/4), in *CAP* B VII. 3–4 (*CSEL* lxv. 166).
3. Fragment from *Ad Ossium de Vincenti ruina* (AD 353/4), in *CAP* B VII. 5–6 (*CSEL* lxv. 167).
4. *Liberius episcopus dilectissimo fratri Eusebio* (AD 353/4; before Lucifer arrives in Vercelli), in the Eusebian corpus ('Appendix II. B', *CCSL* ix. 121–2).
5. *Liberius episcopus dilectissimo fratri Eusebio* (AD 354; follows letter 1, commends Lucifer), in Eusebian corpus ('Appendix II. B 2', *CCSL* ix. 122).
6. *Liberius episcopus dilectissimo fratri Eusebio* (AD 354; Liberius is responding to a letter (non-extant) from Eusebius; Lucifer has arrived in Vercelli), in Eusebian corpus ('Appendix II. B 3', *CCSL* ix. 122–3).
7. *Ep. ad Eusebium, Dionysium et Luciferium*, 'Quamvis sub imagine' (AD 355; just before Liberius was about to go into exile), in *CAP* B VII. 1–2 (*CSEL* lxv. 164–6) and in the Eusebian corpus, 'Appendix II. B 4' (*CCSL* ix. 123–4).
8. *Ad orientales episcopis*, 'Pro deifico timore' (AD 357; Liberius has capitulated to the condemnation of Athanasius), in *CAP* B VII. 8 (*CSEL* lxv. 168–70).
9. *Ad Ursacium et Valentem*, 'Quia scio' (AD 357; now that Liberius has entered into communion with them, he seeks political mediation from Ursacius and Valens for his release from exile), in *CAP* B VII. 10 (*CSEL* lxv. 170–2).
10. *Ad Vincetium*, 'Non doceo' (AD 357; written from exile, Liberius seeks Vincentius' petition to the emperor for his release), in *CAP* B VII. 11 (*CSEL* lxv. 172–3).
11. *Ad orientales episcopos*, 'Studens paci' (AD 357; Liberius now returned from exile), in *CAP* B III. 1 (*CSEL* lxv. 155).
12. *Ad catolicos episcopos Italiae* (AD 362/3; written after synod of Alexandria), in *CAP* B IV. 1 (*CSEL* lxv. 156–7).

A Chronology of Letters Related and Attributed to Eusebius of Vercelli

1. Eusebius to Liberius (AD 354/5; non-extant) after Lucifer's arrival in Vercelli ('Liberius episcopus dilectissimo fratri Eusebio', *Ep.* 3. 1; *CCSL* ix. 123. 6–8).
2. 'Eusebius Constantio imp. Augusto salutem' (AD late 354/5); responding to Constantius' convocation of a council at Milan ('Epistula Prima', *CCSL* ix. 103).
3. 'Domino honorificentissimo Eusebio episcopo Lucifer episcopus, Pancratius presbyter et Hilarius' (AD 355); urging Eusebius to return to the council of Milan ('Appendix II. A 2'; *CCSL* ix. 120).
4. 'Epistola synodica: concilium Mediolanense Eusebio fratri in domino salutem' (AD 355); informing Eusebius about the council's decisions and insisting on his compliance with them ('Appendix II. A 1'; *CCSL* ix. 119).
5. 'Epistola Constantii ad Eusebium: Constantius victor ac triumphator semper Augustus Eusebio episcopo' (AD 355); advising Eusebius not to reject the decisions of the council ('Appendix II. A 3'; *CCSL* ix. 120–1).
6. 'Dilectissimis fratribus et satis desideratissimis presbyteris, sed et sanctis in fide consistentibus plebibus Vercellensibus, Novariensibus, Eporediensibus nec non Dertonensibus Eusebius episcopus in domino aeternam salutem' (AD 355–9); a letter from Eusebius in exile in Scythopolis ('Epistula Secunda', *CCSL* ix. 104–9).
7. 'Domino sanctissimo fratri Gregorio episcopo Eusebius in domino salutem' (AD 360/1); writing in response to Gregory's letter after the council of Ariminum ('Epistula Tertia', *CCSL* ix. 110; *CSEL* lxv. 46–7).

Eusebian Authorship of *De trinitate*, I–VII

With the publication of the *CCSL* ix edition (Turnhout, 1957), Bulhart revived the idea, as advanced in the beginning of the seventeenth century by Jean Étienne Ferreri and later expounded by Morin ('Les Douze Livres sur la Trinité', *RB* 15 (1898), 1–10), of Eusebian authorship for the first seven books of *De trinitate*. This has evoked criticism, specifically from M. Simonetti ('Qualche osservazione sul *De trinitate* attribuito a Eusebio di Vercelli', *Rivista di cultura classica e medioevale*, 5 (1963), 386–93), who expressed his surprise at Bulhart's lack of acknowledgement that the manuscript evidence was too weak to establish Eusebian authorship on this basis alone with any certainty. There is the further problem that no precise means exists to compare the *De trinitate* with Eusebius' other writings, since his literary remains consist only of three letters in which doctrinal matters were not discussed ('Qualche osservazione', 388). Any external verification of a Eusebian style is thus made very difficult. It is significant to Simonetti that Jerome never mentions in *De viris illustribus* 96 that Eusebius wrote such a work. Of course the strength of this argument is only as good as the general accuracy of Jerome's notices, which is itself a questionable assumption, and must not be given undue weight.

Simonetti's real concerns are with Bulhart's acceptance of P. Schepens's controversial dating of the shorter or first recension of *De trinitate* to AD 345–7 (in 'L'Ambrosiastre et saint Eusèbe de Verceil', *RSR* 37 (1950), 295–9). From purely internal considerations, Simonetti argues that the *De trinitate* can hardly be dated to these years, which were just following the council of Serdica (343). The work is characterized by the continual insistence on the absolute equality of the three divine persons in the unity of nature; and especially the Holy Spirit is treated by the *De trinitate* with qualifying terms that once were used of the Son only. Such interest in the nature of the Holy Spirit with respect to Trinitarian polemics is not seen until much later, well beyond Hilary's *De trinitate*, such as in Athanasius' letter to Serapion or Ambrose's *De spiritu sancto* of 381. This too is a major point in L. Dattrino's arguments against Bulhart's chronology. And, according to Dattrino, the Christology of *De trinitate* exhibits a certain theological maturity. The third book of *De trinitate*, for example, which addresses 'De adsumptione hominis', is devoted to establishing the presence of two natures in Christ by means of explaining that what is attributed to one is to be attributed to the other. Indeed, the preoccupation of the writer is to safeguard in Christ his divinity, before and after the incarnation, and thus to distinguish it carefully from the effects of his human nature (*Pseudo-Atanasio: la Trinita* (Rome, 1980), 19 ff).

Does the type of Christology in the *De trinitate* provide sound enough evidence to date the document to the last couple of decades in the fourth century as Dattrino asserts? Even the latter admits that the *De trinitate* manifests 'a simple Christology, typically subdivided, explicitly anti-Arian'. There is very little in *De trinitate* that has not already appeared in the anti-Arian works which we have examined in the two decades after the council of Ariminum (359). Simonetti also concedes that there is nothing in the pneumatology of *De trinitate* which mandates a chronology beyond *c.*380. The theological disputes to which *De trinitate* alludes are certainly issues which were the subject of the second half of the fourth century, but they hardly vindicate what is the heart of Dattrino's thesis, that the work should be placed near the end of the fourth century and probably originated in Spain or Gallia Narbonensis (p. 14). Nor does the fact that the treatise was concerned with combating hostile theories against Nicene orthodoxy assist in placing the work geographically or chronologically with any precision. Dattrino characterizes Spain and Gallia Narbonensis in the last decade of the fourth century as a period 'quantomai fecondo di pressioni ereticali che insidiavano la vita dei fedeli' (p. 13). But how is this any different from the ecclesiastical climate which we have seen in Illyricum or north Italy during 360–80?

If Bulhart's (Schepens's) chronology is rightly rejected, then what alternatives can we offer with the limited sources at our disposal? It is important at this point that we distinguish between the issues of chronology and matters of authorship. Once we discount the arguments that the *De trinitate* must be theologically limited to a very late date in the fourth century, there is no reason why the first recension could not have been written between the years 365–80; a period which saw an increased polarization and compartmentalization between competing theologies and perceived opponents. In fact, the frustration which the writer expresses in VII. 1, in which he longs for the removal of those perpetrators of madness who ought to be eradicated and destroyed, may be due to the lack of official action against the writer's heretical enemies—a complaint which could just as easily pertain to Valentinian's or Gratian's early policies concerning religion.

With regards to authorship, Bulhart's suggestion that there was one author for books I–VII, a probably different writer of book VIII, and an unknown redactor of all eight books ('Praefatio', pp. xxxiii–iv) has received little opposition. Was Eusebius of Vercelli the author of the original seven books? Apart from the problems of chronology, the strongest objections levelled against Eusebian authorship are those which attempt to argue that the work originated from Spain and/or from the pen of a Luciferian. It can be shown, however, that such arguments have virtually no substance, and it is just as possible that the *De trinitate* was written in south or north Italy.

The actual evidence which has been advanced for Eusebian authorship is admittedly slight and inconclusive. We cannot hope to solve all the problems of authorship here, but a few additional points can be made. First is the general observation that there is nothing in the *De trinitate* which Eusebius could not have said. Another way to say this is to ask what we would expect to find if the treatise were from Eusebius' hand. Assuming that the work was written after his return to the west, we should expect it to bear traces of a broadened theological perspective as the result of its writer having been in exile in the east for over seven years. Like Hilary of Poitiers, Eusebius would have become much more informed as to the complexity of certain contemporary issues, Trinitarian and Christological, at a date probably earlier than his western colleagues. More specifically, we know that Eusebius attended at least one eastern synod, since he was present at Alexandria in 362 and was jointly responsible for the decisions which that assembly concluded. He lived for almost another decade after this synod. One would envision that there should be some resemblance between the doctrine promulgated in the synodical letter, the 'Epistola Catholica', and especially the *Tomus* from Alexandria, and the theological ideas expressed in the *De trinitate*.

Parallels of similiar content between these works can be found: explicit condemnation of any view which separates the Holy Spirit from the essence of the Son and the Father ('Epistola', 5 (as enumerated by Tetz, 'Ein enzyklisches Schreiben', 271–3); *Tomus*, 3; 5; *De trin.* II. 30–4; IV. 17; VII. 5. 6); aggressive opposition to any separation of the persons of the Trinity (*Tomus*, 3; 'Epistola', 1; *De trin.* I. 69–70, and *passim*); stern warnings against the 'Arriomanitae' who misuse the doctrine of the three hypostases (*Tomus*, 3; *De trin.* I. 59 [16]); that the Son is not a creation of God, nor is the Holy Spirit to be counted among created things ('Epistola', 5; *De trin.* II. 21–2; 30), and a concern to maintain the full humanity of the incarnate Christ (*Tomus*, 6; *De trin.* II. 40–1, 44).

Comparison of these works is not without problems. For instance, if the *De trinitate* is authored by Eusebius, it is curious that the work appeals to no conciliar authority as a basis for its doctrinal assertions, and there is an absence of any direct reference to the Nicene creed (despite one mention of the council of Nicaea)—a surprising omission in light of the high visibility which the creed enjoys in the documents from Alexandria. Moreover, the one place in the *Tomus* where Eusebius personally expresses his own interpretation of the doctrine of the incarnation (i.e., that it was the assumption of a full humanity yet without sin; *Tomus*, 10), is not found in a lengthy discussion of the incarnation in *De trinitate* (III. 22 ff.).

Apart from these discrepancies, the sensitivities in the *De trinitate* to reputed Arian views about the creaturehood of the Holy Spirit, dividing the members of the Trinity in a hierarchical fashion, the denial that the Son possesses an identical nature to the Father, as well as having a conscious 'anthropos-sarx' model of the incarnation, correspond to the assertions found in the *Tomus* and the 'Epistola'. It is quite plausible for Eusebius of Vercelli to have brought back to the west awareness of such theological developments, since he was, after all, commissioned by the synod as its delegate to disseminate its decisions in the west (Rufinus, *HE* I. 29). In this regard it is also significant that the writer of the *De trinitate* levels a series of anathemas against those 'who believe that grace should not be bestowed upon the penitent who lapsed' (VI. 16. 2). This is an obvious reference to the controversy which racked eastern and western churches after the capitulation of so many bishops to the Homoian decrees propounded at the dual councils Ariminum/Seleucia, and it rules out that the work was by the hand of a Luciferian. Of course the admission of bishops who had lapsed in 359 but sought communion later by disavowing allegiance to any creed but Nicaea was the primary concern of the synod of Alexandria as clearly evidenced in both the 'Epistola' (4; 7) and the *Tomus* (1; 5), and was the decision with which Eusebius returned to the west. To this may be added Morin's still viable arguments, that (1) the biblical citations in *De trinitate*, especially from the Gospels, indicate the usage of texts as found in MSS Vercellensis (a) and Monacensis (q), both of which originate from north Italy; (2) there are a remarkable number of citations parallel with those of Hilary of Poitiers; (3) there is the mention of a Eusebius, almost certainly Eusebius of Vercelli, by Ambrosiaster (in *Quaestiones veteris et novis Testamenti*, 125) who is said to have composed a treatise in which he claimed the Holy Spirit was consubstantial with the Father and the Son ('Les Douze Livres', 8–10).

We may conclude that there are no sustaining reasons which forbid Eusebian authorship of the *De trinitate* and, on the contrary, there exists certain evidence in its favour, quite apart from the kind of arguments adduced by Bulhart.

Credal Documents of Latin Homoianism

The following is a list of the major credal documents which are Homoian or produced by authors who were at one time Homoian.

1. The Sirmium Manifesto of 357 (Hilary, *De synodis*, 11 (*PL* x. 487-9); Athanasius, *De synodis*, 28 (*PG* xxvi. 740D-741D; 744A); Socrates, *HE* II. 30 (*PG* lxvii. 285B-289A)).

2. The Dated Creed from Sirmium, 359 (Athanasius, *De synodis*, 8 (*PG* xxvi. 692B-693C); Socrates, *HE* II. 37 (*PG* lxvii. 305A-308A)).

3. Niké creed brought back to Ariminum (Theodoret, *HE* II. 21. 3-7 (*GCS* xliv. 145-6)). See synodical letter from the second session of Ariminum, 359 (Hilary, *CAP* A VI (*CSEL* lxv. 87-8)).

4. Acacian creed from Seleucia, 359 (Athanasius, *De synodis*, 29 (*PG* xxvi. 744B-745C, partial); Socrates, *HE* II. 40 (*PG* lxvii. 340AB)).

5. Constantinopolitan creed, 360 (Athanasius, *De synodis*, 30 (*PG* xxvi. 745C-748C); Socrates, *HE* II. 41 (*PG* lxvii. 348B-349B)).

6. Auxentius' statement of faith, 364 (Hilary, *Contra Auxentium*, 13-15 (*PL* x. 617-18)).

7. Germinius' confession of faith, 366 (Hilary, *CAP* A III (*CSEL* lxv. 47-8)), and an expanded explanation of his confession to Rufianus, Palladius, *et al.* (Hilary, *CAP* B VI (*CSEL* lxv. 160-3)).

8. Ulfila's creed, *c.*383 (*Scholia*, 308ʳ. 63 (Gryson, *Scolies*, 250)); cf. further elaboration of Ulfila's beliefs by Auxentius (*Scholia*, 304ᵛ-305ʳ. 42-6 (Gryson, *Scolies*, 236-8)).

9. 'Adversus Orthodoxos et Macedonianos', frag. 2 (*Fragmenta theologica ariana* (*CCSL* lxxxvii), 231-2).

10. 'Instructio verae fidei', frag. 14 (*Fragmenta theologica ariana* (*CCSL* lxxxvii), 250; frag. 22 (ibid. 263-4); cf. frag. 17 (ibid. 254-6) for detailed explanation of the relation between Father and Son.

Documents (9) and (10) are preserved in the Bobbio palimpsests. Both are dated by Gryson to sometime after 380, and have different authors (*CCSL* lxxxvii, p. xxv).

BIBLIOGRAPHY OF SECONDARY SOURCES

ARMSTRONG, C. B., 'The Synod of Alexandria and the Schism at Antioch in A.D. 362', *JTS* 22 (1921), 206–21, 347–55.

AUBINEAU, M., 'Jean Damascène et "l'Epistula de interventione Gervasii et Protasii" attribuée à Ambroise de Milan', *Analecta Bollandiana*, 90 (1972), 1–14.

BAGNALL, R. S., *et al.*, *Consuls of the Later Roman Empire* (Atlanta, 1987).

BARDY, G., 'Sur un synode de l'Illyricum (375)', *Bulletin d'ancienne littérature et d'archéologie chrétienne*, 2 (1912), 259–74.

—— 'L'Occident et les documents de la controverse arienne', *RSR* 20 (1940), 28–63.

BARNARD, L. W., 'Athanasius and the Emperor Jovian', *Studia Patristica*, 21 (1989), 384–9.

BARNES, M. R., and WILLIAMS, D. H. (eds.), *Arianism after Arius: Essays on the Development of the Fourth Century Conflicts* (Edinburgh, 1993).

BARNES, T. D., 'Proconsuls of Africa, 337–392', *Phoenix*, 39 (1985), 144–53.

—— 'The Consecration of Ulfila', *JTS* (1990), 541–5.

—— 'Hilary of Poitiers on his Exile', *VC* 46 (1992), 129–40.

—— *Athanasius and Constantius: Theology and Politics in the Constantinian Empire* (Cambridge, Mass., 1993).

BEATRICE, P. F., *et al.*, *Cento anni di bibliografia ambrosiana (1874–1974*, (Milan, 1981).

BIDEZ, J., *La Vie de l'empereur Julien* (Paris, 1965).

BIGELMAIR, A., *Zeno von Verona* (Münster, 1904).

BIRLEY, A. R., 'Magnus Maximus and the Persecution of Heresy', *Bulletin of the John Rylands University Library*, 66 (1983–4), 13–43.

BONNER, G., *St Augustine of Hippo: Life and Controversies* (1963; Norwich, 1986).

BORCHARDT, C. F., *Hilary of Poitiers' Role in the Arian Struggle* (The Hague, 1966).

BOWERSOCK, G. W., *Julian the Apostate* (Cambridge, 1978).

—— 'From Emperor to Bishop: The Self-Conscious Transformation of Political Power in the Fourth Century A.D.', *Classical Philology*, 81 (1986), 298–307.

BRENNECKE, H. C., *Hilarius von Poitiers und die Bischofsopposition gegen Konstantius II: Untersuchungen zur dritten Phase des arianischen Streites (337–361)* (Berlin, 1984).

—— *Studien zur Geschichte der Homöer: der Osten bis zum Ende der homöischen Reichskirche* (Tübingen, 1988).

BROWN, P., *The Cult of the Saints* (Chicago, 1981).

—— *The Body and Society: Men, Women and Sexual Renunciation in Early Christianity* (New York, 1988).

—— *Power and Persuasion in Late Antiquity: Towards a Christian Empire* (Madison, Wis., 1992).

BURKHARDT, J. D., 'Les Ariens d'Occident', *Revue d'histoire et de philosophie religieuse*, 51 (1971), 169–74.

BURNS, A. E., 'On Eusebius of Vercelli', *JTS* 1 (1900), 592–9.

BURNS, T. A., 'The Battle of Adrianople: A Reconsideration', *Historia*, 22 (1973), 336–45.

CAMERON, A., 'Gratian's Repudiation of the Pontifical Robe', *JRS* 58 (1968), 96–102.

CAMPENHAUSEN, H. VON, *Ambrosius von Mailand als Kirchenpolitiker*, Arbeiten zur Kirchengeschichte 12 (Berlin, 1929).

CAPELLE, B., 'Un homélaire de l'évêque arien Maximin', *RB* 34 (1922), 81–108.

—— 'La Lettre d'Auxence sur Ulfila', *RB* 34 (1922), 224–33.

CATTANEO, E., *La religione a Milano nell'età di sant' Ambrogio* (Milan, 1974).

CAVALLIN, S., 'Die Legendenbildung um den Mailander Bischof Dionysius', *Eranos*, 43 (1945), 136–49.

CHADWICK, H., 'The Origin of the Term "Oecumenical Council"', *JTS* 23 (1972), 132–5.

—— *Priscillian of Avila: The Occult and the Charismatic in the Early Church* (Oxford, 1976).

—— 'The Role of the Christian Bishop in Ancient Society', in *The Center for Hermeneutical Studies in Hellenistic and Modern Culture: Protocol of the 35th Colloquy* (Berkeley, Calif., 1979), 1–14.

CHADWICK, N. K., *Poetry and Letters in Early Christian Gaul* (London, 1955).

CHAPMAN, J., 'The Contested Letters of Pope Liberius', *RB* 27 (1910), 325–40.

CLERCQ, V. DE, *Ossius of Cordova: A Contribution to the History of the Constantinian Period* (Washington, DC, 1954).

—— 'Eusebius of Vercelli', *New Catholic Encyclopedia*, v. 637.

CORBELLINI, C., 'Sesto Petronio Probo e l'elezione episcopale di Ambrogio', *Rendiconti: Istituto Lombardo di Scienze e Lettere*, 109 (1975), 181–9.

CORTI, G., 'Lo sfondo Ambrosiano del concilio di Aquileia', in *Atti del colloquio internazionale sul concilio di Aquileia del 381*, Antichità Altoadriatiche 16 (Udine, 1981), 43–67.

COURCELLE, P., 'L'Invention et la translation des saints Gervais et Protais (17–19 juin)', in *Recherches sur les confessions de St Augustine* (Paris, 1968), 139–42.

—— *Recherches sur saint Ambroise: vies anciennes, culture, iconographie* (Paris, 1973).

CUSCITO, G., 'Il concilio di Aquileia del 381 e le sue fonti', in *Aquileia nel IV secolo* (Udine, 1982), 189–223.

—— 'Atti del concilio di Aquileia', in *Aquileia nel IV secolo* (Udine, 1982), 224–54.

—— *Fede e politica ad Aquileia: dibattito teologico e centri di potere (secolo IV–VI)* (Udine, 1987).

DELEHAYE, H., *Les Légendes hagiographiques* (3rd edn., Brussels, 1927).

DOIGNON, J., *Hilaire de Poitiers avant l'exil* (Paris, 1971).

DUCHESNE, L., *Histoire ancienne de l'Église*, vol. ii (Paris, 1908).

DUVAL, Y.-M., 'Sur l'Arianisme des Ariens d'Occident', *Mélanges de science religieuse*, 26 (1969), 145–53.

—— 'Comptes rendus', *Latomus*, 26 (1969), 237–42.

—— 'La "Manœuvre frauduleuse" de Rimini à la recherche du *Liber adversus Vrsacium et Valentem*', in *Hilaire et son temps: actes du colloque de Poitiers, 29 septembre–3 octobre* (Paris, 1969), 51–103.

—— 'Vrais et faux problèmes concernant le retour d'exil d'Hilaire de Poitiers et son action en Italie en 360–363', *Athenaeum*, NS 48 (1970), 251–75.

—— 'Traduction latine inédite du symbole de Nicée et une condamnation d'Arius à Rimini: nouveau fragment historique d'Hilaire ou pièces des actes du concile?', *RB* (1972), 7–25.

—— 'L'Influence des écrivains africains du IIIᵉ siècle sur les écrivains chrétiens de l'Italie du nord dans la seconde moitié du IVᵉ siècle', in *Aquileia e l'Africa*, Antichità Altoadriatiche 5 (Udine, 1974), 191–225.

—— 'Ambroise, de son élection à sa consécration', in G. Lazzati (ed.), *Ambrosius episcopus* (Milan, 1976), ii. 243–83.

—— 'Le Sens des débats d'Aquilée pour les Nicéens: Nicée Rimini Aquilée', in *Atti di colloquio internazionale sul concilio di Aquileia del 381* (Udine, 1981), 67–96.

—— 'La Présentation arienne du concile d'Aquilée de 381', *RHE* 76 (1981), 317–31.

EDBROOKE, R. O., 'The Visit of Constantius II to Rome in 357 and its Effect on the Pagan Roman Senatorial Aristocracy', *American Journal of Philology*, 97 (1976), 40–61.

EHRHARDT, A., 'The First Two Years of the Emperor Theodosius I', *JEH* 15 (1964), 1–17.

ENSSLIN, W., *Die Religionspolitik des Kaiser Theodosius der Grosse* (Munich, 1953).

FALLER, O., 'La data della consacrazione vescovile di sant'Ambrogio', in A. Faccioli (ed.), *Ambrosiana: scritti di storia archeologia ed arte* (Milan, 1942), 97–112.

FREND, W. H. C., *The Early Church* (Philadelphia, 1965).

FRITZ, G., 'Rimini (concile de)', *DTC* xiii. 2708–11.

GALTIER, P., *Saint Hilaire de Poitiers: le premier docteur de l'Église* (Paris, 1960).

GANSHOFF, L., 'Note sur l'élection des évêques dans l'Empire Romain au IVᵉ et pendant la première moitié du Vᵉ siècle', *Revue internationale des droits de l'antiquité: mélanges Fernand de Visscher*, 3/4 (1950), 476–98.

GAUDEMET, J., *L'Église dans l'Empire Romain (IVᵉ–Vᵉ)* (Paris, 1958).

GIBBON, E., *Decline and Fall of the Roman Empire*, vol. ii (London, 1781).

GIRARDET, K. M., 'Constance II, Athanase et l'Édit d'Arles (353)', in C. Kannengiesser (ed.), *Politique et théologie chez Athanase d'Alexandrie* (Paris, 1974), 63–91.

GLAESENER, H., 'L'Empereur Gratien et saint Ambroise', *RHE* 52 (1957), 466–88.

GOTTLIEB, G., *Ambrosius von Mailand und Kaiser Gratian*, Hypomnemata: Untersuchungen zur Antike und zu ihrem Nachleben 40 (Göttingen, 1973).

GRAY, P., ' "The Select Fathers": Canonizing the Patristic Past', *Studia Patristica*, 23 (1989), 21–36.

GREEN, M. R., 'Supporters of the Anti-pope Ursinus', *JTS* 22 (1971), 531–8.

GREGG, R. C. (ed.), *Arianism: Historical and Theological Reassessments: Papers from the Ninth International Conference on Patristic Studies* (Philadelphia, 1985).

GRIFFE, E., *La Gaule chrétienne à l'époque romaine* (2nd edn., Paris, 1964).

GRILLMEIER, A., *Christ in Christian Tradition: From the Apostolic Age to Chalcedon (451)*, trans. J. S. Bowden (London, 1965).

GRUMEL, V., La deuxiéme Mission de saint Ambroise auprès de Maxime', *Revue des études byzantines*, 9 (1951), 154–60.

—— 'L'Illyricum de la mort de Valentinien I (375) à la mort de Stilicon (408)', *Revue des études byzantines*, 9 (1952), 7.

GRYSON, R., *Le Prêtre selon saint Ambroise* (Louvain, 1968).

—— *Scolies ariennes sur le concile d'Aquilée*, SC 267 (Paris, 1980).

—— *Le Recueil de Vérone (MS LI de la Bibliothèque Capitulaire et feuillets inédits de la collection Giustiniani Recanati): Étude codicologique et paléographique* (The Hague, 1982).

GWATKIN, H. M., *Studies of Arianism, Chiefly Referring to the Character and Chronology of the Reaction which Followed the Council of Nicaea* (Cambridge, 1882).

HAAS, C., 'The Alexandrian Riots of 356 and George of Cappadocia', *Greek-Roman and Byzantine Studies*, 32 (1991), 281–301.

HAERINGEN, J. H. VAN, 'De Valentiniano II et Ambrosio: illustrantur et digeruntur res anno 386 gestae', *Mnemosyne*, 3rd ser. 5 (1937): (1) 'Valentinianus II basilicam adornitur (de Ambrosii epistula XX)', 152–8; (2) 'De Ambrosii epistula XXI', 28–33; (3) 'De Ambrosii epistulis XX et XXI: temporum descriptio', 229–40.

HALL, S. G., 'The Creed of Sardica', *Studia Patristica*, 19 (1989), 173–84.

HAMMOND-BAMMEL, C. P., 'From the School of Maximinus: The Arian Material in Paris MS. Lat. 8907', *JTS* 31 (1980), 391–402.

HANSON, R. P. C., 'The Arian Doctrine of the Incarnation', in R. Gregg (ed.), *Arianism: Historical and Theological Reassessments* (Philadelphia, 1985), 181–211.

—— 'A Note on "Like according to the Scriptures" ', *ZKG* 98 (1987), 230–2.

—— *The Search for the Christian Doctrine of God: The Arian Controversy 318–381* (Edinburgh, 1988).

HARNACK, ADOLF VON, *History of Dogma*, trans. from the German 3rd edn., by N. Buchanan, vol. iv (New York, 1961).

HEFELE, C. J., *Historire des conciles*, 2 vols. (Paris, 1907).

Hilaire de Poitiers: Contre Constance, ed. A. Rocher, SC 334 (Paris, 1987).

HOLMES, T., *The Origin and Development of the Christian Church in Gaul* (London, 1911).

HOLUM, K. G., *Theodosian Empresses: Women and Imperial Dominion in Late Antiquity* (Berkeley, Calif., 1982).

HOMES DUDDEN, F., *The Life and Times of Saint Ambrose*, 2 vols. (Oxford, 1935).

HUNT, E. D., 'Did Constantius II Have "Court Bishops"?', *Studia Patristica*, 21 (1989), 86–90.

JONES, A. H. M., 'Were Ancient Heresies National or Social Movements in Disguise?', *JTS* 10 (1959), 296–302.

—— 'Collegiate Prefectures', *JRS* 54 (1964), 78–89.

KANNENGIESSER, C., 'L'Héritage d'Hilaire de Poitiers', *RSR* 56 (1968), 435–56.

—— '(Ps.-)Athanasius *ad Afros* Examined', in C. Brennecke, E. L. Grasmück, and C. Markschies (eds.), *Logos: Festschrift L. Abramowski*, Beihefte zur Zeitschrift für neutestamentliche Wissenschaft 67 (Berlin, 1993), 264–80.

KAUFFMANN, F., *Aus der Schule des Wulfila: 'Auxentii Dorostorensis epistula de fide, vita et obitu Wulfilae' im Zusammenhang der 'Dissertatio Maximini contra Ambrosium'*, Texte und Untersuchungen zur Altgermanischen Religionsgeschichte I (Strasbourg, 1899).

KELLY, J. N. D., *Early Christian Creeds* (3rd edn., London, 1972).

—— *Jerome: His Life, Writings and Controversies* (London, 1975).

KING, N. O., *The Emperor Theodosius and the Establishment of Christianity* (London, 1961).

KOCH, H., 'Philastrius', in *Realencyklopädie der klassischen Altertumswissenschaft* xix. 2. 2125.

KOPECEK, T. A., *A History of Neo-Arianism*, 2 vols. (Philadelphia, 1979).

LABRIOLLE, P. DE, *The Life and Times of Saint Ambrose*, trans. Herbert Wilson (New York, 1928). Original French edition *Saint Ambroise* (Paris, 1908).

LAMIRANDE, E., *Paulin de Milan et la 'Vita Ambrosii': aspects de la religion sous le Bas-Empire* (Montreal, 1982).

LANZONI, F., *Le origini delle diocesi antiche d'Italia: studio critico* (Rome, 1923).

LAZZATI, G. (ed.), *Ambrosius episcopus: Atti del congresso internazionale di studi ambrosiana nel XVI centenario della elevazione di sant' Ambrogio alla cattedra episcopale*, 2 vols. (Milan, 1976).

LENOX-CONYNGHAM, A., 'A Topography of the Basilica Conflict of A.D. 385/6 in Milan', *Historia*, 31 (1982), 353–63.

—— 'Juristic and Religious Aspects of the Basilica Conflict of A.D. 386', *Studia Patristica*, 18 (1985), 55–8.

LIENHARD, J., 'Patristic Sermons on Eusebius of Vercelli and their Relation to his Monasticism', *RB* 87 (1977), 164–72.

—— 'Recent Studies in Arianism', *Religious Studies Review*, 8 (1982), 333.

—— 'Marcellus of Ancyra in Modern Research', *Theological Studies*, 43 (1982), 486–503.

—— 'Acacius of Caesarea: *Contra Marcellum*: Historical and Theological Considerations', *Cristianesimo nella storia*, 10 (1989), 1–22.

—— 'Basil of Caesarea, Marcellus of Ancyra and "Sabellius"', *Church History*, 58 (1989), 157–67.

LOGAN, A. H. B., 'Marcellus of Ancyra and Anti-Arian Polemic', *Studia Patristica*, 20 (1989), 189–97.

LÖHR, W. A., *Die Entstehung der homöischen und homöusianischen Kirchenparteien: Studien zur Synodalgeschichte des 4. Jahrhunderts* (Bonn, 1986).

LYMAN, R., 'A Topography of Heresy: Mapping the Rhetorical Creation of Arianism', in M. R. Barnes and D. H. Williams (eds.), *Arianism after Arius* (Edinburgh, 1993), 45–62.

MCCLURE, J., 'Handbooks against Heresy', *JTS* 30 (1979), 186–97.

MCCLURE, R. M., 'Studies in the Text of the *Vita Ambrosii* of Paulinus of Milan' (Ph.D. dissertation, University of California, 1971).

MACHIELSEN, L., 'Fragments patristiques non-identifiés du ms. Vat. Pal. 577', *Sacris erudiri*, 12 (1961), 487–539.

MCLYNN, N., 'The "Apology" of Palladius: Nature and Purpose', *JTS* 42 (1991), 52–76.

MARTROYE, F., 'L'Affaire Indicia: une sentence de saint Ambroise', *Mélanges Paul Fournier* (Paris, 1929).

MATTHEWS, J., *Western Aristocracies and Imperial Court A.D. 364–425* (Oxford, 1975).

MEIJERING, E. P., *Hilary of Poitiers: On the Trinity, De trinitate 1. 1–19, 2, 3* (Leiden, 1982).

MESLIN, M., 'Nationalisme, état et religions à la fin du IVᵉ siècle', *Archives de sociologie des religions*, 9/18 (1964), 3–20.

—— *Les Ariens d'Occident 335–430* (Paris, 1967).

MOINGT, J., 'La Théologie trinitaire de S. Hilaire', in *Hilaire et son temps* (Paris, 1969), 159–73.

MORIN, G., 'Les Douze Livres sur la Trinité attribués à Vigile de Thapse', *RB* 15 (1898), 1–10.

—— 'Les Nouveaux "Tractatus Origenis" et l'héritage littéraire de l'évêque espagnol Grégoire d'Illiberis', *Revue d'histoire et de littérature religieuse* (1900), 145–61.

—— 'Autour des "Tractatus Origenis"', *RB* 19 (1902), 225–45.

NAUTIN, P., 'Candidus l'Arien', in *L'Homme devant Dieu: mélanges offerts à Henri de Lubac*, vol. i (Lyons, 1963), 309–20.

—— 'Les Premières Relations d'Ambroise avec l'empereur Gratien: le *De fide* (livers I et II)', in Y.-M. Duval (ed.), *Ambroise de Milan: XVIᵉ centenaire de son élection épiscopale* (Paris, 1974).

NORTON, N., 'Prosopography of Pope Damasus', *Folia*, 4 (1950), 13–31; 5 (1951), 30–55; 6 (1952), 16–39.

O DONNELL, J. J., 'The Demise of Paganism', *Traditio*, 35 (1979), 45–88.

O FLYNN, J. M., *Generalissimos of the Western Roman Empire* (Edmonton, 1983).

OOST, S. I., *Galla Placidia Augusta* (Chicago, 1968).

PALANQUE, J.-R., 'La *Vita Ambrosii* de Paulin de Milan: étude critique', *Revue des sciences religieuses*, 4 (1924), 26–42, 401–20.

—— 'Un épisode des rapports entre Gratien et saint Ambroise: à propos de la Lettre I de saint Ambroise', *Revue des études anciennes*, 30 (1928), 292–7.

PALANQUE, J.-R., 'Sur la date d'une loi de Gratien contre l'hérésie', *Revue historique*, 168 (1931), 87–90.

—— *Saint Ambroise et l'Empire Romain: contribution à l'histoire des rapports de l'Église et de l'État à la fin du quatrième siècle* (Paris, 1933).

—— 'L'Empereur Maxime', in *Les Empereurs romains d'Espagne* (Paris, 1965), 255–67.

PAREDI, A., 'Paulinus of Milan', *Sacris erudiri*, 14 (1963), 206–30.

—— 'L'esilio in oriente del vescovo Milanese Dionisio e il problematico ritorno del suo corpo a Milano', in *Atti del convegno di studi su la Lombardia e l'Oriente* (1963), 229–44.

—— *Saint Ambrose: His Life and Times*, trans. M. J. Costelloe (Notre Dame, Ind., 1964). Trans. from *S. Ambrogio, e la sua età* (Milan, 1960).

PELIKAN, J., *The Emergence of the Catholic Tradition (100–600)*, vol. i (Chicago, 1971).

PIETRI, C., *Roma Christiana: recherches sur l'Église de Rome, son organisation, sa politique, son idéologie de Miltiade à Sixte III (311–440)*, 2 vols. (Rome, 1976).

PIGANIOL, A., *L'Empire chrétien (325–395)* (2nd edn., Paris, 1972).

POHLSANDER, H. A., 'Victory: The Story of a Statue', *Historia: Zeitschrift für alte Geschichte*, 18 (1969), 588–97.

PRESTIGE, G. L., *Fathers and Heretics* (London, 1958).

RAIKAS, K., 'St. Augustine on Juridical Duties: Some Aspects of the Episcopal Office in Late Antiquity', in J. C. Schnaubelt and F. Van Fleteren (eds.), *Collectanea Augustiniana* (New York, 1990), 467–83.

RICHARD, M., 'La Lettre "Confidimus quidem" du Pape Damase', *Annuaire del'Institut de Philologie et d'Histoire Orientales et Slaves*, 11 (1951), 323–40.

RITTER, A. M., 'Arius redivivus? Ein Jahrzwölft Arianismusforschung', *Theologische Rundschau*, 55 (1990), 153–87.

RUGGINI, L. C., 'Ambrogio e le opposizione anticattoliche fra il 383 e il 390', *Augustinianum*, 14 (1974), 409–49.

RUSCH, W., *The Later Latin Fathers* (London, 1977).

SALTET, J., 'La Formation de la légende des Papes Libère et Félix', *Bulletin de littérature ecclésiastique*, 3/7 (1905), 222–36.

—— 'Fraudes littéraires schismatiques lucifériens au 4ᵉ et 5ᵉ siècles', *Bulletin de littérature ecclésiastique*, 3/8 (1906), 300–26.

SANSBURY, C., 'Athanasius, Marcellus, and Eusebius of Caesarea: Some Thoughts on their Resemblances and Disagreements', in R. C. Gregg (ed.), *Arianism: Historical and Theological Reassessments* (Philadelphia, 1985), 281–6.

SAVON, H., 'Quelques remarques sur la chronologie des œuvres de saint Ambroise', *Studia Patristica*, 10 (1970), 156–60.

SCHEPENS, P., 'L'Ambrosiastre et saint Eusèbe de Verceil', *RSR* 37 (1950), 295–9.

SCHWARTZ, E., *Über die Bischofslisten der Synoden von Chalkedon, Nicaea und Konstantinopel* (Munich, 1937).

SEECK, O., *Geschichte des Untergangs der antiken Welt*, vol. v (Stuttgart, 1923).

SETTON, K. M., *Christian Attitude toward the Emperor in the Fourth Century* (New York, 1967).

SHERIDAN, A., 'The Altar of Victory: Paganism's Last Battle', *Antiquité classique*, 35 (1966), 186–206.

SIMONETTI, M., 'Qualche osservazione sul *De trinitate* attribuito a Eusebio di Vercelli', *Rivista di cultura classica e medioevale*, 5 (1963), 386–93.

—— 'Osservazioni sull'Altercatio Heracliani cum Germinio', *VC* 21 (1967), 39–58.

—— 'La politica antiariana di Ambrogio', in G. Lazzati (ed.), *Ambrosius episcopus*, (Milan, 1976), i. 266–85.

—— *La crisi ariana nel IV secolo*, Studia ephemeridis 'Augustinianum' 2 (Rome, 1975).

—— 'L'arianesimo di Ufila', *Romanobarbarica*, 1 (1976), 297–323.

SMULDERS, P., *La Doctrine trinitaire de S. Hilaire de Poitiers* (Rome, 1944).

—— 'Remarks on the Manuscript Tradition of the *De trinitate* of Saint Hilary of Poitiers', *Studia Patristica*, 3 (Text und Untersuchungen 78) (1961), 129–38.

STEAD, G. C., 'The Platonism of Arius', *JTS* 15 (1964), 16–31.

STEIN, E., *Histoire du Bas-Empire*, French trans. and ed. J. R. Palanque, vol. i (Paris, 1959).

STEPANICH, M., *The Christology of Zeno of Verona* (Washington, DC, 1948).

SZIDAT, J., 'Zur Ankunft Iulianus in Sirmium 361 n. Chr. auf seinem Zug gegen Constantius II', *Historia*, 24 (1975), 375–8.

TAVANO, S., 'Una pagina degli scolia ariana la sede e il clima del concilio', *Atti del colloquio internazionale sul concilio di Aquileia del 381* (Udine, 1981), 145–65.

TEILLET, S., *Des Goths à la nation gothique* (Paris, 1984).

TETZ, M., 'Über Nikäische Orthodoxie: der sog. Tomus ad Antiochenos des Athanasios von Alexandrien', *Zeitschrift für neutestamentliche Wissenschaft*, 66 (1975), 194–222.

—— 'Ein enzyklisches Schreiben der Synode von Alexandrien (362)', *Zeitschrift für neutestamentliche Wissenschaft*, 79 (1988), 262–81.

THELAMON, F., 'Une œuvre destinée à la communauté chrétienne d'Aquilée: l'Historique ecclésiastique de Rufin', in *Aquileia nel IV secolo*, Antichità Altoadriatiche 22 (Udine, 1982), 255–71.

THOMPSON, E. A., 'Early Visigothic Christianity', *Latomus*, 21 (1962), 505–19.

—— *The Visigoths in the Time of Ulfila* (Oxford, 1966).

TURNER, C. H., 'On Eusebius of Vercelli', *JTS* 1 (1900), 126–8.

—— 'II. Makarios as a Technical Term', *JTS* 23 (1921–2), 31–5.

—— 'On MS Verona LI', *JTS* 24 (1922–3), 71–9.

VANDERSPOEL, J., 'Themistius and the Imperial Court', Ph.D. diss. (Toronto, 1989).

VERA, D., 'I rapporti fra Magno Massimo, Theodosio e Valentiniano II nel 383–4', *Athenaeum*, 53 (1975), 267–301.

Vita di S. Ambrogio: introduzione, testo critico e note, ed. M. Pellegrino (Rome, 1961).

VOKES, F. E., 'Zeno of Verona, Apuleius and Africa', *Studia Patristica*, 8/2 (1966), 130–4.

WALPOLE, A. S., *Early Latin Hymns* (Cambridge, 1922).

WARDMAN, A. L., 'Usurpers and Internal Conflicts in the 4th Century A.D.', *Historia*, 33 (1984), 220–37.

WILES, M., 'The Philosophy in Christianity: Arius and Athanasius', in G. Vesey (ed.), *The Philosophy in Christianity* (Cambridge, 1989), 49–52.

WILLIAMS, D. H., 'A Reassessment of the Early Career and Exile of Hilary of Poitiers', *JEH* 42 (1991), 212–17.

—— 'The Anti-Arian Campaigns of Hilary of Poitiers and the "Liber contra Auxentium"', *Church History*, 61 (1992), 7–22.

—— 'When Did the Emperor Gratian Return the Basilica to the Pro-Nicenes in Milan?' *Studia Patristica*, 24 (1993), 208–15.

WILLIAMS, R., *Arius: A Heresy and Tradition* (London, 1987).

—— *The Making of Orthodoxy: Essays in Honour of Henry Chadwick* (Cambridge, 1989).

WITTIG, J., 'Filastrius, Gaudentius und Ambrosiaster: eine literarhistorische Studie', in *Kirchengeschichtliche Abhandlungen*, viii (Breslau, 1909), 3–56.

WOLFRAM, H., *History of the Goths*, trans. T. J. Dunlap (Berkeley, Calif., 1988).

ZEILLER, J., *Les Origines chrétiennes dans les provinces danubiennes de l'Empire Romain*, Studia Historica 48 (1918; Rome, 1967).

—— 'La Date du concile d'Aquilée (3 septembre 381)', *RHE* 33 (1937), 39–45.

ZIEGLER, J., *Zur religiösen Haltung der Gegenkaiser im 4. Jh. n. Chr.*, Frankfurter althistorische Studien 4 (Frankfurt, 1970).

INDEX OF NAMES

ANTIQUITY

Acacius (of Caesarea) 32–3, 35 n.
Aetius 6, 143, 147
Ambrose (of Milan) 11, 31, 33–4, 36, 87,
  91, 98–9, 101; hagiographic portrait
  8–9, 104–12, 153, 234; episcopal
  election 112–27; baptism 117–19; early
  episcopate 116–28, 135–40, 152–3; in
  Sirmium 122–6; early relations with
  Gratian 132–3, 141–5; 151–2; attacked
  by Homoians 136–40, 142, 151–3; *De
  fide* I–II 111 n., 128–30, 141–8; loss
  and return of basilicas 139–40, 144,
  153–5, 166–8, 203, 210–15; conflict
  with Palladius 148–51, 186–90; council
  of Aquileia 169–85; *De incarnatione*
  190–4; conflict with Arian
  Chamberlains 110 n., 185, 190–1;
  Contra Auxentium 204, 208–13, 215;
  Altar of Victory controversy 195,
  201–2; embassies to Trier 198–200,
  217, 223–6; use of relics 86, 218; with
  Theodosius 229
Ammianus Marcellinus 42 n., 130 n.,
  131 n., 138 n., 139 n.
Andragathius 196, 229
Anemius (of Sirmium) 73, 123–5, 128 n.,
  143
Arius 1, 5, 16, 24, 30, 135, 143, 178–9,
  183, 187, 189–90, 194
Asterius 13, 66
Athanasius (of Alexandria) 2, 4–5, 14–18,
  20, 23 n., 24 n., 26 n., 27 n., 51, 53,
  57–65, 68–71, 75–7, 80, 97, 101
Athanaric 166–7
Attalus (presbyter) 137, 176, 180, 186,
  233
Augustine (of Hippo) 36, 84–5, 86 n., 87,
  89, 106–8, 113–14, 117–19, 126, 169 n.,
  210 n., 214 n., 220–1
Ausonius 131–3, 157 n.
Auxentius (of Durostorum) 3 n., 36,
  85 n., 160, 170, 204–9, 212–15,
  234

Auxentius (of Milan) 2, 11, 24 n., 36, 46,
  59, 67, 71 n., 72, 76–83, 86–8, 104,
  112, 119, 121, 136, 143, 151, 186

Basil (of Ancyra) 21
Basil (of Caesarea) 13, 15 n., 68 n., 71 n.,
  119–21
Bauto 168, 198–99, 202
Benivolus 213

Caecilianus (of Spoletium) 53
Cassian, John 47 n.
Cassiodorus 81 n.
Chrystosom 84
Constantine, emperor 8–9, 13
Constantius, emperor (II) 5, 17, 21, 22 n.,
  24, 27, 37–8, 43, 59, 61–3, 65, 68–9,
  70, 73, 77 n., 102, 201, 233; as
  anti-christ 44–5, 48–9, 53 n., 54–7
Cyprian (of Carthage) 91 n., 105–6,
  116 n., 189, 222

Damasus (of Rome) 36, 72, 76, 80, 82,
  113 n., 124–5, 138, 141, 158 n., 164,
  167, 195 n.
Demophilus (of Constantinople) 85 n.,
  142, 151, 165, 167, 173, 186
Dionysius (of Milan) 18 n., 58–9, 76–7,
  112–13, 119–21, 220

Epictetus (of Centumcellae) 75
Epiphanius (of Salamis) 13, 25 n., 60–1,
  89, 90 n.
Eudoxius (of Germanicia) 55, 57
Eunomius 72, 143, 147, 161
Eusebius (of Caesarea) 13, 108
Eusebius (of Nicomedia) 15 n., 206
Eusebius (of Vercelli) 9, 17, 38–9, 49 f.,
  79, 233, 239–42; his writings 50–52;
  De trinitate 51, 96–102, 118, 239–42;
  council of Milan 52–8; in exile 58–62;
  synod of Alexandria 62–6; return to
  west 66–8

MODERN

INDEX OF SUBJECTS